Reki

FRANK W. PIERCE MEMORIAL LECTURESHIP
AND CONFERENCE SERIES NO. 11

Rekindling the Movement

Labor's Quest for Relevance in the Twenty-First Century

Lowell Turner,
Harry C. Katz, and
Richard W. Hurd

ILR Press
an imprint of
Cornell University Press
Ithaca and London

First published 2001 by Cornell University Press
First printing, Cornell Paperbacks, 2001

Printed in the United States of America

Library of Congress Cataloging-in-Publication Data

Turner, Lowell.
    Rekindling the movement : labor's quest for relevance in the twenty-first century / Lowell Turner, Harry C. Katz, and Richard W. Hurd
        p. cm.—(Frank W. Pierce memorial lectureship and conference series ; no. 11)
Includes bibliographical references and index.
    ISBN 0-8014-3874-8—ISBN 0-8014-8712-9 (pbk.)
    1. Labor unions—United States. 2. Labor movement—United States.
I. Katz, Harry C. II. Hurd, Richard W. III. New York State School of Industrial and Labor Relations. IV. Title. V. Series.
    HD6508 .T87 2001
    331.88'0973—dc21   00-011823

Cloth printing   10 9 8 7 6 5 4 3 2 1
Paperback printing   10 9 8 7 6 5 4 3 2 1

FSC FSC Trademark © 1996 Forest Stewardship Council A.C.
SW-COC-098

Contents

Acknowledgments   vii

Introduction: Revival of the American Labor Movement:
Issues, Problems, Prospects   I
    Lowell Turner, Harry C. Katz, and Richard W. Hurd

Part I: Reinventing the Labor Movement

1. Building Social Movement Unionism: The Transformation of
the American Labor Movement   9
    Lowell Turner and Richard W. Hurd

2. Organize for What? The Resurgence of Labor
as a Citizenship Movement   27
    Paul Johnston

3. Living with Flexibility   59
    Charles Heckscher

4. Lost Ways of Unionism: Historical Perspectives on
Reinventing the Labor Movement   82
    Dorothy Sue Cobble

**Part II: Organizing Upsurge: Strategic and
Structural Innovation**

5. Organizing Immigrant Workers: Case Studies
from Southern California   99
    Ruth Milkman and Kent Wong

6. Structural Change in the AFL-CIO: A Regional Study
of Union Cities' Impact   129
    Jill Kriesky

7. Confronting the Dilemmas of Organizing: Obstacles and
Innovations at the AFL-CIO Organizing Institute   155
Amy Foerster

8. Overcoming Obstacles to Transformation: Challenges
on the Way to a New Unionism   182
Bill Fletcher, Jr., and Richard W. Hurd

Part III: New Strategic and Institutional Orientations

9. The Evolution of Strategic and Coordinated Bargaining
Campaigns in the 1990s: The Steelworkers' Experience   211
Kate Bronfenbrenner and Tom Juravich

10. Union Mergers and Union Revival: Are We Asking
Too Much or Too Little?   238
Gary Chaison

11. Building the High Road in Metro Areas: Sectoral Training
and Employment Projects   256
Eric Parker and Joel Rogers

Part IV: Politics and Policy

12. Organized Labor versus Globalization: NAFTA, Fast Track,
and PNTR with China   275
James Shoch

13. Free Trade, Fair Trade, and the Battle for Labor Rights   314
Lance Compa

Afterword: Whither the American Labor Movement?   339
Harry C. Katz

References   351
Biographies   375
Index   381

Acknowledgments

In addition to thanking each other for occasional praise and much mutual criticism (the academic way of expressing affection), the editors and authors of this book would like to thank the following colleagues for advice and comments: Lee Adler, Martin Behrens, Alex Colvin, Maria Cook, Dan Cornfield, Jefferson Cowie, Robin Gerber, Jack Getman, Pat Greenfield, Peter Katzenstein, Risa Lieberwitz, Nathan Lillie, Manfred Muster, Bruce Nissen, Jonas Pontusson, Jim Rundle, Nick Salvatore, Paul Sawyer, Sidney Tarrow, Robert Taylor, Brian Towers, and Kirsten Wever.

For excellent logistical and administrative support from start to finish of this project, and with good humor and courage in the face of great adversity, Lori Ard earned our deepest thanks. Brigid Beachler came aboard just in time to help us down the home stretch and across the finish line with consistent competence. Thanks also to Robin Givens and Cathy Mooney, who each made important contributions at critical moments.

At ILR Press, Fran Benson shepherded this book through the publication process, making it relatively painless and sometimes even enjoyable for the rest of us. Mario Bognanno and Margaret Hallock, reviewers for the press, gave us critical support and excellent suggestions, most of which we tried to incorporate. Do Mi Stauber produced yet another first-rate index.

This project was funded by a grant from the Frank W. Pierce Memorial Lectureship and Conference Fund at Cornell University's ILR School.

Revival of the American Labor Movement

Issues, Problems, Prospects

Lowell Turner, Harry C. Katz, and Richard W. Hurd

Despite the American labor movement's loss in the bruising battle over the China trade bill, supporters and opponents of the movement agree that after years of decline, labor has once again become a powerful political force. "It's like night and day comparing the AFL-CIO's political operations today with those in the 1994 elections," said Charles Cook, who publishes a nonpartisan political report. "It's like comparing a Model T with a Ferrari." In other signs of labor's strength, white-collar workers, including doctors and psychologists, are flocking into unions as never before, and labor registered its biggest organizing victory in sixty years by unionizing 74,000 Los Angeles home-care workers in 1999.[1]

Since the 1970s, researchers have chronicled the decline of the labor movement and the shrinkage of collective-bargaining coverage to a small fraction of the American workforce. For those who believe that strong unions and collective bargaining agreements are essential characteristics of a healthy and economically just democratic society, these have been gloomy times indeed. And not only have talented researchers explained the decline, many have implied or even openly argued that decline is inevitable, that labor unions are relics of an earlier industrial era and on their way to obsolescence in a modern high-technology and service-based global economy.[2]

Quite surprisingly, however, from the depths of despair, a strange and unexpected series of events emerged into public view by the mid-1990s. From a few organizing unions of the 1980s (SEIU, AFSCME, ACTWU, CWA, and others), from the new AFL-CIO Organizing In-

---

[1] Steven Greenhouse, "Despite Defeat on China Bill, Labor Is on Rise," *New York Times* (May 30, 2000): A1, A18.

[2] See, for example, Troy 1986.

stitute founded in 1989, from the rise to prominence of a new generation of energetic and progressive union leaders, emerged a wave of fresh activist energy throughout the American labor movement. The most dramatic indication of revitalization came with the 1995 watershed victory by John Sweeney, who headed an insurgent slate in a contested election for AFL-CIO leadership. The "New Voice" candidates campaigned on a platform calling for massive additional resources and energy for both organizing and political action, a platform that has since been widely implemented. By the turn of the millennium it was not yet clear whether this new activism would be enough to launch a full-fledged labor movement revival. But it was clear that new hope was present and realistic, with the challenge of revitalization now at the top of the agenda for a once demoralized labor movement.

The purpose of this book is to examine union revitalization efforts: to identify central developments, to analyze strengths and weaknesses in the new initiatives, and to assess progress made and prospects for the future. We ask questions such as: Can union decline be reversed? Are there serious indications of revitalization beyond new leadership and publicity? What accounts for successes and failures so far, and what strategies have shown the most promise for future success? Can innovations in areas such as vocational training consortia contribute to labor movement revitalization? Are there ways to reconcile the contradictions between an "organizing model" of unionism and the traditional member-focused "servicing model" of the postwar era? Can unions successfully target relevant groups (beyond the existing blue-collar and public-sector bases) such as women, minorities, service employees, semiprofessionals, and professionals? Can political action and legislative campaigns on issues such as trade contribute to reversing the decline, or is this only a way to hold the line (or even worse, an inadequate strategy of the past)?

This book is designed to target these and related questions by bringing together the work of highly regarded experts whose research and analysis indicate contrasting answers and perspectives. There is, to be sure, a great deal of opinion trumpeting on many of these questions; the focus here, by contrast, is on research: hard evidence and causal analysis provide grounded answers and realistic perspectives. We hope that the analysis presented will offer meaningful signposts for future research as well as for policymakers and union leaders regarding what is and is not possible, what may and may not work.

Admittedly, this is a partisan book, just as it also is a collection of scholarly work. The authors, without exception, believe that a viable, independent labor movement is essential in a democratic society. We are all close observers of industrial relations and the labor movement, and much of our research is informed by close personal contact with unionists and the processes we describe. The closeness to practice combined with the analytical tools of academia provides a richness of perspective that is often missing in dryer, more detached scholarly writing. Crossing the boundaries of fields including industrial relations, sociology, political science, and economics, we believe that research breakthroughs and theoretical advances are most likely in interdisciplinary analysis that targets and builds upon day-to-day realities. It is in this spirit of broad inquiry and close observation that we work and offer our research findings and analysis.

Although the authors and editors of this collection agree on the importance of unions, a range of views is represented regarding the efficacy of current efforts at renewal. Some of the authors focus on successful initiatives consistent with the AFL-CIO's strategic approach and offer or imply an optimistic appraisal of labor's future. Others applaud current efforts but are less enthusiastic because of institutional inflexibility that stands in the way of effective strategic reorientation. A few of the contributors present alternative conceptions involving redefinition of the role of unions and how they relate to workers, employers, and the government.

The chapters in the first section of this volume address the problems, prospects, and alternative scenarios and strategies facing labor. Here the key question is whether a particular strategic reorientation holds the key to labor's revitalization and the terms of that reorientation. The chapter by Lowell Turner and Richard Hurd as well as the one by Paul Johnston argues that in order to revitalize, the American labor movement will have to transform itself into "social unionism" and link up with broader social movements throughout American society. While Turner and Hurd emphasize the rise, fall, and rise again of social movement unionism, Johnston sees labor movement growth in campaigns for the expansion of citizenship.

Charles Heckscher presents an equally bold and controversial vision for the labor movement when he asserts that the key to the future growth and success of unions lies in their ability to create representation structures that accommodate the needs of the increasingly mobile American workforce. Heckscher sides with those who believe that workers' attachments to any particular firm are likely to be short-lived, and therefore new forms of "associational unionism" are needed.

Dorothy Sue Cobble makes a more modest, though related, claim by stressing that unions should become more sensitive to the needs of workers who feel strong occupational links rather than ties to a single employer or job site. Cobble claims that occupational unionism could draw lessons from the craft unionism that stood as a real alternative to the industrial union model that became predominant in the post–World War II period.

The chapters in the next section have a more empirical focus in their examination of the recent organizing efforts within the American labor movement. They provide rich additions to the growing literature assessing these efforts. Ruth Milkman and Kent Wong trace the complexities of organizing among low-wage workers in Los Angeles and show that neither top-down nor bottom-up styles provide a simple prescription for success. They also hint at the long-term problems unions face in sustaining activism and cohesion after an organizing victory. The chapter by Amy Foerster and the one by Bill Fletcher and Richard Hurd report the tensions created within the ranks of American unions because of the top-down and directive nature of the Organizing Institute and a number of other AFL-CIO initiatives. Jill Kriesky examines the AFL-CIO's recent union cities initiative focused on local labor councils, and clarifies both what is new in these efforts and the problems confronted to date.

While organizing is clearly at the center of the American labor movement's current agenda, in recent years unions have also adopted new collective-bargaining tactics and restructured through mergers as part of revitalization efforts. The chapter by Kate Bronfenbrenner and Tom Juravich reports how the steelworkers linked corporate campaigns to more aggressive bargaining approaches that in some important demonstration cases stopped the near automatic success employers had been having through the use of permanent striker replacements. Gary Chaison evaluates the extent of recent union mergers and the various factors that motivate them. Mergers, he argues, appear to work best when motivated by the advantages gained from administrative coordination and economies of scale. Eric Parker and Joel Rogers describe successful local coalitions in Wisconsin involving unions, employers, and labor-market intermediaries to promote economic development and worker training.

Union revitalization in the United States also has included politically oriented initiatives that seek to influence international trade rights and global labor conditions as revealed by the papers in the final section of this volume. James Shoch describes the ebb and flow of labor's fortunes in fights over free trade agreements, indicating both the conditions necessary for labor's "fast-track" legislative victories and the problems inherent in building similar future coalitions. Lance Compa analyzes union efforts to influence international rights and standards. Whether at the domestic or international level, Shoch and Compa describe how through practical and pragmatic political activities and compromises labor has scored limited but important successes in the international arena.

We hope this book will convince you of the richness of innovation now under way within the American labor movement. At the same time, new strategies and possibilities make it essential to discuss the strengths, weaknesses, and the prospects for expanded revitalization. The book closes with Harry Katz's reflections—an assessment of the prospects as well as a reminder of the limitations and critical problems of recent efforts.

The renewal of the labor movement, we believe, is a precondition for both the revitalization of American democracy and the democratization of our increasingly global society. If this book contributes in some small way to a broadening and deepening of contemporary union efforts aimed at modernization, reform, and renewed influence in the American political economy, it will have served its purpose.

PART I

Reinventing the Labor Movement

Building Social Movement Unionism

The Transformation of the
American Labor Movement

Lowell Turner and Richard W. Hurd

L abor movements long in decline in many industrial democracies are now on the move. They are developing new strategies, pursuing internal reform, restructuring, and seeking new ways to gain members and influence. This is an exciting and, in some ways, unexpected development, and it is an important one in this global era in which governments and unions appear to have lost much of their power in regulating markets. The modernization and revival of national labor movements, which has expanded through cross-national collaboration, could offer a much-needed democratic counterweight to the growing power of capital in today's world economy. The "battle in Seattle" in late 1999 offered a dramatic picture of the alliances and active labor participation that could shape a new democratic force on the global stage.

In the United States, the renewed energy displayed by the labor movement is particularly promising. From organizing drives to strike victories to legislative campaigns, labor's renewed influence in the American political economy is clearly seen. A labor movement that was left for dead by many in the Reagan era has developed new leadership and innovative strategies for rank-and-file mobilization and political clout. In a global economy dominated to a large extent by American-based multinational corporations, the world needs a strong American labor movement. The goal of the new activists, young and old, who drive today's labor campaigns, is the rebirth of modernized, mobilized, powerful American unions.

We suggest that innovations at the heart of the current revitalization are part of a broad shift away from traditional postwar unionism to a new social movement unionism. The transformation occurs in a weak institutional context in which experimentation and innovation are possible. Driving the change are two generations of activists: veterans of the social movements of the 1960s, now in leadership positions at the American Federation of Labor–Congress of Industrial Organizations (AFL-CIO) and in many member unions, and a new generation of campus and workplace activists.

Strategies for Revitalization

The 1990s witnessed the growth and expansion of important strategic innovations in the U.S. labor movement (Bronfenbrenner et al. 1998; Fraser and Freeman 1997; Nissen 1999). The most significant of these are organizing of the unorganized, grassroots political action, coalition building, labor-management partnership, union mergers and internal restructuring, and international solidarity.

Most of the new strategies are connected, directly or indirectly, to a new emphasis on rank-and-file participation or mobilization, the essence of social movement unionism. Current organizing and grassroots political efforts are founded on expanded member activism. Coalition building mobilizes other groups and their members to support union campaigns such as organizing and trade legislation. Environmental, campus, religious, human rights, and other groups have increasingly joined with unions and their members in campaigns and actions from local to national levels. Successful partnerships encourage expanded workplace participation, and national level agreements at firms such as Kaiser Permanente and Levi Strauss provide for company neutrality in union-organizing drives. Much of today's internal restructuring in unions is aimed at reforming the organization to make expanded rank-and-file participation and new organizing drives possible. Growing international solidarity ranges from high-level junkets to networks of activists, with various types of rank-and-file mobilization typically necessary in winning campaigns.

Mobilization efforts have clearly led the recent revitalization, marking off current AFL-CIO strategies from those of previous decades. Although rank-and-file and grassroots mobilization produces excitement and great promise for the future, the road to a fully revitalized labor movement is a long one full of obstacles—from employer antagonism to internal resistance to change. Transformation may well require the powerful cleansing action of a broader society-wide social movement upsurge, well beyond specific efforts to build social movement unionism.

Social Movement Unionism and Organizational Change

Broadly speaking, the shift to an emphasis on rank-and-file mobilization in organizing, grassroots politics, and elsewhere can be characterized as a shift from business to social movement unionism. Both business and social movement unionism are "ideal types," but the direction of change in the 1990s is of great historical and current significance. From the point of view of today's union activists, the transition from the social movement unionism of the 1930s to the business unionism of the 1950s to 1980s left American unions demobilized and to a large extent defenseless in the face of growing employer opposition from the 1970s on. One could also argue that labor law reform failed in 1978 and 1994 because unions lacked the will or capacity to mobilize large-scale support. Leaders of the current shift in union priorities, from John Sweeney on down, aim to revitalize the labor movement through active organizing, political action, and the rebuilding of a strong social movement dimension, a capacity for rank-and-file mobilization and ongoing involvement (Sweeney 1996).

There is a difference between social movements and social movement unionism. Social movements are broad society-wide phenomena that rise and fall in unpredictable historical waves. Social movement unionism, by contrast, is a type of unionism based on member involvement and activism. Although it is possible to build social movement unions in the absence of the broader social movement, as many local unions have shown, the broader movement more easily sweeps away obstacles and breaks down resistance from entrenched officeholders and conservative forces inside and outside of unions. Current strategies aimed at building social movement unionism thus address an interactive process: broad, powerful social movements, when they do come along, can drive institutional change (including labor law reform), thereby supporting activists at the local and national levels. By the same token, current efforts to build social movement unionism, by opening up possibilities for involvement and mobilization, may help lay the groundwork for the next social movement wave.

American unions, both local and national, are in effect joining in an attempted expansion of democratic participation in the workplace and society. The preponderance of elements in current strategies contributes to the push in this direction. In the end, the success of each strategy may well depend on the success of the others in a broader social movement context.

From Business to Social Movement Unionism

The history of the American labor movement is long and varied. At one extreme, labor activism has taken shape as vast, turbulent, and short-lived social movements; at the other, unions have consolidated their influence over the decades as stable institutional forces. In the rise and fall of the labor movement, these two forces—social movements and institutions—have repeatedly interacted to shape union prospects and the range of strategic choices available to union leaders and their activist members.

Over the past hundred years, the American labor movement has gone from craft-based occupational unionism to transforming social movement (1930s) to social contract incorporation (1940s) to business unionism (1950s–1990s) to a major contemporary push toward renewed social movement unionism (Brody 1980; Green 1980; Fraser and Freeman 1997; Boyle 1998). Labor's upsurge in the 1930s helped to build new institutions for collective bargaining as union membership and influence grew (Gross 1974, 33–37). On the other hand, when labor missed the next social movement wave in the 1960s, unions lost the opportunity for revitalization and, under the weight of an escalating employer offensive, fell into long-term decline and decay. A companion effect has been growing economic and social polarization in American society. Today's revitalization efforts are bred of both desperation and the examples of a few organizing unions that did ride the 1960s wave. Just as the popular upsurge of the 1930s helped to build and then breathe life into new workers' rights and institutions of industrial relations, so the organizing activists of today aim to build the collective power necessary to reform, rebuild, and revitalize labor's institutional supports for the challenges of the global economy.

The story of labor's social movement and institutional success in the 1930s is well known. Led by rank-and-file activists and union leaders in mass production industries who had been excluded from membership in the old AFL, American workers across the country demanded union membership and recognition. The National Labor Relations Act (NLRA or the Wagner Act), passed by Congress in 1935 and upheld by the courts in 1937, gave union recognition and collective bargaining rights to any workers who could gain majority workforce support. Organizers from CIO and AFL unions alike fanned out across the country to take advantage of popular sentiment and readiness to mobilize. In a few years, union membership more than doubled. Rising working-class protest demanded and gave political backing to Senator Wagner's promotion of the new labor laws, and these same movements of protests then gave substance to the laws and made the institutions work. Beyond a doubt, social movements in this case shaped institutions (Gross 1974; Green 1980).[1]

Wartime solidarity incorporated the newly strengthened unions into the political economy through the War Labor Board, informal access to President Roosevelt, new influence in Congress, and in other ways. Union leaders assumed that this implied "social contract" would carry over into the postwar era—and it did, but in a more limited way. Labor's influence was restricted through Taft-Hartley legislation and in compromise strike settlements in which labor's power was confined to collective bargaining and shopfloor enforcement at the expense of

---

[1] The relationship, to be sure, was interactive: Once growing protest gave leverage to political forces to pass the new legislation in 1935, the NLRA (especially after clearing the Supreme Court in 1937) opened the door for more union organizing. Thus, beneath the causal relationship social movements > institutions lies a more complex picture: mass protest > new legislation > more mass protest and organizing, which in turn helped to consolidate the new institutional framework (see, for example, Gross 1974, 33–37; Hurd 1974; Green 1980; Lichtenstein 1995).

greater voice or codetermination in company decision making (Brody 1980; Gross 1995). In the context of the new cold war, many labor leaders consolidated control of their own organizations through a purge of the left (communists and noncommunists alike) that eliminated internal opponents at the cost of stripping the labor movement of many activist-minded local, regional, and even national leaders.

For the most part, the capacity to promote renewed social movement unionism disappeared, replaced by what came to be known as business unionism: collective bargaining, enforcement of the contract, and representational and other group services (health plans, insurance, group legal services) for the union member. Although the new rights and services were important and valuable to the members, the life went out of the unions. People began to see them as service agencies and stopped going to meetings or otherwise participating except for occasional activism at contract time (which did show mobilization potential for those who might want to tap into it). Although union membership density was near its peak (around 34 percent) by the time the AFL and CIO merged in 1955, the stage had already been set for the long-term dominance and eventual decay of a nonparticipatory business unionism.[2] While economic restructuring and labor market changes, which accelerated by the 1970s, made it essential that unions organize new industries and groups of workers, a consolidated contract-oriented unionism had little capacity to organize and entrenched leaders had little interest in organizing the new sectors of the economy.

What could have revitalized such unions for the increasingly difficult challenges of the 1970s and beyond? Perhaps the civil rights movement, antiwar movement, women's movement, or even the environmental movement (see, for example, Isaac et al. 1998). Institutions can be reinvigorated by social movements; in the politics of conflict, however, it is also possible for entrenched interests to beat back social movement influence—almost always to the detriment of the institutions.

Why did American labor miss the boat—the same boat that revitalized the German, British, and Italian labor movements in the 1960s and 1970s? To a large extent, it was the conservatism bred by business unionism in which many labor leaders presided over increasingly nar-

---

[2]Maurice Neufeld warned of precisely this as early as 1950 (Neufeld 1951).

row member-oriented organizations that had lost a broader vision and passion for social justice. This combined with ideologically intense cold war anticommunism made many labor leaders (led by George Meany of the AFL-CIO) suspicious and at times quite hostile to new political stirrings on the left, whether it was civil rights, antiwar protests, or the women's movement.

There were important exceptions, and these show the lost potential. Martin Luther King was killed in Memphis in 1968 while supporting the union recognition strike of a thousand black sanitation workers against a white racist city council. The movie *At the River I Stand* beautifully demonstrates how the power of this labor protest was magnified by the power of the civil rights movement and vice versa. The national union involved—the American Federation of State, County, and Municipal Employees (AFSCME)—used the strike victory in Memphis as a springboard for organizing other municipal employees across the South; and a cohort of AFSCME activists, empowered and radicalized by this experience and the power they saw and felt in the convergence of these two popular movements, would go on to lead many successful public sector organizing drives in the 1970s and 1980s.

The labor movement supported the passage of civil rights legislation, and particular unions such as AFSCME and UAW participated actively in the civil rights movement. But the exclusion of black and Hispanic workers from skilled jobs in construction and other industries continued, as did the segmentation of jobs in the public sector and elsewhere—often with the collusion of unions whose first loyalty was to their existing (mostly white) members. Most labor leaders, in other words, gave their primary loyalty to the status quo, at a moment in history when a powerful movement was transforming society and could well have transformed and reinvigorated labor as well (Isaac et al. 1998).

The story is similar for the women's movement, itself to some extent a product of the civil rights and antiwar movements (led in its early years, in many cases, by women who had been active in those earlier movements). Outside the public sector, most unions had little interest in organizing female occupational categories such as clerical workers and nurses. Again, there were exceptions, as reflected in the public sector, the growing interest of SEIU and other unions in organizing the healthcare industry, CWA's commitment to organizing telephone operators and new telecommunications occupations, and the growth of AFT and NEA organizing in the public schools. But the larger picture was the same: conservative male labor leaders, threatened by the rising new women's liberation movement (as it was then called), showed little interest in bringing this potentially revitalizing force within the apparently stable house of labor.

For the anti–Vietnam War movement, the problems were political and generational. With a few exceptions (Walter Reuther of the UAW after 1968, for example; Lichtenstein 1995, 420–38), top labor leaders were so deeply anticommunist they could not link up with this truly (and unruly) mass American movement. With its foreign policy funded by the State Department (part of the cold war Red purge deal), the AFL-CIO supported the war in Vietnam well after most Americans had come to realize it was a mistake. Media images of New York City construction workers beating up antiwar demonstrators reflected a broader feeling among labor leaders that the protesters were privileged, un-American college kids, anathema to labor's interests.

While labor leaders resisted, a vast swath of an entire generation was swept up in the antiwar movement—and many of these bright, young activists came to see unions not as allies but as barriers to change. Far from discovering a source of reinvigoration in the swelling activism of American youth, labor leaders lost credibility with much of that energetic, activist-minded, up-and-coming generation.

From this cross-movement hotbed of activism in the 1960s and 1970s, a new and reinforced environmental movement also emerged. Here too the reaction of labor leaders was broadly negative. Far from working with environmental groups to find common interests (to develop, for example, a social-ecological reform strategy for the future of industry on a small planet as German unions have done), labor leaders reacted to demands for environmental preservation in many cases solely as attacks on union jobs. Bumper stickers on the pickup trucks of construction workers chiding "Sierra Club take a hike!" reflected the lack of vision in a politics of reaction. Once again, unions alienated a good part of an activist generation.

Social movements can revitalize institutions, and one way they do this is by sweeping away entrenched officeholders. But such revitalization is a political process and can also be blocked by defensive, threatened leaders—in this case aided by the fact that the new social movements were not for the most part targeted at the workplace, employers, or unions, but at government policy. This allowed existing union leadership, from George Meany on down, to cordon off their organizations from the radical currents of change.

The main exception to this predominant pattern for the 1960s and 1970s lay in the public sector. Here, new enabling legislation (national, state, and local) combined with the contagious activism of the era (an activism that mobilized blacks, Hispanics, women, and youth) to produce something of a social movement unionism in many places (Johnston 1994; Isaacs et al. 1998). Here in a more benign environment, with less employer opposition, unions grew rapidly in the public sector throughout the 1970s, contrary to the opposite trend in the private sector. By the 1980s, union membership density in the public sector was more than double that in the private sector. In the public sector, the movements of the 1960s in many cases did revitalize unions and the institutions of industrial relations, showing the potential had this happened on an economy-wide scale.

In the long run, however, the activism of the 1960s may yet save the American labor movement. Many young rank and filers were strongly influenced by the social movements of their formative years and became a constituency inside their unions for change and for greater openness.[3] And many activists in the course of the 1970s did find unions in which they could work and even thrive. John Sweeney, one could argue, leads the AFL-CIO today precisely because he was not threatened by the activists of the 1960s, and in fact began to hire them in the 1970s, knowing that these were people committed to social justice who would work hard for the cause if allowed to do so. Such activists, at Sweeney's SEIU and at other unions such as AFSCME, ACTWU, and CWA, would in the 1980s and 1990s play major roles in the organizing drives that laid the groundwork for a broad "changing to organize" campaign by the mid-1990s.

---

[3]See Heberle (1951, 118–127) on the concept of a "political generation," shaped by the experiences of its formative years (ages 20–30) and ready to rely on that learning when it becomes the "ruling generation" (circa ages 40–65).

It wasn't that business union leaders didn't try to reverse decline. By the 1980s, it was no longer possible to pretend that things were fine. An employer offensive against unions had gathered force; starting on a large scale in the 1970s, it received official blessing in President Reagan's firing of the PATCO workers in 1981 and contributed to the rapid decline in private-sector union membership in the 1980s and 1990s. In a context of globalization and economic restructuring, union decline was driven by employer opposition and backed by the state; but because labor in the private sector had missed the social movement boat, unions were more vulnerable to attack than they otherwise would have been. By the 1980s, they had neither strong supportive institutions, as employers and government had whittled away at labor laws and their enforcement and interpretations (Gross 1995), nor the force of widespread collective action.[4] Labor leaders responded to the crisis in the areas they knew best—through concession bargaining and expanded services to members—and they moved beyond such modifications to experiment with labor-management cooperation. In all of these areas, modest gains were made in some cases, but nothing came close to turning the tide. Decline persisted (Kochan, Katz, and McKersie 1986).

Labor refocused its efforts on keeping Democratic Party friends in Congress (the last barrier, perhaps, against union extinction) and getting a Democratic president elected (Dark 1999). In 1978, with a Democratic Congress and president, they had come close to getting some relief in modest labor law reform, only to be thwarted by a Republican filibuster in the Senate. With Democrats forever (it seemed) in control of the House, even with Reagan in power, they had high hopes for a renewed push for labor law reform under the next Democratic presidency. They campaigned hard for Mondale in 1984, for Dukakis in 1988, and for Bill Clinton in 1992.

In the meantime, however, a push to organize the unorganized developed within the labor movement at the grassroots level, which was led in many cases by activists of the 1960s generation. Some unions

---

[4]Note the parallel here to an earlier era. Kim Voss (1996) argues that the 19th-century Knights of Labor failed because of employer countermobilization and because the KOL as an organization was unable to develop and implement appropriate new strategies to counter the employer offensive.

began to shift resources toward organizing. For the most part, the unions that grew in the 1980s while others declined were the organizing unions. Within the councils of the AFL-CIO, facing failure in so many areas, the new voice began to be heard. In an effort to consolidate what had been learned and to train new organizers, the AFL-CIO founded an Organizing Institute in 1989 directed by Richard Bensinger (himself a veteran of the 1960s social movements). As graduates of the Institute proved their worth in organizing drives, demand for their services rose and the Institute expanded. A new beachhead for organizing was carved out, and the dialogue and mutual learning grew among the Institute, the organizing unions (such as SEIU, AFSCME, CWA, ACTWU, HERE, UAW), and other unions that wanted to organize (Hurd 1998).

Against this backdrop, when Bill Clinton and a Democratic House and Senate took office in early 1993, traditional labor leaders were elated. They had contributed to the Democratic victory and expected it to pay off (Friedman et al. 1994). Although they had no coherent strategy of their own for labor law reform, many had hopes for the Commission on the Future of Worker-Management Relations (the Dunlop Commission), appointed by Clinton to study and propose win-win reforms for labor-management relations and workplace regulation (Kochan 1995). The commission heard thousands of hours of testimony and studied long and hard, finally coming up with a consensual but rather watered down package—too watered down for labor but not watered down enough to please employers. In any event, the ink was barely dry on the commission's report when the Gingrich revolution swept into Congress, immediately foreclosing the possibility of any union-friendly legislative reform.

What was missing in 1994 was the same as in 1978: strong, popular pressure in favor of reforms aimed at reducing the barriers to union organizing success. The AFL-CIO and some member unions organized letter-writing campaigns but showed no inclination either to consult the members on this issue or to mobilize vast support, the support that a social movement unionism might have achieved. In any case, after decades of business unionism, it is unlikely that rank-and-file support would have been there to mobilize.

Union organizing activists, meanwhile, carried on with their work. They had looked skeptically at the Dunlop Commission from the start, and now, bolstered by successes in the field and by the failure of just about every other approach, they began to talk more openly about in-house revolution and a massive shift of resources from servicing to organizing. When Newt knocked the final props out from under the aging "our Democratic friends will take care of us" crowd—the labor equivalent in the political arena to business unionism in the economic arena—John Sweeney in 1995 announced his candidacy for president of the AFL-CIO.

In his winning campaign, Sweeney and his slate partners, Linda Chavez-Thompson and Rich Trumka, rode the crest of a growing internal reform movement. Upon taking office, the new leaders swept house at the Federation, brought in younger activists and staff members (most AFL-CIO departments are now headed by former social movement activists), cleared the red-baiting, movement-debilitating cold warriors out of the International Affairs Department, and announced a massive $20 million shift of resources into organizing.[5] Since 1995, expanded training programs and hiring incentives for organizers, new union education programs, central labor council reforms and mobilizations, countless organizing drives, and grassroots political campaigns have taken shape across the country. High-profile organizing, strike, and political victories have raised labor's visibility and strengthened its role as a newly fortified actor in the political economy.[6]

This is a heartening story as far as it goes, and clearly offers the best—and perhaps last—hope for the revival of the American labor movement. Activists and leaders, however, have much more in mind than a simple turnaround in declining union membership. What many

---

[5]Thus, veterans of earlier social movements help to promote new social movements (or in this case awaken a slumbering labor movement to its social movement potential), a pattern well known to social movement theorists (McAdam 1988; Voss and Sherman 1998).

[6]Watershed victories, none of which would have been possible in the 1980s, include the union representation election victory in early 1999 for 74,000 homecare workers in Los Angeles, the result of a long but relentless SEIU organizing drive; a major strike victory at UPS in 1997 as the Teamsters campaigned around the broad issue of part-time work with widespread public support; and the fast-track victory in Congress, also in 1997, led by the AFL-CIO in alliance with environmental groups, placing an important obstacle in the way of free-trade agreements lacking labor and environmental protections.

of them seek is nothing less than a widespread, full-fledged social movement unionism, one that can translate at the appropriate time into an even wider social movement coalition—with environmental, religious, human rights, consumer, women's groups, and others—fueled by two decades of growing inequality. New labor progressives believe conditions are right for such a social movement, and that indeed it will take the power of such a movement to transform the institutions, to reestablish the right to organize, and to overcome the "representation gap" and the general powerlessness so widespread in the economy and society (Sweeney 1996, 154–57; Bronfenbrenner et al. 1998). They also believe that in so doing, they will not only reduce America's extraordinary inequality but will push firms toward the high road, adding important social value at and beyond the workplace, compatible with strong economic performance (Wever 1998).

Causal Forces: Social Movements and Institutional Change

To summarize, social movements have shaped democratic institutions of workplace representation; in the absence of renewed social movement energy, these institutions in the postwar era have stagnated and decayed. The current hope and strategic orientation of many American labor leaders and activists is for the organizing energy of a new social movement unionism to build the broad power necessary for institutional reform and even transformation, to revitalize the labor movement, and to combat economic and social inequality.

In our effort to draw on and synthesize theoretical perspectives from several disciplines, we find insights from industrial relations, political science, and sociology all useful in making sense of the above story, including contemporary attempts at labor movement revival. From industrial relations we draw on the framework known as "strategic choice," which emphasizes the critical decisions made by key actors such as business, labor, and government (Kochan, Katz, and McKersie 1986). Thus, employer opposition played a major role in driving down union influence and numbers from the 1970s to the 1990s. This was not the only available option for American business and not the choice that all firms made, yet the institutional framework—weak labor laws, business unionism—made anti-unionism a viable option. Employer opposition was successful in part because the union response was so weak. Mired in bargaining concerns and day-to-day contract enforcement, unions responded to the new employer challenge defensively without well-articulated, proactive union strategies to counter the threat. The choices of employers and unions, in other words, help explain the decline of the labor movement and collective bargaining coverage in the 1970s and 1980s.

From political science (comparative political economy) and industrial relations, we draw on the important recent literature of the "new institutionalists" (such as Hall 1986; March and Olsen 1989; Steinmo, Thelen, and Longstreth 1992). Building in part on older industrial relations traditions (Perlman 1928; Commons 1934), these contemporary theorists emphasize the importance of institutions in accounting for economic, political, and social outcomes. The central argument is that institutions shape behavior. From this perspective, an institutional framework was consolidated in the 1940s and 1950s in the wake of the social movement upsurge of the 1930s, one that shaped the behavior and decisions of industrial relations actors throughout the postwar period. Collective bargaining, the NLRA and NLRB, industrial unions in mass production industries dominated by large firms all combined to shape the choices and decisions of unions and employers in relation to one another. Unions were lulled into a businesslike relationship with companies, helping to regulate the workplace through contract negotiation and enforcement. Employers accepted such arrangements until it became clear beginning in the 1970s that NLRA interpretation, NLRB enforcement, and business unionism together meant that other options were viable. Firms learned, for example, that they could open new facilities and keep them union-free, challenge union certification, defeat union-organizing drives, and press existing unions for major concessions. In this view, the industrial relations framework encouraged employer opposition to unions, which further weakened both the unions and the framework itself.

A shortcoming of the institutional literature is that it doesn't tell us how institutions come to be or how they change. Here we need to study social movements and draw on insights from sociology and social history (Johnston 1994; Kelly 1998; McAdam, McCarthy, and Zald, 1996; Tarrow 1994) because social movements are one important source of institutional change: social movements shape institutions. While social movement theorists primarily debate the origins and characteristics of social movements, our concern is also with the effects. The labor upsurge of the 1930s played a major role in shaping the institutions of industrial relations that would in turn shape labor-management relations throughout the postwar period. When labor to a large extent missed the social movement wave of the 1960s, unions lost the opportunity for an organizational revitalization that could have provided stronger mobilization against mounting employer opposition. By the 1990s, institutional atrophy and chronic union decline led a new generation of trade unionists to push for renewed social movement unionism, aimed at mobilizing the rank and file to combat employer opposition and fight for institutional reform. The renewed movement was especially aimed at strengthening the right to organize.

To sum up the current situation using all three theoretical perspectives, unions are now shifting their strategic orientation and promoting a new social movement unionism. This is aimed at organizing the unorganized and taking political action to strengthen union influence. The ultimate objective is to reform labor laws with new protections for workers and unions and to reform the institutions of industrial relations.

Social movement unionism is not the same thing as a social movement, to be sure. The former is a type of unionism that mobilizes the rank and file for specific actions and gains; the latter is a broad, often uncontrollable social phenomenon that comes along at particular periods of history. While social movement unionism can make specific gains in organizing or politics, a widespread social movement is a force that can reform or transform institutions. Labor activists in the United States promote social movement unionism in the absence of a broader social movement—but with the explicit goal of instigating that wider movement to provide the power necessary for institutional change.

Assessing the Prospects

We have laid out an optimistic scenario, arguing that a return to social movement unionism has the potential of saving and revitalizing the American labor movement. But what are the realistic prospects? Can the change in attitude and perspective at the AFL-CIO serve as a coalescing force? Can institutional inertia and conservative tendencies be overcome? Can the internal culture of unions adapt to a more freewheeling participatory style that welcomes activists and militants? Can women, people of color, and immigrant workers find a home in unions and achieve more prominent leadership roles? The transformation of unions from insurance agencies to centers of working-class activism has proven complicated. There are notable examples of unions that have shaken off institutional rigidity and redefined themselves, but at least as common are those that have clung to traditions while changing only at the margins.

A brief review of developments over the past few years is sobering. The level of activity has certainly been raised in the effort to promote organizing at the AFL-CIO and in many national unions. In one promising sign, union membership grew by 265,000 in 1999, the largest increase in twenty years. Nonetheless, union density stayed at 13.9 percent overall and dropped to 9.5 percent in the private sector (Hirsch and Macpherson, 2000, 11–12), the lowest level since before the Great Depression. Although much has been made of the increase, we should point out that since 1980 this is the fifth time that membership has increased and the third time that density has failed to decline. It seems that the increase in organizing ability has not yet been sufficient to overcome the tremendous hurdles of employer opposition, an unfriendly labor law, and deunionization through downsizing, outsourcing, and privatization.

Along with efforts at organizing, there have been signs of success on the political front. Efforts by the Sweeney administration to centralize control of political strategy have been supported broadly. The most notable change has been a dramatic increase in funding for the AFL-CIO political operation. In 1996 affiliated unions agreed to a special assessment (above normal dues) totaling $35 million to finance expanded electoral activities. The funding was renewed in comparable amounts for the 1998 and 2000 election cycles.

Major accomplishments of the heightened political involvement, however, have been largely defensive: defeat of "paycheck protection," defeat of "fast track," forestalling Republican attacks on unions (such as the Team Act). The major positive accomplishments have been on legislation only indirectly beneficial to unions, such as increases in the minimum wage. Nonetheless, the effort to build a lasting political presence continued with grassroots operations in one hundred districts in the year 2000. In an effort to boost political influence, the 1999 AFL-CIO convention took the unusual step of endorsing Al Gore for president prior to the primary season. This type of top-down political effort is quite distinct from rebuilding labor's political strength at the grassroots. Whether the centralized approach represents a change in philosophy or a bow to pragmatism is perhaps unimportant. What is more significant is the need for labor to crack through the seemingly impenetrable wall of resistance to any effort to create a union-friendly legal environment. In the long term, labor's ability to sustain its effort to build grassroots political operations may have more impact on laws and institutions than candidate endorsements. While the political strategy shows promise, its movement-building potential may be thwarted if grassroots components are delegated to the back burner.

In spite of mixed results, the very fact that unions are more active in organizing and politics, including new overtures to mobilize members in support of these efforts, offers an encouraging sign of movement-building potential. In late 1999 proponents of social movement unionism received a major boost in the "battle in Seattle." In a truly impressive and high-profile campaign, American unions brought tens of thousands of demonstrators to Seattle for the World Trade Organization meetings held the week of November 29 to December 3. Remarkable was the wide range of participants active and present in this coalition effort, including environmental, student, consumer, human rights, and religious organizations, along with hundreds of trade unionists from other countries.

The Seattle events gathered so much attention precisely because this was the first large-scale popular protest on American soil focused on the issue of democracy in the global economy. The demonstration demanded a social dimension to expanding international trade and asked, "What kind of global society is being created?" A major new front has opened in struggles for democratic and human rights, one that includes international labor solidarity as a central feature, and one that may be with us for years to come. American unions have arrived on this post–cold war international stage, showing a capacity to mobilize members and to build broad, influential coalitions addressing the very nature of the new global economy. Seattle may well turn out to be a key step forward for the revitalization of the American labor movement.

In the absence of convincing evidence that labor has, as a broad force, reinvented itself as a social movement, we can conclude only that the prospects are uncertain: much activity, many new initiatives, and mixed results. Examples of renewed activism are plentiful and exciting, yet in the absence of a broader social movement they are often limited in effect. The future depends on the decisions of leaders, the resolve of members, and the ultimate strategic direction adopted by unions. The barriers to internal reform, rank-and-file mobilization, broad coalition building, and international solidarity are high. As learning processes and activist experiences develop, however, there is reason for hope for the future of the American labor movement, far more reason than we have known in many years.

CHAPTER TWO

Organize for What?

The Resurgence of Labor as a Citizenship Movement

Paul Johnston

The most urgent question facing workers' movements in both North America and Europe as the new century dawned, therefore, was whether democracy could be rescued by extending its scope into the forbidden gardens of the market itself.

> —David Montgomery, in *Citizen Worker: The Experience of Workers in the United States with Democracy and the Free Market during the Nineteenth Century* (p. 162)

Yes, we know, it has finally sunk in: organize or die. But organize for what? What kind of unions do we want to build? Where do we want to take our workplaces, our communities, our country, our world? Yes, we know, we want to take our wages and conditions of employment out of competition. But if competition is the place we want to leave, what is the place we want to go?

No social movement can thrive without a shared self-understanding: a common vocabulary of meaning and action; shared questions; a collective learning process; and clear, common, and useful ideas that resonate among our ranks about what is wrong, what we want to do about it, and what part our movement has played and can play in making history. And this is the main missing ingredient in today's embryonic labor movement revival—what social movement scholars following Erving Goffman (1974) call a social movement frame—an orienting, motivating, and unifying idea; a story we tell about ourselves that identifies who are we, what we are doing, the challenges we face, and the ways in which we respond to those challenges. To the extent that we are engaged in an open and tolerant dialogue that explores answers to these questions, the new labor movement can become not only a movement in itself, but also a movement for itself. This is an old agenda, to be sure, but it is time to try again.

Social movement scholars typically consider social movement frames as the naive self-understanding of participants, or perhaps as interpretations that serve (or fail to serve) as strategic resources for the activists they study. Their own scholarly analysis, on the other hand, is framed as an objective outsider account. Regardless of their own naive self-understanding, however, scholars have long been, for better and for worse, active frame makers within the world of industrial relations, and the frames they have produced have reflected their own interests, identities, and assumptions. This scholarly participation continues.

Today, however, not only is the labor movement disoriented, but also those whose work it is to study it; so we lack not only social movement frames but also credible theories of the labor movement. And on the assumption that neither scholar nor activist has a monopoly on either insight or naïveté, we consider both problems as one. We need social movement frames based on our best social research, and we need theories of the labor movement based on the experience of practitioners. To achieve this—to ignite our collective learning process—we need to challenge and reject assumptions widely held on each side of the divide between theory and practice regarding the irrelevance of theory on the one hand and the naïveté of practitioners on the other. To the extent that we fail to do so, both scholar and activist will continue to fulfill each other's pessimistic expectations.

The term *social movement unionism* as used here is not a theory of labor relations but a descriptive term for an observable social force that occasionally, and recurrently, surfaces in a variety of different employment situations. This is only a beginning for our analysis, because it invites us to ask, "What is labor when it is a social movement? How does it vary, and why?" Moreover, the term allows us to distinguish between labor as a social movement and what is usually labeled "the labor movement", that is, labor as a field of organization associated with labor relations.

Labor organization may be shaped by social movements, and may even at times lead them. But labor organization is also shaped by many other influences in the world of labor-management relations. And although we tend to take our current form of labor organization for granted (as the only "sensible" way to do things), labor relations take many different forms in different countries and over time. Today's labor organization is partly a product of labor movements of the past, partly a product of employer and governmental responses to those movements and to the challenges of workforce administration more generally, and partly an arena within (and sometimes against) which new labor movements may emerge.

When labor surfaces as a social movement, on the other hand, it typically produces and in turn depends for its development on a very specific type of labor organization: labor as a social movement organization. Social movement organizations broadcast agendas for social change and mobilize, support, and deploy networks of membership and collective action in support of those agendas. In this sense, the current challenge of organizational transformation for those of us who are interested in labor movement revival is to build social movement organizations.

Our argument has two parts, one that stresses diversity and one commonality. The goals, resources, shared identities, forms of organization and collective action, patterns of discourse and change over time, and ultimately the historical possibilities of labor movements vary depending on the kind of employment relations and the historical circumstances within and against which they surface. Despite this diversity, we argue, labor movements all appeal to, rely upon, and seek in some sense to achieve the promise of citizenship. This is understandable, because citizenship refers to our position and behavior in the public institutions that, in part, orient, inform, and support labor's occasional challenge to the dictatorship of capital.

We begin by briefly reviewing the recent resurgence of social movement unionism in the United States. Then we argue that citizenship can serve as a powerful framework for research and practice in this field, while briefly relating this notion to the great body of citizenship theory and suggesting avenues for research and practice. The following section reviews labor movement activity in four main sectors—public workforce, corporate unionism, immigrant and other low-wage movements, and temp unionism—finding in each patterns of interest, action, and identity associated with the promise of citizenship. The final section discusses the convergence of these movements in local communities and considers the implications for labor councils and the possible emergence of new urban agendas.

The Resurgence of Social Movement Unionism

Every historical era is a crucible of change for labor both as a social movement and as an organization. Here in the United States and around the world, the past two decades of crisis have been no exception. Decline, defeat, and demoralization have driven us through a collective learning process. Painful confrontations with the failures of old union agendas have led us, helped us, forced us to challenge old assumptions about unionism. Assisted by the passage of an aging generation of leaders in so many locals, labor councils, international unions, finally in 1995 at the peak of the AFL-CIO itself, this process led to the emergence of a new cohort of activist leaders, themselves the product of social movements of recent decades. Consequently, there are more activists today dedicated to the revival of labor as a social movement in rank-and-file and staff and other leadership positions than in any period since the 1930s.

The gradual nature of this change makes it less visible to many who have joined the labor movement in recent decades. However, unionists and others who have observed the U.S. labor movement since mid-century can attest to profound changes in the composition, orientation, politics, policy, and practice of those staffing labor's organizational infrastructure since the post–World War II era.

To be sure, it would be easy to overstate this claim. Despite the argument made below for labor as a democratic social movement, today's labor union bureaucracy remains riddled with mini-fiefdoms, ruled by one union boss and administered by staff in ways that assume incompetence and exclude participation by ordinary union members. But the new AFL-CIO has also escaped from the clutch of cold war politics, overcome its conservative cultural politics, and abandoned its adversarial relationship to other social movements. Today many unions, some labor councils, and a lively crop of new community-based labor organizations are exploring new methods of organizing and new ways of representing people: innovating, testing new strategies for power, building new coalitions, and rethinking their agendas. We have been reshaped by a globalizing economy and an increasingly transnational workforce, and this process will continue. If the basic orientation of a labor federation or labor union organizational infrastructure makes a difference in a country's historical development, then the consequences are likely to be even more profound than now seems evident.[1]

These recent changes in the personnel and leadership of U.S. labor organization have been accompanied in recent years by encouraging evidence of a renewal of social movement unionism in the United States. This long-developing but still-embryonic renewal has so far only succeeded in stopping the downward trend in labor movement strength most cited by scholars and commentators: the rate of union membership. Membership in the private sector now hovers at the depths of its long decline which began in the 1950s. But union membership growth is less a measure of social movement unionism than a sign, after the fact, of its success. Strike activity might be a better measure, but the Department of Labor has stopped collecting data on most work stoppages. Moreover, the last two decades have produced deep reservations about the strike even among more militant union leaders.

No social movement, moreover, can take root and grow without access to effective levers of power and the disruptive, expressive, and transforming experience of collective action. As a result, in a learning process that may have decisive effects on the direction and the prospects for labor movement revival, labor union leaders and activists are today groping for new strike strategies and other more viable forms of collective action. The explosion of strike activity that began in 2000 has provided an arena for this learning process to unfold.

Before this recent upsurge of militancy, however, the beginnings of labor movement resurgence were mainly evident to participants and mainly expressed in pervasive organizational crises and changes, occasional surges of collective action, and new organizing and other initiatives that occasionally succeeded and more often failed. Even now labor has by no means erupted once again as a history-shaping social movement in the United States. But gradually, unevenly, with advances only slightly more common than setbacks, the institutional apparatus of the

---

[1]An example is the current shift in the stance of the AFL-CIO toward immigrant workers' rights, which has further destabilized an already crisis-ridden immigration policy domain and is likely to lead to significant policy change at the federal level. If the economic and political exclusion of first-generation immigrants has been an important factor in the past century of U.S. economic and political development, then this shift may produce a radical change in the direction of development over the coming decades.

U.S. labor movement is restructuring in a manner that strengthens its capacity to function as a network of social movement organization.

Significantly, in contrast to past history, this resurgent unionism is finally opening the doors of labor to immigrant workers, and also taps into the energies of civil rights and other social justice movements. Also evident is a new commitment to organizing, including ambitious industry-wide organizing drives and some even more ambitious regional campaigns. Other evidence includes a revitalized and growing labor movement in building maintenance, agriculture, and hotel and restaurant industries, and surges of organizing among Latino immigrants in low-wage industries; on the strike front, a trend away from the debacles of the post-PATCO era, which appears to have sparked renewed worker confidence and has recently led to a greater volume of strike activity; in local government across the country, a wave of "living wage" initiatives and home healthcare campaigns, both targeting contracted public workers; on college campuses, a steady pattern of militancy among graduate student employees; among temporary employees and other occupational groups, a variety of new worker associations often not affiliated with the AFL-CIO; at all levels of electoral action, sharply intensified grassroots mobilization; on the international front, a break with the past half-century of collaboration with reactionary and repressive forces against progressive unionisms and the beginnings of cross-border organizing and global solidarity; quietly and behind the scenes, a new degree of nonsectarian cooperation among the networks of longtime left-wing activists now well entrenched in unions formerly hostile to their involvement; and now in community after community across the United States, the emergence of a great variety of creative new labor-community organizing projects and coalitions addressing social and economic justice issues in arenas extending far beyond the old scope of bargaining over wages, benefits, and working conditions.

The central role of social movements in this process might best be illustrated by imagining the state of the unions in the United States today were it not for social movements among just two groups of workers. Before the recent emergence of their labor movements, both public workers and low-wage immigrant workers had long been scorned by the labor establishment. Now, despite real vitality in a variety of other sectors, it is probably fair to say that labor clings to life thanks mainly to the phenomenal growth of public service unionism from the 1960s to the 1980s and to the renewal of industrial organizing among immigrant workers in a variety of industries, from agriculture to the service sector, in more recent years. These energies have surfaced in several international unions, but they intersect in the Service Employees International Union, with its strong public-sector and private health and building maintenance divisions. Were it not for these episodes of social movement unionism, the successful challenge to Lane Kirkland and his anointed successor for leadership in the AFL-CIO in 1995 would have been unlikely to occur, and SEIU's John Sweeney might well be the failed leader of a second-rate international union.

The Challenge of Diversity

Labor relations today are characterized by extraordinary diversity, and both scholars and practitioners can be faulted for drawing conclusions about all work and labor relations from one piece of the workforce. Too often, for example, scholars focused either on trends observable in the higher waged corporate workforce (e.g., Kochan et al 1986) or on contingent employment in the new informational workforce (e.g., Hecksher 1988) tend to generalize from that part to the whole of the workforce and its labor movements. Meanwhile, "in the real world," unionists relying on repertoires similarly transplanted from one sector to another have frequently paid a more painful price.

The public and the private sector, for example, have displayed contrary patterns of change for decades, with crisis coming in the former and relative stability in the latter during the expansive 1960s and 1970s, followed by crisis in the private sector and unprecedented stability and union security in the public during 1980s. Despite this, most industrial relations scholars (and organizational researchers more generally) neglect the sectoral difference. And within the public and private sectors, trends in employment and labor relations have also displayed wide and sometimes contrary patterns of variation: intense and bitter conflict alongside consolidated labor-management partnerships, the growth of "union-free environments" alongside fully reorganized industries, unprecedented union security and job security alongside massive subcontracting of professional work for still higher wages and low-wage work for still lower wages, the wholesale expulsion of many workers from the organization into contingent status, and the simultaneous expansion of both high-wage high-skill and low-wage manual and service work.

Also, labor movement activity in the United States lately has been concentrated in the service sectors, and conventional wisdom remains convinced that the time of industrial unionism among semiskilled blue collar workers—with its historic contribution to democratic development—is long dead.[2] But clearly, oppressive industrial employment concentrated in closely knit ethnic communities continues alongside all these postindustrial workplaces. These conditions continue and expand, of course, throughout our increasingly integrated global economy and society. They continue and are continuously renewed here in the United States as well, fed in part by in-migration to work in agriculture, food processing, light manufacturing, hotel and restaurant, building maintenance, health services, and virtually all of the lowest wage positions in a wide variety of other industries.

Moreover, virtually all these patterns of diversity coincide with and are reinforced by basic fault lines of racial and ethnic differences. Among the various segments of the U.S. workforce, labor movements typically surface within groups bounded by language, culture, residential, and other circumstances associated with race and ethnicity. As a result, within a given urban region, participants in different labor movements typically inhabit radically different social universes.

How, then, in the face of all this diversity, is it even conceivable that we might both analyze and orient our practice with a single theory of the labor movement?

This diversity is more than a theoretical challenge. It is also a serious practical problem. It can produce competing leadership groups, conflicting interests or agendas for labor, competing claims for labor movement resources, and other barriers to coalition building. Also, assump-

---

[2]Aging scholars have (since Kerr et al. 1960) concluded that the traumas of early industrialism have long been left behind in advanced countries like the United States. In a parallel vein, the younger generation of new social movement scholars and post-Marxist radical intellectuals similarly pronounce the labor movement passé.

tions and strategies taken for granted and transplanted from one context to another frequently lead to catastrophe for workers and their unions. And again, our ideas about the labor movement are not only analytical and strategic tools but also, as social movement frames, social and cultural forces uniting or dividing us and orienting or disorienting us. Paradoxically, then, this diversity makes a coherent theory of the labor movement not only more difficult but also more necessary to achieve.

Labor as a Citizenship Movement

Our argument is that despite the diversity, the different labor movements emerging in each of the circumstances we have discussed all seek to defend, exercise, and extend the boundaries of citizenship, and all these labor movements converge with other citizenship movements that seek to develop public institutions that defend and rebuild local communities in an increasingly globalized public order. Practically speaking, this implies a new way of framing our claims and orienting our strategies: no longer is the fate of a particular bargaining unit at stake, but the status and future of a community; no longer does our power depend mainly on market position or on homogenous coalitions with similar workers in the same labor market, but also on heterogeneous coalitions assembled around a vision of the future or, implicitly at least, a potential governing agenda.

To forestall misunderstanding, citizenship refers not only to formal political participation but also to a variety of forms of membership, use of public resources, and other kinds of participation in public life. Citizenship rights refer not only to legally sanctioned rights but also to rights that may be denied but are nonetheless claimed by participants and so may orient and motivate social movements. Moreover, citizenship refers not only to the status of U.S. citizens, but also to the citizenship status, behavior, and claims of citizens of all countries. Although mainly associated with the nation-state today, citizenship also surfaces within other politically regulated institutions, from the labor union and local government to the transnational and global levels. Here, citizenship is defined in this expansive and developing sense, as our relationship to public institutions.

Historically, citizenship has always meant exclusion as well as inclusion. Citizenship is always the imposition of an extreme power upon a population. Citizenship always legitimizes a power, which, behind the veil of "the public good," always favors one private interest over another. But from a strictly scientific point of view, the question is not whether we like citizenship but whether it is a social force moving in our world and informing our labor movements. The promise of citizenship may still be valid if we can discern a developmental logic within which the hidden tyrannies, biases, hypocrisies, and other boundaries implicit in citizenship are challenged by social movements which themselves arise from, appeal to, and seek to strengthen the institutional structure of citizenship. Citizenship's critics, it seems, are themselves oriented by the promise of citizenship.

This perspective does not privilege the labor movement above all other forces for social change. It suggests, in fact, that the labor movement achieves its full potential only when it aligns itself and even merges with other democratic social movements or when it enables its participants to express themselves and act not only as workers but as members of a community with multiple interests and identities. This family of social movements does not necessarily embrace all of today's emancipatory social movements. Although citizenship movements are frequently often also women's movements and environmental movements, for example, some feminist and ecological insights and agendas are beyond the scope of citizenship. Nor does this perspective claim that so-called citizenship movements understand themselves as such, although when they are in motion, something approaching this language does typically appear. But this perspective does propose to anchor the labor movement in the broader and still far-from-finished movement for expanded democracy. Citizenship theory, we claim, offers a unifying social movement frame, an essential explanatory tool, and a practical and strategic orientation for scholars and other participants. Successful labor movement initiatives, we argue, draw upon the resources, resonate with the themes, and defend or extend the boundaries of citizenship.

Moving as it does around and against rather than through the exercise of market power, this citizenship movement frame certainly does not fit the familiar inherited routines, organization, and self-concept of business unionism in postwar America. It points, in fact, to connections with historical processes beyond the conventional boundaries of the labor movement and the realm of industrial relations. The citizenship frame also resonates with other approaches that similarly link labor movement revival to broader agendas (Brecher and Costello 1990; Banks 1991; Waterman 1993; Sweeney 1996; Eisenscer 1999; Fine 1998; Scipes 1992). Most, though not all, of these views also anchor resurgent unionism in the defense of local communities. The citizenship frame resonates with the social movement unionism of countries such as Brazil, Mexico, South Africa, South Korea, and the Philippines, where the most dynamic and powerful labor movements in the world today take on issues of democracy, human rights, and social justice not only in the context of labor relations but also in the larger society (Foweraker and Landman 1997; Scipes 1992). It reclaims our roots in the citizenship movements of the nineteenth century, as revealed by social historians tracing the relationship between class conflict and the emergence and development of citizenship (Marshall 1950; Hobsbawm 1968; Thompson 1974; Barbalet 1988; Rueschemeyer, Stephens, and Stephens, 1992; Montgomery 1993; Steinberg 1995). It observes, however, that the western European and U.S. path through industrialization to expanded citizenship is neither unique nor the final expression of this force for global democratic development. And it lends support to the already-evident notion that this larger democratic revolution is an unfinished business and we are participants in it.

Labor Relations and the Civic Regime

For reasons rooted in a half-century of social and intellectual history, research on contemporary labor relations, social movements, citizenship, political processes, public organization, and the state is not well integrated. I am convinced that citizenship theory can produce historic breakthroughs both in social theory—which has for centuries wrestled unsatisfactorily with the problem of the state—and in social practice, long haunted as well by the problem of power in political organizations ranging from the labor union to the political party to, most tragically, the socialist state. But given the wide range of views and the amount of dialogue needed to fully realize the promise of citizenship theory, it would not be useful to attempt to survey the field here. Nor is it possible, in this context, to consider how to grasp the relationship between citizenship and various kinds of labor in concrete detail. Rather, we can refer to a set of widely shared understandings about the institutions of citizenship and point to fairly obvious connections between them and the challenges faced by the labor movement.

Participants in today's dialogue and struggle over citizenship are generally familiar with several basic dimensions of citizenship, each of which is associated with a particular set of institutions. Although interpretations vary, most would agree that these include the triad of basic civil rights, political rights, and social welfare rights, which were the focus of T. H. Marshall's (1950) classic theory of citizenship. Each are associated not only with a particular set of rights but with a particular set of complex public institutions, and each can be easily associated with a particular type of "pro-citizenship" social movement.

Civil rights are associated with individual rights and the civil and criminal legal system. Political rights are concerned with electoral processes and other forms of participation in the political system. Social welfare rights are associated with "family needs" for social insurance and the social welfare programs that comprise much of local and state government. Most citizenship scholars follow Marshall by including educational resources in the last category on the grounds that, like minimal subsistence, education is a necessary condition of political participation. We will not address the merits of this approach, but simply consider that as the informational revolution accelerates and as struggles over educational opportunities become pervasive, there may be good reason to follow Talcott Parsons (1966) in treating educational institutions, status, and opportunities as a distinct field of citizenship or stratified inclusion and exclusion from public rights or resources.[3]

Also, students of citizenship have long recognized labor market institutions, workers' rights, and labor-management relations as a dis-

---

[3]Liberals emphasize civil rights; Republicans, political rights; social democrats and some feminists, social welfare rights. All are of vital interest to the labor movement. Educational radicals may eventually play a comparable part. Pluralist political science, orthodox Marxism, and some feminists, on the other hand, are profoundly cynical about the promise of citizenship. For our purposes here, it is only necessary for them to acknowledge that, although

tinct and particularly problematic domain of citizenship, under the label of "industrial" or "economic" citizenship. The state of our economic citizenship, or economic citizenship status, is observable as the complex of public law, policy, regulation, opinion, interests, identities, activities, and resources that pervade and shape our economic lives. Taken in this sense, variation in citizenship status includes not only differences in whether a constituency has a political voice in a community but also observable differences in personal autonomy and protection from abuses of authority and power, differences in access to social services and health care, differences in informational resources and educational opportunities, differences in coverage by labor relations or related laws, and so on.

From the standpoint of the labor movement, on the other hand, economic citizenship is also an ideal. As an ideal, it is our answer to the question posed above: If we want to take our conditions of employment out of competition, where do we want to take them? Our answers range from a legally enforceable contract to public (or socialist) work to worker control of the labor process to full-fledged "economic democracy" or workers' self-government. Whatever our agenda for economic citizenship might be, however, it is inevitably problematic because citizenship claims conflict fundamentally with the workings of the labor market and the institutions of private ownership.[4] This fault line of conflict between capitalism and democracy is built into the system, so to speak, and produces tensions and other effects in the social structure and at deeper levels of personal experience.[5] It results in struggles that may drive changes not only along the boundaries of

---

promises may be illusory, movements that appeal to them may not be. Two other schools of thought are less likely to follow this argument: "civil society" enthusiasts for whom civil society is not part of public institutions but an independent social order, and a certain strand of neo-institutional organization theory (e.g., Soysal 1994) which holds that citizenship simply expands inexorably through the force of its own rationality.

[4]Although beyond the scope of this discussion, economic citizenship is also problematic because of other internal contradictions and historical processes.

[5]Marshall concludes his famous discussion of citizenship with a discussion of this tension as reflecting a "basic conflict between social rights and market value . . . not an invention of muddled brains [but] . . . inherent in our social system." (1950:68–74). Bendix (1964), Giddens (1982), Bowles and Gintis (1986), Turner (1986), Barbalet (1988), Held (1989), and Janoski (1998) all wrestle with this issue.

industrial citizenship but also in other citizenship domains, and so has been associated with citizenship development from its earliest known emergence in ancient Greece to the modern world. Such conflict may lead, for example, to changes in the social wage. An expansive social wage can change the economic balance of power by changing workers' vulnerability to unemployment, while the political determination of public policy (or the battle over the definition of the public interest) draws all parties into public life.

Connections should also be clear between the status and rights of workers and their unions, or economic citizenship more generally, and each of the other citizenship domains. Thus, for example, whether workers enjoy basic civil rights such as freedom of association and travel or freedom to enter into and to leave employment will have a decisive effect on their conditions of employment (as is evident in recent patterns of change in the status of unauthorized immigrant labor in the U.S. and elsewhere). Whether and how political processes produce public policies that regulate labor unions, capital mobility, employment practices, labor-management relations, the social wage, apprenticeship and training programs, and the direction of economic development itself obviously have a profound effect on the status of workers and the interests of their unions. Whether workers have access to educational resources in today's increasingly flexible and skill-centered labor markets, and who controls these resources and the learning that occurs within them, and whether and how these educational resources mediate between the needs of workers—especially educationally disadvantaged workers—and those of employers, are of tremendous interest to workers and workers-to-be and of increasing interest to labor unions and other worker organizations as well.

Finally, anthropologists and others have advanced the concept of cultural citizenship, through which groups claim space for the expression of their identities and recognition of their own membership in public life (Flores and Benmayor 1997). Rather than just another subdivision of citizenship, this is an important crosscutting concept. Historically, democracy has always emerged in institutions that seek to impose a homogenous cultural identity on their citizenry. The incompatibility of homogenous cultural identities with core principles of citizenship is evident, however, in today's multicultural and increasingly transnational society. So the concept of cultural citizenship is a useful way to grasp the struggle by excluded groups and their allies for public institutions that embrace heterogeneity or a more fully developed citizenship. This is a recurrent struggle in a country like the United States, continuously transformed due to war, conquest, slavery, and immigration. Consequently, even as cultural pluralism repeatedly defines fault lines of conflict in U.S. society, it also offers openings for citizenship development toward a "Durkheimian moment" of less particularistic, admittedly tenuous, but a more consistent and universalistic form of citizenship.[6]

The assertion of cultural citizenship and struggles for institutions that embrace a multicultural, often racialized membership are certainly visible in today's unions, not only in struggles for recognition, membership, and leadership by (and among) previously excluded groups, but also in efforts to open them up to participation and leadership of women. Once again, recent gains on these fronts are mainly the product of social movements among public workers and immigrants.

Thus, we have six distinct concepts of citizenship. Four of these—civil, political, social, and educational—are indirectly important, particularly in circumstances in which crisis drives workers and their unions to grope for ways to outflank employer power. The fifth concept, economic citizenship, is in perpetual tension with capitalism and clearly central to labor's agenda whatever it might be. A final crosscutting dimension refers to the diverse cultural identities that must be recognized and expressed throughout a democratic public order.[7]

We do not suggest that this descriptive list is a theory of citizenship; for that, we would need to treat public institutions as a whole. But we can observe that every set of public institutions is characterized by a particular set of such arrangements, which together might be termed "the civic regime." It should be clear that this territory is sufficiently

---

[6]The implicit "progressivism" of this view may grate upon some postmodern sensibilities, but the appearance of an evident logic of development in a process such as citizenship implies only a possible historical direction, which may well be blocked or subverted by other historical forces.

[7]We neglect here the important and contested arena of environmental rights and ecological identity (Van Steenbergen 1994).

broad and its geography sufficiently varied and complex that it might give rise to a variety of different struggles over the terms and conditions of citizenship, not only a variety of labor movements, but also other social movements expressing the interests and identities of other groups within the framework of public life. For our purposes, it should be clear that the civic regime is the terrain on, through, and against which such movements emerge and develop, at least in part. It is also a product of such movements, at least in part, and certain changes in the civic regime are the goal of democratic social movements, at least in part.

This suggests the notion of a family of social movements shaped by the citizenship status of their participants and distinguished by their appeal to the promise of democracy. According to a compelling current of social movement scholarship, these democratizing social movements are evoked, oriented, and sustained by a particular kind of conversation that occurs within and is evoked around them. In these public conversations, people address one another in a manner that assumes a fundamental equality and openness to dialogue over questions of common concern. In this kind of encounter, issues are decided on the basis of argument rather than authority or tradition. These conversations may help to constitute people as citizens of a shared public and equip democratic social movements with exceptional learning and adaptive abilities.[8]

Other such citizenship movements can include movements for democratic revolution or reform, consumer rights, welfare rights, corporate accountability, international human rights, student movements, movements for racial justice, some urban social movements, and some currents of feminist, gay, lesbian, and environmentalist movements. By no means homogenous or oriented toward a single vision, all these democratic social movements are informed by a culture of critical discourse (Gouldner 1976). All share a commitment to communicative competence (Habermas 1979), which drives a collective learning process (Elder 1993). All are best evoked or organized by methods that

---

[8]These practices suggest discursive modes of citizenship organizing and participatory social research which may help to constitute and reconstitute public life and are corrosive and potentially subversive to more hierarchical groups.

rely on such discourse to challenge conventional codes in ways that constitute and reconstitute public spaces (Melucci 1996). Because of the instability of any definition of "the public" or its "interest," all share a tentative, de-centered attitude that leaves them always incomplete, nicely postmodern.

A Unifying Agenda for a Diverse Movement

The U.S. workforce appears to face at least four radically dissimilar types of labor relations environment: public employment, low-wage work in a wide variety of industries with high concentrations of African-American and immigrant labor, corporate employment in large organizations, and slicing across all three of the above sectors temporary employment, including work for a contractor or temporary service provider.

These four categories are neither exhaustive nor exclusive, but because they are defined by basic patterns of economic differentiation, they do allow us to capture much of the patterns of recent labor movement activity in the United States. To what extent, then, do variations within and among the labor movements that surface in these settings reflect changes and differences in the civic regimes that constitute them, and to what extent can all be grasped as citizenship movements that converge on the defense of local communities? A systematic answer to these questions is beyond our capabilities here, but a very brief overview of developments in each of these arenas will at least suggest an answer.

Public Service Unionism

The only truly significant U.S. union growth of the past half-century came, of course, in the public workplace, mainly in schools and other local government, formerly despised and excluded in the house of labor. Recent progress in health care and educational organizing continues this trend.

Public workers occupy a unique economic position, since they are employed in the production of politically defined "public needs," and so they have a unique relationship to the local communities through the local agencies where they are concentrated. The labor movements of these "citizen workers" follow a distinct logic of labor-management relations, defined by their emergence in political bureaucracies. Their movements surface and their strategic coalitions are located in the differentiated political universe that surrounds each single agency, rather than homogenous labor markets that slice across organizations. Public workers are empowered mainly by their status in political coalitions and by their capacity to articulate their particular claims as legitimate public interests.[9]

Sectoral differences have had decisive consequences for patterns of change over time in public- versus private- sector labor relations. While the private-sector labor movement drifted into steady decline in the 1960s and 1970s, those parts of the public workforce empowered by growth in the social welfare state and the racialized, gendered, urban upheavals of that era produced new labor laws, explosive union growth, and a new species of adversarial employee associations. Public organizations grew not so much through conventional organizing strategies, but through the transformation of long-existing (and essentially similar) employee associations and unions into social movement organizations. They achieved the first major beachheads of clerical and professional unionism, established new work environments of freer speech and less arbitrary and abusive supervision, and proved themselves powerful new constituencies for expanded (and occasionally for improved) public services.[10] They produced new African-American and female union leadership, and in the comparable-worth or pay equity movement a wave of feminist unionism. Despite the often bureaucratic character of the organizations they left in their wake, these public worker movements rearranged the political and organizational landscape not only of unionism but also of urban life, creating the possibility—still unrealized—of progressive new urban coalitions between labor and

---

[9]Public employee strikes are more likely to succeed, for example, when they combine economic with noneconomic demands, frame economic demands as legitimate claims or principles of good government, and ally different kinds of workers in collective action. On these and related generalizations about the public workplace, see Johnston 1994.

[10]Today's correctional officers' unions have similarly benefited from and increasingly organized the "law and order" coalition of recent decades, which provides the effective political demand for expansion of the prison-industrial complex.

neighborhood movements, with far-reaching implications. And they disclosed a dimension of public life still unrecognized in political theory—the status, organization, and activity of the working people who produce what in the very heart of politics is defined as "the public interest."

By the time of the PATCO strike, however, most public employee unions had already experienced their own PATCO-like traumas at the local level, typically brought on by their own mechanical application of radically inappropriate bargaining agendas and strike strategies borrowed from the private sector.[11] By and large they failed to fully grasp the power of labor-community coalitions in campaigns for good government. For the most part, they were relieved to join in new labor-management coalitions against the Republican assault of the Reagan era alongside their erstwhile adversaries in local government. Their newly empowered leaders closed down the drive for more democratic public workplaces, turned away from developing labor-community coalitions, and consolidated their own positions. Without the emergence of extraordinary leadership, these more recent trends are unlikely to be reversed until a new period of recession triggers fiscal crises that again spur attacks on organized public workers.[12]

Although most public worker movements have subsided to a simmer, the unions they left in their wake represent a distinct kind of unionism, uniquely related to local communities, which continues to play a powerful role in the defense of local government, universities and other education, health care, and social services.[13] Moreover, as we will see below, the more recent emergence of new urban leadership out of the private-sector labor movement may provide yet another opportunity to assemble these new resources into progressive new urban coalitions.

---

[11]These traumas were promoted by a main current in the industrial relations research of that era which was dedicated to the development and diffusion of strategies to contain those troublesome public worker movements (e.g., Wellington and Winter 1971; Kochan 1974; Sumners 1976; Katz 1984.)

[12]Education may depart from the trajectory of the rest of the public sector in intelligible ways, as demographic trends, racial differences, generational politics, and informational development also affect wages, class size, and the politics of educational production.

[13]See, for example, Piven and Cloward (1988).

Community-Based Corporate Unionism

Then out of the private sector came the great resistance movements sparked by the failure of the industrial relations model of bargaining unionism by the early 1980's: resistance to concession bargaining, two-tier wage systems, plant closures, and subcontracting. Early on these mainly took the form of movements within unions to vote down concessionary agreements and to unseat those who had negotiated them. More often than not they failed, but they still began to transform unions into arenas for participation. Increasingly, though, local unions began to take a stand against concessions and plant closures. In case after case, beleaguered workers and their unions discovered new resources as they reached out for support to other community members in their churches, schools, neighborhood organizations, and across the country and the world in "corporate campaigns" patterned on the early efforts of the United Farm Workers (UFW).

These were, and are, often poignantly painful battles mobilizing whole communities against the seemingly inexorable logic of capitalist development, and more often than not they failed and continue to fail. Catastrophic defeats like the mid-1980s strike by Local P-9 of the United Food and Commercial Workers union at the Austin, Minnesota, Hormel plant and the six-year-long Caterpillar strike by the United Auto Workers Local 751 in Decatur, Illinois, displayed both the challenges facing this segment of the workforce and the response by labor organizations shaped in previous decades of collective bargaining. Both local unions resisted the tide of concessionary bargaining, both inspired broad support among grassroots labor activists across the country, and both were ultimately abandoned by their respective international unions.

On the other hand, the 1988–90 Pittston coal miners' strike showed that other directions are possible. In that successful struggle, whole communities mobilized in defense of their right to health care, deploying tactics and discourse consciously adopted from the civil rights movement and the UFW union. In contrast to the P-9 and Caterpillar debacles, they were solidly backed by an international union with its leadership already renewed through internal rebellion. More recently, the massive Teamsters strike at United Parcel Service in 1997 also ended in success. Again, not coincidentally, the strikers framed their claims as a public issue, and again they enjoyed the solid support of an international leadership renewed through internal upheaval.[14] That strike emboldened other workers and their unions such as the United Auto Workers in Flint, Michigan; their eight-week 1998 strike snowballed into a massive shutdown of GM production and secured similar public support through its challenge to downsizing and sub-contracting. It ended in a standoff rather than a union victory, but this was still a far cry from the wrenching Caterpillar debacle.

In every case in the process of articulating their appeals, these union-ists found their particular concerns translated into the general inter-ests of their community. Most of these campaigns did little more than slow the erosion of labor's industrial base, and even as they began to take up the tools of grassroots political action to moderate the impact of plant closures and even began to envision new institutions that would allow local communities to control capital investment, partici-pants did not always rely on the language of citizenship. Among union-ists, however, these experiences produced a radically new grasp of the relationship between corporate decision making and community in-terests and new language linking their claims to those interests. New levers of power began to become visible, and this stimulated a great deal of innovation as organizers groped for new strategies to outflank the overwhelming bargaining position of corporate employers. These strategies involved growing recognition of the potential power of labor-community coalitions and recognizing the importance of economic development planning, the value of research (not only for strategic planning but also for identifying avenues of political action to influ-ence employer decisions), and the imperative of transnational solidar-ity in the face of global competition.

Then a hiatus ensued. The volume of traditional economic strikes declined still further, and many wondered whether the strike was per-haps dead after all. Even as the economic strike continue to fade away,

---

[14] It may be a mistake to assume that recent changes in the leadership of the Teamsters Union will reverse these trends. The Hoffa administration will face election and must cover its left flank. The apparently enduring achievement of what is in effect a loose two-party sys-tem in the Teamsters Union falsifies longstanding claims by venerable sociologists regarding the death of union democracy (Lipset et al. 1956)

however, the political strike increasingly took its place. The April 2000 Los Angeles–area strike victory of the Justice for Janitors campaign, discussed below, was a dramatic demonstration of the power of the political strike.[15] As of this writing, pioneering local unions once again are experiencing "the school of the strike." There they are relearning old lessons about strike organization and strategy and exploring new possibilities for the political strike in the informational age.

Low-Wage and Immigrant Workers' Movements

As suggested by our repeated reference to the UFW, Chicanos and first- and second-generation Mexican immigrants have been a repeated source of inspiration and innovation for the new labor movement. Most of the innovations employed in today's labor movement were developed decades ago by the UFW, which maneuvered as we maneuver today to outflank the superior market position and political power of employers.[16] Agriculture differs from other low-wage sectors in terms of labor law or more generally in terms of the civic regime confronting immigrant workers.[17] Despite this, similar patterns of labor movement activity in agriculture, building maintenance, and hotel and restaurant industries suggest that we revise the common view of the UFW as a unique case and see it rather as a pioneer.

Some of the earliest and least-noted movements for union democracy and against concessions occurred among Latino and African-American custodians in the Service Employees' frequently corrupt building maintenance unions, which in many cities had been forced to adopt two-tier wage agreements by the mid to late 1970s. Stimulated by racial succession in the workforce, those developments sparked

---

[15]In Los Angeles in 2000, SEIU campaigners finally demonstrated that it was possible to win the second stage in the Justice for Janitors campaign. The three stages were (1) win recognition, (2) achieve significant improvements in wages and working conditions in the heavily competitive building maintenance industry, and (3) start dealing with the "social wage" or conditions of urban life faced by low-waged and immigrant workers (e.g., housing costs), develop a political agenda, and seek to become part of a new urban governing coalition.

[16]The United Farm Workers Organizing Committee (UFWOC, predecessor to the United Farm Workers Union) was conducting fully developed corporate campaigns by 1970.

[17]Within agriculture, variations in wages, working conditions, and other employment relations are powerfully affected by variations in labor law.

democratic reform movements and other upheavals, to which the international union responded, as was its practice, with trusteeships and mergers.

By the mid-1980s, however, organizers influenced by the UFW and by organizing experience in comparable conditions in the garment industry assumed responsibility for SEIU's organizing department, and they in turn launched the Justice for Janitors campaign.[18] By the early 1990s, "J for J" had demonstrated in city after city the power of direct and disruptive collective action, oriented by careful strategic planning, armed with corporate campaign tactics, allied with community coalitions, and framed as campaigns for economic and social justice, to tap the social movement potential of this workforce and the larger community in locally based industry-wide organizing campaigns. The campaigns would generate economic and political power and use them to secure contracts with building maintenance firms through tactics targeting both the major companies behind the building maintenance contractors and the public agencies that contracted for their services.

Significantly, these campaigns reorganized the building maintenance industry during a period when a labor surplus in this low-wage labor market made it a poor target by conventional standards of union strategic planning. More than any other factor, the Justice for Janitors campaign legitimized SEIU's John Sweeney in his 1995 bid for leadership in the AFL-CIO.

The Justice for Janitors campaign was only the most visible of a series of immigrant workers' movements that effectively rebuilt declining unions in this period. These movements included hotel and restaurant employees in San Francisco, Los Angeles, Boston, and elsewhere; drywall workers in southern California's construction industry; democratic upheavals in the Teamsters' food industry unions; and following Cesar Chavez' death, the resurgence of a somewhat more strategic and less sectarian UFW union. Also in this era, labor organizers launched a variety of new community-based organizing projects targeting im-

---

[18]In a set of comparative studies centered on strikes, Johnston (1994) examines the character and course of public worker movements, the history behind the emergence of Justice for Janitors in California's major building maintenance union, and the surge of feminist unionism associated with the pay equity movement in both sectors.

migrants and other low-wage workers outside the framework of collective bargaining.[19]

Along with the new organizing agenda and, most recently, the Living Wage campaign, these initiatives are bringing into focus an important feature of the new labor movement: it mobilizes and represents working people beyond the boundaries of the bargaining unit, in dealings not limited to employers and on issues not limited to the scope of recognition. This is dismissed as a digression by some organizers, who prefer to go straight for the membership cards and the union contracts. The next several years should show whether these "community-oriented" efforts can facilitate organizing and serve as a viable mode of labor organization and civic participation, or indeed if they can survive.

The 1990s were also a period of dramatic change in the formal citizenship status of immigrant workers, especially for Mexican immigrants concentrated in California. If, as we have argued, the labor movement is both strongly shaped by the citizenship regime and in turn a force for the expanded development of citizenship, then those changes should be closely related to variations in labor movement activity among these immigrant workers. When analyzed, the social history of the period reveals this to be the case.

Specifically, for example, we find that patterns of industrial militancy across different industries and over time are directly related to the citizenship regime in effect in those industries and at those periods, including both citizenship status and the intensity of enforcement. Evidence includes data on union membership trends in the 1980s, when lax Immigration and Naturalization Service enforcement practices were accompanied by a 16-percent increase in Latino union membership

---

[19]Jennifer Gordon (1999) provides a partial list that includes the Workplace Project in Long Island, the Latino Workers Center, the Chinese Staff and Workers Association, and the Workers Awaaz in New York City; the Tenants and Workers Support Committee in Alexandria, Virginia; the Korean Immigrant Workers Association in Los Angeles and the Asian Immigrant Women's Advocates in Oakland, California; the Workers Organizing Committee in Portland, Oregon; La Mujer Obrera in El Paso, Texas; the Immigrant Workers' Resource Center in Boston, Massachusetts; the Mississippi Workers Rights Project in Oxford, Mississippi; and the Coalition of Immokalee Workers in Immokalee, Florida. The author's own work is based at the Citizenship Project, a Mexican immigrant labor-community–based organization dedicated to expanded citizenship, broadly defined.

while union membership rates collapsed in the rest of the private-sector workforce (Freitas 1993). The Mexican and Central American workers' movement surged still further in the early 1990s among workers benefiting from the amnesty provisions of the 1986 Immigration Reform and Control Act and the continued lax enforcement regime of the period. A sharp decline in the propensity to organize started in 1995, reflecting the passage of Proposition 187 and subsequent exclusionary legislation and intensified border enforcement and employer sanctions. While that legislation and enforcement failed to slow the flow of undocumented labor, it dramatically increased the likelihood and consequences of deportation, loss of access to health care, isolation, and general vulnerability of undocumented immigrants. The result was, in effect, a new apartheid, which affected workers in major portions of the low-wage labor market and their families.[20] These exclusionary trends directly affected unauthorized immigrants but also indirectly affected all lower-wage workers. In case after case, union organizers reported that the increased vulnerability of this segment of the workforce had a general demoralizing effect and undermined organizing efforts in workforces with mixed citizenship status.

Legal permanent residents and their unions, however, were deeply involved in mobilizations in the late 1980s in response to the amnesty process, and since 1995–97 they were represented in a huge surge of demand for naturalization, expanded voter registration, language and social welfare rights, and political participation. The link between the labor movement and the broader citizenship movement among Mexican immigrants was strongest in those unions in which immigrant leadership was itself the product of democratic upheaval. Unions char-

---

[20]The more accepted view in industrial relations research on immigrant workers relies on one case of qualitative research among undocumented immigrants in the late 1980s era of amnesty and lax enforcement to conclude that what we term here the civic regime is not a significant factor in the propensity to organize (e.g., Delgado 1993; Milkman and Wong 2000). We claim that, on the contrary, it was as significant then as it is today. Its significance is painfully obvious today and was "the dog that didn't bark" a decade ago. The practical impact of such well-intentioned efforts to downplay the significance of citizenship status is that they minimize the need for immigration policy change. Rather, under the banner of "organize immigrants as workers, not as immigrants," they inadvertently discourage activists from identifying the labor movement with the immigrant rights movement and so tapping the power of the larger citizenship movement in immigrant communities.

acterized by more paternalistic and authoritarian rule, on the other had, failed to tap into the power of the citizenship movement and continued to be dogged by their own internal democratic distemper.

Throughout the entire labor movement, unionists began to grasp the importance of organizing among immigrant workers and to share firsthand experience of the challenges of citizenship status among organizing workers. Early in 2000, this learning experience led to the adoption of a new more inclusive stance toward immigrants by the executive council of the AFL-CIO. By then, proposals by major agricultural employers and their Republican allies in Washington D.C. for a limited amnesty for agricultural workers had already generated intense interest among undocumented workers. The AFL-CIO's February 2000 call for "a new amnesty" both reinforced that interest and contributed a significant new change to the policymaking equation in Washington D.C. As the previous exclusionary stance of the AFL-CIO had been an essential ingredient in current federal immigration policy, this new stance is likely to trigger change in policies and practices affecting immigrants, or what Soysal (1994) terms the "incorporation regime." And if such institutions (immigration policy, citizenship status, labor movement openness to immigrant workers) do indeed significantly influence employment relations, then equally significant changes are likely to follow in this and other arenas.

Elsewhere I examine the emergence of transnational citizenship in the most significant bloc of immigrant labor, Mexican immigrants in California (Johnston 2001). In realms that range from labor to education and local government, recent years have witnessed the greatest expansion in the circle of citizenship, or participation in public life, since the similar African-American citizenship movement of the civil rights era. If economists and historians such as Piore (1979) and Mink (1986) are correct, this shift may have still more profound consequences for U.S. political, social, and economic development. As they argue, the segregation of recently arrived immigrants from rural areas into low-wage, less politically regulated labor markets and, in many cities, into politically marginalized urban settlements have been essential ingredients in an entire century of development characterized by deep inequalities or dualism in the U.S. economy, polity, and urban life. This suggests, then, that new horizons may now be opening toward a period of possibility for a more inclusive and egalitarian civic regime in the United States.

Temp Unionism

Still on the margins but increasingly the focus of innovation in organizing is the growing "permanently temporary" workforce of peripheralized employees. Temporary employment and contracted-out production is nothing new in agriculture, of course. Such a resurgence of contracting has sharply reduced wages and benefits over the past decade. But now major slices of the temp workforce can also be found in diverse occupational groups and subsectors, from the construction trades (the one great success story for temp unionism) to white collar and technical service work to colleges and universities. During the last decade, a wide array of new temporary workers' organizing projects have surfaced across the country. Like the UFW in agriculture, many consciously or unconsciously imitate the craft union model of organizing their labor market through a hiring hall. These include a variety of local advocacy groups and worker-owned temp agencies; home health-aide organizing campaigns; and unions of cab drivers, freelance writers, and high-tech contract employees. The New York–based Working Today is a rapidly growing online network of independent workers and their associations, which to date operates mainly as a consumer group of temporary workers and their associations. Although this workforce cuts across all sectors, the centrality of its information-age segment is underscored by the new academic underclass of temporary faculty, which matched or surpassed the building trades in its rate of union membership in the 1980s.

Although an intense focus of innovation and organizing today, it remains to be seen whether temp unionism will thrive. If the rise of a network society means that peripheral, boundary-spanning positions will acquire a new centrality, then these marginal efforts to organize this marginalized workforce may move to the center of the labor movement. If that is the case, then a particular vanguard role may fall to the part-time instructors—overwhelmingly public employees and typically leaders in their own trade or profession—who provide most postsecondary education and training to working adults. Regardless, for our purposes it is useful to note that all these efforts seek to replace the lost infrastructure of membership in the organization with a local structure of information, training, and job opportunities—all new avenues for new ways of organizing—not unlike the locally rooted building trades unions.

If this new infrastructure does develop, it is likely to do so through citizenship movements and will also serve as a base for them. Historically, the craft unions that represent contingent workers in the building trades have been deeply engaged in public life through their stake in the jobs associated with local development and redevelopment and in state and federal construction projects. If labor movements based on the new temp workforce burst into public discourse, they are likely to do so through demands for public health and other social insurance and efforts to reregulate their employment relations. In addition, owing to their public-sector status, contingent academic workers are likely to contribute campaigns in defense of public education and for educational equity and opportunity.

Convergence in Community Unionism

From the local to the global level, the phenomenon of citizenship is becoming increasingly complex, overlapping, and differentiated. At the same time that globalization drives the development of increasingly transnational citizenries, however, local public spaces remain at the center of much citizenship movement activity. This pattern holds with most varieties of social movement unionism. The beginnings of resurgence in the U.S. labor movement are associated, accordingly, with a new emphasis on local organizing and local political action based in neighborhoods as well as workplaces. Infused with the promise and the claims of citizenship, this new image of labor movements that defend the local community and offer their own vision of its future can help to tie together what seem to be a bewildering variety of trends in our extraordinarily diverse workforce. In all strands of the new labor movement, these two themes—citizenship and local communities—converge because, in a variety of different ways, each addresses what is in effect the same quintessentially political question: "What kind of community do we want to live in?"

A focus on local communities runs through all the strands of labor movement revival reviewed above. Public workers, for example, have become central players in the never-ending struggle over the local definition of the so-called "public interest" that they themselves produce. Movements to limit disinvestment and plant closures and concessionary contracts with major local employers—and even among auto and related workers in higher wage industries whose bargaining structures extend across the country and around the world—are increasingly driven by the local defense of jobs and communities. Both the resurgence of industrial unionism among immigrant workers and alternative approaches to labor organization and representation, such as workers' rights centers among immigrants and in the right-to-work south, draw upon and reinforce the bonds of solidarity that still anchor many workers in beleaguered neighborhoods. And efforts to organize the growing ranks of temporary workers invariably seek to replace the lost infrastructure of the organization with a local structure of its own.

This shared urban space is the basic site and this common urban future is the actual stake in today's organizing drives. Through today's local "Living Wage" campaigns, public- and private-sector organizing agendas have finally begun to converge. To the extent that they move beyond the contracted-out public workforce, tie organizing to living-wage initiatives and, perhaps, healthcare responsibility campaigns targeting employers that do not provide healthcare coverage, they may even evolve into labor's rejoinder to welfare reform. From this point of view, today's organizing campaigns are themselves urban agendas. They respond to the rise of low-wage and increasingly part-time and temporary work with a fight for an urban future that will permit families to support themselves.

Although the new AFL-CIO's organizing agenda has drawn much attention, perhaps as important is its Union Cities program. This eight-point agenda both incorporates and refocuses the organizing agenda within a framework that may unfold into a new urban agenda. As it stands, the Union Cities program is no more than a starting point. But because it resonates with all the strands of innovation in the house of labor today, the program may become a vehicle for deeper and broader realignment and redefinition of the labor movement as an urban social movement.

Both the Union Cities program and all the disparate movements mentioned above move the center of decision making and responsibility for leadership down from the international unions to the local unions, and at that level channel labor union activities beyond relatively homogenous workforces and across diverse local communities. As a result, everything converges at the local labor council. And, as a result, labor councils are themselves in renewal today. After decades in which the international unions (each narrowly focused on its own interests in its own nationwide jurisdiction) served as the central institution in the house of labor, the local labor council is increasingly reemerging as a center of labor movement activity.

Thus, it falls to labor councils to broker and hold together common or complementary organizing campaigns that mobilize the same allies, publicize the same themes to organize workforces residing in the same neighborhoods, and align this force with the complementary resources of the public workers and others whose efforts similarly focus on the fate of local places (on this topic see Gapasin and Wial 1998 and Kriesky 1998). In this increasingly central local forum, that quintessential question—"what kind of community do we want to live in?"—must be answered in a manner that speaks to all of these labor movements and their allies.

The significance of this trend may best be grasped when it is viewed within the history of urban social change and approached with the conceptual tools of urban political theory. These too are beyond the scope of our discussion here, but several observations may stimulate some useful thought. First, almost universally, the regimes governing, shaping, and reshaping urban life in the United States over the past half-century have been centered on property or commercial development (Molotch and Logan 1987, Stone 1989). Second, these regimes have been recurrently challenged both by justice-oriented movements based in African-American and other dispossessed communities and other neighborhood movements based among new middle class constituencies concerned about their quality of life. Both are typically infused, we should note, with a grassroots feminist assertion of deeply gendered claims (Johnston 1994:17–17, 100–104). To date, these challenges have either failed, been co-opted, or achieved power only to find themselves paralyzed due to the absence of their own viable governing agenda

(DeLeon 1992). Third, in the postwar period these contests occurred in circumstances in which public- and private-sector unions were alienated from one another. Private-sector unions were politically dormant and largely contained by collective bargaining, and public employee unionism was dominated by police and construction trades groups allied with the pro-business status quo (Mollenkopf 1983). Fourth, since the 1970s the addition of progressive (and again, deeply gendered) public service unionism to the urban mix has produced the potential to tilt the balance of power toward the challenging groups through labor-community coalitions (Johnston 1994). Fifth, we argue here, the new political energies and local focus of a resurgent private-sector labor movement has further swung the potential balance of power toward the challengers. Sixth, we also claim, the emergent political voice of immigrants, now achieving U.S. citizenship and registering and voting in unprecedented numbers, further strengthens the hand of neighborhood groups and both public- and private-sector unions.

As a result, people who participate in various forms of community-based unionism, especially in local labor councils, are beginning to grapple with the challenge of coalition building around a new vision of the city. Also as a result, local labor movements are beginning to think in terms required for participation as more than junior partner in governance.

Current and previous patterns of local political incorporation are essential parts of state and federal political alignments, so the long-term implications of these trends extend far beyond the local level. In California, for example, the pendulum has only begun to swing away from the right with the election of a centrist, Gray Davis. Now, emerging new labor and Latino political majorities in the rural regions that have long been secure power bases for Reaganite conservatism are likely to ally with the growing strength of progressives in the urban centers. This new urban-rural coalition in turn may produce the possibility, perhaps sooner than now seems likely, for a statewide multicultural governing coalition that is unabashedly progressive.

Experience in the United States and elsewhere suggests that new perils await labor and its allies when it seeks to govern. In particular, there is an urgent need to develop alternatives to the inherited and too often taken-for-granted menu of policy options. We need a network of local policy resources that can arm labor's local leadership with "good government" and "livable city" policy agendas that are more than oppositional in nature and yet help us avoid becoming the defenders of an indefensible status quo. These developments coincide with the devolution of decision making for much social policy to the local level. The result is a vital strategic opportunity for the development of a network of local labor-community–based policy institutes: a new incarnation of the nationwide network of Municipal Affairs Bureaus of the Progressive Era. If they can avoid the powerful pull to serve as instruments of factional power within their broad and diverse potential constituencies, such institutes can help broker the new urban agendas now on the horizon.

CHAPTER THREE

Living with Flexibility

Charles Heckscher

*D*espite flashes of energy and enthusiasm in the past few years, the prospect for unions and the traditional system of labor relations remain bleak. The focus on organizing by the AFL-CIO in the last few years has clearly not uncapped a powerful wellspring of desire for unionization. Labor advocates increasingly hang their hopes on reform of existing labor laws; but the Dunlop Commission early in the Clinton administration only showed how difficult it would be to build a social consensus around labor law reform. All that remains from that experience is bitterness and closed doors. If Dunlop, the master negotiator of our era, could not find a common ground on these issues, it is probably not there to be found.

What is still more disturbing is the lack of agreement and common cause among labor's natural allies. More than fifteen years ago the Solidarity Day march tried to bring together a wide range of social-action groups, but it never built a sustained unified movement. Today community action groups are more likely to maintain a careful distance than to follow labor's lead, and liberal political figures are cautious about too close a relationship.

This is not a recent problem. The paralysis of the labor relations scene dates back at least to the late 1970s, when President Carter failed to win passage of a mild labor law reform measure. It can probably be traced back another decade to the fissures that developed around the Vietnam War and the youth movements. In any case, for twenty or thirty years we have been going around in the same circles. That is not a sign of health.

Psychologists tell us that those caught in repeating circles need to reframe their view of the world. In the case of labor relations, it is largely a matter of taking seriously the evidence of upheaval in the economy. Most of us believe in a general way that big changes are going on in business—major shifts in markets, new technologies, increased capital mobility, and the like. We also should know that the labor relations system is part of a larger system, analyzed so well by Dunlop (1958), which, since the defining moment of the 1930s, has centered on large, industrial, vertically integrated, bureaucratic companies. If that has changed, then the labor relations system must also change.

The emergence of large industry in the early part of this century gave rise to an industrial relations order in which the primary strategy of unions was to take wages out of competition through industry-wide agreements, and their primary weapon was the mass strike. This system displaced, though did not completely replace, another that had existed long before and was centered on small craft-based companies in regional networks. Craft unionism is based much less on strikes and pattern contracts than on controlling labor markets and the power of local bargaining agents. It continues in industries that have maintained the old structure, particularly the building trades.

It seems probable that these two familiar modes of capitalist organization are now being absorbed into something different. The argument about a "paradigm shift" has been made so often that I will not try to repeat it here, except to evoke the main forces of technological change, globalization, maturing consumer markets, and an increasingly skilled and entrepreneurial workforce. In combination, these forces are scrambling industry and market boundaries throughout the economy.[1]

Yet the dominant arguments about strategies for labor, at least among its friends, ignore such fundamental system changes and treat the problem as essentially tactical. There are various strands of this view, which may conflict: leftists often argue that unions need to go back to mobilizing their base, unionists often argue the need to shore up the sanctions underlying labor law. But under the apparent conflict is a

---

[1]Of course an argument can be made that these "new" forces are merely slight variations on old patterns. This argument is, however, seldom made explicit. I am going to assume for the purpose of this paper that the changes are fundamental; I make the argument more explicitly in *The New Unionism*.

shared view that this war has been fought before, and all we have to do is to go back and rediscover the old life springs of the movement.

When this assumption is made explicit, few would say they believe it without major qualification. Almost everyone accepts the significance of economic changes, especially since the early 1970s. What has not happened, however, is a Dunlopian reassessment of what this means for the labor relations system.[2] What I want to begin here is an effort to take the idea of economic transformation seriously, rather than merely acknowledging it and then returning to familiar paths, looking to old institutions for solutions.

Taking transformation seriously involves, first, a close analysis of the current scene; second, a pulling back from existing institutions, which are familiar but particular, to the underlying and universal problem of employment representation. Above all, if there is a transformation, it is not assured that the labor movement as we now know it—existing unions, the AFL-CIO—will be a part of a rebuilt system. It is essential to confront this possibility. If we restrict ourselves from the start to the question, What should unions do?, it becomes impossible to make any clear assessment of how the system is changing. The core question is rather, What form of employment representation will produce workplace justice and dignity in the current conditions? The answer may well involve institutions on the margins of or even outside organized labor.

Unions and the Economy

Let me start with some general propositions about the relations of worker representation to the economy.

First, I assume that worker representation is part of an economic and political system. This is a Dunlopian point of view, rather than a Marxist one: if one sees unions as aiming to replace the current system with another one in which they are the primary drivers, the analysis

---

[2]Dunlop had the great advantage of writing during a time when the system was fairly solid and complete. Today, if we are to adopt a systems perspective, we have to imagine a prospective system that has not yet been built.

must be completely different. In the perspective I am taking, however, unions specialize in two key aspects of the society as a whole: the interests of employees and the value of social justice. This means that someone else has to specialize in running the economy,[3] and unions or employee bodies have the same kind of tension that exists for any social institution: they have to push their specialized interests in a way that also maximizes the interests of the whole.

Two more propositions follow: First, institutions of worker representation cannot survive unless they are widely perceived as contributing to economic growth as well as economic justice. In the New Deal era they were linked to the Keynesian economics of demand stimulus. Since the late 1970s, however, the public focus has shifted to concern about inflation and competitiveness. Higher wages for union members are no longer widely seen as translating into prosperity for all; this is a fatal weakness that tends to isolate unions during defining moments of conflict. Second, and related, unions can succeed only if they essentially contribute to good management, not if they fundamentally undermine it. In fact, they have functioned by making deals that are in the long-term interests of management as well as employees; in part, they force management to act in its own interests.

That management does not consistently act in its own interests can be derived from a couple of major tenets of psychology and sociology. First, people and institutions tend to maximize their own interests at the expense of the whole, especially by trying to get away with a little more than the others while hoping that they don't try to do the same; this is known as "the tragedy of the commons." Second, those in power come easily to believe that they know the right answers and that they must therefore exercise their power to get people to accept them. These patterns operate quite independent of malice or evil, and they are observable in all societies and periods. They are the core reasons why some check on power, some sort of "deal" among social stakeholders, is essential to the stability and growth of any social system.

---

[3] I do not mean to imply that the relationship between unions and business leaders must necessarily be arms' length and oppositional; any system is better if there is open interaction and cooperation among the different functions. Nevertheless, the function of maximizing economic production is distinct and should not simply be annexed onto the role of unions.

During the main industrial phase of economic development in this country, from about the 1930s to the 1960s, large companies began to value stability and predictability more than cost cutting. They structured themselves as bureaucracies and oriented to mass markets. They therefore valued clear, stable jobs; long-term, loyal employees; and predictable labor relations. They began to provide much of the social support needed by employees throughout their careers, from training to medical insurance to pensions to psychological support to job ladders that sequenced challenges in ways that kept people productive and motivated over long periods. Although these benefits were won in the unionized sphere only with conflict, it is important to note that they were extended without conflict to nonunion employees—lower and middle managers as well as lower level employees in some industries where unionization made few inroads. Thus, in the 1950s especially, we saw a system that was successful from all perspectives.

Although management benefited from this order, it would not have gotten there on its own. In every industrialized country in the world the same story played itself out: management had to be compelled to create and sustain the system. Unions took on the task of forcing management to live up to its own bureaucratic principles of predictability and clarity by defining close job descriptions. They forced managers to abandon personalistic control, which the business schools were telling them to do anyway, and to provide the kind of job security that produced loyalty. This is why a major Harvard Business School study from 1960 concluded that unions made companies manage better.[4] If that had not been true, the labor movement would not have been able to survive and succeed.

I am not implying that representative institutions need to aim directly at economic growth, trying to outdo management. Their value is in their focus on worker interests and justice. I have taken this for granted and have emphasized only the less-familiar side of the tension that must be managed by the system. Employee bodies must pursue justice, and be seen as doing it, in a way that advances the interests of

---

[4]Slichter, Sumner H.; Healy, James J.; and Livernash, E. Robert (1960).

the whole. The strategic problem lies in the paradox of opposing management in a way that does not fundamentally undermine companies and the economy.

The Current Transformation

The heart of the economic transformation of our time, at least from the perspective of workers, is the familiar issue of flexibility, or responsiveness. This is the core strategic focus and the driving passion of most top managers. There is no worse sin from the point of view of Wall Street and of economic analysts than inflexibility and the inability to respond rapidly to changing demands. My argument is that since flexibility isn't going away—and no one has found a way of making it go away—we had better learn to live with it.

Flexibility is not a passing fad; many deep and convergent currents drive it. First, we are going through one of the great historical periods of technological discontinuity: microprocessors already touch almost every aspect of the economy, and most of the implications have not yet begun to be felt. This is certainly as big a change as the steam engine a century and a half ago. Right on its heels is coming the biotechnology revolution, which will probably have an even greater impact. Furthermore, there is reason to believe that the pace of scientific invention has reached a permanently higher plateau, so that the pauses between major innovations are likely to be shorter and shorter.[5]

A second crucial factor is the maturation of capitalist markets. In the first generations of industrialization the problem was to produce and distribute enough mass consumer goods for everyone. In the advanced economies, however, people have enough of the basics; they want customized products and responsive services that keep up with the latest developments and meet particular needs.

These are just the biggest of a set of forces pressuring management to respond quickly to environmental pressures and to structure themselves for sustained change. They explain why the language of flexibil-

---

[5]For some data on the increasing pace of scientific progress, see Bell, Daniel (1973).

ity is both so long lasting and so widespread. It has been growing steadily for at least twenty-five years. A multitude of specific fads have reflected the same basic tendency. It has been as visible in Sweden and Japan as in the United States; and if those countries have resisted the pressures somewhat longer, they appear to be moving rapidly in this direction now, and perhaps with even more pain than we.[6]

Flexibility also, however, presents major problems for industrial relations. In fact, it is at the center of almost every labor-management dispute today. The current structure of industrial unionism is designed to create stability and predictability, and is therefore radically out of synch with the new emphasis. In recent years unions have consistently traded wage and benefit increases for the fundamental protection of job security, yet they have been unable to stop the erosion. They have on occasion slowed job losses for the term of a single contract, but the essential trend has continued inexorably. The outcome of union strategies focused on job protection has therefore been losses in all domains.

Companies have clearly and widely moved away from taking responsibility for long-term careers. There is a whole set of reasons why career security used to be more or less in the interests of companies but is no longer. These certainly include crude cost-cutting considerations, but they also reflect the deeper economic changes just sketched. With skills and demand metamorphosing so rapidly in so many domains, it is often more effective to look for those with needed skills on the open market rather than developing them internally. Once companies begin to do that, they tend to break the whole pattern of expectations and commitments that grounded the classic system.[7] Today, even in a very tight labor market, companies no longer hesitate to lay off middle managers as well as blue-collar workers whenever they feel they need a change in strategy or a boost in their stock price. And the contingent workforce, which has reached over 30 percent of the total workforce in this country, continues to grow not only

---

[6]See, for example, *Wall Street Journal Interactive Edition,* June 4, 1998: "Europe Firms Lift Unemployment by Laying Off Unneeded Workers." See also fn 8.

[7]This was at the core of my argument in White-Collar Blues (Basic Books, 1995).

here but even more rapidly in Europe.[8] This is an irreversible sea change that we need to examine.[9]

Employee Responses

The fact that companies are no longer prepared to take responsibility for careers doesn't mean that people don't need the kind of support that they once got from them. Where can they find it now?

One model—in concept the easiest—is to turn back the clock by forcing companies to provide more security and more employee services. That would require policies of reregulation and protectionism. When looked at directly, however, this seems to be an implausible approach. The current political resistance to following this road is not only vociferous but also long lasting (going back at least twenty years) and widespread (equally visible throughout Europe, including countries with strong social-democratic histories). We therefore should look

---

[8]France, Spain, and the Netherlands have had very rapidly growing temporary-employment sectors in the past decade; Sweden and even Germany have also bent considerably under the pressure. See *Wall Street Journal Interactive Edition,* June 4, 1998: "Europe Firms Lift Unemployment By Laying Off Unneeded Workers."

See also Rothstein (1998) citing data from *The Economist* (1997): "Part-time employment in the Netherlands for all occupations is almost 40%. Britain is next at nearly 25%, then France and Germany at 15%, and Japan at about 13%. Spain and the U.S. are next at about 8%."

[9]Few in the corporate world would question the basic fact that commitment to long-term employee loyalty has declined, but some academics of course have. A few years ago there was a small rush of papers claiming that the trumpeted growth of downsizing and contingent work was not showing up in the data, and that job tenures did not seem to be decreasing. This appears, however, to be simply a case of data taking a while to catch up: More recently the trends have begun to make it into the peer-refereed world. For example, Hank Farber, long a skeptic, recently found that after declining only slightly from the late 1970s to 1992, the percentage of the workforce with long-tenure jobs fell sharply since then, despite the tightest labor market in thirty years (Farber 1997b).

The trend toward layoffs and job cuts has continued in the last year or two despite an extraordinarily tight job market—another strong indication of permanently increased flexibility rather than punctual moments of cost cutting. During the first eight months of 1998—a period of extraordinary economic prosperity—the total number of job cuts were about 37 percent higher than for the same period in 1997 according to Challenger, Gray & Christmas (survey reported in *Dow Jones Newswires,* September 8, 1998).

hard at the alternative rather than paying lip service to the idea that the world is fundamentally different and proposing solutions that follow the familiar patterns.

First, a society of relatively mobile, flexible employees without a lifetime tie to a single firm could be good. The old bargain, remembered nostalgically now, had many bad aspects. It was fundamentally paternalist, demanding in return for security and support a level of submission to corporate demands, which is increasingly unacceptable. It squelched diversity, invaded private lives, and reduced people to positions on organization charts. And, of course, it produced fragmented, alienated work lives.

A more flexible economy might strike a different bargain, one we can already see in certain innovative companies. In this best-case scenario, from the point of view of employees, the deal offers important benefits:

- The ability to make more active choices about jobs. Even without romanticizing a notion of fishing in the morning and philosophizing in the afternoon, a model of mobility offers at least a greater balance between the interests of employers and those of employees, because the option of leaving is a viable one.
- Personal development—the opportunity to develop personal skills and interests through sequences of jobs rather than letting a single company "mold and shape you" (as one middle manager put it).
- Less fear and subordination. In the traditional system, advancement often hung on the ability to please a single boss. Such concentration of power invites abuse, and even in the best of circumstances inexorably creates an atmosphere of craven eagerness to please. With multiple bosses and frequent opportunities to prove themselves in varying situations, employees can establish far more independence.
- Greater participation in defining the nature of work and decisions that affect it. This is another consequence of the need for rapid response: Companies have found that top-down control is far too slow and inward-looking for today's circumstances, and so they have moved —painfully and reluctantly, but steadily—to involve people more in decision making on the job.

- More acceptance of diversity. One of the strongest forces working against new entrants in workplaces has been the strong corporate culture created from the long-term paternalistic
  relations. Mobility opens up new opportunities and also
  reduces the power of entrenched resistors.

This scenario will not happen automatically; it requires an effective
system of representation to balance differing interests. What is needed
is a system that can deal with decentralized, flexible management, integrate semiprofessional and "knowledge" employees, and generate real
political support. It should be compatible with economic needs for innovation, involvement, and flexibility rather than stability.

Representation in a Mobile Economy: A General Model

With this focus on mobility, we need to refine our question: What
would be required for employees to have good working lives in a truly
mobile economy? Can we construct a system that would enable people to construct satisfying working lives, and to pressure employers to
maintain high standards, without trying to reconstruct an image of stable internal labor markets, high regulation, and protection?

Existing industrial unions have trouble with this question because
they focus on the negotiation of multiyear contracts that guarantee a
maximum of predictability for members, in effect forcing the employer
to be consistent about the loyalty bargain. This strategic focus is reflected in industrial union structures (generally centralized around contracts) and in skills (stressing bargaining and grievance handling).
Unions know how to bargain a contract and to enforce it, but this
works only when they are pushing in a direction that already makes
sense in terms of the general needs of the economy and of management, which is no longer the case.

Thus, a union that contributes to a mobile economy would need a
different set of strategic foci. It would need to support mobility among
its members, and find ways to pressure employers through methods
other than collective bargaining.

Support for Mobility

The first thing people need for mobility is support for careers that span several companies and skill sets.

Locked into traditional models of "good" work, we rarely ask what it would take for people to feel comfortable in changing jobs. If we do ask this, the answers come flooding in. People would need the following:

- Portability of benefits such as health insurance and pensions.
- Information about job opportunities, company reputations, salary norms, and so on.
- Access to continuing education and developmental opportunities for specific skill training, and more general education on social and economic developments which open new horizons.
- Help with financial planning: planning for retirement, children's education, and other savings needs. In a mobile economy people should be assisted especially with planning for likely periods of unemployment. These concerns were more or less "automatically" taken care of in the paternalist bargain, but are no longer.
- Social and psychological support in dealing with change and instability.
- Mentoring about career paths and possibilities.

These factors could produce a situation in which people were relatively well prepared for a career with twists and turns and without long-term security or predictable movement through a hierarchy. With increased preparedness, they would be relatively able to defend themselves from abuse and to negotiate effectively with employers; in effect, they would gain some of the advantages now enjoyed by a relatively small number of high-tech employees in Silicon Valley.

There is no basic reason why these items could not be provided by unions or other employee organizations rather than employers or independent firms. In fact, there is a long history of unions playing this kind of role, particularly in crafts where people naturally move frequently from job to job. These traditions have been submerged by the "industrial" deal, but they are closer to the mark for the current situation. Below I describe some efforts to re-create this function today.

Pressure

Support for mobility is far from enough. I have argued that no economic system can work effectively without some ability to push back against the desires of employers, in part to stabilize the system and thereby fulfill employers' own long-term interests. However, even though increased mobility gives employees some leverage, it is generally a weak form; only in rare cases of extremely tight labor markets can employees get what they need simply by threatening to leave. Therefore, a piece of the system has to be some kind of organized pressure on employers.

Here again we tend to be limited by familiar images. Organized pressure in the last fifty years has meant the strike; the right to strike has become an article of passionate belief in the labor movement. Yet in many, if not most, situations today, the strike is ineffective, and it is hard to direct toward the real issue. Despite some much-trumpeted exceptions, strike rates continue to decline: In 1999 the number of workers idled by work stoppages dropped to the lowest level since the government began keeping records in 1947. These are reasons for looking for other ways to bring worker influence to bear.

Two major forms of pressure, with deep historical roots but less salience in the current system, have been slowly developing in the last twenty years, and a third has some potential. These are publicity, lawsuits, and financial leverage.

Publicity gains in effectiveness in the modern economy because company reputation has become an increasingly important competitive factor. As mass production is replaced by services and customized products, the ability to respond quickly to customers and to provide innovation in usable forms has become more central to corporate success. Such tight relations to customers, however, makes companies more vulnerable to concerted attempts to undermine their reputations. Unions have occasionally used this weapon, in boycotts or corporate campaigns, but it is far from a central part of the arsenal.[10]

---

[10]"Big companies today have to be seen as responsive and socially and politically correct. They know their image is at stake," said Wendy Liebmann, president of WSL Strategic Retail consulting group. In today's competitive retail environment, she adds, such perceptions can determine the brand a consumer will choose (*The Wall Street Journal Interactive Edition,* April 10, 1997: "Sweatshop Pact: For Workers or Apparel Makers' Image?").

Lawsuits have become a powerful weapon, of course, because of the enormous increase in employee rights legislation and court rulings of the last thirty years. For most human resources directors, the threat of litigation is far more worrisome than the threat of unionization or strikes—and with reason: The rate of legal action against companies continues to increase steadily and quite rapidly.[11] This leverage, however, is seldom used in a strategic way. Most lawsuits are filed on behalf of individuals by lawyers seeking contingent fees; if the plaintiff wins, lawyers and clients walk away with a lot of money but nothing else changes much. Occasionally unions, notably AFSCME and SEIU, have filed comparable worth and other suits on behalf of members or potential members, but the tactic remains rare.

Jesse Jackson has been most public in showing an alternative possibility. Rather than trying to use publicity and lawsuits to get specific remedies—a tactic that is clumsy at best—he uses these background threats as a way of getting to the table for negotiation about policy changes. This allows him to open up the field considerably and to conduct something approaching collective bargaining in situations in which there is no NLRB-recognized bargaining representative and no credible strike threat.[12]

The third nonstrike form of pressure also has a long history but also needs adaptation to the modern milieu: coordinated use of employee financial resources. Peter Drucker (1976) pointed out long ago that pension funds control large shares of total capital; since that writing, the growth of 401(k) plans and their relatives have shifted much of these funds toward individualized and portable buckets of money. Although garment and other unions have often used the financial leverage of their union-owned pension funds in the past to pressure

---

[11]"In 1996, American workers brought more than 23,000 lawsuits alleging race, sex, disability or age discrimination to federal courts, more than double the 10,771 that were brought in 1992, according to the U.S. Courts' administrative office. In the last two years, job discrimination lawsuits have been rising about 20% a year" (*Los Angeles Times Online,* May 12, 1997: "Job Discrimination Lawsuits on Upswing").

[12]For example, at Mitsubishi, Texaco, Con Edison, and Freddie Mac (Barron's Online, June 15, 1998: "Jesse Jackson Takes Aim at Freddie Mac, Alleging Employment Bias"; *Wall Street Journal Interactive Edition,* January 15, 1997: "Jesse Jackson, Mitsubishi Unit Reach Accord to End Boycott"; *Dow Jones Newswires,* April 13, 1998: "Jesse Jackson Investigates Possible Con Ed Discrimination").

their employers, no one has to my knowledge figured out how to use the much larger pool of individualized funds as leverage. The idea is simple: to get a large number of people to invest their pensions in a fund controlled by an employee-oriented organization that can then, within the limits of fiduciary responsibility, invest them to maximize employee interests. The implementation is, however, only rudimentary so far.[13]

What could these forms of pressure be used for? They are clearly quite well adapted to pressing employers for good working conditions. Employment rights laws, for example, effectively extend a de facto right of due process to all employees; the problem has been enforcing them. If employee bodies systematically use the threat of lawsuits to force the adoption of internal policies to prevent violations of these laws, they are going "with the grain" and, if anything, they are simplifying things for their employers. Lawsuits, then, seem to be a plausible tactic.

Similarly, the threat of negative publicity can be quite effective when employer rhetoric about participation and empowerment fails to match the reality. This is in fact the case in many workplaces today: Management recognizes verbally the need for teamwork and involvement but fails to create the conditions for them. Employee groups that make the discrepancy public—especially internally—have some leverage.

Wage negotiation is a harder problem. In the areas I have just mentioned, the interests of employees and employers are not objectively that far apart; the conflicts tend to come from habits of control and hierarchy rather than from real contradictions. But wages involve a more serious collision, an essentially zero-sum distribution. There is reason to doubt that the kinds of pressure I have discussed are strong enough to do this job.

I have no sure answer to the wage problem. The difficulty is that there is no accepted version of a good wage distribution. Unlike in the

---

[13]However, for a recent example of a union using pension funds in this way, see *The Wall Street Journal Interactive Edition,* February 19, 1997, "Pension Fund Tells Maxxam to Avoid Logging Redwoods." Religious groups have also used this approach: *The Wall Street Journal Interactive Edition, Dow Jones Business News,* April 18, 1997: "Church Group Targets Wal-Mart To Push Sweatshop Reforms."

1930s, economic theory and political wisdom are not converging in a sense that workers need a larger share of the pie (or a smaller one, for that matter). Without consensus there has been a relatively slow but steady erosion of wages for some twenty-five years.

It is far from clear, however, that a life with fewer strikes—to put the problem in its simplest form— would necessarily be a life of declining wages. Other forms of leverage have worked in the past, most notably the control of labor markets by craft and guild structures. Boycotts have occasionally been successful in ending severe wage injustices.[14] Full employment policies are possibly the most reliable way to raise wages, and they make any kind of employee pressure much more effective.

Nor is it clear that an increase in strikes would succeed in setting the wage balance right. The point is that wage setting has never been just an outcome of unions' power to strike: It has always been a matter of union and management power regulated by a social consensus about fair wages. Since the 1930s, that social consensus has been centered on issues of inflation and deflation. When the latter was seen as the greater danger, government and other social institutions swung toward the worker side; but when inflation became the primary threat, they swung the other way. This has been a crude way of managing the overall social wage by adjusting the balance of power.[15]

Thus, until there is a convincing argument that wage increases will not restart inflation, there will be little support for them no matter what unions do. Because some economists believe we may be entering a deflationary period, the pendulum could be on its way back as of this

---

[14]Wal-Mart, for example, in dealing with religious and stockholder groups criticizing labor conditions at its suppliers, has agreed that "suppliers are required to meet a number of standards, including 'fairly' compensating workers at the higher of legally required minimum wages or the prevailing industry wages" (*The Wall Street Journal Interactive Edition, Dow Jones Business News,* April 18, 1997: "Church Group Targets Wal-Mart To Push Sweatshop Reforms").

[15]Not that inflation and deflation are the only factors in play: There is no question that the general employer hostility to unions in the United States is higher than in most other industrialized nations, so that even in the depths of the Depression there was fierce resistance to unionization. But the inflation-deflation condition clearly tipped the balance even in this country.

writing. Then new mechanisms of wage regulation will need to be created that have scarcely been hinted at, but which are not likely to center on stable industry-wide agreements, not in a world where industries are constantly being scrambled by new markets and technologies. They may well center on improved labor-market management by government and employee associations.

These are just indications; let me leave this issue as a serious lacuna in a theoretical model of representation in a mobile economy, not one that is demonstrably insoluble.

The forms of pressure I have described—legal action, publicity, and financial leverage—are types of conflict, but they are possibly more sustainable forms of conflict than the strike. They appeal more centrally to public opinion and are, I think, somewhat less subject to hijacking by narrow interest groups. But whether you accept this or not, the central issue is that they *are* ways in which conflict is often structured nowadays. They have shown some effectiveness, and it is easy to see how they could be far more effective.

Such effectiveness depends mostly on organization; these methods do not work on an individual basis. Suits can be filed by individuals, but such suits are usually available only to the relatively wealthy and do not usually produce solutions that improve things for everyone. Similarly, financial action and publicity have to be collective to work. A major part of the problem of representation today is to organize the power of legal action and publicity in ways that lead to widely beneficial results.

Real Current Developments

I have been talking about the abstract requirements of a system of representation that would enhance mobility and flexibility; now I am going to describe some reality.

First, a little-recognized fact of the current employment scene is that there are thousands of associations springing up in every sector. Some of these are identity associations: African Americans, women, gays, the disabled. Some are professional associations: computer programmers, artists. Some are geographic. And some are combinations: African-American small business owners of New York. Some bring together laid-off workers from particular firms or regions for very preliminary versions of the kind of support and portability sketched above.[16]

These associations provide some of the functions that I have described: mentoring, information, and psychological support for career transitions. They sometimes provide benefits and financial instruments. More rarely, but often enough to show it can work, they exert pressure on employers by unifying individual voices.[17] These associations are the major force behind the developing law of employment rights, which is today probably more important than union contracts as a shaper of labor relations. This is where a great deal of the energy is. When people say that workers aren't organizing nowadays, one can properly reply that they are organizing; they just aren't organizing unions.

This pattern—local associations backed by employment rights—is not in any sense a solution by itself. Employee associations are generally small, weak, and isolated. Employee rights law often leads to a chaotic mess, with various factions claiming particular benefits and competing with each other. But even if they are not solutions, they cannot be ignored; they are sources of real energy that should be mobilized.

Working Today

Finally, we look at the nascent organizations that are trying to pull these forces together—to use new forms of leverage in mobile labor markets and draw on natural associations. In different ways one can see such efforts within the formal labor movement, in organizations such as

---

[16]It is easy to document that a lot of such associations exist but difficult to get any reliable numbers. Hundreds of pages of these employee groups can be found on the Internet, and one can safely assume that there are a lot more that do not yet have web pages. Ray Friedman has tried to document the extent and nature of these groups in some areas; for example, he surveyed the Fortune 500, the Executive Leadership Council, and the National Black MBA Association, and found that somewhere between 29 and 43 percent of companies in these samples had network groups, mostly among African Americans and women. There was a substantial increase in formation of such groups between 1987 and 1991, which was the end of his study (Friedman and Carter 1993).

[17]A well-documented instance is the Black Caucus at Xerox. See Deinard and Friedman (1990).

Local 1199 of the National Union of Hospital and Health Care Employees in New York, who have used their healthcare plan not only to draw members but also to leverage employers;[18] or the Florida Education Association, which has established financial-planning services for its members and is backing portable pension arrangements. Similar efforts can be seen at the edges of the labor movement in organizations such as Working Partnerships, a San Francisco–based organization that organizes contingent workers linked to the local labor council, or Jobs With Justice, a coalition of labor and community groups partly supported by the AFL-CIO. At times these organizations stand clearly outside, although allied with, the movement; other examples include the Talent Alliance and the Employment Project.

I will detail one such example, an organization in which I am involved that aims ambitiously to pull together the forces I have discussed. Started two and half years ago by a former union organizer, the organization is called Working Today. Its goal is to become nothing less than the "one big union" for a mobile workforce. Although it stands outside the labor movement, it does not compete with unions: One could easily be a member of a traditional union for collective bargaining with a particular employer and of Working Today for career support as one moves among employers. A number of union leaders have expressed great interest; Morty Bahr, the President of the Communications Workers of America, is on the board.

The organization seeks to develop the dual functions described earlier: first, to provide through collective organization a network of support to strengthen the security, and therefore the negotiating power, of individuals as they move between companies; second, to develop a collective voice that, rather than negotiating in a traditional sense, can set standards for industries and the economy as a whole. Its experience so far helps clarify the promise and the problems of the model of representation I have sketched.

First, the promise. The network of support was the easiest place to begin in the development of this organization, although it involved a

---

[18] *New York Times,* September 16, 1998, Wednesday: "Union Will Steer Members to Rite Aid in Return for Promise Not to Fight Organizing Drives."

great deal of entrepreneurship and invention because the pieces did not exist in the past. Working Today already provides an excellent portable healthcare package for its members. It recently opened a financial planning service. It is developing a database of employers, which tells employees where the jobs are and identifies good and bad employers. It is involved in discussions with organizations that are interested in coordinating continuing education for mid-career adults. These pieces are certainly still very incomplete in terms of providing a full range of support for mobile employees, but this area has seen rapid progress and is likely to continue to do so.

The response to the basic idea of Working Today has been encouraging, especially given the rudimentary nature of its operations. The positive reaction has included the following:

- Substantial support has come from a number of foundations, including MacArthur, Ford, and Stern.
- An impressive group has joined the Board of Advisors. In addition to Morty Bahr, Bill Bradley (who hosted an educational session for us), William Julius Wilson, Jeremy Rifkin, Paula Raymond, and Tom Kochan are now members.
- There has been a tremendous amount of positive publicity, including major pieces in the *New York Times,* the *Los Angeles Times,* and other print venues; radio appearances on *All Things Considered* and *Talk of the Nation*; and a segment on the ABC nightly news.

The most important response, however, has been from employees. The organization has grown quite rapidly despite the fact that there has been no organized membership drive and there is so far only a small amount to offer in tangible benefits. Today the organization counts about 90,000 members and affiliates. About 5,000 of these are direct members who came in response to the various media stories. About eight months ago Working Today began to develop members by reaching out to associations such as Asian Women in Media, Women Employed, the Graphic Artists' Guild, TempAide, and the World Wide Web Artists' Consortium; over 85,000 people have now been affiliated in this way.

The goal of the association strategy is not to establish a huge AARP-style organization, but rather a federation of associations, with associations serving as locals and possibly national groups (e.g., African Americans, women, professionals) as internationals. A large range of needs could be addressed through this kind of arrangement: Associations could learn from each other, they could gain in power through systematic alliances and coordinated actions, and they could exchange resources. Through scale the possibilities for pressure could be enormously increased: by creating investment fund pools on a vast scale, by mobilizing large numbers of people for legislative lobbying, by publicizing to the members lists of good and bad employers. Such an organization, in short, would use the building blocks of the current chaotic situation to construct a more coherent and unified structure.

The Problems

Any organization of this kind faces a major chicken-and-egg dilemma: Until it reaches a critical membership mass, it cannot provide the services and economies of scale, or develop the clout, that is needed to attract those members in the first place. Working Today has so far relied on the help of more powerful sponsors: money from foundations, a reputation boost from its advisory board, and the interest of the media. It has also benefited from a large number of members who like the idea, even though they do not yet get direct benefits from it. So far these areas of support are so strong that the organization has pulled through challenge after challenge and supported the rapid growth. This is a primary indication that it is on to something, touching themes that are vital to the current economic situation. But these offerings of trust and encouragement will need to be repaid in hard accomplishments before too much longer.

Of even more concern, I think, are some basic challenges. On the service side, there is a risk of becoming merely a provider of services, thus competing with the rapidly growing sector of for-profit operations offering everything from health care and financial advice to job postings to discount buying. Working Today provides no special value in this arena unless it also brings a reputation for concern about the interests of its members as employees. This means that it has to create more than an economically self-interested bond; members have to see themselves as part of a larger community with a sense of shared values and interests.

A sense of community exists to some extent among current members based on the vision that Working Today has presented: encouraging mobility and flexibility while helping people navigate through such a world. It is in fact this vision that has drawn most members so far, since the organization hasn't had many tangible benefits to offer them. But it will not be easy to develop and maintain this rough solidarity as the organization becomes larger and more complex.

It seems likely that the basic glue holding people together will come not through the central body, but through the associations that compose it. It is these associations that, in many cases, provide a sense of community and social solidarity and are currently looking for ways to pursue their shared vision. Thus, the problem now is for Working Today to create itself as a coordinator and link among associations, with the goal of trying to give them avenues for developing their own power.

A key aspect of this challenge is whether (and to what extent) Working Today can draw on member solidarity to cross-subsidize its activities, not only to support political action, but more important to help lower income members through the pooling of resources. For example, a portable healthcare system, if it is to move in the direction of justice, will require this kind of redistribution; otherwise, low-income members just won't be able to afford it. But what would hold the high-income members into a plan that costs as much or even more than the competition? This can only work if the health care is linked to something else: to a coordinated set of services that advance members' interests in diverse ways, or to a vision of a society that people care about.

The development of solidarity and organizational reputation will also depend in large part on the second leg of the strategic structure: the kinds of pressure exerted. So far Working Today has done very little in this area. It has defined a few legislative positions on fairly technical issues of tax laws to reduce the discrimination between independent employees and those employed in corporations, but it has not taken a stand on more complex and visible issues, nor has it yet put pressure on employers. When it does, it will mobilize its membership but create the risk of splits.

These tensions go to the core of the enterprise: Is there a sufficient sense of shared interest to sustain an organization of this type? Craft unions built communities of occupation, and industrial unions built communities, albeit much weaker ones, around the companies and industries they represented. An associational union that encourages flexibility and mobility and involves a very diverse set of organizations can't rely on either of those. The answer is too far away to be clear, but it is likely to lie in the kind of solidarity that has already brought together the member associations. By analogy with the AFL-CIO, Working Today needs only to provide the extra benefits of scale and coordination; the true identification and energizing of members would lie with the core associations, which have already shown considerable ability to arouse the passions of their members.

I focus on Working Today because I know it well and because it is one of the most comprehensive efforts to date. But it would not be worth paying attention to if it were not part of a much larger set of similar activities. The large number of employee associations and employment rights groups are the base; Working Today and cognate organizations are seeking ways to build a coordinated structure.

Conclusion

Those who worry about injustices tend to want to stop them. They pursue relatively simple strategies: either looking backward toward a better age in the past or constructing a simple conceptual model of a better world. But change does not usually move in either of those directions, as we have seen from much recent history. Effective social action has to come from understanding the basic nature of the current forces and the choices they allow; and then working toward the better options. If the center of the current changes is an increase in economic and social flexibility, it is not likely to be useful to wish for something different, whether a utopia from the past or an invented future. The question has to be whether there are good versions and bad versions of the current developments. There are certainly bad versions of flexibility—those in which all the benefits redound to the employers, where rhetoric covers a reality of tight control. "Bad" means bad not just from the point of view of a different group or of justice, but bad for the ability and survival of the system. A good version would be one in which real flexibility is encouraged by making mobility attractive and engaging employees fully in the tasks of creating knowledge and service. Then we need to ask how to make that happen.

The strategy I have put forward is intended to go with the flow, to turn the dangerous currents of the present economic scene in good directions and to build on the energy of associations outside the labor movement rather than forcing them into the existing framework. There is much uncertainty about it, as about all labor strategies, but now there are real experiments of this type worth observing, analyzing, and testing, and these should be the focus of our attention.

CHAPTER FOUR

Lost Ways of Unionism

Historical Perspectives on Reinventing the Labor Movement

Dorothy Sue Cobble

The history of the American labor movement is replete with surprising twists and turns—occurrences no one could have predicted
and often with consequences no one intended. Perhaps one of the more
famous stories illustrating the labor movement's unpredictable course
is the one historians often tell of the multiple and solemn pronounce-
ments made by august labor experts in 1932 heralding the certain death
of the labor movement. These dire predictions, of course, were issued
literally on the eve of the dramatic and widespread upsurge of labor
organizing that began in 1933 (Brody 1993, 82–119).

History, then, serves as a warning to those who would predict the
future: the naysayers who rule out rebirth as a possibility as well as those
who think we can *will* a reenactment of the turbulent social movements
of the 1930s. Many of the economic, political, and cultural forces that
spur the birth of mass social movements are beyond the control of organized labor. What can make a difference, however, and in fact is possible to will is the reinvention of the labor movement from the inside,
or what could be called institutional redesign. Institutional innovation
by itself is not sufficient to revitalize the labor movement, but it is an
essential precondition. As the twenty-first century dawns, organized
labor must reposition itself to survive droughts of conservative ascen-
dancy. At the same time, when the opportunity for dramatic advance
once again arises, the labor movement must be poised for takeoff—
ready to ride, or even lead, the next wave of social reform.

The institutional redesign I have in mind involves fundamentally rethinking the house of labor. I'm not talking about adding a new wing or applying a new coat of paint. I'm talking about rethinking the movement from the foundation on up, about reinventing the labor movement so that it can be the vehicle for the aspirations of the twenty-first century workforce. The industrial form of unionism dominant today may continue to be viable for some groups of workers in some sectors of the economy, but if the labor movement is ever to appeal to the majority of today's workers, it must transform itself radically. New models of unionism must be invented—specifically, models more appropriate for a mobile, service-oriented, and knowledge-based economy in which women, immigrants, and people of color are in the majority.

Like many other theorists, I see us at a historical divide—like the 1880s if you will or the 1930s (Piore and Sabel 1984; Heckscher 1988; Cobble 1991b, 1994). We are living through a period of profound technological, economic, and political restructuring. Labor must change to meet these new realities, and it must once again let old forms of unionism give way to new. The issue, however, is not simply how to reinvent a new unionism; it is how to reinvent new *unionisms*. Academics and activists both must resist the siren call of the "one right way"—or as AFL-CIO president John Sweeney calls it, the "one-size-fits-all"—approach to unionism (Sweeney 1996). History shows that the labor movement thrived when it tolerated and even nourished multiple, and at times competing, models of unionism. Today, as in the past, we need union institutions that are suited to workers in a wide range of jobs—from cappuccino maker to computer programmer to dependent-care provider. Moreover, the labor movement of the twenty-first century must be responsive to the multiple and overlapping identities of a culturally and racially diverse workforce. It must be a means to end discriminations based on race, gender, sexual identity, and other invidious social distinctions as well as a vehicle to rectify class inequities. In short, organized labor must create new institutions and broaden its animating philosophy.

In this essay I will draw on historical research to offer some possible directions for institutional and cultural change within the labor movement. I will focus on the labor movement in two very different historical contexts—both eras that have heuristic value for us today. First, I look at the organizing and representational efforts of the early craft unions and the American Federation of Labor (AFL) before the New Deal. Then I shift to the more recent past to examine the unionism of women service workers in the 1930s and after. Both discussions raise and help partially answer three questions that I think are fundamental to labor's future: (1) How should labor organize itself, that is, what institutional forms will be most effective? (2) Who should belong to the movement, that is, what should be the criteria for membership? (3) What are the issues around which the new workforce will rally? These questions I believe must be posed and answered anew if the labor movement is to redesign its institutions and practices for a new century.

Beyond Industrial Unionism

The early craft unions and the AFL under Samuel Gompers may seem like odd places to look for new models of a revitalized unionism. Most historians and activists tend to turn first to the industrial unionism of the CIO when searching for clues about rebuilding and expanding the labor movement. After all, the labor movement grew exponentially after John L. Lewis and other labor leaders set up their own rival federation in the 1930s dedicated to organizing mass production workers along industrial lines. But I would argue that today's postindustrial workforce may have as much, if not more, in common with the workforce of the nineteenth and early twentieth century as with the industrial factory workers who built the CIO. Further, the older forms of unionism such as the guilds, associations, and self-help groups of the nineteenth century and the craft unions of the pre–New Deal AFL have more to offer as alternative models of collective representation for today's workers than do the industrial unions of the more recent past.

The majority of workers who organized successfully before the New Deal practiced a very different form of unionism than the industrial unionism that became dominant with the rise of the CIO. Building tradesmen, garment workers, restaurant employees, performing artists, and others recruited and gained recognition on an occupational basis rather than by industry or individual work site. I call this occupational rather than craft unionism because it was not necessarily exclusive or limited to skilled craftsmen, and I argue that aspects of occupational unionism have much to offer today's workforce (Cobble 1991a, 1991b, 1994). With the growth of a mobile, "contingent" workforce, the decline of internal labor markets, and the rise of new crafts, occupations and professions in which worker identity is primarily horizontal (with other workers in the occupation) rather than vertical (with those working for a single employer or company), a unionism emphasizing cross-firm structures and occupational identity appears viable once again.

Occupational unionism was not a work-site or firm-based unionism with wages, benefits, and job security dependent on organizing an individual employer. Rather, the strategy of occupational unionists was to gain market power by organizing the labor supply; that is, they focused on gaining the allegiance of all those who did the work of a particular trade or occupation within a given labor market. Occupational unionists offered a number of services that helped create ongoing ties between workers and their union. They ran hiring halls and employment bureaus and agencies; they also provided training—what we would now see as professional development—as well as job placement for their members. Benefits and union membership were portable (they moved with the worker from job to job). Occupational unions sought employment security for their members rather than job security. The issue was not fighting for seniority or tenure at an individual work site but increasing the overall supply of good, well-paying jobs and of providing workers with the skills to perform those jobs (Cobble 1991a, 1991b, 1994).

Further, occupational unions routinely took on responsibilities that later came to be seen as exclusively management functions. In many instances, they embraced an approach I term *peer management*. In contrast to the industrial union practice, common by the 1930s and 1940s, in which management disciplined and the union grieved, occupational unionists preferred to both write and enforce their own workplace rules rather than simply react to those created by management. Together, workers decided upon acceptable performance standards, how to divide up work time and tasks, which union members would staff certain assignments, and many other work organization and quality questions. What we now commonly think of as managerial "rights" were for them subject to peer control: Union members saw it as exercising their craft prerogatives—not unlike what persists today among some professional groups that determine and monitor the standards for their profession (Cobble 1991a, 1991b).

Despite the current severe legal limitations on occupational unionism (Cobble 1994), unions increasingly are attempting to revive some of these historic practices. The National Educational Association and the American Federation of Teachers, for example, held their first joint national conference in October 1998. The primary agenda item was how teacher unions could move beyond the old industrial unionism and embrace a craft/professional model that would emphasize teacher training, peer-established workplace performance standards, and improving the quality of service. The "new unionism" (as it has been dubbed by teacher unionists) was the subject of intense debate on the local and regional level for some time before the 1998 national conference (Kerchner, Koppich, and Weeres 1997; Rideout 1998). Since 1998, both teacher unions have held major national conferences to further the development of the new unionism among teachers and to help invent new models of unionism for the growing numbers of doctors, psychologists, and other knowledge workers who desire collective representation (Maitland 1999; Kemble 2000).

Other initiatives are under way to introduce worker- and union-run hiring halls and temporary agencies among contingent and mobile workers, the most successful of which operate in a well-defined geographical area and confine themselves to a single sector, such as farm labor or telecommunications. Local 164, International Brotherhood of Electrical Workers in New Jersey, for example, has drawn on its craft traditions representing electricians to organize teledata workers. Local 164 set up a state-of-the-art training program, provided continuous upgrading to journey-level employees, and monitored the performance standards of the workers they trained. They have created an employer demand for unions: employers in the area now seek out the local, eager to sign union agreements that will ensure them a steady source of competent skilled labor (Powers 1998; Merrill 1999). The sectoral labor-management partnerships pioneered in Minnesota and elsewhere also are reviving important elements of occupational union strategy, as is Working Today, A National Association of

Employees with its emphasis on portable benefits and occupational advancement (Parker and Rogers, this volume; Heckscher, this volume; Horowitz 1999).

The Early AFL and Lost Forms of Organizing

There are other aspects of pre–New Deal unionism that warrant attention in addition to the representational practices of occupational unionists. The Federation itself, especially in its early years in the late nineteenth and early twentieth century, experimented with a wide range of organizing and representational strategies that have gone largely unacknowledged by researchers. Most historians assume that the early AFL resembled the lackluster, organizing-averse fossil of the late 1920s and early 1930s with which we are so familiar. Yet my research suggests a somewhat different story.[1]

Indeed, throughout much of its history, the Federation along with its state and local affiliates took considerable initiative in organizing; organizing was simply too important to be left to the Internationals. The Federation coordinated a far-flung and extensive network of AFL volunteer and paid organizers. These AFL organizers helped build up the membership of existing Internationals. They also had the authority to charter new local unions and directly affiliate these new locals with the Federation. By my estimates, from the founding of the AFL in 1886 to its merger with the CIO in 1955, the AFL chartered some twenty thousand federal or directly affiliated local unions (Cobble 1997: figures 1–4; Cobble 1996b, 1–3).

The history of this strange anomalous creature—an AFL-affiliated local union but without a parent International—is both fascinating

---

[1] The following paragraphs are based on a range of archival sources including AFL, AFL-CIO Charter Books, 1890–1966, Collection 18, George Meany Memorial Archives, Silver Springs, Maryland [GMMA]; Directly Affiliated Local Unions, Charter Files, 1900–1965, Microfilm 22, GMMA; Collection 40, AFL, Federal Local Unions Charter Records, 1942–1981, GMMA; American Federation of Labor Records, Part I: Strikes and Agreements Files, 1898–1953, Microfilm Edition. For a fuller discussion see Cobble 1996b and Cobble 1997.

and instructive. The 1886 AFL constitution provided for the formation of "a local body, to be known as a 'Federal Labor Union'" and authorized any group of "seven wage workers of good character and favorable to Trade Unions" to petition the national Federation for a local union charter (AFL 1886). And, as the AFL charter books reveal, thousands did petition for AFL membership, and the vast majority received charters. Many groups of workers simply self-organized; others had assistance from an AFL organizer or a subnational body such as a central labor council (CLC), state federation, or another AFL local union.

These locals demonstrated a remarkable range of institutional forms. Many organized along craft lines: Their membership belonged almost wholly to a single trade. Others were more industrial, representing different types of workers within a single industry. And some were both multicraft and multi-industry—chartered, in essence, as geographic unions because their jurisdiction covered every worker in a particular town, community, or region.

The representational strategies pursued by these locals varied just as widely. Some focused primarily on local legislative initiatives; for example, minimum wage ordinances; others emphasized benevolent functions, offering unemployment assistance or income supports for the sick and disabled. Still others provided job training and employment referrals. A few locals established community mediation and arbitration boards that interceded in labor-management disputes. For a brief period in the early 1890s, the Federation even chartered a number of "nonpartisan social reform clubs" in which "persons of various vocations . . . in favor of union labels, the trades union movement in general, and such economic reforms as will serve to leave to the worker the wealth which he produces" could join together "for mutual aid and instruction" (AFL 1897, 46).

But what is the relevance of this aspect of AFL history today? It bears directly on the questions posed earlier concerning who should be a union member and what institutional structures are appropriate as work and employment relationships transform. The federal locals of the past were *self-constituted* communities; union membership was not dependent on securing employer recognition or qualifying as an employee under the law. Rather, the labor movement itself determined who was eligible for membership. The AFL issued charters not on the basis of bargaining-unit status or legal classification, but because a group of workers pledged and demonstrated their allegiance to the principles of the labor movement.

The labor movement once again must define its own membership boundaries, and it must once again open up its ranks to a broad cross section of the American workforce. We live in a world in which so-called "employees" are disappearing. According to my calculations, close to one-third of the private-sector workforce is no longer defined as an employee under the NLRB, and the number of nonemployees are growing every day (Cobble 1994, 290). As work is being reorganized, more and more workers no longer fit the mold of the traditional employee directed by others and dependent on a single employer. Many are assuming managerial responsibilities, working in teams that are self-regulating and formed around particular projects or tasks. Others are moving into self-employment or independent contractor status. Granted, many so-called independent contractors are misclassified and more properly resemble traditional employees in their lack of autonomy at work and their economic dependence on a single employer. But others are indeed no longer employees in the traditional sense; they may hire or supervise others or may negotiate a fee for their services with multiple employers rather than receive an hourly wage for their labor from a single employer.

The early AFL and the labor movements that preceded it represented nonemployees: They organized the self-employed, the unemployed, contractors who hired others, foremen, and supervisors—indeed, whoever needed to organize in order to control the market and reform the larger economic and political system (Cobble and Vosko 2000). Today, the labor movement must not limit itself to representing only those who qualify as dependent employees. The goal of labor historically has been to help workers achieve economic independence and greater control of the work process. Wouldn't it be ironic if the labor movement ended up fighting to ensure that workers remained dependent employees? To appeal to today's workforce, the labor movement must not be seen as a conservative force wedded to the constraining work arrangements of the past but as a vehicle for creating more humane and flexible work. Economic restructuring opens up opportunities for workers (and for reviving organized labor) as well as dangers. An economy in which workers have more autonomy and skills, for example, is also an economy in which the bargaining power of labor, both individually and collectively, is enhanced.

Moreover, the labor movement needs to move beyond contract unionism and broaden the current definition of what constitutes a union. The labor movement in the past did not restrict itself in this way. Historically, collective bargaining was one of many methods used by unions to raise the living standards of American workers. Similarly, securing a formal trade agreement with an employer, while desirable, was not the defining feature of unionism. Why should the current labor movement limit itself only to those groups who see securing contracts with individual employers as their primary tactic and who have the power and leverage to win such a contract? The definitions of the movement must be expanded: Why exclude community groups who are organizing around labor issues, for example? In one sense, there is quite a simple answer to declining union membership: Any organization doing the work of the labor movement should be part of the labor movement. Let the ends be the measure of unionism, not the means.

Finally, the history of federal labor unions reveals a structural relationship and a power dynamic among the various union bodies—Federation, International, and state and local bodies—that differs from the current situation. The Federation *itself* initiated organizing directly; it did not see organizing as a function solely of the Internationals. The subnational bodies (the state federations, CLCs, and local unions) also had greater power and autonomy. For example, the CLCs and state federations often organized and affiliated local labor groups as a way of expanding their dues-paying ranks and increasing their economic and political clout at the local and regional levels. These local union groups, federal locals included, could join the AFL and its state and local bodies whether or not they had parent Internationals. It was not until the late nineteenth and early twentieth century that the national unions began assuming authority over the membership rules of subnational structures and asserting, for example, that CLCs and state federations affiliate only local bodies chartered through a national or international union (Ulman 1955).

As political and economic decision making are pushed to the local and regional levels in response to market restructuring and government decentralization, community-centered unionism and community-based organizing efforts become increasingly important. Witness the crucial role played by the local community in winning the 1998 dock workers lockout and strike in Australia: The community—family members, neighbors, and friends of the strikers—thronged the docks and made it impossible for replacements to get through. Opening up membership at the subnational level and allowing the CLCs and state federations to become more proactive in setting up and affiliating local labor groups could help foster this necessary resurgence of union power at the state and community level.

Representing the New Service Workforce

The last set of historical examples I will discuss are reconstructed from my research on the organizing concerns and strategies initiated by women service workers in the 1930s and after. These examples suggest some of the new issues that need to be embraced as more and more people, men and women, take on jobs in the service sector of the economy.

Daniel Bell (1973) and other commentators (for example, Drucker 1993) stress the centrality of knowledge work in the new economy. I agree. Yet, of equal importance, especially given their numerical dominance, is the new emotional proletariat—the front-line service workers and paraprofessionals engaged in interactive work (Macdonald and Sirianni 1996, 3). Service work, sociologist Arlie Hochschild (1983) tells us, is primarily about emotional labor not mental or manual work. It involves the expenditure of energy to create an emotional state in the customer, client, patient, or passenger. Or to reach back to an earlier sociological theorist, C. Wright Mills (1951) eloquently explained that in the new white collar economy people are asked to sell themselves—their personalities, sexuality, and appearance—not just their brains or their brawn. Service workers, then, especially those engaged in person-to-person or voice-to-voice encounters, have new and particular concerns arising from their particular circumstances. The issue is not just controlling the boss-employee relationship but influencing the customer-employee encounter. Service workers want to affect the rules governing employee-customer relationships; they also want to limit management's intrusive regulation over their personality and appearance. Let me offer some examples from the history of organizing among women service workers that point to the salience of these issues.

As early as the 1930s, union leaders like Myra Wolfgang, later vice president of the Hotel Employees and Restaurant Employees (HERE), recognized these concerns as legitimate organizing issues and built a sizeable union constituency based on that realization. Wolfgang moved from organizing dime store clerks and soda counter waitresses in the 1930s to organizing Playboy Bunnies in the 1960s. She helped secure the first union contract at the Playboy Club in Detroit in 1964 and later saw HERE win a national contract covering all Playboy Clubs in the country. Before the contract, bunnies received tips but no wages, and she organized the Detroit Club by sending her own seventeen-year-old daughter in as a union "salt" by picketing the club with signs reading, "Don't be a bunny, work for money," and by the astute use of publicity. Her quips were legion. She once testified before Congress, for example, that Hugh Hefner's philosophy was "a gross perpetuation of the idea that women should be obscene and not heard" (Wolfgang 1972, 31–33; Cobble 1991a; Cobble 1996a, 346–47).

Wolfgang and HERE continued to address the particular needs of their service-sector workers after securing representational rights at the Playboy Clubs. HERE kept the loyalty of the workforce by negotiating new *customer* rules of behavior such as the "look but do not touch" rule, by redesigning bunny uniforms to cover more of the worker's body and by contesting management definitions of attractiveness. The union also defended bunnies who were fired for "loss of bunny image"—a dischargeable offense that often occurred in a bunny's thirties but could happen earlier if management noticed such defects as "crinkling eyelids, sagging breasts, and drooping derrieres" (Cobble 1991a, 128–29; Cobble 1996a, 347).

What servers would wear at work was another contested issue. In national negotiations during the 1970s, HERE and the Playboy Clubs International debated just how much of the server's body would be revealed by the bunny costume. In other less publicized negotiations in the 1970s involving cocktail waitresses and barmaids, HERE restricted employer choice of uniform. They argued in one case, for example, that the employers provide "uniforms that fit" (some employers refused to buy uniforms over a size 12) and "adequately covered all parts of the body normally covered by personal clothing" (Cobble 1991a, 131; Cobble 1996a, 347).

Other service workers have raised similar concerns. Flight attendants, for example, knew the importance of challenging employer control over customer encounters and employee appearance (Nielsen 1982; Rozen 1988). One of the more interesting chapters in their history occurred in the 1970s in response to the increasing sexualization of flight attendant work. When the airlines shifted away from the marriageable-girl-next-door image to the "Fly Me" come-on (pioneered by National Airlines) and the not-so-subtle ads paid for by Continental with flight attendants promising to "really move our tail for you," stewardesses fought back (Cobble 1999, 28–30).

In 1972, flight attendants formed the first national organization for "stewardesses and their allies," the Stewardesses for Women's Rights (SFWR). SFWR wanted equal wages and promotional opportunities, but their central concern was to control their image and end what they called "sexploitation." The airlines created the expectation among the flying public that flight attendants were there for passenger titillation rather than passenger safety. Stewardesses wanted to substitute their own image of professionalism for the sexualized one perpetrated by the airlines. Instead of wearing the required "Fly Me" buttons, they distributed new ones reading, "Don't Fly Me, Fly Your Self." They also handed out "National, Your Fly is Open" bumper stickers. They filed lawsuits alleging that airline ads created a hostile work environment. They also left their male-dominated unions in droves in the 1970s, setting up independent, female-led organizations in which issues of professional image, control over one's appearance (part of what I call "body rights"), and the character of customer interaction would be taken seriously as issues (Cobble 1999, 28–30).

These issues remain very much alive today. In 1998, for example, grocery clerks of the United Food and Commercial Workers (UFCW) local in Oakland, California, sparked a media firestorm by protesting Safeway's new "smile rules" for employees. Grocery store clerks were required to smile and make extended eye contact with all customers. They must also offer to carry groceries into the parking lot for anyone needing assistance. Management's substitution of its own rules for service workers' own highly developed nonverbal and verbal methods of controlling interactions with the public, especially with aggressive men, had disastrous results. Worker job satisfaction declined, sexual harassment increased, and, in one case, a female employee was sexually assaulted in the parking lot when management insisted, over her objections, that she help two male customers carry their groceries to the car. The UFCW's complaints did not generate much of a response from Safeway. But local radio call-in talk shows, newspaper editorial columns, and Internet sites buzzed with opinions about whether "smile rules" were a serious labor issue and who had the right to set the rules of social encounter in the workplace (for example, Veverka 1998; Mc-Nichol 1998).

Of course there are issues other than the employee-customer relationship that will be crucial concerns for the twenty-first-century workforce. Issues of economic justice, opportunity, and security will not disappear. Raising wages for the vast army of low-paid service workers, ending unfair and discriminatory treatment, and establishing labor protections and benefits as a right of citizenship rather than as a function of employment will all be important reform priorities.

Yet it is important for the labor movement to acknowledge that the concerns of large numbers of today's workers, service and otherwise, are as much psychological as economic. Since World War II, the numbers of college-educated workers have increased significantly. That shift along with other social and cultural changes has meant that more workers now expect jobs that offer autonomy, variety, and the opportunity for self-development. They also want work lives that are compatible with their family and civic commitments.

The Harvard Union of Clerical and Technical Workers (HUCTW) is one example of a union responding to this wide range of worker concerns. They have pushed aggressively on economic issues such as wages and benefits, winning major monetary gains for the clerical and health-care workers they represent. Yet as Kris Rondeau of HUCTW recently explained, the union's current goals, generated in response to member priorities, involve "work redesign," creating opportunities for "deep learning," and negotiating release time for what she called "community building." This latter provision would allow workers paid time off from the job so that they could remain active in vital community institutions such as the Parent Teacher Associations in their local public schools (Rondeau 1998).

A unionism reconceived to meet the needs of the new workforce will move away from treating people as interchangeable units and focus on representing the *individual* as well as the *collective* interests of employees. That shift of course is a fundamental challenge to many current union practices, from seniority to across-the-board wage packages. Yet there are alternative labor movement traditions to draw on. The performing arts unions, for example, still negotiate a collective contract that sets minimum standards while allowing individuals to bargain supplemental enhancements (Gray and Seeber 1998). And, as Pat Armstrong (1993, 308–12) maintains in her work on nurses, the strongest representational strategy for nurses has been and continues to be one that blends concern for individual and collective needs. Nurse unionism builds on the best of the professional traditions— that is, a concern for "collegial participation, individual rights, and influencing public policy"—without abandoning the traditional union emphasis on "equity, collective rights, and improving conditions of work and pay."

In conclusion, this essay has raised and attempted to answer some fundamental questions facing a labor movement in need of revival— questions about how the movement should be structured, who should join, and what issues should lie at its core. I have relied on examples from labor's own history to help suggest alternatives to current union practice and to identify some past practices that warrant reclaiming. What are these best union past practices? Let me offer four as a partial summary: (1) a unionism with fluid, porous membership boundaries that shift as the nature of work shifts; (2) a unionism with the structural capacity to organize occupationally and geographically as well as industrially; (3) a movement with a structure in which all levels—national, local, state, and regional—are activated and empowered economically as well as politically; and (4) a movement open to diverse means as well as diverse ends.

History makes it clear, however, that the solutions for one generation were never wholly the solutions for the next. The unionism of the future may look in part like the unionism of the past, but it also will transcend that past in ways we have yet to imagine. Our task, then, if a new and revitalized labor movement is to be built for the twenty-first century, is to have the courage to risk change and the courage to think beyond our traditions, past and present.

PART II

Organizing Upsurge: Strategic and Structural Innovation

Organizing Immigrant Workers

Case Studies from Southern California

Ruth Milkman and Kent Wong

F oreign-born workers, especially those from Mexico and Central America, are the core of the low-wage workforce in contemporary southern California, and they have been the focus of many recent union recruitment efforts there. The regional landscape, like the national one, is littered with organizing failures, but there have also been some spectacularly successful efforts to bring Latino immigrants into the union fold during the 1990s. This chapter considers the two best-known success stories—one involving janitors who clean office buildings in Los Angeles and another concerning drywall hangers in the region's residential construction industry. We compare these two cases to two instances of large-scale immigrant organizing efforts that have yet to achieve their goals. One case involves garment workers employed by Guess, Inc. and the other concerns truckers servicing the Los Angeles–Long Beach port. On that basis we explore the conditions that have facilitated, and those that have impeded, recent efforts to unionize immigrants in the region, focusing particularly on the role of union commitment and strategy.

In all four of our cases, as in most manual occupations in late twentieth-century southern California, the labor force consists overwhelmingly of foreign-born Latinos. Thus, in our analysis the presence of an immigrant-dominated workforce is a constant, not a variable, and we cannot assess systematically here the relative "organizability" of foreign- and native-born workers. However, our research does confirm Delgado's (1993) claim that immigrant workers, despite their obvious vulnerability to deportation and other limits on their legal rights (especially for the undocumented), are by no means impossible to unionize. Anyone who doubts this need only consider the two cases of success, which created widespread awareness of the potential for immigrant unionization within southern California's labor movement in the early 1990s. Local 399 of the Service Employees International Union's (SEIU) Justice for Janitors (J for J) campaign won a contract from a major building cleaning contractor in the summer of 1990, the triumphal conclusion of a two-year Los Angeles–based organizing drive that brought janitorial membership in Local 399 to 8,000, up from about 1,800 five years earlier. This was the largest private-sector union organizing achievement involving Latino immigrants since the United Farm Workers' victories of the early 1970s. Two years after the janitors' victory, a five-month strike by thousands of Mexican immigrant drywall hangers (workers who install the sheetrock panels that make up the interior walls of modern buildings) halted residential construction throughout southern California. This yielded a union contract that doubled drywallers' wage rates in Los Angeles and surrounding counties and brought 2,400 previously nonunion workers into Carpenters Local 2361.

These impressive victories appeared to lay the foundation for a broader effort to unionize the region's vast population of foreign-born workers, and hopes that this might occur were bolstered by the ascent of new, more progressive leaders to top positions in the national AFL-CIO in 1995. And yet, a decade after these two strikes, the vast bulk of the immigrant workforce in southern California remains outside the union fold. There have been scattered immigrant organizing successes in the area since 1992—most notably the 1999 union election that added 74,000 Los Angeles home-care workers to the ranks of the SEIU, many of them foreign born—as well as many campaigns ending in failure or stalemate. Our third and fourth case studies are high-profile examples from the latter group. One is the effort launched in the mid-1990s by the International Ladies' Garment Workers' Union (ILGWU) and then continued by the Union of Needletrades, Industrial and Textile Employees (UNITE) to unionize Guess, Inc.[1] The other case is the

---

[1] UNITE was formed in 1995 by a merger between the ILGWU and the Amalgamated Clothing and Textile Workers (ACTWU).

grassroots organizing effort among the thousands of truck drivers who service the Los Angeles–Long Beach waterfront, now the world's third-largest port. These drivers launched a series of work stoppages in the 1980s and 1990s, culminating in a massive and highly effective strike in 1996 whose main goal was to secure union representation with the Communication Workers of America (CWA). However, both the Guess workers and the port truckers, despite energetic and imaginative organizing efforts, remain nonunion today. By dissecting the problems these two campaigns confronted and comparing them to the successes of the janitors and drywallers, we hope to illuminate the factors that shaped the disparate outcomes.

Our basic claim is that internal union problems, which led to inadequate strategies or compromised commitment, was the key factor undermining the Guess campaign and the collapse of the 1996 port truckers' strike. The comparison to the janitors and drywallers suggests that unionization can be and has been achieved among immigrant workers under conditions generally similar to those that prevailed in the garment and truckers' cases. To be sure, there were some notable additional obstacles that organizers had to confront in the latter campaigns. The most obvious of these is the vulnerability to capital flight in the garment case. Unlike janitorial, construction, and trucking work, which are not geographically mobile, garment firms can and often do move work to new and sometimes distant locations to cut labor costs and to avoid or resist unionization. Indeed, Guess ultimately did relocate much of its production to Mexico in the face of the ILGWU/UNITE organizing drive, although this was as much a result as a cause of the campaign's weakness. Even with the constant threat of capital mobility, there is more apparel employment in greater Los Angeles today than anywhere else in the United States and more employment in apparel than in any other manufacturing industry in the area, so that there is no shortage of garment workers for union organizers to target. Moreover, immigrants have been successfully unionized in manufacturing settings in Los Angeles in recent years (see, for example, Delgado 1993 and Zabin 2000).

The Los Angeles–Long Beach port truckers also face some special organizing obstacles, most important the fact that as independent contractors the majority are legally ineligible for conventional forms of unionization. Yet this did not prevent the truckers from forming a number of independent labor organizations in the 1980s and 1990s nor from launching several large-scale strikes, culminating in the huge 1996 walkout that nearly succeeded in winning union recognition. Again, we argue that the negative outcome was due primarily to strategic weaknesses within the union, not to the peculiarities of the industry or the independent contractor problem.

Our effort draws inspiration from and in many respects is analogous to Bronfenbrenner's (1997a) pioneering research on union strategies, which seeks to specify the characteristics of organizing campaigns that are most likely to yield success. However, there are at least two important differences between her work and ours. First, whereas Bronfenbrenner's methodology is largely quantitative, based on analysis of hundreds of organizing campaigns, ours is qualitative and includes only a few cases. Second, whereas Bronfenbrenner analyzed unionization efforts culminating in elections held under the auspices of the National Labor Relations Board (NLRB), the traditional route to union recognition in the United States, none of our four cases involved NLRB elections. In all of the occupational groups involved, this approach was ruled out by the particular organizational features of the industries in which they were embedded. Because building services, residential construction, and garments all rely on extensive subcontracting, a union electoral victory at any given firm would merely lead the building owner, housing developer, or clothing manufacturer to shift work to nonunion subcontractors, typically putting the newly unionized firm out of business and its employees out of work. NLRB-oriented organizing also is impractical in intermodal trucking, both because of the large number of firms in the industry and because the owner-operators that now dominate the occupation are not legally "employees" and thus are not eligible to vote in NLRB elections. Thus, in all four of our cases, the campaigns necessarily departed from the traditional unionization model oriented toward NLRB elections, relying instead on innovative strategies and tactics.

The alternative organizing approaches that were used in launching these campaigns can be divided into leadership-initiated and bottom-up initiatives. Both the janitors' and the garment workers' campaigns were initiated by union leaders and were strategically designed to exert intensive pressure on the powerful individuals and groups within each industry to win union recognition. While these two campaigns also included grassroots organizing among workers, both were launched by established union leaders and based on careful research. By contrast, the drywallers' and port truckers' organizing was begun by rank-and-file workers—including, to be sure, key individuals with strong leadership skills. Although the drywallers and truckers did seek and ultimately receive support from established union organizations, in both cases the involvement of established labor unions was limited and relatively belated. Indigenous organizing efforts among workers themselves were the main force propelling these two campaigns forward.

Based on this four-way comparison, we argue that what really matters is not whether a union organizing campaign begins as a strategic effort to put pressure directly on the decision makers in an industry or as a bottom-up, grassroots mobilization of workers on the ground. Rather, success seems to depend on effectively combining the two approaches into a comprehensive strategy. Both the janitors and the drywallers managed to bring these two crucial elements together, even though one began as a leadership-initiated effort and the other as a bottom-up campaign. In the Guess case, largely for reasons related to the 1995 union merger that made the ILGWU part of UNITE, what was originally conceived as a comprehensive campaign devolved into a more limited, publicity-driven effort; here the weakness of the grassroots organizing proved fatal. For the port truckers, the converse was true: The campaign's strength was at the level of bottom-up mobilization, while the CWA's coordination efforts at the top foundered, again leading to an unsuccessful outcome.

In both of these cases, internal union problems were the critical obstacles to success. Given the intense employer opposition that faces virtually all union organizing in the late twentieth century, any lack of resolve or strategic weakness on the union side can easily undermine a campaign. Although it is impossible to know with certainty what the outcome would have been if the organizers had done everything right at Guess and in the port truckers' campaign—and surely there are cases of organizing efforts in which the union does everything right but is nonetheless outmaneuvered by powerful employers—our comparison to the janitors and drywallers suggests that determined and skillful organizing, backed up with adequate financial and legal resources, can make or break unionization efforts among immigrant workers in southern California.

This seemingly voluntaristic analysis is not entirely without a structural dimension, however. Indeed, there were particular economic, political, and social factors that made these four occupational groups ripe targets for organizing in the first place, and thus it is hardly accidental that organizing efforts *emerged* in these four cases and not in others. However, our focus here is not on this question, but instead on explaining what happened after these highly promising efforts began, and specifically on the factors yielding success or failure. Before considering each case in detail, in the next section we briefly sketch out the key common background factors that the four share. Despite their location in different industries and sectors, all of the occupational groups involved were highly unionized in the southern California region prior to the post-1965 surge in immigration (although garment workers less so than the others). In all four, union density declined drastically before the immigrant influx, and the resulting deterioration in wages, benefits, and working conditions then led native-born workers to abandon these occupations in the late 1970s and early 1980s. They were soon replaced by low-wage immigrants, and as employment skyrocketed in all four fields, vigorous new organizing efforts emerged among the newly recruited foreign-born workers. These processes of union decline and immigrant incorporation into the labor market were remarkably similar across these otherwise diverse cases, and in all four, serious unionization efforts emerged in this context.

Union Decline and the Immigrant Influx

Southern California historically was a bastion of the open shop, where unions never penetrated as deeply as in the northern part of the state. However, organized labor did gain a foothold in the 1930s and 1940s in many industries, janitorial, garments, trucking, and construction among them. By the early 1970s, union density (union members as a percentage of all nonfarm wage and salary workers) in the Los Angeles–Long Beach metropolitan area was roughly equivalent to that in the state of California as a whole, hovering around 30 percent. About 80 percent of residential drywallers and nearly all of the truckers servicing the Los Angeles–Long Beach port were unionized by the Carpenters and Teamsters unions, respectively. SEIU Local 399 had about 5,000 janitorial members in the mid-1970s, including nearly all of those who cleaned the major downtown Los Angeles office buildings as well as some in surrounding areas. And although union density was less extensive in garments than in these other fields, the ILGWU had about 4,000 to 5,000 members in Los Angeles in the mid-1970s.

In all four cases, however, as employers went on the offensive both nationally and in the southern California region, union power collapsed in the late 1970s and early 1980s, precipitating deep cuts in wages, the virtual disappearance of fringe benefits, and dramatic deterioration in working conditions. In the Los Angeles-Long Beach area, union density fell from 30 percent in 1967 to less than 20 percent twenty years later; over that same period the decline was from 24 to 14 percent in the Anaheim-Santa Ana-Garden Grove metropolitan area of Orange County (just south of Los Angeles), and from 31 to 19 percent statewide (California Department of Industrial Relations, various years).

Capital mobility was often cited as the force behind union decline in the garment industry, yet regional employment in the industry expanded rapidly in this period even as the union virtually collapsed. Moreover, in building services, residential construction, and trucking, none of which can be relocated to take advantage of cheaper labor costs elsewhere on the globe, unions were equally devastated during this same period. In all these cases, employer determination to weaken or eliminate unions, along with an increasingly inhospitable political environment (leading to deregulation in trucking, among other factors), were the key forces propelling deunionization. Nonunion firms came to dominate all four industries in the region by the mid-1980s, despite their otherwise varied characteristics. This in turn led to the exit of massive numbers of native-born "Anglos" (and in the case of janitors, African Americans as well) from the workforce. But in the meantime, demand for labor in all four industries was expanding dramatically, so employers turned to the vast and growing supply of Latino immigrants.

The region, and Los Angeles in particular, was the destination of choice for both documented and undocumented post-1965 immigrants, especially those from Latin America, and their arrival radically altered the composition of southern California's working class. By 1990, one in three Los Angeles county residents was born outside the United

States. And whereas as recently as 1970, only 12 percent of employed persons in the five-county Los Angeles area (Los Angeles, Orange, Riverside, San Bernardino, and Ventura counties) were foreign born; by 1990 the figure had shot up to 33 percent. Most immigrants in the region are Latino, and within that category they come primarily from three countries: Mexico (with by far the largest share), El Salvador, and Guatemala. In low-wage manual and service occupations like garment, janitorial, trucking, and drywall work, Latino immigrants are especially predominant (see Waldinger and Bozorgmehr 1996).

Native-born workers rapidly exited all four fields of employment as a *result* of union decline and the accompanying deterioration in wages and benefits, not the other way round. Some workers and union officials, particularly in the drywall case, blamed the decline in union strength on the availability of cheap immigrant labor in the region. But when we compare southern California to other parts of the United States, this view loses credibility. For example, in New York City, there was an influx of immigrants into janitorial work only slightly below the level in Los Angeles, yet there was no significant erosion in the union's strength, and wages remained relatively high. Similarly, in garments, the New York union declined far less than in Los Angeles, despite a massive increase in immigrant employment in both cities. By contrast, in both trucking and construction, there was a national process of sharp deunionization, yet in most parts of the country immigrants were not a significant part of the workforce. In construction, for example, nationally 90.6 percent of unionized workers were white in 1977–78 and 89.0 in 1989; similarly, nonunion construction workers were 91 percent white at both dates (Allen 1994, 415).

Native-born workers thus exited all four occupations in southern California in response to the changes induced by union decline. It was not immigrant competition that induced union decline, but union decline that led natives to exit and immigrants to enter these fields. Indeed, natives remained numerous in sectors in which unions maintained a presence (public-sector janitorial work, long-distance trucking, and commercial drywalling), while leaving the less attractive, newly deunionized positions to recent immigrants, who eagerly filled the void. Even in the garment trade, in which immigrants were a longstanding presence, native-born workers exited in the wake of the union's utter collapse, and immigrants became even more dominant.

By the late 1980s, then, all four of these occupations had been ut-
terly transformed. The unions had been crippled, wages and benefits
had declined dramatically, and the composition of the workforce had
shifted toward nearly complete reliance on Latino immigrants. It was
against this background that new union organizing campaigns were
launched in the 1990s within all four industries. Long presumed to be
"willing" to work for low pay and to be generally tractable, immigrant
workers suddenly emerged as a core source of union militancy in the
1990s, to the surprise of most observers. In addition, Latinos rose to
prominent leadership positions in the local labor movement, most notably with the (contested) election in 1996 of Miguel Contreras to head
the Los Angeles County Federation of Labor, the first non-Anglo to
hold that position (Sipchen 1997). These many parallel developments
in our four cases notwithstanding, the effort to revive unionism in each
moved along distinct trajectories and with divergent outcomes. We are
now ready to consider each of the cases in more detail.

Successful Leadership-Initiated Organizing: Justice for Janitors

In the 1980s, then-SEIU president John Sweeney (who now heads the
AFL-CIO) began a concerted effort to revitalize the union. He increased the resources devoted to organizing and recruited scores of new
staff members, many of them progressives with experience in the social movements of the 1960s and 1970s. Among other initiatives,
Sweeney aimed to reorganize what had once been the SEIU's primary
base, namely, building services, which had been severely eroded in
many cities (although not in New York, Chicago, or San Francisco).
The result was the national J for J campaign, which arrived in Los Angeles in 1988 after some modest successes in smaller cities, most notably Denver.[2] The leadership and most of the financial resources devoted to the effort came directly from SEIU headquarters, and in Los
Angeles as in other cities where J for J was launched, the campaign proceeded not because of support, but rather active resistance, from many

---

[2]For a more detailed account of this case, see Waldinger et al. 1998.

established local union officials. Nor did this campaign originate at the grassroots level; it was the brainchild of a national, highly centralized leadership.

Both nationally and in Los Angeles, J for J deliberately steered clear of the NLRB representation election process for several reasons. Not only did that process increasingly favor employers in this period, but also, in the organizers' view, it unduly distanced the union from rank-and-file workers. "[NLRB] elections are controlled by the bosses," one organizer said. "It's an alienating process for workers and . . . separates the union from the workers." The NLRB process was in any case problematic in this industry, simply because most building owners' contracts with cleaning firms included 30-day cancellation clauses. If the union won a representation election, the building owner could simply switch to a new, nonunion cleaning contractor to effectively void the result. The architects of J for J, then, needed a non-NLRB organizing strategy that would target the building owners as much as the immediate employers (i.e., the cleaning contractors). What gradually emerged was the "comprehensive campaign," which one J for J organizer defined as "a war against the employers *and* the building owners, waged on all fronts [without] leaving any stone unturned." In the words of one Los Angeles janitor, "The strategy was attack, attack, attack." This was an industry-wide organizing strategy—essential given the building owners' ability to rapidly shift work from one contractor to another—and was designed to gain control over all the key players in a local labor market so that wages were taken out of competition.

One of J for J's major strengths was a business-oriented understanding of the industry. As one organizer put it, "We always try to understand the industry as it understands itself." From its inception, the Los Angeles campaign had a full-time research/corporate person, whose job was to gather information—later supplemented by data supplied by researchers at SEIU headquarters in Washington. One impressed management informant observed that the SEIU had the ability to "ferret out the weaknesses" of the ownership/management structure in any particular situation. This effort depended on access to highly skilled, often college-educated organizers and researchers, combined with the technological resources that enabled them to be effective. Once again this underscores the critical role of the progressive national leadership in J for J's effectiveness.

Research was important not only for targeting building owners and other key players in the industry, but also for activating the membership base. "Our economists know how to crunch the numbers. . .the real numbers," one organizer said. "Someone will get pissed if they learn that it costs the owner one cent to give them a raise." Understanding the industry, then, was a tool in the hands of the workers, allowing them to see how and why they had the potential to turn things around.

J for J also relied heavily on guerrilla-style legal tactics: While studiously avoiding representation elections, Local 399 did file complaints with the NLRB over discrimination against union activists and other "unfair labor practices." Organizers also pursued legal redress through other government agencies in protest of health and safety violations and the like. These efforts put economic pressure on the contractors, whose legal costs quickly mounted, and at the same time allowed the union to serve as the effective representative of the workers even without official recognition. "We called it 'acting union without a contract,'" an organizer explained. "That was what we tried to do with the workers of the nonunion companies. It didn't require a contract for them to redefine their relationship to their employer and to defend their rights." Filing unfair labor practice complaints also permitted janitors to go on strike under certain conditions with legal protection against being permanently replaced.

J for J also became highly skilled at orchestrating "in your face" media-oriented events. For example, a demonstration at a building that was profiled in the television series *L.A. Law* and was being cleaned by a nonunion firm dubbed the structure the "Home of the L.A. Lawless" in a publicity stunt that focused on various legal violations. In other instances, J for J took a group of workers to the country club frequented by the owner of a cleaning firm, where they raised a ruckus, chanting and screaming, and they performed street theater in front of a restaurant while an industry player dined inside. At the glitzy Century City complex adjacent to Beverly Hills, where the Los Angeles J for J campaign ultimately focused much of its energy, a series of such publicity stunts were staged to draw attention to the janitors' plight. "The denizens of Century City were not interested in having a bunch of Latino janitors out there in the daytime screaming and yelling," an organizer recalled. "It's fine for us to come in at night and clean their buildings, but they didn't want to look us in the face during the daytime." Such tactics publicly embarrassed key individuals in the industry while also making life difficult for building tenants.

Another critical element of the J for J strategy involved mobilizing political allies. The organizing campaign took place in the context of a massive building boom in downtown Los Angeles. As construction could not begin without approval from the city's Community Redevelopment Authority (CRA), the union had a powerful lever on which to lean. During this period the head of the Los Angeles County Federation of Labor sat on the CRA's board, as did other potential allies; consequently, no office tower built after 1987 opened up without a unionized cleaning crew. Similarly, the union could exert political pressure on developers and owners in many instances. "The only people with money to own buildings are banks, insurance companies, and pension funds," one organizer noted with only slight exaggeration. Such institutions often were vulnerable to the union's political leverage. An organizer recounted one example involving the ARCO Center, a huge office tower in downtown LA that was built with pension-fund money. "The owner didn't call us back. We found out that the pension funds invested in the project came from Ohio PERS [Public Employee Retirement System]. We called the union rep in Ohio, who called the real estate administrator, who then called the development partner, who then called the union."

The union was also able to mobilize linkages to local political leaders. In 1990, after the Los Angeles police violently attacked demonstrating janitors at Century City, the union, with help from the County Federation of Labor, contacted then-mayor Tom Bradley, who phoned the principal ownership interests at Century City to voice his concern over the incident. Yet another source of strength was support from unions representing janitors in other cities. Most important, the powerful leader of the giant SEIU Local 32B-32J in New York, Gus Bevona, lent a hand after viewing on video the Los Angeles police beating of the Century City strikers and putting pressure on the main cleaning contractor in Century City, International Service Systems (ISS), which was headquartered in New York and under contract with Local 32B-32J. "Bevona called the president of ISS into his office, and after making him wait for two and a half hours, threatened that if he didn't recognize the Los Angeles union, all hell would break loose [at ISS buildings in New York]," an organizer recalled. "The contract with ISS was signed that day."

Although all these elements of the campaign were critically important, ultimately J for J's ability to put pressure on employers also relied on its success in galvanizing the rank and file into action. For example, Bevona would not have intervened had it not been for the previous mobilization of strikers on the ground three thousand miles away. That the Los Angeles janitorial workforce was made up largely of Latino immigrants facilitated the mobilization process. Although J for J has enjoyed some victories in cities where immigrants are not a major presence in the janitorial workforce, the Los Angeles campaign was by far the most successful. "The reason that Los Angeles is the shining star of the union is that we've had the highest percentage of workers' participation, have the highest worker turnout, and the highest percentage of workers going to jail and getting arrested," an organizer explained. "At heart and soul, there has to be a mobilized workforce."

The social structure of immigration involved a series of interlocking networks that were central to the union-building process. In addition, the peculiar conditions of building service work helped create a sense of occupational community: Working at night, unlike most workers, the janitors were thrown together as a group. Many lived in the same neighborhoods or even the same buildings and rode the buses to work together. As an organizer put it, "even though L.A. is famous for no community, we found a community of janitors." Class consciousness may also have been higher among these particular immigrants, both because of their experiences in their home countries and because of the stigmatization that they suffered in the process of immigration. "If you ask, 'Que piensa de la union?' [What do you think of the union?], they answer, 'La union hace la fuerza' [Union is power]," an organizer recalled. Among the Central American janitors there was also a sizable group of seasoned activists who had been involved in left-wing or union activity back home. That experience did more than impart organizing skills or a proclivity toward activism; it put the risks entailed in a union drive into an unusual perspective. "With the Salvadorans, you find different attitudes," an organizer noted. "There, if you were in a union, they killed you. Here, you lost a job at $4.25 an hour." If, as this suggests, the social processes underlying immigration had the potential to facilitate union organizing, that potential was not always realized, as our next case study shows.

An Unsuccessful Leadership-Initiated Campaign: Organizing Guess

In the mid-1990s, the ILGWU decided to make a concerted effort to organize one of the major players in the Los Angeles garment industry, namely, the designer jeans manufacturer Guess, Inc.[3] In contrast to the janitors' case, the national union leadership did not impose the organizing campaign on a reluctant local leadership; rather, the Los Angeles organizing staff, working closely with the ILGWU's national organizing director, persuaded the top union leadership in New York to provide resources to launch the campaign. The impetus within the union was thus different than in the J for J case, emerging from mid-level leaders rather than at the top of the organization. But like J for J, the Guess campaign was an effort conceived by union leaders as part of a strategy for labor movement revitalization.

By the 1990s Los Angeles had emerged as the nation's largest center of apparel manufacturing. But the ILGWU's membership in the West had been declining since the 1970s, so that only a few hundred garment workers in Los Angeles were unionized—not even one percent of the industry's rapidly growing workforce of well over 100,000. The ILGWU leadership, headquartered in New York, still viewed Los Angeles as a remote hinterland and did not see the crisis there as an especially pressing concern. But locally, the ILGWU had accumulated an impressive record of experience in organizing the immigrant workers who had come to dominate the low-wage workforce in Los Angeles. Back in the mid-1970s, the union's Western organizing director developed a program targeting immigrant workers for recruitment and hired a cadre of about ten young, progressive Latino organizers for this purpose. They succeeded in winning union representation elections at

---

[3]This section is based on the authors' interviews with organizers as well as newspaper accounts of the Guess campaign and other documents.

a substantial number of immigrant-employing plants in the vast industrial plains crisscrossing Los Angeles. Virtually all of these plants were outside the garment industry, however, including a muffler factory, a furniture shop, a plant that made pillows, and even a firm that manufactured tombstones. "We were not targeting any industries," one organizer recalled. "It was more, 'This has to be a movement of immigrant workers' than 'This is the garment workers' union.' We didn't concentrate on garments."

This effort did nothing to reverse the erosion of unionism in the Los Angeles garment industry, which continued apace. However, it had other important results. It offered a means of maintaining the ILGWU's Los Angeles presence, providing a new constituency that gradually replaced the members continually being lost in the garment shops as intense competition from offshore garment contractors fed employers' determination to eliminate the union from those few shops where it still had a foothold. The effort also helped shape a new generation of Latino union organizers, many of whom would devote their lives to the local labor movement and some of whom later became prominent local union leaders. Perhaps most important, this vigorous initiative targeting foreign-born workers in the late 1970s established the ILGWU's reputation in the local community as a union committed to organizing immigrants and addressing their particular needs. This was a path-breaking move in the context of the larger Los Angeles labor movement, which as yet had no serious interest in recruiting immigrant workers and many segments of which were overtly xenophobic.

Despite their success, many of the ILGWU's new organizers soon became frustrated. "It was like a revolving door, where we were bringing members in and members were going out the other door," an organizer recalled. "There were a lot of problems, internal problems, with the leadership. . . . We had business agents who didn't speak the language [Spanish] . . . so the shops that had Latino members were not serviced properly." The problem was that any organizing effort that targeted one garment shop was doomed to failure. The cutthroat competition that prevailed in the industry meant that keeping the union out was, from the employers' perspective, a matter of survival. If the union did succeed in organizing a subcontracting shop, the manufacturer could simply shift work elsewhere, forcing the shop to close down.

As in the building services industry in which J for J emerged, this meant NLRB-oriented strategies were an exercise in futility. Cohort after cohort of ILGWU organizers came to the same conclusion: The only hope of organizing garment workers in Los Angeles was to organize industry-wide, or at least to target a whole subindustry making a particular product line, with the goal of taking wages out of competition. But this was a daunting prospect, for by the 1980s Los Angeles was the single largest garment manufacturing center in the United States, with rapidly growing employment. It did not help matters that back in New York the ILGWU leadership was slow to abandon its view of Los Angeles as just one more outpost on the vast nonunion periphery.

Finally, however, in the mid-1990s, the union decided to launch a major organizing campaign in the Los Angeles garment industry, targeting Guess, Inc., one of the largest firms producing in L.A., with approximately 3,500 workers, including those employed by subcontractors. As in the J for J case, the union organizers who proposed this campaign devoted extensive efforts to researching the garment industry in the region as well as Guess in particular. The firm's high visibility and high-profile public image were important considerations in choosing it as the target, since the union envisioned from the start a two-pronged approach that would include publicity about sweatshop conditions, and possibly a boycott, as well as a bottom-up organizing effort among Guess workers on the ground. In addition, the choice was appealing because Guess was highly profitable and thus could easily afford to pay union wages and to absorb the costs of its subcontractors' doing so. Another plus was the fact that nearly all of Guess's production was located inside the United States and concentrated in downtown Los Angeles. "Our feeling was that organizing Guess would be an awfully good alternative to organizing the whole sportswear industry in L.A., and it would give us a base," one organizer recalled. "It would be a launching pad to do something even bigger than that, which is what our goal was."

Although it was conceived as a prelude to something even more ambitious, the Guess campaign itself was a formidable organizing project. The fact that the company had such a large number of subcontractors—around 70—was the most obvious challenge because, as the organizers knew, unless they attacked on multiple fronts simultaneously, the company would be able to shift work around quite easily in response to a strike at any given contractor. "We called it the octopus," one organizer explained. "It has all these tentacles. If you grab hold of one, it just sheds that one and kills you with the other ones." In an effort to address this problem, the union developed a limited, strike-based strategy. The plan stopped short of attempting to take the entire workforce—those employed at all 70 contractors along with those directly employed by Guess at the "inside shop" where sample making, distribution, and other activities were located—out on strike. Instead, the idea was to generate unfair labor practice strikes (in which, unlike "economic" strikes, employers are legally prohibited from hiring "permanent replacements" for strikers) at the inside shop and a few key contractors. "We wanted to have an army of 500 to 1,000 workers on strike from all those shops together and use them to picket all the others, and they would be the backbone of the campaign," an organizer recalled. Simultaneous with this "ground war," the ILGWU planned an "air war," a publicity campaign exposing the industry's sweatshop conditions, focusing on Guess in particular.

Like the J for J effort in Los Angeles, the Guess campaign was an initiative launched by union leaders rather than emerging from the grassroots. The ILGWU organizers who conceived the campaign, however, well understood the importance of rank-and-file mobilization. Had they carried out the plan originally envisaged, the Guess organizing effort might have closely paralleled that of the janitors. However, a number of developments intervened to put the Guess campaign on a very different, and as it turned out, far less auspicious, path. The most important of these was the merger between the ILGWU and ACTWU into UNITE, which took place just before the effort was slated to be launched. The internal politics of the merger and the attendant power shifts led to a significant scaling back of the original commitment to the Guess campaign, as different groups within UNITE scrambled for resources for the projects and agendas each wanted to pursue. The original plan for the Guess campaign had entailed a commitment of thirty highly experienced organizers, but in the end, as one staff member recalled, "We didn't get them. We got fifteen, half of whom were extremely inexperienced." And crucially, UNITE's top leadership in New York decided that the strike strategy originally envisaged was not viable and should not be pursued, and that instead the campaign should concentrate on the air war.

The campaign got off to a good start in the summer of 1996, when UNITE complained to the U.S. Department of Labor that Guess contractors were illegally involved in industrial homework, just before the privately held firm was scheduled to launch its initial public stock offering. UNITE picketed the Waldorf-Astoria in New York where Guess was holding a reception for potential investors, and distributed a "white paper" detailing various alleged labor law violations the company and its contractors were engaged in. Soon after, UNITE filed a class action suit on behalf of a group of garment workers for labor law violations. These efforts generated a great deal of national publicity, thanks to Guess's high-profile product line, and at first the air war seemed to be going quite well for the union. The stock offering was postponed, and Guess launched its own public relations countercampaign. "We had a tremendous impact on them . . . at the level of their image, which is their single biggest vulnerability," one organizer recalled. "They were infuriated and scared."

But then Guess began to fight back against the union's various efforts with renewed vigor. The firm shifted work away from contractors where the union seemed to have some strength, which led to layoffs, with devastating effects on morale. A few months after UNITE's campaign began, Guess filed the first in what would later become a long series of lawsuits against the union. Shortly afterward, in January 1997, the company announced that it was going to begin shifting a major component of its production, almost all of which had been in the United States before, to Mexico. Although the union filed charges with the NLRB, arguing that this was illegal retaliation against the union's effort to organize, the effects of this announcement were devastating. "It's basically a death blow," one organizer said. "We have moved the work out of the country, fuck you! You know, you may fight us with some lawsuits for a while, but it's over. Workers know it's over. Society knows it's over. We do have the right to produce wherever we want, and if you don't like it, too bad."

The company poured millions of dollars into legal maneuvers, and the union likewise was forced to devote enormous sums of money to what can only be described as a legal morass. Although the union has never abandoned the effort entirely, no one expects a victory, and the campaign made no headway whatsoever toward reversing the longer-term failure to organize the garment industry in Los Angeles. UNITE did a great deal of creative publicity in this campaign, and succeeded in building alliances in the wider community, involving students as well as a range of other supporters in its boycott efforts and even attracting support from public figures who urged consumers not to buy Guess products. All this paved the way for the anti-sweatshop campaigns which have taken off since. The Guess campaign was far less successful on the ground, however, partly because of the decision not to engage in strike activity and partly because of the limited number of organizers assigned to the effort. While the union spent millions of dollars on the legal side of the campaign, this was entirely involuntary. At the outset, they were unwilling to pour funds into rank-and-file mobilization, or the "ground war" in UNITE's terms. This is the most striking point of contrast to J for J, which committed extensive resources and energy to rank-and-file mobilization as well as to the other elements of its campaign.

Successful Bottom-Up Organizing: The 1992 Drywall Strike

Whereas the J for J and Guess campaigns were launched by experienced union leaders, the drywallers' organizing began at the grassroots.[4] The story begins in October 1991, when Jesus Gomez, an immigrant from El Maguey, a small village in the Mexican state of Guanajuato, complained of being cheated out of some of his pay by a drywall contractor. Residential construction was severely depressed at the time, and the piecework rates for drywall hangers had fallen to a new low of about 4 cents per square foot, which meant earnings of only about $40 to $75 for a ten-hour day. Gomez, then 33 years old, who had been hanging drywall since 1975, vividly remembered the days when the industry was unionized and when pay rates were double that. Along with several other experienced drywallers who became leaders of the strike— most of them also from Gomez' hometown of El Maguey—he had suffered the consequences of the union's decline for a decade, and now he

---

[4]For a detailed and fully documented account of this case, see Milkman and Wong 2000.

decided it was time to fight back. He contacted some Carpenters union officials, who offered him meeting space in their Orange County union hall. Gomez began visiting job sites and talking up the idea with other drywallers he knew, many of them old friends from home.

Immigrant networks were as crucial here as in the J for J campaign, perhaps even more so. Although these immigrants from a small village in western Mexico lacked the political sophistication and experience of the Salvadorans who were involved in the janitors' campaign, the drywallers' social cohesiveness was even stronger. The fact that at least a few hundred men from El Maguey worked in the drywall trade and were bound by close kin and friendship ties was a critical source of the solidarity that emerged in the organizing campaign. "That was the key, right there," recalled a drywaller who accompanied Gomez on some of the early organizing rounds. "Having that big group from one area." After many months of meeting, first in Orange County and then throughout southern California, drywallers were recruited into the campaign by the hundreds, and finally they struck on June 1, 1992.

Although the Carpenters union did make meeting space available for the organizing effort, the union members and staff—at this point still heavily Anglo and far more conservative than the SEIU leaders who orchestrated the J for J effort—were sharply divided in their views of the emerging drywallers campaign. While some saw the potential of the movement, many others were hostile to the Latino workers who now dominated the industry, seeing them as responsible for the deterioration of pay and working conditions that had occurred in the 1980s. Most were deeply skeptical about the prospects of the new organizing drive that Gomez had launched. "They said, 'No, you can never organize those guys,'" recalled a Latino member of the Carpenters' staff and an early supporter of the effort. "'You're beating your head against the concrete.'"

This was, then, a bottom-up campaign which the Carpenters simply would not have initiated on their own. As it turned out, however, the union's coolness toward the effort proved quite fortuitous. The fact that Gomez and his allies, who called themselves the "Movement of Drywall Hangers," were not affiliated with any "labor organization had one key advantage: They were not subject to the 30-day legal limit on picketing for union recognition in construction (after which the law requires that a petition be filed for an NLRB representation election).

Indeed, when the anti-union Building Industry Association filed unfair labor practice charges against the Carpenters, the complaints were dismissed for lack of evidence, precisely because the union was not an official sponsor of the strike. Employers did get temporary restraining orders in some cases, but even this was more difficult than usual, thanks to the strikers' independent status. As management attorneys pointed out later, the "strategy of declining representation by a traditional labor organization in the early stages of the strike was an important tactic."

Initially, the walkout was extremely successful, shutting down virtually the entire industry from Ventura County (just north of Los Angeles) to the Mexican border. There were many allegations of intimidation and violence from the outset. Although it is difficult to know how extensively such tactics actually were used, they were particularly potent in the context of the immigrant networks within which most drywallers were enmeshed. "The Hispanic community is pretty tight; most of these people know where everyone lives," one contractor explained. "The guy down the street is a union supporter, you want to go to work, he sees you leave in the morning with your tools, he's going to report you to the union thugs, that you're working. They're going to threaten you."

Solidarity began to falter, however, as the employers began to defend themselves more effectively, and the strike wore on into a second month. Increasingly desperate for income, some of the strikers began drifting back to work. Things improved somewhat when the AFL-CIO regional office set up a "Dry Wallers Strike Fund," soliciting contributions to help strikers pay their rent and other bills, as well as donations of pro bono legal assistance. This appeal ultimately yielded over $2 million from over twenty different unions, with the Carpenters contributing easily the largest share. Food and money were also donated by a range of community and church groups. As the police began to arrest and jail strikers by the hundreds, the AFL-CIO fund became increasingly critical for bail purposes. Legal assistance was coordinated by the California Immigrant Workers' Association (CIWA), an organization founded by the AFL-CIO in 1989. The combination of funding for bail payments and sophisticated legal assistance proved highly effective. "The thing that really helped us was being able to bail leaders out of jail and keep 'em on the ground," an organizer explained. "That kept the morale going. As we accelerated the strike and pulled more workers off the job sites, it was the ability of those workers to look out there and constantly see their leaders willing to take the risk, going to jail."

As in the janitors' campaign, the role of the media was also important. The strike began only a few months after the Los Angeles "riots" in the spring of 1992, so that the sensitivity of the police to media scrutiny was at its peak. The strike organizers and their supporters in the AFL-CIO and CIWA took full advantage of this. "We said, 'It's a Latino Rodney King,'" an organizer recalled. In part because of this, the strikers were able to win highly sympathetic media coverage. "There were just great articles talking about the conditions these workers were in," an AFL-CIO staff member said. "And it was front-page stuff, and it was on television, and here we were in the midst of this hostile, anti-immigrant community, and yet there was such solid public support for these strikers. . . . The media coverage was outstanding."

In late July 1992, after the strike had been going on for about two months, CIWA-funded attorneys filed unfair labor practice charges against several builders and contractors with the NLRB, alleging that the temporary restraining orders the employers had obtained to restrict picketing at job sites violated the strikers' constitutional rights. At the same time, in what would prove a far more important legal offensive, the same attorneys complained to the U.S. Department of Labor that drywall contractors had violated the overtime pay provisions of the 1938 federal Fair Labor Standards Act (FLSA). These complaints to the Labor Department were soon followed by dozens of class-action lawsuits seeking back pay for these alleged FLSA violations. By all accounts these suits played a pivotal role in the strike, ultimately bringing the contractors to the bargaining table and leading to a strike settlement agreement in November 1992. There were large sums of money at stake here, not only back pay for unpaid overtime over a three-year period, but also punitive damages and attorneys' fees. The employers' potential liability in these suits decidedly tipped the balance in favor of settling the strike, which they now sought to do after months of intransigent refusal to negotiate. "Once those [suits] were filed," a drywall executive recalled, "there were some people that had great exposure and some of those people with great exposure very quickly decided that maybe we should find a way to settle this lawsuit and the strike. It became in their interest to become a union contractor and have all this go away."

Starting in September, the Pacific Rim Drywall Association

(PRDA), a trade group comprised of nonunion residential drywall contractors, which previously had no involvement in labor issues, began meeting with strike leaders and with representatives of the Carpenters union, who only at this point stepped forward with an offer to represent the strikers and help them obtain a union contract. By November, when the settlement agreement was concluded, the PRDA had grown substantially, embracing an estimated 75 percent of the drywall industry in the five-county Los Angeles area. In November they agreed to recognize the Carpenters as the exclusive bargaining agent for the drywallers (without a representation election); the strikers became dues-paying union members; and employers signed a two-year union contract providing for higher wages and medical benefits in exchange for withdrawal of the FLSA suits against the signatory firms.

Although the contract represented a substantial improvement from the viewpoint of the immigrant workers involved in that it doubled wages relative to prestrike levels, neither the wages nor the benefits were comparable to what drywall hangers had enjoyed in the earlier union era prior to the 1980s. Wages had already risen during the strike and thus were not perceived as onerous by the employers. "It was a good agreement," a drywall contractor said. "It did have health insurance but the men had to pay for half of it. And there was no pension, none of the things that you normally associate with a union." Moreover, there was an unusual clause in the contract, providing that if the market share held by union drywall firms in the area fell by 20 percent or more, wage rates would be determined by market conditions. Another limitation was the refusal of the drywall employers in San Diego, who had resisted the strike far more vigorously from the outset, to join in the PRDA-brokered settlement. Instead, with financial support from the anti-union American Builders and Contractors (ABC), they filed a massive lawsuit against the Carpenters union under the Racketeer Influenced and Corrupt Organizations (RICO) Act in November 1992, just after the strike was settled to their north, accusing the union of orchestrating the strike and the violence associated with it. The RICO suit was settled two years later but still casts a dark shadow over union organizing in construction and elsewhere (Brody 1995). Yet by any standard the drywallers strike was a massive victory for organized labor, and along with the janitors' success should have put to rest any doubts about the "organizability" of immigrant workers in contemporary Los Angeles.

The Port Truckers' 1996 Strike:
A Bottom-Up Campaign That Fizzled

Our fourth and final case study involves another case of bottom-up organizing, in many ways very similar to the drywallers case in its origins, though without a comparably triumphal conclusion.[5] In the
spring of 1996, about 5,000 Latino truck drivers who haul freight from
the port of Los Angeles–Long Beach to warehouses, rail terminals, and
other destinations, went on strike. Like the drywallers, they were initially self-organized; also like the drywallers, they eventually turned to
organized labor for assistance. In this case the workers did not link up
with the union which traditionally had represented workers in their
occupation (the Teamsters) but instead with the CWA, which took up
the organizing opportunity energetically despite its lack of previous experience with this segment of the workforce.

In an earlier era, virtually all the truckers servicing the port had been
Teamsters union members. But in the late 1980s, the combined impact
of deregulation of the trucking industry and the nationwide employer
assault on organized labor led to a rapid process of deunionization. Accompanying this was a shift away from conventional forms of employment, as the trucking firms increasingly used independent contractors
to haul freight. These were owner-operators who leased or owned the
vehicles they drove, although more often than not all the arrangements
were made by the trucking firms who also controlled the flow of work.
The employers initially benefited from the new arrangement because it
transferred many of the risks of the industry to the drivers. But this organizational shift also reduced the barriers to entry and soon led to the
proliferation of smaller and smaller trucking firms servicing the port.
The ensuing cutthroat competition produced a spiral of declining pay
rates and deteriorating working conditions, even as demand for truckers boomed as the Los Angeles–Long Beach port emerged as the nation's largest. The pay system changed from hourly to per-load rates,
which spurred a dramatic decline in efficiency in the freight-loading
process, because once the drivers themselves were forced to absorb the

---

[5]This section is based on the authors' interviews with organizers as well as newspaper
accounts of the truckers' strike.

costs of waiting time, neither the shippers nor the trucking companies had an incentive to maintain a centralized dispatching system.

As in the janitorial, drywall, and to a lesser degree even garment cases, deunionization and the accompanying devolution of pay and working conditions led many native-born workers to leave port trucking jobs, shifting to long-distance trucking or other pursuits. Latino immigrants rapidly poured into the vacancies thus created. By the late 1980s this new workforce had already begun to organize itself—a process greatly aided, ironically, by the long periods of time drivers spent waiting for their loads at the port, which was also one of the main issues that galvanized protest actions. A two-and-a-half week strike in the summer of 1988 launched by the independent Waterfront/Rail Truckers Union (WRTU), for example, focused primarily on the issue of excessive waiting time. The WRTU was no longer a visible presence when the port truckers walked out again in November 1993 in a more loosely organized protest action sparked by diesel fuel price hikes and environmental regulations. Another group, the Latin American Truckers' Association, emerged in the aftermath of this strike.

Such fleeting episodes of solidarity failed to produce any lasting organization, and on occasions when the truckers made overtures to unions, they were apparently rebuffed. But these strikes demonstrated the potential disruptive power of this occupational group, who were capable of bringing the region's entire transportation network to a standstill. A series of independent truckers' organizations emerged in the industry over the years, some of which explored the possibility of unionization, but none gained a firm footing. Then, in the mid-1990s the truckers made a bid to affiliate with CWA Local 9400, whose membership is comprised primarily of telephone workers. This unlikely affiliation came about because one of the rank-and-file trucker activists had a personal contact in CWA, and because unlike other unions the truckers had approached, this one proved receptive.

With rudimentary help from the CWA staff, the rank- and-file activists recruited members steadily in 1995 and 1996, and as in the drywallers case, they gradually drew more and more truckers to their meetings. Starting with a small group of fifteen workers, they built the organization until thousands of truckers were in regular attendance at meetings. Unlike the drywallers, however, the truckers had no concentration of immigrants from a single area or even from a single country (they included Mexicans as well as Central and South Americans); more dispersed immigrant networks nevertheless helped in the organizing process. Another important factor facilitating the organizing was the continual close contact truckers had in the physically isolated space of the port terminals, where organizers were able to make excellent use of the long hours truckers were compelled to spend idly waiting for their loads. In addition, as they waited and as they worked, they continually had before them the example of durable unionism *inside* the port, where the International Longshore and Warehouse Union (ILWU) had long represented the well-paid cargo handlers within the shipping terminal gates.

With help from the CWA, the truckers launched a series of demonstrations to publicize their plight and to seek support from the wider community. In October 1995 they organized a giant convoy of trucks from the port all the way to downtown Los Angeles, where they extracted a supportive resolution from the Los Angeles City Council; in February 1996 they organized a similar convoy in Long Beach. There were also various political efforts to challenge the legal definition of the truckers as independent contractors, which was the most basic obstacle to unionizing them. As they were not employees as such, they were not legally eligible for unionization, and might even be vulnerable to sanction under antitrust law if they organized. Because the union made little progress on this front in the political arena, they turned to direct action once again.

In planning the May 1996 strike, the CWA developed a two-pronged strategy to overcome the independent contractor problem. First, they decided to strike for union recognition against the dozen or so trucking companies operating at the port that still had traditional employment structures. Second, and simultaneously, they encouraged workers to become part of a scheme developed by Donald Allen, an entrepreneur who approached the CWA in early 1996 with the idea of establishing a new firm, the Transport Maritime Association (TMA), which would hire the truckers as conventional employees and recognize CWA Local 9400 as their union. TMA would then lease the truckers' services to the existing trucking companies, thus short-circuiting the independent contractor problem. Although the prices shippers would have to pay for trucking initially would be higher, this plan had the potential of rationalizing the system by creating a new dispatching system that would compensate for the additional costs and lay the foundation for higher wages and benefits.

Lured by the promise of a substantial increase in pay and a generous fringe benefit policy, and with active encouragement from both rank-and-file organizers and CWA officials, over 4,000 truckers signed up to work for Allen. Although they could not legally go on strike as independent contractors, they were perfectly free to decline offers of work and to accept TMA's offer of employment. The May 1996 "strike," which was the result of some nineteen months of careful planning, involved thousands of independent contractors who did precisely this, along with a handful who simultaneously struck for union recognition against the small number of firms with conventional employment arrangements. It was a formidable show of strength for the truckers, by far the most effective of the strikes they had launched over the 1980s and 1990s.

The shipping companies, alarmed by the specter of unionization, responded initially by rerouting some ships to other West Coast ports and won court injunctions barring mass picketing in front of the terminal gates. The trucking firms consistently refused to employ CWA-affiliated truckers employed by TMA, and began to recruit replacement workers from out of the area. Allen then threatened to operate as a rival trucking company, rather than as a labor-leasing operation. There was extensive support for the strike from the church and community groups, who organized food banks and the like. The CWA offered funds to strikers threatened with foreclosure or facing other financial problems due to the loss of income associated with the walkout. Other local unions also endorsed the strike.

This highly innovative strategy for overcoming the legal issues surrounding the status of independent contractors helped galvanize the most effective of the series of strikes the port truckers had mounted in the 1980s and 1990s. However, a number of unexpected developments undermined the effort. One of the top CWA leaders who had been involved in the organizing from the outset had a heart attack due to the excessive heat at an overcrowded union meeting in the early days of the strike, which was demoralizing and disorienting for the strikers. More important, it turned out that Donald Allen lacked the capital to carry out his promises, and in any case the trucking firms refused to do business with him, so that ultimately the entire TMA scheme collapsed. The CWA had never really investigated Allen's financial situation, although questions had been raised about this in the press. There were other problems as well. It might have been possible to time the strike in tandem with the ILWU's contract dates which would have allowed longshore workers to walk out in support of the truckers, but the CWA declined to do this. (In the end the only organizational gain to emerge from the strike was that the ILWU won the right to represent intra-harbor truckers, those hauling freight within the port from one terminal to another, a previously unorganized group.) It didn't help matters that the CWA officials who were at the helm of the effort were non–Spanish-speaking Anglos, although they did put some rank-and-file truckers on staff in the course of the campaign.

Thus, as in the Guess case, this organizing effort was undermined by a series of internal union difficulties. There was no lack of commitment to strikes on the part of CWA in contrast to UNITE, but a combination of bad luck and inadequate planning on the part of a union that was trying its best to organize an industry in which it had no previous experience and limited knowledge paved the way to defeat. In contrast to the extensive research effort behind the J for J and Guess campaigns, here the CWA was operating with a limited staff and had no prior experience in the industry. The union had the best of intentions but proved ill-equipped to mount the kind of serious investigation of the industry as a whole or of the financial viability of TMA on which the strategy depended so centrally. The immigrant workforce was keenly motivated and had basically organized itself, but they needed the guidance and expertise of an established union to confront effectively the multibillion-dollar shipping industry, which had long resisted unionization. CWA did attempt to rise to the occasion, but without the research capacities of SEIU or even UNITE, and without the legal leverage that proved so pivotal in the drywallers strike, it could not bring the campaign to a successful conclusion, and instead the rank-and-file enthusiasm gradually dissolved into disillusion and defeat.

Conclusion

As all four of these cases illustrate, Latino immigrant workers in southern California are capable of extraordinary militance. In the wake of the janitors and drywallers victories in the early 1990s, it seemed that Latino immigrant unionism had a bright future. As one janitors union activist put it, "We Latino workers are a bomb waiting to explode!" Yet whether this potential can become the basis of durable labor organization depends on the ability of experienced leaders (most likely, but perhaps not necessarily, based in preexisting unions) to channel it into a viable strategic direction, rooted in a careful analysis of the economic context and of the industry power structure. What can we learn from the janitors' and drywallers' success, and the Guess campaign's and port truckers' lack of it, that might facilitate such efforts in the coming years?

Despite their contrasting initial organizing approaches, there were many common elements in the two successful campaigns. Both involved industry-wide organizing: The janitors organized the entire building cleaning market in downtown Los Angeles and Century City, and the drywallers organized the vast bulk of workers in their trade in the wider region's residential construction industry. Both overcame the many obstacles to unionizing industries in which subcontracting plays a major role, by using strategies that avoided NLRB elections and instead finding means to pressure employers. In both cases union recognition was directly linked to contract negotiation; thus, the long delays that so often plague even highly successful NLRB-oriented campaigns were avoided. Both unions built alliances in the wider community and used highly creative tactics to win public support and to put pressure on the employers, including media-oriented efforts that were critical in responding to the police activity directed against both strikes. In both, too, immigrant networks played an important role. Both campaigns galvanized workers, trained new union leadership, and resulted in workers developing a strong sense of ownership of the campaign.

Successful unionizing efforts, at least those conducted outside the conventional NLRB representation election framework, must contain *both* serious commitments of resources, leadership, *and* expertise from the existing labor movement and extensive mobilization from below. It is less important whether the union leadership component or the grassroots mobilization effort comes first (the two cases of success are opposites in this respect) than having one stimulate the other. Immigrant workers are ripe for organization, but success is unlikely without a strong commitment and adequate leadership from existing unions. In the Guess case, UNITE's commitment was insufficient, particularly to bottom-up organizing; in the case of the port truckers, the rank-and-file mobilized themselves but the CWA proved ill-equipped to coordinate a winning campaign. Thus, our comparison suggests that union capacity and strategic planning matter; indeed, they can make the difference between success and failure.

Even our two successful cases are problematic in that the consolidation of unionism in the immigrant workforce after the initial organizing victory encountered serious difficulties. The Carpenters failed to sustain the share of the market it had at the time of the strike settlement, and SEIU Local 399 was plagued by internal factionalism. The Los Angeles janitors were later incorporated by the International SEIU (after Local 399 was placed in trusteeship) into Local 1877, and then in April 2000 went on to launch another successful strike ten years after the original organizing strike.

The revitalization of the labor movement in southern California, where the working class is increasingly dominated by foreign-born workers, will require not only more organizing victories like those of the janitors and drywallers, but also effective reshaping of the institutional life of unions so that immigrants are at the vital center. Winning union recognition, however, is only the first step in labor organizing. Among other things, consolidating immigrant unionism means effectively incorporating immigrants into leadership at all levels and building on the dynamism evident in the rank-and-file mobilizations that emerge in organizing campaigns to strengthen and consolidate the new unions. And the labor movement must signal its support of immigrant workers on a broader level, as the new AFL-CIO leadership did in February 2000, in a historic reversal of its previous policy, calling for a new amnesty for undocumented immigrants and for an end to legal sanctions against employers who hire them (Greenhouse 2000a). Only this kind of comprehensive effort can fulfill the potential for immigrant organizing that our case studies document. The revitalization of organized labor in southern California, and perhaps even in the United States as a whole, may hinge on whether unions are able to rise to this challenge.

CHAPTER SIX

Structural Change in the AFL-CIO

A Regional Study of Union Cities' Impact

Jill Kriesky

*I*n its quest to renew and rebuild the U.S. labor movement, the New Voice leadership elected to lead the national AFL-CIO in 1995 has proposed a dramatic change in the role of the more than six hundred central labor councils (CLCs) across the country. In recent history, advancing labor's electoral and legislative agendas and sharing information and support on common and individual union issues have comprised the primary duties of most CLCs. Their council committee structures and functions have evolved to meet these needs. Now AFL-CIO President John Sweeney and his administration are urging these county or multicounty confederations of local labor unions[1] to join them as "the building blocks and the foundation of our revitalized movement" (Rosier 1996, 10) in "a society that has lost all respect for workers and the jobs they do" (AFL-CIO nd(a)). Thus, the Sweeney administration's new charge demands changes in both function and structure of the CLCs.

The purpose of this chapter is to identify the functional and structural changes that the national AFL-CIO leadership is encouraging

---

[1]The definition given here is not precisely accurate. The jurisdictional boundaries may cut across counties. Some states do not currently have any chartered CLCs. Occasionally, this chapter labels CLC as large, medium, and small. According to the designations of the AFL-CIO Field Mobilization Department, a large council is one with potential per capita payments on 80,000 or more local union members, a medium council per capita range is 25,000 to 80,000, and a small council's potential per capita payments are less than 25,000. Most councils fall into the small category, although the large councils' jurisdictions encompass the vast majority of union members.

CLCs to pursue to make the New Voice's vision a reality. The first section defines the main vehicle for these changes—the Union Cities initiative supported by the AFL-CIO Field Mobilization Department. Next, a preliminary assessment is given of the progress made toward these changes and the obstacles impeding that movement. The study's third objective is to evaluate whether the changes under way are sufficient to achieve the AFL-CIO's goals for the councils. The final section of the chapter offers conclusions and outlines the future research that will rely on this preliminary study.

Methodology

The observations made in this study are based on information gathered from four sources. First, in editing *Working Together to Revitalize Labor in Our Communities: Case Studies of Labor Education—Central Labor Body Collaboration* in early 1998, I began collecting, largely from other labor educators who work directly with CLCs across the country, anecdotes about the functional and structural transformations with which these bodies are grappling (Kriesky 1998). In addition, I attended the September 1997 Joint State Federation/Central Labor Council Conference, the University and College Labor Education Association (UCLEA) Task Force on CLCs and State Federations meeting in May 1998, and the June 1998 Central Labor Council Best Practices Conference for CLCs in the Mid-Atlantic Area of the Northeast Region. All provided additional case study reports that focused more specifically on council work relating to the new Union Cities initiative. Materials prepared and disseminated by the national AFL-CIO Field Mobilization Department, newspaper reports, and published and unpublished accounts of CLC activities comprised a third data source. The fourth information source was a series of interviews conducted with ten of the AFL-CIO's Northeast Region staff members in the fall of 1998 and two interviews—one with a Northeast Region staff member and one with a CLC Advisory Board member—in the spring of 2000. These were heavily relied on in analyzing the progress and obstacles to activities and structural changes, potentials, and the role CLCs play in advancing the New Voice agenda.[2]

Functional and Structural Changes Proposed in the New Voice Vision

To comprehend the significant changes posed by the CLC charge to become "the building blocks and the foundation of our revitalized movement" requires an understanding of the roles CLCs have served over time. Although there are few analyses focused specifically on the early development and roles of CLCs, those that exist identify these councils as pivotal in union struggles at the turn of the century. The councils inserted themselves in local collective bargaining by offering the use of arbitration committees to reach contract settlements, or if that failed, by providing strike support or coordinating boycotts or sympathy strikes by member locals. In addition, many turn-of-the-century CLCs invested considerable resources in organizing new locals

---

[2]Maine, New Hampshire, Vermont, Massachusetts, Connecticut, Rhode Island, Delaware, New York, New Jersey, Pennsylvania, Maryland/D.C., West Virginia, and Puerto Rico (because of its population's ties with Northeast states) comprise the Northeast Region. The author conducted telephone interviews with the Northeast Region Field Mobilization director; state Field Mobilization directors for Maine, New Hampshire/Vermont, Massachusetts, New York, Maryland/D.C., Delaware, Connecticut, and Pennsylvania (acting director), and the state Field Mobilization staff member for West Virginia. Interviews ranged from thirty minutes to one and a half hours. They were conducted in preparation for a more comprehensive and methodologically rigorous survey of CLC officers which the author expects to undertake in the future.

The Northeast Region is more geographically compact and urban than the other three regions (South, Midwest, and West), and the region's economic transformation differs from that in other regions. Thus, the results found here may not be indicative of developments elsewhere. Critics of this study might argue that because Field Mobilization staff are charged with (and evaluated on) implementation of the national AFL-CIO's vision of CLCs' performance, their observations and interpretation of CLC progress toward the new goals may be more sympathetic than those of other analysts outside of the process. However, this bias does not appear to have occurred. The anonymously contributed comments made by field staff included significant criticisms as well as support for activities which in no way seem to overstate labor's progress. Further, additional sources of information corroborate conclusions based on these interviews.

of workers, some of whom fell outside of the jurisdictional boundaries of existing national unions. (For example, according to Forsythe (1956), the St. Louis central body unionized unskilled waiters and waitresses into a local directly affiliated with the AFL.) Finally, historical records indicate that these regional organizations participated heavily in public policy debates on general workers' rights issues such as public education, hours of work, and women and child labor. Involvement in partisan politics occurred, but its level appears inconsistent from election to election (Eimer 1997, 17).

Despite some impressive successes on these fronts, since its inception, the AFL sought to limit the central bodies' autonomy. The initial AFL voting structure allowed national unions representation proportional to their membership size, but CLC bodies each held only one vote (Ulman 1955, 3790). Later restrictions on CLC activities included the requirement that CLC-organized locals had to join an international union (although they were not similarly required to belong to central bodies) and limitations on CLC-initiated sympathy strikes and boycotts (Ulman 1955, 383). The CIO similarly sought to curb the power of its regionally based bodies, the Industrial Union Councils (IUCs). Their work, at least in some locations, was similar to their AFL counterparts (Foner 1990). In 1946 the CIO executive board directed the IUCs to focus on "their primary function [which] was to implement national CIO policy, and . . . [to avoid] associating with organizations whose goals and objectives the CIO had not officially endorsed." (Zeiger 1995, 272). Although this and subsequent rules were proposed to eliminate communist influence in councils, they likewise decimated local autonomously determined initiatives by IUCs.[3]

By the time of the AFL and CIO merger which marked the start of organized labor's "modern" era, local central bodies' power relative to the federation and its international union constituents was well contained. Lens (1959, 62) describes them as a "negligible force confined to minor legislative and lobbying actions." While significant counterexamples existed, the national federation apparently fostered CLC

---

[3]In the analysis of the Union Cities agenda below, we will examine the important question of why this subordination occurred.

interest in these limited roles for many years. In the AFL-CIO's 1973 publication *Rules Governing Local Central Bodies,* two of the six enumerated purposes related the legislative and electoral duties. Two others encouraged councils to "exchange information" among themselves and "provide aid, cooperation, and assistance" to affiliated locals. The final two generally mandated "furthering the appropriate objectives and policies of the AFL-CIO . . . and "to engage in other activities as are consistent with the objectives and principles set forth in" the AFL-CIO's constitution and policies (AFL-CIO 1973).

More than a decade later, the authors of *The Labor Council in the Community: A Guide to Local Central Bodies* similarly concluded that "[t]oday, the primary focus of local councils is in the area of political and social action, with international unions bearing primary responsibility for organizing and collective bargaining functions" (Hindman and Patton 1986, 6). It is not surprising, then, that the CLC structures discussed most fully in these publications and staffed most consistently in councils include the Committee on Political Education (COPE), legislative, and community services committees.

By the end of the 1980s, a revised vision of CLC responsibilities emerged in the *AFL-CIO Handbook for Central Labor Councils.* It proclaimed that "[t]he mission of the AFL-CIO Central Labor Council is to organize the community to promote social justice for all working people" (AFL-CIO Department of Organization and Field Services and George Meany Center nd, cover page). Yet with little commitment to fostering this vision with either rhetoric or resources, the role of CLCs did not change substantially. Further, with the deindustrialization of the 1970s and 1980s, many councils lapsed into inactivity or were merged under pressure from the national AFL-CIO.

With the election of the New Voice slate in the fall of 1995, the focus on changes in the functions and structures of CLCs sharpened quickly to support the New Voice goals of union growth and renewal. Shortly after Sweeney's inauguration, Marilyn Sneiderman, a longtime activist and author of the *AFL-CIO Handbook,* was appointed director of the newly formed Field Mobilization Department. A product of the consolidation of the former Field Service and COPE regional offices, the new department's job was to "forg[e] a new partnership with state and local central bodies" (Rosier 1996, 10). Sweeney then appointed a twenty-two member Advisory Committee on the Future of Central Labor Councils from a mix of large, medium, and small councils. Along with the Executive Council Committee on State and Local AFL-CIOs, the advisory committee's role was to counsel the leadership on new structures and policies. Less than nine months after the election, the new administration assembled representatives from almost two hundred CLCs in Denver, Colorado, for the first-ever national conference focusing on the potential strength and the resources needed for CLCs to contribute to the labor movement's revitalization and growth.

The next major development, led primarily by the advisory committee, was perhaps the most significant in promoting the structural and functional changes of the CLCs. Over a period of months in late 1996 and early 1997, field mobilization staff and CLCs were introduced to Union Cities. The importance of this initiative to the national AFL-CIO is captured in the subtitle of one of its pamphlets: "A Guide to Greatness for Local Unions and Their AFL-CIO Central Labor Councils" (AFL-CIO nd(a)).

The eight points that define Union Cities appear in table 1. The field mobilization state directors and staff in each state spent the following months introducing the concept and steps to the CLCs in their jurisdictions. Councils opting to pursue an official Union City designation must pass a resolution and submit a work plan. The latter is typically based on daylong or multiday strategic planning sessions, typically facilitated by the state field mobilization director, staff, and/or local labor education program faculty. This process alone represents a significant new function for most councils which have infrequently, if ever, made a systematic analysis of their strengths and weaknesses and strategies related to specific objectives for each year. As of August 1998, 150 CLCs, about one-fourth of all councils, had passed the resolution (AFL-CIO 1998). Considerably fewer are actively planning and working on the Union Cities goals. Approximately 60 percent of councils in the northeast region that passed the resolution consciously work toward its goals. However, field mobilization staff and labor educators alike note that many councils that, for a variety of reasons, have not formally sought the Union Cities designation are in fact carrying out one or more of the eight steps.

Table 6-1 Eight steps to rebuild the labor movement from the bottom up and help improve the lives of working families

1. Promote organizing as the labor movement's top goal and get half of the local unions in the jurisdiction to sign up for the AFL-CIO "Changing to Organize, Organizing to Change" initiative, which shifts resources into organizing.

2. Mobilize against anti-union employers by recruiting and activating at least 1% of union members for *Street Heat*, the AFL-CIO's new solidarity and rapid response team.

3. Organize grassroots lobbying/political action committees to work on local, state and national issues, build community alliances and support political candidates who champion working families, and then hold those candidates accountable once they are elected.

4. Organize community allies in support of economic development strategies that create jobs and growth, while establishing workers and family-friendly community standards for local industries and public investment.

5. Sponsor the new AFL-CIO Economics Education program for at least a majority of local unions in the geographic area so union members can understand why workers and their families are suffering, who did it to them, and what can be done about it.

6. Persuade city or town councils and county governmental bodies to pass resolutions supporting the right of workers to organize and insist that political candidates do likewise as a condition of endorsement.

7. Work to make sure that all official central labor council bodies—executive board, committees, officers, delegate bodies—are as diverse as the membership represented by affiliated unions.

8. Encourage all unions to increase their membership so that a three percent growth rate becomes a reality in the CLC jurisdiction by the year 2000.

Source: Union Cities, Strong Communities, AFL-CIO, nd.

Specific Structural and Functional Changes

Each of the eight steps requires a change in the way CLCs function; most encourage a change in their structure. However, because Union Cities is essentially in its infancy, councils and staff have worked most specifically on structural and functional changes in three areas. Two of these areas—mobilization and organizing—are themselves major Union Cities goals closely related to the labor movement's overall goal of resurgence. The third—council resources—underlies the ability to achieve all Union Cities goals. A comprehensive, though not exhaustive, list of the current structural and functional changes proposed or under way in CLCs in each area is examined below.[4]

According to the Northeast field mobilization staff, the most obvious and significant functional change CLCs need "to help rebuild the labor movement from the bottom up" is the mobilization of rank-and-file members to support local labor struggles. Dubbed "Street Heat," labor leaders view the pressure applied by such large turnouts of union members for rallies, picket lines, campaign phone banks, and at the polls on election days, as an effective tool to advance labor's organizing, community, political, and legislative goals. Several state directors agreed that "if you have good mobilization, it takes care of the rest." Accompanying this functional change is a multifaceted structural one. Field Mobilization published *AFL-CIO Street Heat: Mobilizing to Win* (AFL-CIO 1997), a handbook describing how to set up a committee in a council to oversee the use of Street Heat. The handbook covers the frequency of its use, the issues on which it is used, its availability for coalition partner use, and so forth. It also describes how constituent locals of the council, in turn, establish and build support for a communication structure within their unions to alert member activists of Street Heat activities in a fast and efficient manner. The size of the commitments—both to creating the CLC and multiple local union-based structures and to establishing a smoothly functioning relationship between them—is considerable. It stands in stark contrast to the attention that the CLC delegate participation in monthly business meetings has required from local union members and officers in the past.

---

[4]Many AFL-CIO leaders view the new approaches to political and legislative action that councils are developing as equally important to their organizing and mobilizing activities. Likewise, progress made in the delivery of Common Sense Economics across the country represents significant change in council activities. Neither assertion is disputed here. However, due to space limitations and consideration of organizing and mobilization as the top two Union Cities steps, they are the primary focus of this study.

Sharpening the focus on new member organizing represents the second significant change required by the Union Cities approach. It encourages council leaders to develop a greater awareness of the organizing potential that exists in their communities and to analyze the role their CLCs can play in supporting it. At a minimum, this assignment demands that councils use their newly developed mobilization structure to provide visible support for local workers exercising their right to organize and condemnation of local employers who violate that right. A more activist approach to promoting organizing requires additional structural changes—most typically forming an organizing committee that can provide organizing leads, staff, campaign coordination, leverage for employer neutrality, and/or training of volunteer organizers.

Perhaps the most challenging aspect of Union Cities to councils is the need to acquire or reallocate significant financial, physical, technical, and human resources to achieve the eight steps. Securing these resources dictates that virtually all councils undertake new activities to raise money, recruit volunteers, and develop technical skills (such as one-on-one organizing, preparing for rallies, grant writing and administration, etc.) or at least redirect resources toward those needs. Some councils, particularly those with limited financial resources that are typically small CLCs, must consider organizational changes that will increase resources available to them so that they can function more effectively than in the past. Suggested structure changes include pooling per capita council membership payments among several CLCs to hire shared staff, merging councils, and "chapter" or consortium arrangements that would facilitate sharing of a variety of resources. The New Alliance Proposal adopted by the national AFL-CIO convention in October 1999 is, in part, an attempt to address the resource question for councils and state federations of all sizes and the closely related issue of labor's clout on economic, social, and political issues. By encouraging fuller participation of international unions and their locals, the AFL-CIO expects greater resources from them to support locally developed strategies for addressing labor's organizing and community agendas (Goldstein and Crosby 2000, 12).

Functional and Structural Change: Advances and Obstacles

Mobilization

In keeping with the field staff's observation about the changes in CLC activities needed to help rebuild the labor movement, the most obvious change these bodies have accomplished over the past two years relates to the size and frequency of Street Heat demonstrations. All of the Northeast Field Mobilization staff interviewed named such actions among the "most notable" activities of the CLCs in their states in the last year. The breadth of issues on which mobilizations have occurred is impressive. Organizing (including both national AFL-CIO–sponsored community campaigns—the nationwide Strawberry Campaign and the Day to Make Our Voices Heard, Our Choices Respected), strikes (including the national United Parcel Service and Overnite strikes and local works stoppages), unfair labor practices, support for fired workers, and other campaigns drew hundreds of union participants. Predictably, some large councils had many more activities than a typical small council.[5] For example, the Boston CLC holds one per month on average, while most small councils support approximately two or three per year. Yet most staff reported that councils of all sizes succeeded in reaching the Union Cities goal of attracting the participation of one percent of local union members or more.

Further, as suggested above, Street Heat has helped CLCs achieve other Union Cities goals. In New York, Vermont, and New Jersey, Street Heat activities have prodded politicians to publicly commit to the rights of organized workers. Through mobilization in support of hospital workers on Martin Luther King Day and events incorporating the Labor Council for Latin American Advancement (LACLA), the A. Philip Randolph Institute (APRI), and the Coalition of Black Trade Unionists (CBTU), the Hartford, Connecticut, council has

---

[5]The Northeast Region examples given here do not represent an exhaustive list of all councils participating in the particular types of activities. Time constraints in the interviews limited data collection, and space limitations here demand a less-than-complete summary of information collected.

worked on the diversity issue. Indeed, several Field Mobilization staffers noted that these events generally increased participation by previously inactive rank-and-file members, especially younger ones, people of color, and women.

Structurally, CLCs have made advances as well. Field Mobilization staff in all but one state surveyed report evolving mobilization structures in the councils. The most advanced among these are truly impressive. The Boston CLC's Mobilization Committee boasts members from fifty local unions with attendance of thirty or more at each meeting, a well-developed set of criteria for determining whether the Street Heat structure should be used, and even the beginning of the development of "substructures" focusing on the issues within particular Boston communities. The DC Metro council has likewise built the capacity to contact hundreds of union members for Street Heat and to determine criteria for its use, and it continues working with affiliates to develop communications networks within locals.

Further, councils appear to be figuring out how to "cut the pattern to fit the cloth" where union density and limited resources pose significant obstacles to mobilization. In rural Vermont, one or more CLCs may join in the efforts already in progress under direction of the Central Vermonters for a Livable Wage, a coalition of citizens interested in local and statewide measures designed to raise all workers' wages. In New Hampshire, the state federation helped establish a mobilization mechanism in Manchester when council resources were insufficient to do so. In mid-state New York, several councils (all small and mid-size) are starting to look to collaboration on mobilizations to increase their turnout and influence.[6]

These experiences are similar to those found by the national Field Mobilization office in their "Union Cities Progress Survey." Based on the responses of 108 CLCs nationwide (all but a few of which are en-

---

[6]In addition to the initial attempts to coordinate activities reported to the author in 1998, these councils will participate in developing strategies involving all CLCs, the state federation, and point people from international unions as part of the New Alliance pilot program put in place in New York in May 2000.

rolled in Union Cities), the study reports that almost two-thirds had actions in support of organizing, and a larger (unspecified) number rallied in support of striking workers. Fifty-eight of the 108 councils reported establishing Street Heat mobilizing structures.

While the results are impressive, discussions with Field Mobilization staff and conference presentations uncover some persistent obstacles. Councils have an easier time of developing their mobilization committees, with a representative of affiliated locals, than that representative does in establishing the structure within the local. Some local officers (and some CLC officers) apparently do not oppose actions, and indeed have historically worked hard to turn workers out for rallies. However, the loss of personal control that institutionalized mobilization structures could incur may keep at least some leaders from encouraging their establishment.

As CLCs begin to build and flex their muscle, tensions between them and their respective state federations have increased. Many historically weak councils have depended on their state federations for leadership and/or resources to meet their objectives. In other cases, statewide officers have long recognized (sometimes based on their own experiences) that successful CLC leaders become likely challengers for their federation positions. The potential loss of power posed by increased labor council activity has strained the relationships between the organizations in some states (both within and outside of the region). Further exacerbating the tensions is the belief by some state AFL-CIO leaders that the national organization prefers working through CLCs and seeks to limit state-level power.[7]

Organizing

Despite the primary focus of councils on politics in recent history, it appears that councils are willing to widen their scope to include organizing. Northeast Field Mobilization staff repeatedly named actions in support of organizing as many of the CLCs' "most notable" events. Three

---

[7] These officers typically point to the nationwide gathering of CLCs at the Denver conference in July 1996 before a similar event was scheduled for state federations. The latter event was held in November 1996.

types of activities are particularly common in the region. First, councils of all sizes have sponsored rallies in support of local and national organizing campaigns. Scranton, Pennsylvania; Portland, Maine; Washington, D.C.; Boston; Baltimore; and New York City are only a few sites in the Northeast Region where CLCs have rallied for their neighbors' right to organize. Small councils in Vermont, Maine, and Connecticut have held informational picketing at grocery stores on behalf of the California strawberry workers, sometimes in coalition with community partners with whom they have had little previous contact. The latter is a particularly significant accomplishment given the remoteness in distance and local impact of the strawberry workers' struggle to these CLCs.

Second, councils in several states including New York and New Jersey have engaged elected officials in public debate about organizing in their communities. Others have pushed for "right to organize" resolutions in city councils and have written letters to local newspapers in support of organizing campaigns. The Pioneer Valley CLC in western Massachusetts put an interesting twist on this strategy, convincing two employers seeking contracts with local governments that they would need the council's assistance to do so. To get this help, both agreed to union recognition for their employees based on a majority of them signing union authorization cards (Bennett 1998, 10).

The third type of organizing support—direct participation in campaigns in the community—requires a structural component of CLCs. So far, the development of council-based organizing committees is far more likely to occur in large councils with financial resources, locally based union organizers, and multiple ongoing campaigns. CLC representatives have discussed committee development in cities including New York, Buffalo, Boston, Worcester, Washington, and Baltimore. However, state directors in Maine, Pennsylvania, and Connecticut have also mentioned plans to establish medium or small CLC-based or statewide committees in the near future.

To date, CLC support for organizing committees falls into two categories. In some instances, the councils offer support through their sponsorship of organizers' meetings. They provide meeting space, support staff, and most important, the opportunity for dialogue. The Buffalo, New York, committee has served in this capacity. In others, council delegates or their designees comprise the organizing committee's membership and are setting the course for campaigns in their areas. They are beginning to develop organizing targets, strategic planning, and training. The Boston, Worcester, and Washington organizing committees all report such activities.

Although there are no published estimates of the contribution CLC activity has made to organizing nationwide, many councils of all sizes have embraced the challenge. Models of "best practices" for councils with varying access to human and financial resources are beginning to emerge. As already mentioned, Field Mobilization's national survey of CLCs found significant mobilization of Street Heat in support of organizing. It recorded more than 400 Strawberry worker actions and seventy-five events on Right to Organize Day of Action nationally. Additionally, some councils' organizing committees are seeking to improve organizing opportunities in their communities by pushing for local ordinances or resolutions requiring employer neutrality in campaigns in which employers are government sponsored or supported. In Denver, the CLC and the Colorado AFL-CIO succeeded in a similar effort when it pressured the Adam's Mark Hotel to pledge neutrality in exchange for the conclusion of an extended boycott ("Adam's Mark Inks Neutrality Pact with Labor" 1998, 1). Finally, Gapasin and Wial (1998) have examined CLCs across the country that promote organizing with activities beyond basic support and information transmittal to internationals. They conclude that some impressive examples of CLC organizing activity exist, and they suggest that the number of councils involved could increase with full-time staff or volunteer delegate resources, leadership dedicated to CLC participation in organizing, and affiliated unions and a local community with interest in forming new units. More recently, in June 1999 CLCs across the country rallied behind the AFL-CIO's new Voice@Work campaign and held actions around the June 24th national day of action in support of organizing (Colburn and Reynolds 2000, 3).

Again, despite the successes in incorporating organizing into the CLCs' agendas, several obstacles exist. Primary among them is the shortage of all types of resources to carry out the work. The overwhelming majority of councils still operate with no paid staff to develop organizing structures, plans, research, or leads. Likewise, most council delegates lack organizing tools—the ability to analyze targeted employers, strategic planning skills to develop campaigns, and experience in one-on-one communications with potential union members. With legislative/political and collective bargaining issues competing for councils' mobilization capacity, even CLCs' ability to deliver bodies to organizing rallies or picket lines consistently is not certain.

There are also structural obstacles to the role of local central bodies in organizing. As two state directors and the history above noted, most "modern-era" councils have not handled organizing. Because the relationships, whether good or bad, among international unions attempting to organize in a particular area have developed outside the CLC structure, these bodies are likely to ignore or resist CLC participation in brokering organizing opportunities. Indeed, since many international unions set their organizing targets, plans, and goals regionally or nationally, they may have no interest in discussing these issues with a local CLC structure. Additionally, CLC organizing committees will have to figure out how to assist organizers whose modus operandi is to keep activities extremely low profile and confidential in the formative stages.

Resources

While they have clearly wrestled with the problem of securing the financial, physical, technical, and human resources needed to carry out the Union Cities agenda, Northeast Field Mobilization staffers admit that they have made limited progress on this front. Here, as elsewhere, the councils' main source of financial resources is the per capita dues paid by member local unions. Field Mobilization staff report increased affiliation in many of their councils, although few have focused on this effort with a systematic campaign. A few councils, again, usually larger ones, also pursue grant funding to underwrite projects and staff. Some councils sponsor fund-raising activities—dinners, golf tournaments, raffles—although few staff identified new initiatives. Central Maine CLC is one exception. It has held, with community coalition partners, various fund-raisers to finance the mobilization committee's work around plant closings in the region. (One innovative community-based event was a fund-raising hunters' breakfast scheduled during the fall hunting season.) Another exception is the United Labor Council of

Reading and Berks County, in Pennsylvania. In recent years it has started raising money by selling ads for a special Labor Day edition of the local newspaper, and it has formed a 501(c)(3) organization to solicit money for some projects (Bussel 1998).

Technical resources for councils have also increased with the new emphasis on increased activism. National Field Mobilization has pledged that each state will have a full time staff person to assist CLCs and state federations. The staff interviewed described their roles in various ways, including adviser, support staff, confidant, "nudge" or "haunt," and leadership mentor for the CLCs. In addition, in the Northeast Region, university-based labor education centers function in all but three states and Puerto Rico. The type of assistance offered to Field Mobilization staff and CLCs varies significantly across the region, from courses on leadership development to strategic planning facilitation and advice. Finally, within the last year, the Northeast Region Field Mobilization staff has sponsored three subregional conferences at which CLCs exchanged "best practice" case studies on their Union Cities goals and discussed the existing obstacles. Similarly, Field Mobilization staff in Vermont and Pennsylvania have held their states' first meetings designed specifically for CLC officer interaction. Since 1996 the West Virginia Field Mobilization representative has co-taught a course on skills for CLC officers with a labor educator at the state federation's weeklong summer school. The contacts made at these meetings represent another resource to leaders as they to implement the Union Cities initiative.

The most promising expansion of human resources are developing along with structural change. Street Heat committees, while still in formative stages, have substantially increased the "people power" and time commitments made to some councils. One state director explained that delegates who historically were not encouraged to attend council sessions are now participating because their mobilization committee meetings are held in conjunction with the former. Another pointed out that different delegates, including younger activists, now view the council with more interest because it is a place where solidarity actions are planned.

Other changes are evolving more slowly. A few councils are starting to work collaboratively to share resources. Councils in New York

and West Virginia have held joint activities, including labor education courses and political events. Beaver County and Butler County
CLCs, two small central bodies in Pennsylvania, are working toward
jointly hiring a staff person to advance their Union Cities agendas.
The Mid-State (New York) CLC has hired a staff member from the
jurisdiction of a neighboring council with which Mid-State is building a collaborative relation. In Pennsylvania the Field Mobilization
representative reports that community services liaisons have assisted
in their Union Cities efforts. Similarly, in locations where paid local
or international union staff are stationed, as in Reading, Pennsylvania, they have been able to use the flexibility in their schedules to move
the Union Cities activities forward. Finally, in at least three Northeast
states, small councils are examining the possibility of merging to combine resources. Two states, New York and Maryland, are likely to consider options for consolidating or coordinating efforts as pilot states
for the New Alliance. But for every story of pending or complete structural change there is a staff-related failed attempt or, even more commonly, a lack of time to work through possible structural changes with
councils for which raising the subject abruptly would alienate the affected council leaders.

The CLCs' lack of resources is a phenomenon identified by the nationwide survey. But limited efforts similar to those in the Northeast
are increasing councils' capacities. Field mobilization staffing in each
state is virtually complete. The national survey found that CLCs are
also finding ways to reallocate resources. For example, community service liaisons are assisting seventy of the 108 respondents in Union Cities
activities. While recognizing that it cannot force its affiliates to require
CLC or state federation membership for their locals, the national AFL-
CIO continues to press the issue through its direct dialogue with international officers and the AFL-CIO Executive Council Committee
on State and Local Central Bodies.

In addition to staff, the national Field Mobilization office has pro-
vided CLCs with various documents containing technical advice on
Union Cities activities, including "Why Union Cities?" (AFL-CIO
Department of Field Mobilization 1997c), "Union Cities Planning
Guide for Central Labor Councils" (AFL-CIO Department of Field
Mobilization 1997b), "The Road to Union Cities: Your Resource Map

to Rebuild the Labor Movement" (AFL-CIO Department of Field Mobilization 1997a), "AFL-CIO Street Heat: Mobilizing to Win" (ALF-CIO 1997), and "June 24: A Day to Make Our Voices Heard, Our Choices Respected: Tools and Resources for Organizers" (AFL-CIO 1998). All of these provide practical suggestions for council work. Recently, the advisory committee produced a two-page resource guide with brief descriptions of councils that have increased their resources through community service liaisons, affiliation growth, grant funding from private and public sources, using labor education centers creatively, and affiliate funding for special projects (Crosby nd). In implementing the New Alliance proposal, Field Mobilization leadership state that leadership development through workshops and on-the-ground training or mentoring will be critical. The department has already prepared materials including guidelines for building the communication linkages between international union point people at the national and local offices and CLCs and state federations that will be critical to developing the strong working relationships proposed (Colburn and Reynolds 2000, 5).

National Field Mobilization has also offered networking opportunities for council leaders. In July 1996 and again in July 1998, Field Mobilization hosted multiday conferences in Denver and Chicago, respectively. Prior to the national AFL-CIO Convention in September 1997, it held the first joint State Federation/Central Labor Council Conference in Pittsburgh. Hundreds of council representatives gathered at these meetings to learn about "best case" practices; to design future actions which delegates committed to carry out upon returning to their councils; and to plan strategically for "building vibrant, proworker communities over the next several years" (Sneiderman 1998a). Field Mobilization held regional CLC meetings in May and June 1999 to cultivate further exchange of ideas on how councils can best meet Union Cities goals. In an effort to integrate Field Mobilization training with other AFL-CIO initiatives, the Field Mobilization department sponsored a one-day workshop for women officers of state and local central bodies in conjunction with the Working Women's Conference in March 2000.

Clearly, however, several major obstacles remain. Many Field Mobilization representatives made the point that labor council activity is the primary concern for virtually none of the CLC presidents in their states. Almost all are officers in their local unions; some are members of regional boards of internationals or state federation committees. Most are not employed by their union and thus work (for pay) forty or more hours per week. They usually attempt to maintain family and social responsibilities and lack the time to undertake strategic thinking, planning, and actions to increase resources.

Further, the ambitious breadth of Union Cities leads some council leaders to believe that it is simply another effort to force small councils to merge. This attitude is partially an artifact of AFL-CIO history. In late 1980s the national AFL-CIO launched a campaign to merge some of the smaller and less active CLCs. Council leaders have related stories about the top-down manner in which representatives from the national AFL-CIO attempted to force these changes without support from the CLCs. Many councils resisted, and the efforts were only marginally successful. As a result, however, CLC officers and delegates who witnessed the efforts remain skeptical about the national AFL-CIO's motives even though top leadership has changed.

But as Northeast Regional Director Joe Alvarez has stated, councils must have a "critical mass"—an ability to represent the labor movement and advance its organizing objectives effectively—to achieve Union Cities goals. He emphasizes that this is not necessarily related to council size. Further, as described above, mergers are only one of several ways of sharing resources to reach a critical mass. For example, the New Alliance proposes a somewhat different method of creating area labor federations to which existing CLCs would presumably belong. The fact remains, however, that the resource question requires special care and attention if the Union Cities goals are to be reached.

The Adequacy of the Union Cities Agenda Implementation to Achieve New Voice Goals

The question of whether the Union Cities approach can contribute to the current AFL-CIO administration's goals is, in fact, a two-part query. First, can councils engaged in the Union Cities process overcome the obstacles they face in developing mobilization and organizing structures and functions? Second, even if they can clear existing hurdles, is the Union Cities approach one that will "change the labor movement to create a new voice for working families in our communities?" (AFL-CIO nd(a))

Conditions for Overcoming Obstacles to Union Cities

Because Union Cities is a relatively new program, a definitive answer to the first question is not yet possible. However, at least four conditions must prevail for this initiative to flourish. First, expectations for Union Cities change for various-sized councils need clarification. Several state staff noted that the magnitude and complexity of the tasks suggested by the eight steps overwhelm many councils, particularly the small ones. Moreover, recently published case studies, best practice materials, and conference presentations, which the CLCs are more likely to read or see, frequently discuss the more sophisticated efforts of mid-size and large councils with greater resources. At best, this makes the small councils timid about embracing the effort. At worst, it raises suspicions that the initiative, and any resources available for it, belongs to big-city CLCs.

Field Mobilization never expected all CLCs to become Union Cities. However, the wide adoption of some of its principles and actions is certainly desirable. In informal conversations, Field Mobilization leadership have emphasized that the successes by CLCs with greater resources should serve as starting points for councils with fewer, not models requiring exact replication. They have lauded the creative but limited activities in support of organizing and other Union Cities goals of less well-endowed councils (Sneiderman 1998b). Field Mobilization must make this case more frequently and publicly. Further, providing more models of success achieved in limited-resource councils or assistance in analyzing how to pattern success in smaller councils after those of resource-rich councils is essential to the widespread adaptation of the process.

Second, at the same time it builds leadership capacity, Field Mobilization must continue to curry support or acceptance of its agenda in the CLCs. From interviews with staff in the Northeast region, a spectrum of council leadership affinity with Union Cities emerges. At one end of the spectrum are the CLC officers who embrace the process. They use their energy and develop skills to move the agenda. At the spectrum's opposite end are the councils who either oppose or are unaware of Union Cities. (At least in the Northeast, most CLCs appear uninterested or unable to resist the initiative.) The critical location on the spectrum at this point in Union Cities' development is in the middle. Several regional staff located one or more of their councils here. While the central body leaders either do not support the AFL-CIO administration and goals or lack the energy or skill to enact its agenda, they are willing to allow the structures and activities to develop around them. Convincing others closer to the negative end of the spectrum to allow such development may be key to spreading the Union Cities agenda.

"Common Sense Economics" (AFL-CIO Education Department 1998), "Why Union Cities?" and similar presentations prepared by the national AFL-CIO departments offer convincing evidence for why community-based action around organizing must be the labor movement's top priority and how mobilization increases effectiveness on this and other issues. Because virtually all central body leaders possess a strong commitment to the labor movement, at least some without energy or skills (or time) who hear these appeals will agree that Union Cities–style activities are imperative. Thus, two more important "next steps" emerge. The first is an effort to encourage such leaders to make room for others in their council who are willing to spearhead the initiative. This is a delicate task which may dictate a transfer in decision-making authority, leadership training for delegates, and considerable assistance by state directors. But again, it is imperative for Union Cities principles to take hold across the region. Second, Field Mobilization and other AFL-CIO departments should continue to produce educational materials similar to those described above. The diversity of conditions experienced by CLCs across the country guarantees that they will not be equally receptive to the appeals based on the need to organize, economic conditions, or any single topic. But the plethora of issues affecting working people guarantees that each program will strike a responsive chord with some CLCs and spark their move on the spectrum away from the unaware and resistant toward activism.[8]

---

[8]The recently announced effort to educate and mobilize working families for the 2000 elections through various membership outreach strategies provides a natural fit for many CLCs comfortable with the role of participation in partisan politics (AFL-CIO 1999, 1).

A third condition that would help Union Cities overcome many of its present obstacles is the provision of basic leadership skill development for council leadership. Virtually all of the state staff interviewed talked about their informal and ongoing efforts to develop the leadership capacity of council officers. As the roles and goals of councils have changed, it is not surprising that even longtime officers do not have the leadership, organizational, and technical skills to establish mobilization and organizing structures, goals, and activities. Even in the smallest of states (by population or geography), the job of overseeing the Union Cities process is too large for the assigned Field Mobilization staff. In the Northeast, most staff admit that some councils—either those that are "getting by okay," those that are inactive and not in strategic locations, or those resistant to the AFL-CIO's new direction—simply don't get their attention, because there isn't sufficient time. Providing inexpensive, easily accessible leadership development programs and encouraging attendance in them would help council officers acquire basic tools for handling their new responsibilities and may foster interest in new activities.[9]

A final condition, one that emerges from the above three, also deserves mention. To varying degrees, all of the above steps require new financial resources. Whether it is the time needed for developing small council approaches to Union Cities; instructors to deliver leadership training; or presentations, one-on-one discussions, or other strategies to remove impediments to new functions and structures, money to hire staff to complete these tasks is at least part of the solution. To believe that the fundamental transformation of CLC structures and

---

[9]University-based labor education centers throughout the region already offer leadership training in various formats and with varying degrees of regularity at low cost. Because Field Mobilization leaders view the skills of labor educators as an extension of their resources, these groups could collaborate to design a leadership skill course tailored to the needs of CLCs. Agendas for the 1999 regional CLC meetings included some such training. However, the questions of how to deliver such a full curriculum of leadership training and how to provide ongoing mentoring for developing leaders as they learn by doing is unresolved. As one leader noted, competent CLC presidents and state federation officers may be capable mentors for new leaders. As in many organizations, however, maintaining power and/or office is a strong labor movement tradition and the current system does not support seasoned leaders if they choose to move out of office into a mentoring role.

functions will transpire without significant money dedicated to it is self-deceptive. The Union Cities goals clearly rely on the continued search for new resources and increasingly effective distribution of existing ones.

Traditionally, CLCs have noted that if all eligible locals affiliated with them, at least the financial resource shortfall would be much smaller. That all but a few international unions continue to balk at the prospect of requiring their locals to affiliate (and enforcing that requirement) suggests that more fundamental issues of the CLCs' roles may still exist. The discussion below considers this debate more fully.

The Contribution of Union Cities to a Larger, Revitalized Labor Movement

Whether Union Cities is an appropriate initiative for the ambitious goals of the Sweeney administration is a complex issue that merits analysis of a myriad of historical and contemporary factors upon which this chapter cannot comment exhaustively. However, at least three observations are in order in the context of the material presented here. First, given the large and spirited turnouts for council-sponsored mobilizations, both the capacity for community-based bodies to tap the participation of rank-and-file workers and the effectiveness of most of these actions are evident. Northeast Field Mobilization staff speak enthusiastically about the growth they have witnessed in CLC activities, attributing it alternatively to the Union Cities initiative, the excitement generated when people *do* something, and the sense of hope provided by the new administration. The impact created by CLC involvement in recent mobilizations around trade issues in Seattle and Washington, D.C., suggests that local central body participation is indeed an important strategy for labor movement renewal.

However, a related, second observation is that a structure (or a variety of them) that can sustain that participation over an extended period of time is not yet in place in most, if any, CLCs. Observers of council activities admit that in the past virtually all CLCs had peaks and valleys in their activities based on the perceived needs of the community, the time and energy of key officers and activists, and similar factors. In the Northeast, Field Mobilization staff recognizes that the current attempt at establishing institutional structures for mobilizing, organizing, and consolidation of resources that might prevent such a bumpy ride is a painstakingly slow process. It will require patience and focus by the national organization to allow nurturing of this process. This is a difficult task given the legitimate temptation to concentrate staff on critical battles that inevitably spring up in hot spots across the nation. Even with persistence in fostering the structural changes, there is no irrevocable proof that these structures will sustain CLC efforts.

Third, even if the councils succeed in instituting sustainable structures capable of advancing the New Voice goals, the tension between the national AFL-CIO's organizing goals (and the CLC role in them) and those of its international union affiliates require examination and resolution. As mentioned above, the current lack of support for mandatory CLC affiliation among international unions leaves one with the uneasy feeling that many are not ready to design a substantive role for the local central bodies in their strategic plans. Indeed, a return to the history of CLC autonomy identifies sources of friction that appear unresolved.

The national unions bear responsibility for limitations on CLC activities that rendered most of them ineffective on issues outside of legislative lobbying or electoral politics. Ulman (1955, 382) claims that "national unions were opposed to [sympathy strikes and boycotts] . . . holding in effect that the good union doctrine of 'sanctity of contracts' should take working precedence over the good union doctrine of 'an injury to one is the concern of all.'" Thus in 1898 and 1901, respectively, the AFL constitution limited central bodies' ability to conduct sympathy strikes and boycotts without international union approval. Although unions depended upon labor councils to assist with union organizing in the 1930s and 1940s, that role also virtually disappeared over time in favor of international union–based campaigns (see Cobble 1997). Major unions even attempted to curtail CLC involvement in legislative advocacy. In the 1920s some AFL unions argued that central bodies were pushing too hard to secure through social policy legislation what unions might instead secure for their members through collective bargaining (Lorwin 1933, 410). In the late 1940s and 1950s, CIO unions curbed the IUC's role in political issues to rid them of Communist influence (Zeiger 1995, 271–3).

Although the parameters of the international unions' limitations might be different, the core control issues may remain the same. For example, even without staging sympathy strikes or boycotts, are international unions ready to allow CLCs to determine (or even participate in determining) the focus or timing of actions against the employers with whom they bargain? Will they respond to a CLC-initiated request for organizing resources when it conflicts with their own strategic choices? And if local central bodies choose to endorse a congressional candidate or political party or a position on an environmental issue that runs counter to that of major international unions or the national AFL-CIO, how will the contradiction be resolved?

To prevent CLC-organizing structures from underuse as so-called rent-a-rallies or the potentially destructive clashing of CLC and international union organizing goals at the local level, or even diverse goals in the political arena, internationals' organizers and Field Mobilization representatives at all levels must intensify initial efforts to figure out what the nexus between these organizations should be. Both the national CLC Advisory Committee and the Committee 2000 are attempting to resolve these sticky issues. The involvement of CLCs, state federations, and international unions in determining local strategies through the New Alliance represents a bold attempt to address these issues. Although it is far too early to determine the success of this effort, the willingness to undertake it demonstrates a determination to attack head-on one of the labor movement's most significant organizational issues.

Conclusions and Next Research Steps

That many of the structural and functional changes required of CLCs to master the eight steps to Union Cities will require a long and arduous process is evident from even a cursory examination of the initiative. That more than one-quarter of all active councils have formally engaged in the effort, and many more of all sizes are pursuing some of the steps, speaks to the initiative's relevance to rank-and-file union members across the country. As one labor educator commented, the New Voice leaders "may have awakened a sleeping giant." The national

AFL-CIO and Field Mobilization leadership seem cognizant of obstacles to the success of Union Cities and its potential limitations in contributing to the goals of organizing and revitalizing labor's voice in the community. Its support of a wide variety of mobilizing and organizing actions and structures reflects a necessary willingness to reshape and refine the initiative as needed.[10]

To better understand what adjustments will foster the structural and functional changes demanded by Union Cities calls for a further investigation of its acceptance, operation, and obstacles at the local level. The interviews with Northeast Field Mobilization staff suggest that acceptance short of support has allowed significant progress in some CLCs. To learn from council leaders what motivates them to embrace Union Cities or at least allow it to "happen around them" is a first step in determining how to draw more central bodies into the process. Providing new ideas on alternative ways of structuring councils and their relations with each other and their state federations to increase council resources can help identify the means of creating a critical mass for action. Learning from council officers and delegates participating in the mobilization and organizing activities in councils of all sizes (and with varying levels of access to resources) can help to identify the leadership skills and other resources needed in inactive councils to spark UC activities. Finally, a systematic and comprehensive examination of the contribution of mobilization and organizing efforts to the achievement of the labor movement's goals is imperative. It will ensure that these seemingly appropriate activities really are "improving the lives of working families and helping them regain control of their future" (AFL-CIO nd(a)).

---

[10]Conversations with local, regional, and national Field Mobilization staff indicate that they are comfortable with CLCs exercising considerable autonomy in choosing the issues around which they mobilize and how they implement other Union Cities principles even though the national AFL-CIO has promoted specific campaigns (e.g., the strawberry workers' organizing campaign, the Day to Make Our Voices Heard, Our Choices Respected, and Social Security reform). Although such local definition of goals may turn out workers for action in the short run, Johnston (1998, 2) correctly notes that without a clear agreed-upon framework of "what is wrong and what we want to do about it," labor's ability to impact society as a social movement is limited (also see Rogers 1995).

CHAPTER SEVEN

Confronting the Dilemmas of Organizing

Obstacles and Innovations at the
AFL-CIO Organizing Institute

Amy Foerster

*I*n recent months both the labor and popular press have engaged in a vigorous debate regarding whether the U.S. labor movement is currently undergoing a revitalization. Those who believe that a revitalization is under way point to a host of events to support their view: the ascent of the New Voice ticket to the top echelon of leadership within the AFL-CIO in 1995, the dramatic organizing victories that have taken place in subsequent years, and the rise of strategic alliances between labor and other activists, particularly in recent struggles regarding globalization and opposition to the World Trade Organization. Perhaps most dramatically, these pundits argue, union membership grew by over 265,000 members in 1999, the largest single year of membership growth since the 1970s. Although these factors certainly allow for cautious optimism, other scholars warn that a variety of obstacles remain before a full-scale revitalization or transformation can be successfully achieved. Structural and institutional factors may hinder a transformation (Fletcher and Hurd 1998, 1999; Glenn 1997), and some warn that the process itself is driven from the "top down" and may result in few changes at the grassroots level (Brecher and Costello 1996; Gapasin and Yates 1997; Moody 1997, 1998). At issue here are disagreements regarding both the structure and nature of the labor movement. Is labor most effective as a bureaucratically organized network of unions controlled by powerful leaders? Or will it achieve greater victories as a grassroots movement controlled by workers? Are these two categories mutually exclusive?

This manuscript has benefited greatly from the helpful suggestions of Richard Hurd, Immanuel Ness, Sidney Tarrow, and Henry Walker.

This chapter will take a new look at these debates by documenting and examining the history of one innovative union program that has played a major role in labor's current attempts at revitalization: the AFL-CIO Organizing Institute. Founded in 1989, the Institute was initially created to assist unions in devising new organizing strategies, to provide strategic analysis of successful and unsuccessful campaigns, and to recruit and train new organizers. In addition to its essential role in organizing, I argue that the process of forming the Institute and attempting to implement its ambitious programs led to significant changes both at the international and local level of union operations. These changes, however, have led to contentious debates regarding the role of centralization and democracy in the movement, as well as the direction the movement should take in the future. Additionally, I argue that the particular obstacles faced by staff and supporters of the Organizing Institute are indicative of the larger structural and cultural problems facing the labor movement as a whole. The manner in which the Institute grappled with these obstacles is therefore indicative of the struggle presently occurring within the house of labor, and proves instructive to those concerned with both the past conditions and future health of the U.S. labor movement.

The remainder of this chapter documents the history of the Organizing Institute's program, explains how expansion of that program led to larger attempts at transformation throughout the labor movement, and outlines the obstacles and conflicts that have marked the Organizing Institute's history. Finally, the chapter concludes by examining what the case of the Organizing Institute can tell us about the larger issues of revitalization and transformation inside the labor movement.[1] How successful will these attempts be, and what obstacles must be overcome before a true revitalization can occur?

---

[1] These issues are addressed through the utilization of in-depth interviews with ten individuals who have been heavily involved in the Organizing Institute since its inception. These respondents were selected after consultation with the director of the Organizing Institute and labor educators who agreed that fourteen individuals were key to the formation and utilization of the Institute. Of the fourteen, ten agreed to be interviewed. It is important to note that although all were intrinsically involved with the Institute in some way, not all were supporters of the organization. The interviews ranged in length, but typically ran between 45 minutes and two hours. Respondents were questioned on a number of issues, including the reasons the Institute was founded, what the initial goals of the Institute were, conflicts and clashes that emerged over the years, and whether the respondents felt that the organization

Formation of the Organizing Institute:
The Recent Past

> Why should we worry about organizing groups of people who do not
> want to be organized? If they prefer to have others speak for them and
> make the decisions which affect their lives, without effective participa-
> tion on their part, that is their right. . . . I used to worry about the size
> of membership. But quite a few years ago I just stopped worrying
> about it, because to me it doesn't make any difference.

This quote, taken from a 1972 *U.S. News & World Report* interview
with former AFL-CIO President George Meany (Anonymous 1972),
is indicative of the problem that faced the labor movement in the 1970s
and 1980s. Not only had union membership and density plummeted
precipitously over the course of the previous forty years, the rate of
union organizing had dropped drastically as well. Chaison and Dhavale
(1990) estimate that the average number of annual elections and employees organized into new units from 1982 to 1987 was less than half
that of 1975 to 1981. This resulted in a union culture that devalued organizing and the work of union organizers, as one founder of the Organizing Institute recognized:

> . . . organizers were typically the lowest paid . . . you know, it was
> historic in my union that if somebody was a bad rep [business
> representative] you dump them into organizing. 'Cause you didn't
> want them to be around the members. And that was true in the
> labor movement—[organizing] was a dumping ground or a step-
> ping stone to something higher, which was servicing (personal in-
> terview, 10/30/97).

Not all labor leaders shared these sentiments, of course. Some in the
movement recognized the seriousness of the organizing crisis at a very

---

had an effect on the goals and priorities of the labor movement as a whole. In addition to
the intensive interviews, supplementary material was gathered to form a more extensive history of the Institute. These materials included training manuals, position papers, press re-
leases, and internal documents garnered from the Institute. These data formed the basis of
a larger research project. For the purposes of this chapter, however, primary attention will be
focused on the results of the interviews.

early stage and advocated increased organizing throughout the 1970s
and 1980s, as the following quotation makes clear:

> Clearly the labor movement was not growing . . . we needed to or-
> ganize more workers to grow. We were winning 50 percent of elec-
> tions—that wasn't good enough. Organizing costs were sky-high.
> . . . there was a desperate need in the labor movement to find the
> keys to successful organizing, to find ways to defeat employer
> campaigns, and to assist national unions in doing that (personal
> interview 9/29/97).

A few early experiments toward organizing were conducted in the
1970s and early 1980s, primary among them the Blue Cross/Blue
Shield campaign and the Houston Organizing Project, which took
place over the course of 1981–82. The Houston project was an "enormous organizing program, funded by the Federation, designed by the
Federation and in partnership with major affiliates who dedicated
staff organizers to the campaign" (Personal interview 10/16/97). Designed to "crack the Sun Belt" (Balz 1982), the project garnered funding from a variety of international unions in order to attack a back-
log of approximately eighty requests for organizing assistance in
Houston-area companies. The Houston project explicitly sought to
increase the AFL-CIO's role in promoting organizing and to sym-
bolize commitment to the organizing function. Although the resources devoted to the project were considerable for the period—a
budget of $1 million and a staff of twenty organizers (ibid.)—the pro-
ject did not prove nearly as successful as planners had hoped. This
was due, in part, to poor timing, as the project began precisely as the
bottom fell out of Houston's oil-based economy, creating an environment even more hostile to unions than was already present. Other
problems proved equally difficult to combat, however, including a
scarcity of trained organizers, which was described by a respondent
familiar with the project:

> . . . the urgency of organizing was upon us in the early eighties . . .
> Houston represented an effort to try to stimulate it. . . . And I
> think it became very apparent that one of the real missing ingredi-

ents was a dearth of good, energetic organizers. I mean, that was one of my most stark realizations from Houston, is that the people that the international unions had organizing—apart from the project staff that we hired directly, [who] were, you know, energetic and enthusiastic, but not particularly effective—but, Jesus, in comparison to the international unions! They had nothing! I mean, they had no resource[s], they had no people who were energetic, they had no people who were self-motivated to organize. And that was really the genesis of the Organizing Institute (personal interview 10/17/97).

The Houston Organizing Project evidently served as a foundation for the inception of the Organizing Institute, and therefore proves instructive for two reasons: The obstacles faced in Houston continued to plague the movement long after the Institute's formation, and the types of individuals recruited into the project provided a blueprint for the recruits later targeted by the Institute. As one of the project's architects recalled:

> . . . we hired a lot of project organizers, many young trade unionists and then a lot of good kinds of people that were something of a precursor to the Institute . . . in that we tried to hire people who had college educations, were articulate. . .most of them had trade union backgrounds, but not necessarily from the shop floor level (personal interview 10/17/97).

Even with the addition of the "good people" hired in Houston, the project ultimately proved disappointing, perhaps in part because a deeper problem lay beneath the surface, one in which the dearth of skilled organizers became a symptom of a larger malady rather than its cause:

> . . . the unions contributed money but they didn't bring skilled organizers there . . . the bottom line is that. . .even with those twenty organizers. . .we couldn't be without the involvement of the local structure and active participation [from locals]. And the local structure was not one that was tuned to organizing. You couldn't overcome that (personal interview 10/17/97).

The results of the Houston Organizing Project demonstrate that the labor movement faced a real dilemma during the 1980s: although reformers sensed that the key to revitalization and rejuvenation lay in the ability of unions to organize and mobilize both new and existing members by using innovative tactics and strategies, the structural mechanisms with which to achieve these goals were sorely lacking. Many local and national unions were stuck in the rut of servicing members and had no real sense of how to extract themselves (Fletcher and Hurd 1998). Many lacked the political will to do so (Fletcher and Hurd 1999). Finally, the scarcity of good organizers severely limited the ability of local unions to achieve organizing victories. All of these forces coalesced in Houston, and created an environment in which labor leaders were compelled to think about new solutions and new ways to organize. One of the results of this reflection was the Organizing Institute.

> We had this idea. There was this constant crisis of organizers . . . the labor movement didn't invest. It had no sense of mentoring or developing people, and there was no outreach into campuses or into community organizations. We were very . . . incestuous; very inward looking in some ways. So we came up with this groovy idea called the Organizing Institute. We didn't know how we were going to do it, but we were going to recruit and train organizers! (personal interview 10/30/97)

Programs and Agenda of the Organizing Institute

The AFL-CIO Organizing Institute officially came to fruition after a series of discussions between the former secretary-treasurer of the AFL-CIO, the assistant to the secretary-treasurer, the former director of organizing and field services, leaders of several affiliated unions, and Richard Bensinger, who was to head the new program. Although the exact date of the decision isn't entirely clear, the Federation and five affiliated unions agreed to fund the new entity, which was set up as an autonomous organization not under the purview of the Department of Organizing and Field Services. This decision caused a certain degree of tension inside the

Federation, primarily because some staff in organizing and field services apparently felt the Institute was unnecessary or extraneous in light of the work already carried out by the department. Although respondents did not come to a consensus regarding the factors that led to the decision to fund the Institute as a separate entity, it does seem that part of the reason was to elevate its stature, as is evident in the following remarks:

> . . . then the decision was made . . . we wanted it to be, to establish it as a separate entity. There was a need to do it, because it had a symbolic importance that established it as a freestanding institute. It showed a commitment to the process (personal interview 10/16/97).

> It gives [the Institute] a certain number one status, stature, to say that it was an independent thing and it didn't get sucked in by the bureaucracy . . .it could be more entrepreneurial and creative. . . . But the Institute was fully funded by the Federation. They agreed to separately incorporate it; they were very supportive of the idea (personal interview 10/30/97).

Once the decision was made to make the Organizing Institute an autonomous unit, a proposal was taken to the executive board of the AFL-CIO, which approved the initiative and created a matching-funds program through which the Institute would be funded by both the Federation as well as the international unions participating in the program.

Despite the conflict and debate that marked the program at its inception, the original goals of the program were very clear. Because there was no systematic way in which to train organizers and no centralized location from which to recruit them, the Institute sought to increase efficiency in both respects. Additionally, once recruits were trained by the Institute, it was then necessary to place the trainees with affiliated unions. The initial structure of the Institute, then, was formulated with the express purpose of achieving all three objectives: recruitment, training, and placement. The RTP program, as it later came to be known, operates through a five-step process: (1) potential organizers are recruited, typically on college campuses or through the efforts of local unions; (2) potential organizers apply for admittance to a three-day classroom session; (3) following admission, recruits attend three days of classroom instruction, which stresses organizing concepts and skills. (4) those evaluated highly by Institute staff are invited to participate in three-week internships with member unions in which they participate in a large-scale organizing campaign; (5) those evaluated highly by supervisors are offered six-to-twelve-week apprenticeships with a member union; upon successful completion they are often offered permanent positions as union organizers.[2]

The RTP program has been highly effective. It has expanded greatly over the years, rising from 25 initial graduates in 1989 (personal interview 10/30/97) to hundreds per year currently.[3] Problems arose, however, as many of the graduates from the Institute's program moved into organizing positions with a variety of unions across the country. Many found it difficult to utilize their skills in locals not fully committed to an organizing agenda, a problem strikingly reminiscent of the difficulties encountered by project organizers employed as part of the Houston Organizing Project. Local unions face a variety of pressures that inhibit them from committing fully to an organizing agenda. Many, for example, face conflicting demands to service existing members while increasing the level of resources (both financial as well as staff allocation) devoted to organizing, educating, and mobilizing (Fletcher and Hurd 1998). In such conditions, it is perhaps not surprising that Institute graduates—most of whom were trained to utilize innovative tactics and strategies—suffered a certain level of frustration when encountering locals that did not seem to explicitly support organizing or increased member involvement in union affairs. Two respondents explained the situation:

---

[2]It is important to note that this process operates a bit differently for rank-and-file workers who are nominated by their local unions. They also attend the three-day classroom training but then typically hone their skills within their home union rather than participating in outside campaigns as interns or apprentices.

[3]This estimate would inflate to thousands per year if Union Summer participants are considered. The Union Summer program was a three-week summer program intended to introduce a large number of college students and activists to the goals and mission of the labor movement. The program provided organizing experience to thousands of young workers, students, and activists who participated as interns on a variety of local union organizing campaigns. Although the program was not directed by the Organizing Institute, its staff was integral in training and placing the recruits.

. . . the tough thing is, people need organizing directors . . . it's critical that we place people where they'll get ongoing training . . . superstar organizers will fail if they're not developed, nurtured, and mentored . . . (personal interview, 10/30/97).

I felt that we had to get into the structure . . . get them [locals] to change their culture. To get the balance of resources towards organizing. It couldn't just be recruitment and training and placement of interns. . . . see the problem is, you just develop good organizers and they get into situations with shits for supervisors. Then you got a problem, because they're just going to die on the vine or quit, you know? (personal interview 10/16/97)

To prevent "death on the vine," Institute staff and supporters began to try to find ways to increase both the effectiveness of organizers as well as the length of time they remained in the field. To do so, Institute staff felt that it was imperative to encourage change at the local level, as is explained in the following statement:

I remember when we talked to organizers, one part we start[ed] realizing is that a lot of people say, "Well, my organizing director will not give me the money. . . ." So the more we started thinking about this, we realized that a lot of this was about not just personal commitment, but institutional commitment, right? . . . I'd say [in] '94 we created this thing called Elected Leader Task Force on Organizing of the OI. . . . Our contention was that . . . if people were developing an organizing program, you couldn't overlook this resource issue, right? So, it was bound to happen that at some point we would take this cultural thing one step further to say that the labor movement has to have a more fundamental, even radical, cultural shift . . . (personal interview 10/30/97).

In an attempt to create organizational change within local unions, the Institute—in conjunction with the larger Federation—implemented the Elected Leader Task Force on Organizing. The task force brought together leaders of several major unions, all of whom shared key characteristics. First, the unions these leaders represented were all considered organizing unions. In addition to a strong financial commitment to organizing, these unions demonstrated the best aspects of what is often termed an "organizing model" of unionism: a strong commitment to member involvement in union affairs, a willingness to utilize new strategies and tactics in organizing, and an understanding that every action taken by the union, from organizing new workers to filing grievances, can be conducted in such a way that it serves to build the union, bring in new members, and most important, develop rank-and-file leadership.[4] Additionally, the leaders recruited into the Elected Leader Task Force on Organizing utilized the Institute heavily, either to train their own members in organizing techniques or by hiring graduates of the Institute and integrating them into their organizing staff.

The task force operated initially as a clearinghouse for information, with leaders from the selected unions discussing how they had created change in their own organizations, and finding commonalties in experience, despite the very different industries in which they organized. Although the leaders did not agree on the specific strategies and tactics that were most useful in organizing, they did recognize that their collective experiences could prove instructive to the many local leaders who had little or no idea about how to transform their organizations from servicing to organizing locals. With this in mind, the task force began to offer three-day retreats to elected leaders, during which the leaders engaged in intense discussion on how to create change in local unions. The program eventually culminated in the Changing to Organize campaign sponsored by the newly created AFL-CIO Department of Organizing.[5] The purpose of these shorter programs was not only to convince a large number of local leaders of the necessity of increased organizing, but also to offer specific guidelines on how to shift resources into such a project. Although it seemed clear that changes had to be

---

[4]It is difficult to summarize the tenets of the organizing model in a brief discussion. For an overview of the model see special issue #17 of *Labor Research Review* (1991). For more recent discussions of the organizing model, including its drawbacks and limitations, see Bronfenbrenner and Juravich 1998; Fletcher and Hurd 1998.

[5]Following John Sweeney's ascension to the presidency of the AFL-CIO, the Department of Organizing and Field Services was split into two separate departments. Shortly after this action, the Organizing Institute came under the purview of the Department of Organizing and moved both their offices and staff into AFL-CIO headquarters.

made at the local level,[6] such a project was, and remains, a delicate undertaking. This is due in part to the particular structure of the AFL-CIO, which is a complex federation of labor organizations, including many autonomous national and international union affiliates. Affiliates join the Federation voluntarily, and pay per-capita dues to the organization in return for access to the services it provides. While the Federation certainly has a role in creating policy and offering resources to its affiliates, it does not have the authority to require affiliates to adhere to Federation recommendations, including recommendations regarding organizing expenditures and resource allocations. For this reason, it was a bit unexpected that the Organizing Institute and the Department of Organizing at the AFL-CIO take such a proactive stance on local union affairs. This was recognized by the architects of the plan:

. . .the [Organizing Institute] has, with the [Elected Leader] Task Force . . . pushed the envelope on . . . this sort of intrusion into the bureaucracy of various unions, and having such a major amount of resources devoted to a bread-and-butter function of an affiliate . . .[is] doing something that intruded upon the bread-and-butter of the international union (personal interview 10/16/97).

. . . that was interesting, because the Federation was normally not engaged. I remember [one union official] saying that this is the first time that affiliates really let us seriously into their business at the local level, that this was good. The reason he was interested is that he thought it really intriguing that. . . we were getting so deep inside the culture and [were] able to raise issues. And the reason we were able to do it is *we* didn't do it! . . . we immediately created a peer relationship. So instead of some AFL-CIO staff guy telling people what to do, it was [an] elected leader, speaking to leaders! (personal interview 10/30/97)

---

[6]The importance of the local union's commitment to organizing cannot be underestimated. First and most obviously, it is at the local union level that most union members—and potential members—make contact with the labor movement. Additionally, some observers estimate that up to 70 percent of the labor movement's resources are controlled at the local level (Anonymous 1996), pointing to the more pragmatic necessity of increasing local unions' commitment to organizing.

The effects of the Elected Leader Task Force on Organizing and its Changing to Organize program are, of course, still too recent to be fully known. What is clear, however, is that the Organizing Institute and the larger Federation made a significant change in the relationship between the Federation and its affiliates, creating a larger role for the Federation in local union affairs. By attempting to change the culture of local unions, the Institute forged a role for itself that was unprecedented. The repercussions of this move are still being assessed throughout both the Institute and the larger labor movement.

What has been argued thus far, then, is that the Organizing Institute has played a key role in the struggle to transform the U.S. labor movement—not only because it has provided the movement with a pool of skilled organizers, but also because its struggle to best utilize those organizers has resulted in significant changes and new initiatives throughout the wider movement. What has not yet been discussed, however, is how successful these attempts at change have been and will be in the future.

Possibilities for the Future

For the most part, labor leaders are guardedly optimistic regarding both the Institute's impact on the union movement and the movement's potential for further rejuvenation. Some leaders believe that the influx of young organizers into the movement—either in the form of students recruited from college campuses or young workers recruited from the shop floor—will spark an era of increased enthusiasm for organizing and increased commitment to improving the lives of workers. The following quotation is indicative:

> I think the short-term and long-term effect . . . of the Institute is, as its graduates move on into positions in national unions, for them to bring to those unions a different kind of spirit. It's a spirit . . . it's the culture of organizing that they bring with them . . . it gives younger people, and younger rank-and-file people a way to move up in the organization. That has to affect the long-term culture (personal interview, 9/29/97).

Another leader, when asked about the most significant changes he has seen in the labor movement during the course of his career, pinpointed the formation of the Institute as the most important change, for the following reason:

> I forget when I got involved in it, whenever [the OI] started . . .
> but that's been the most tremendous change. [It] has created a
> market for organizers . . . but also I think the early work of the Institute in placing good organizers in unions and also placing experienced organizers in the director roles. . . . I mean we never really
> talked about this, but suddenly there were . . . really aggressive organizing people on the inside of these institutions. . . . I really
> think all that helped to move the politics that resulted in
> Sweeney's win [of the presidential elections in the AFL-CIO in
> 1995](personal interview 10/17/97).

What these respondents seem to assert, then, is that organizers recruited and trained through the Organizing Institute bring with them a different culture—a culture of organizing—which has already served to shift the culture of the larger institution significantly.[7] While the long-term effect remains to be seen, these respondents seem to believe that the influence of Institute-trained organizers can only increase as does their tenure in the movement.

Other respondents, while laudatory of the Institute and its programs, are more cautious in their analysis:

---

[7]The "culture of organizing" is a term that was defined differently by the respondents. While many simply defined a culture of organizing as one that "gives credit to people who do organizing" or that "makes organizing a priority in the organization," others claimed that this culture was about more than just gaining new members or increasing the resources devoted to organizing. One respondent summarized this approach as follows:

> If the culture is solely about organizing, what are you organizing for? We think there
> has to be a linkage between process and results, so if a lot of the process is driven by
> organizing, there also have to be results, like a better standard of living. People don't
> live to organize. . . . It's about understanding that we are a grassroots organization
> and that . . . whatever we're going to work on, it needs to be driven by collective action and education and information . . . Our place is to do grassroots work . . .
> That's to me what an organizing culture is about, [but] I don't think it necessarily
> means that [to the rest of the labor movement] (personal interview, 11/19/97).

It [the Institute] may save the labor movement from premature death . . . it won't do that single-handedly . . . it's a partial answer to the puzzle. The puzzle is, how can we figure out what we need to do, and then how can we do it successfully? If we don't grow, for all of our good intentions, then we've had it (personal interview, 10/16/97).

I would like to think that the . . . Organizing Institute will have a long-term effect on the labor movement. But the reason I say it won't is that until and unless each of the affiliates understand and go through their own organization and change it, so that the order of the day is organizing rather than just servicing, nothing will change . . . (personal interview, 10/16/97).

These quotations indicate that while many within the labor movement are hopeful about the future, they recognize that the business of movement transformation is far from complete. The political climate in which unions must organize and operate is still extremely hostile, intransigence on the part of local unions remains a problem, and the Institute's method of training as well the attitudes of some of its graduates have created hostility among both members and local union staff. Finally, conflicts emerging from the Federation's increased role in union organizing and in the affairs of local unions remain both unrecognized and unresolved.

Obstacles to Transformation

One of the earliest obstacles facing the Organizing Institute revolved around criticism regarding the use of organizers recruited from outside the labor movement. Many felt that organizers recruited from college campuses, in particular, had little background in or knowledge of the labor movement, which led to problems when the organizers tried to relate to workers or lead organizing campaigns. Perhaps the most public of these criticisms came in a 1996 piece printed in *Labor Notes,* in which the author declared, " . . . unions should avoid overreliance on young staffers recruited from college campuses, given a crash-course in organizing, and parachuted into workplace campaigns" (Early 1996, 12). Campaigns led by these organizers were doomed to failure, says the author, because members weren't involved at all levels of the cam-

paign, and, in fact, were often left out of the organizing process in all
but the most superficial ways. Instead, organizers were left "frantically
handing out leaflets, ringing doorbells, and driving around with rental
cars and expense accounts 'looking for workers'"(ibid.).

Similar sentiments were found among some of the respondents interviewed:

> . . . we invest, you know, our best efforts, time, and resources in
> those communities and in people who will stay in those commu-
> nities and be sustained by the organizing work and not get burned
> out. So that's not flying around and staying in hotels and renting
> cars. It's building relationships. We also really stress in our
> organizing that organizing is about long-lasting relationships
> based on shared values. . . . Well, if you're zipping around, you're
> not going to have long-lasting relationships (personal interview
> 11/19/97).

It is important to note that this respondent probably did not intend
these comments as a critique of organizers trained by the Organizing
Institute. It is instead a criticism of a specific form of organizing, which
allocates a significant amount of money and staff resources to a campaign without attention to the intensive "bottom-up," worker-inclusive
strategies that researchers and organizers alike are finding to be successful
(Bronfenbrenner and Juravich 1998). Additionally, such campaigns—
and their strategists—are occasionally taken to task for evaluating the
success of a campaign simply in terms of the number of individuals
brought into the union. While quantitative gain is undoubtedly important, some argue that the movement should be equally concerned
with the qualitative changes created in the communities in which campaigns take place, in the individuals involved, or in the labor movement
itself. The shortsighted campaigns described above exist at all levels of
the labor movement, however, and are not specific to the graduates of
the Organizing Institute. The Institute's image, however, quickly became linked both with this type of "blitz" campaign and with organizers recruited from outside the labor movement, forcing staff to expend
considerable energy defending their program against charges that they
were "using union members' money in recruiting people from outside
the movement" (personal interview 10/30/97).

Other issues have arisen to create difficulties for the Organizing Institute as it continues to recruit, train, and place a large number of organizers with affiliated unions. Initially, the Institute hoped to place their graduates in campaigns and permanent positions that would provide the most valuable, and rewarding, training. As the demand for graduates has risen, however, the Institute has faced a great deal of pressure to increase the number of people trained and placed. The results are described below by a founder of the Organizing Institute:

> . . . the [initial] goal was to turn out good organizers, [and] to require unions that were hosting internships or apprenticeships to handle people in a particular way. . . . [It's] expanded pretty dramatically over the past few years. There were political things they had to do too, to accommodate. They have to send people to unions that they know aren't doing organizing that's worth anything. . . . I would say, frankly, given the demands of having to get more people through . . . that the quality of recruit has declined. . . . I think, honestly, since Bensinger left . . . that they've tried to undermine [leadership of the Institute] . . . [and] there's been a real attempt, I think, to control the OI and make it part of a hiring hall that the big thinkers have come up with . . . (personal interview, 10/17/97).

It seems that the Institute's success in achieving its goal to recruit, train, and place organizers has led to a new host of problems affiliated with rapid growth. First, its success has led to increased demand; so much so that the organization has allegedly weakened its standards in accepting recruits. Additionally, as the program has gained notoriety and acclaim, it has apparently come under pressure to accommodate the demands of powerful affiliates, resulting in the placement of graduates in campaigns that may hold a great deal of strategic importance but offer less to the recruits in terms of training or growth. Finally, the success of the Institute resulted in a promotion for the founding director, Richard Bensinger, who became director of the new Department of Organizing following the victory of the New Voice slate of candidates in 1995. Shortly thereafter, the Institute itself became affiliated with the new organizing department, a move that some respondents found ironic, given the initial concern that the Institute be formed outside the Federation.

In addition to criticisms leveled against the Institute and the uncertain consequences of the program's rapid growth, some observers assert that its assistance in creating a larger role for the Federation will create new conflicts, as the interests of members, local unions, internationals, and the Federation clash:

> . . . this whole question of what I would call "top-down" organizing efforts—you have to wonder exactly how that's going to play out, because, ultimately, you can't force local unions [to do what] they don't wish to do. . . . This is the big question for the Federation: What is the role of the Federation in organizing? Is the Federation going to hire organizers? And then who are they going to organize and for what union are they going to organize? . . . When you superimpose the role, the activity, of organizing on top of the labor movement, at what level does it most appropriately reside? And I wonder if that role is appropriately within the Federation's purview (personal interview 10/16/97).

Others assert even more strongly that the Federation's interest in local union affairs is inappropriate and even destructive:

> I remain deeply dedicated to the idea that the Federation is a voluntary association of affiliated unions whose individual autonomy has to be respected. I don't believe you can make the AFL-CIO one big union. . . . I think something will be lost the more and more you centralize power. . . . The more you centralize power, the less attention it's going to be possible to pay to what central power has to regard as the minutiae of membership interests (personal interview, 9/29/97).

The question of concentration and centralization of power is one with which the labor movement must seriously grapple. It is particularly important now, as some observers charge that the path to transformation is blocked by a new leadership that remains firmly encased in the shell of old bureaucratic institutions of the Federation (Brecher and Costello 1996). Although none of my respondents stated matters this strongly, some did question the relevance of the AFL-CIO and also questioned the importance of recent changes in leadership that have occurred at the Federation:

> I think that I would fight against . . . an analysis that the changes in the AFL-CIO are particularly important. . . . It's all grassroots for me, [and] every step that you go from that, you're on thinner ice. And when you get up to the level—up or down to the level— of a national labor center like the AFL-CIO, see, to me, it doesn't add that much value. . . .I think it's changed for the better, by the way, but I don't think it's anywhere near the point where it's adding more than it takes away . . . (personal interview 11/17/97).

Another respondent questioned the commitment of the labor movement both to the project of organizing new members and to the concept of grassroots democracy and empowerment, suggesting that real commitment to these ideals would undermine the bureaucratic foundations on which the labor movement currently rests:

> . . . I don't think these institutions want to change. I think there are institutional prerogatives in these unions, and they have to act in the best interest of the institutions. . . . The institutional prerogative is to make sure the institution survives, and it's been that way for so long that organizers . . . are sort of like a cancer to these institutions. They're constantly looking for ways to survive the cancer or get rid of it. . . . I also believe very strongly that the only way to change these institutions . . . is to bring in huge amounts of new members . . . especially when you are bringing in new members that have just had to go through this horrible fight. They bring a different culture to their local . . . and to the international that they join. They bring a different perspective. . . . How can this possibly be in the best interest of these huge institutions to invite this bottom-up grassroots rebellion? It just ain't gonna happen. And it won't happen with the AFL-CIO. It's not possible (personal interview, 10/17/97).

While these are certainly harsh criticisms, they point to very serious issues that underlie many of the discussions and debates surrounding the attempt to transform the labor movement: just how serious is the commitment to organizing new members? Is the attempt to rebuild the labor movement a "revolution from above," as some have maintained (Gapasin and Yates 1997)? If so, how wise was the Organizing Institute's decision to work in conjunction with the larger Federation? Finally, what can the history of the Organizing Institute tell us about the possibility of revitalization within the larger labor movement?

The answers to these questions are of vital importance, and point to many larger issues that must be resolved before the U.S. labor movement can effectively experience true revitalization. The experience of the Organizing Institute can be illustrative, since the organization's unique history points to several unresolved points of conflict that may prevent the labor movement from achieving the wide-scale transformation many believe to be necessary. As we have seen, the Organizing Institute had two related goals: (1) to create organizational change within the Federation and its affiliates by shifting organizational priorities from servicing to organizing, and (2) to rejuvenate the labor movement by increasing union density. Institute insiders strove to achieve the first goal by reforming the AFL-CIO in such a way that organizing would be exalted, and they hoped that eventually organizing would become the top priority of the entire labor movement. This would involve shifting both resources and staff toward the larger organizing project, as well as training and motivating members of the movement to accept the organizational shift. Reformers hoped to achieve the second goal by waking and mobilizing their "sleeping giant": the estimated 13 million men and women who are members of various labor organizations. In mobilizing these members it was assumed that labor would garner new power in the political and economic realms, and, more importantly, that such a shift would result in a return to the social movement "roots" of labor. This shift and return to social movement activity would then result in large-scale grassroots campaigns that would serve to bring in hundreds of thousands of new members.

The key problem, however, is that the Organizing Institute and its reformers assumed that the achievement of the first goal would automatically and naturally lead to the achievement of the second. It seems, however, that the Institute did not anticipate the particular manner in which the first goal would be attempted or achieved. In promoting its organizing agenda, the Institute forged an alliance with the Federation that served both to institutionalize the Institute and to centralize organizing functions in the labor movement. Although this alliance had some positive benefits for the Institute, the centralization attempt has created severe conflict. Because the labor movement is currently organized as a loose federation of autonomous international and local affiliates, a move toward centralization undermines strongly held beliefs about the nature of the movement itself.

To understand why this problem emerged, we must first reanalyze the process through which the Institute attempted its goal of organizational transformation. We have seen that the Institute was very effective in promoting at least part of its agenda within the larger bureaucratic organization. It recruited, trained and placed thousands of organizers within the labor movement, and also contributed to a setting in which the organizing debate and discussions of organizational change permeated the labor movement. It has run into significant opposition, however, in its attempts to implement organizational change and transformation.

In understanding why this is the case, it is perhaps helpful to turn to the literature addressing organizational behavior. This body of literature, while vast, comes to an agreement on several essential issues. The most recent accounts, for example, assert that organizational stability is more common than organizational flux, and that organizational change presents a difficult undertaking for any organizational actor attempting to implement it (DiMaggio and Powell 1991; Hannan and Freeman 1989). This is because external and environmental forces raise the cost of organizational change, making it extremely risky for organizations to alter their established mode of operation. Primary among these forces are legal and fiscal barriers to change. There are numerous cases in which political and legal decisions prevent organizations from abandoning certain activities or from branching out into new ones. Additionally, acquiring information about new environments and modes of operations is expensive. Personnel specialize in certain information channels, for example, and find it both difficult and costly to find new channels that provide superior information. Finally, organizational change is constrained by factors internal to the organization as well. These factors include the organization's existing investment in equipment and personnel, constraints on information available to organizational leaders, internal politics that resist upsetting the organizational equilibrium, and organizational histories or norms that resist fundamental change (Hannan and Freeman 1989, 67–69).

If this is the case, why would organizations ever attempt to implement change? Several factors, both internal and external to the organization, may influence this decision. Key among these are growth in the organization itself, the size and age of the organization, technological innovations, competitive pressures, shifting access to resources, and, perhaps most important, the threat of extinction (Barnett and Carroll 1995; Haveman 1992; Powell and Friedkin 1987). Greenwood and Hinings (1996) elaborate these processes further and argue that the propensity for organizational change depends on the extent to which groups within the organization are dissatisfied with how their interests are accommodated within that organization. A high measure of dissatisfaction becomes a pressure for change. To actually push for change, however, these organizational actors must recognize the connection between the prevailing organizational template and their position of relative disadvantage inside the organization. But these actors have difficulty prescribing their vision of change if it is based solely on notions of personal or group disadvantage. Instead, leaders within the disadvantaged group must be able to present the entire organization with an articulated alternative, one that appeals to a widely held normative vision of the organization. Additionally, these leaders must be adequately placed in the power or leadership structure to articulate this alternative mode of organizational behavior in arenas that matter. If any of these conditions do not exist, the possibility of successful organizational change is much lower.

On the surface, it would seem that reformers within the labor movement followed the pattern laid out above. Many of the founding leaders and staff members of the Institute were former field organizers or directors of organizing within the labor movement, and they felt continual frustration at the fact that organizing was not more widely valued and practiced within the movement. The majority of these individuals held very strong beliefs regarding the labor movement's role in society, and believed that labor should be concerned with raising the standard of living for all American workers, not just maintaining the standards of current union members. The reformers believed that organizing would provide the impetus for rejuvenation of the labor movement and were frustrated that the movement, as it existed in the mid to late 1980s, seemed more concerned with servicing existing members or exerting influence in foreign affairs. The prevailing organizational template of the labor movement at that time—servicing existing membership and maintaining the organization—was woefully inadequate in addressing the reformers' vision of labor as a movement.

The problem, however, emerged when reformers attempted to present an "articulated alternative" to the way things were run in the labor movement. On the surface, the appeals for increased organizing activity seemed relatively innocuous. In attempting to promote an organizing agenda, however, the Organizing Institute, along with its supporters in the Federation, began to delve into the affairs of local and international unions. While such attempts are certainly understandable—after all, most organizing campaigns are carried out by local and international unions—the ensuing debate engaged deeply held beliefs about the labor movement and the role of the Federation within it.[8]

To understand this better, it is perhaps helpful to briefly revisit the relationship between the Federation and local and international affiliates. Although unions affiliated with the AFL-CIO pay per-capita dues to the organization in return for services provided by the Federation, they are not required to adhere to Federation recommendations or policy initiatives. Affiliates are instead largely autonomous organizations that join the Federation voluntarily; for this reason the role of the AFL-

---

[8]This conflict has played out at least once before. Buhle (1999) documents one occasion in which a national labor leader, Walter Reuther, attempted to institute a large-scale, highly centralized organizing agenda. It failed, however, because, as Buhle comments, "the AFL-CIO could not and should not endorse a powerful 'national trade union center' whose existence and activities threatened the internationals' 'autonomy'" (Buhle 1999, 160).

CIO has historically been as a service provider to its affiliates.[9] It is evident, then, that in forming a larger role for itself—and by extension for the Federation—in organizing, the Organizing Institute challenged deeply held beliefs regarding both the autonomy of local and international affiliates, as well as about the nature of the labor movement itself. In this sense the alternative organizational template promoted by reformers became cast as a template that promoted centralization and a shift to a corporate organizational structure. This template clashed significantly with the existing structure of the labor movement.[10]

Additionally, by framing their organizational template in this way, the Institute and other reformers inside the Federation left themselves open to criticism from two opposing camps. First were those who opposed increased centralization because it would result in a loss of power and autonomy for themselves or their organizations. This camp was typically comprised of staff and leadership enmeshed in the network of local affiliates. Next were those who believed that centralization undermined union democracy and grassroots initiative. This camp included a wide variety of union activists, union members, some staff, and independent labor scholars and journalists.

The first camp, in a sense, was to be expected. Any attempt at organizational change or in a shift in organizational template results in

---

[9]This does not mean, however, that there haven't been significant battles regarding the relationship between the Federation and its affiliates. Buhle's recent work (1999), for example, examines this relationship and asserts that it has been characterized by conflict. In many cases such conflict has occurred because top Federation leadership sought to increase its own power and that of the organization, often at the expense of autonomous locals and grassroots members.

[10]Anxiety regarding the role of the Federation, its new leadership, and the proposed organizational template has been widespread. One recent example appeared in *Counterpunch* magazine, in which the authors ask, "Where is Sweeney taking labor?" and comment that the "proposed reorganization aims at giving the national AFL-CIO greater control." They capture the primary tenets of the debate:

> Proponents of the shake-up, the first in nearly half a century, argue that the task of revitalizing organized labor requires this sort of shift in power towards Washington hq, now ruled by John Sweeney, a man pledged to get labor on the move again. Adversaries fear that the plan would make it easier for Washington to crush any independent local initiatives that lay outside or threatened the strategies decreed in Washington (Cockburn and St. Clair 1999, www.counterpunch.org/sweeney.html).

resistance (Greenwood and Hinings 1996; Kotter 1995). Typically this resistance is based on personal or organizational interest. Staff or leaders of the organization are often quite invested in maintaining the existing organizational template, usually because they benefit from it financially, or simply because they are accustomed to carrying out their tasks in a certain manner. Members of an organization may prefer the existing organizational template because it requires little effort or participation from them. Fletcher and Hurd (1998) explain how this has played out in the context of the debate surrounding organizing:

> Staff representatives are experienced in servicing, and most were hired because of their negotiating skills and expertise in the grievance/arbitration process. They are proud of their work, and many oppose the shift to an approach that may leave them behind if they cannot adapt. These concerns are often mirrored in the initial response of members, who have not been expected to take responsibility and are accustomed to being serviced. The typical member is not interested in the activities of the union except at contract time and when there is a problem at work (Fletcher and Hurd 1998, 42).

Shifting to a new way of doing things involves costs for these actors, either in start-up time to learn new skills or in a downgrading of the skills they already hold. Additionally, changing labor's organizational template would require sharing power; doing so is probably not in the best interest of organizational actors who have benefited from the existing structure. This is particularly the case for leaders at local and international unions; for them there is no guarantee that a move to a more centralized labor movement will have any measurable benefit for their organizations. In fact, they may actually lose power and influence personally; a situation most organizational actors would reject under the circumstances.

Greenwood and Hinings (1996) acknowledge this problem in their discussion of organizational change by asking "under what circumstances and for what reasons do privileged groups accept radical change and diminished privilege?" (Greenwood and Hinings 1996, 1045). Unfortunately, they do not present any answers. Likewise, proponents of centralization in the labor movement have not yet articulated a solution to this problem. Most often the shift in organizational template is presented as a last-ditch effort for the labor movement to save itself. However, if the movement is saved at the expense of those currently most enmeshed within it, can they really be expected to endorse the shift in organizational frame?

Additional resistance, however, was also forthcoming from a second quarter: labor activists, grassroots organizers and proponents of increased union democracy. These actors objected that increasing centralization in the labor movement—even if it occurred in the process of promoting new organizing initiatives—would necessarily result in a loss of democracy at the grass roots. For these actors, the new organizational frame proposed by the Organizing Institute and the Federation violated their notion of labor as a movement. For them, labor is not simply a federation of connected organizations; instead, it is a movement dedicated to improving the lives of all American workers. For individuals holding such beliefs, centralization and increased power for labor leaders are diametrically opposed to grassroots empowerment and union democracy. They worry that increasing power among "labor bureaucrats" will squash the militant grassroots action necessary to create a better society and a better union movement. This is very powerfully stated in a 1996 edition of *Labor Research Review:*

> . . . the new AFL-CIO Executive Council is composed primarily of the same officials who have presided over the last two decades of the labor movement's decline. Few of them have challenged the institutional constraints imposed by labor law, union structure, bureaucratic deadwood, and organizational inertia. While some New Voice leaders have been associated with progressive or reform forces in their unions, others have fought oppositions who have advocated the very changes that New Voice now promotes. Some have silenced rank-and-file initiatives and even broken strikes of their own members. Few have projected an alternative vision for the labor movement, let alone for society (Brecher and Costello 1996, 8).

Because the Organizing Institute was so closely aligned with the Federation—particularly after the New Voice ticket's ascent to power—it became embroiled in, and perhaps a victim of, this move toward centralization. Additionally, the Institute has proven unable to present a workable alternative template to the rest of the labor movement. Its attempts to increase the Federation's role in organizing alienated both the established leadership structure of many local and international unions as well as its own constituency: the legion of grassroots organizers and dedicated activists who hoped to push the labor movement back to its social movement roots. In this sense, the Organizing Institute has been unable, so far, to successfully complete the "frame bending" Greenwood and Hinings (1996) believe is necessary for organizational change.

The preceding paragraphs have suggested that breaking out of the existing organizational frame will be difficult for two reasons: (1) actor-opponents within the existing frame will resist relinquishing their positions and privilege within the network of labor organizations, and (2) the competing frame presented by the Federation threatens labor's notion of itself as a social movement. Both factors will continue to impede labor's attempts at organizational change.

Also, any discussion of organizational transformation is not complete without a discussion of the external and environmental factors surrounding both the Organizing Institute and the labor movement more generally. Although overcoming internal opposition and conflict is undeniably important in creating movement or organizational transformation, we must not forget that external opposition is often paramount both in crushing social movements and in destroying organizations. Employer opposition and legal obstacles to organizing remain problematic, as do judiciary decisions and legislative actions that favor corporations and employers rather than labor and workers. Although the movement has begun addressing these issues, it has not yet led to any real change; for the most part these arenas remain as they have for years—fields in which labor must compete with one hand tied behind its back.

Environmental factors play a large role both in movement success and in organizational transformation; organizational competition from professional associations and employer-sponsored "workplace partnerships" continue to siphon potential members away from the labor movement, as does general disinterest on the part of many American workers. This may reflect in part the fact that labor has proven unable to adapt to an employment market characterized by temporary and contingent work, job mobility, and a shift into the service sector. While the movement has, through its Union Privilege program and other "associational" forms of unionism, made small steps toward adaptability, it has not engaged in serious reflection as to whether the current structure of the labor movement best attracts and serves the legions of American workers who remain unorganized.

All of these factors, however, cannot be adequately addressed until labor confronts its own internal conflicts. The movement must first decide on its direction and its vision, and the method in which it will achieve both. Undeniably, the process of forming the Institute and attempting to implement its goals has already contributed to notable changes. While the significance and impact of those changes may be, and should be, hotly contested, the level of debate and discussion surrounding the movement is both impressive and exciting. Where that debate carries us—as participants in, and supporters of, the labor movement—remains to be seen; what is clear is the importance of the effort. At stake is not only the future of the labor movement, but the future of millions of workers as well.

> We're challenging the labor movement, right? . . . That's what we should be doing. An assessment of the impact of all this is a whole 'nother question. It's a hard, *hard* fight. This will take many years. . . . which means we have our work cut out for us. . . . But that's what's fun! This is a heck of a transformation job. I don't think it's bigger than we can handle; maybe it is. I don't think so. But we'll find out! (personal interview 10/30/97)

CHAPTER EIGHT

Overcoming Obstacles to Transformation

Challenges on the Way to a New Unionism

Bill Fletcher, Jr., and Richard W. Hurd

The U.S. labor movement has been grappling for more than a decade with the complex question of how to generate revitalization. If nothing else, the internal debate has produced consensus that organizing must be at the forefront. The organizing priority was confirmed with the election of John Sweeney as president of the AFL-CIO in 1995, and it has been reinforced by the Federation's unceasing efforts to induce, support, and applaud organizing efforts by affiliated national unions.

The clarion call of "Changing to Organize, Organizing for Change" has been spread to all levels and corners of the labor movement. Given the critical importance of this effort, the AFL-CIO and its affiliates have been working diligently to resolve dilemmas related to implementation. Much of the attention has been devoted to shifting greater resources toward organizing. With a major share of labor's financial resources controlled at the local level, any shift in priorities must be accepted by local union leaders to have full effect. Thus, the AFL-CIO and the national unions have campaigned to persuade locals to embrace the change to organizing and to manifest support by reallocating funds.

Many of the unions most committed to the organizing priority have determined that a top-down process is the most effective mechanism of ensuring change at the local level. Some national unions have mandated a shift of local union resources and staff to support organizing, while others have restructured, forcing locals to merge or otherwise consolidating control over resources in order to facilitate the change. In some unions with decentralized structures, this revolution from above is authorized by the leader of a region, a statewide organization, or a large local with a geographic jurisdiction.

If member approval of the shift of resources is required, leaders pull out all stops to push through the decision. There seems to be a consensus that member support can be secured by appealing to self-interest, in short by arguing that organizing will increase bargaining power and allow the union to take wages out of competition. Little attention is paid to issues of representation in advance of the shift, and indeed, potential problems are ignored, masked, or downplayed. It is the organizing itself that takes priority. There is an understanding among many proponents of the change to organizing that the abrupt reallocation of resources and staff will inevitably lead to crises in representation and other local union functions. The consensus, however, is that it is best to avoid raising red flags on the assumption that organizing locals will adapt and figure out how to handle these challenges as they arise.

Of course, not all unions are as committed to the organizing priority, and not all union leaders are in a position to mandate this type of radical reorientation. At the national level beneath a rhetorical commitment to organizing, many leaders and staff assume that in their unions the shift will be deliberate rather than abrupt. Because gradual change is less threatening, many unionists see it as the most realistic way to establish the organizing priority. In spite of our conviction that the labor movement cannot afford the luxury of a slow and comfortable transition to an organizing priority, it is essential to recognize that for many locals the commitment to organizing is marginal rather than comprehensive. In those unions in which national leaders equivocate, it is difficult and risky for local leaders to embark on their own organizing crusades. Even in unions in which the national leaders are vociferous proponents of organizing, it is our impression that many local leaders are reluctant to abandon traditional approaches and embrace the new priority wholeheartedly.

As experienced by local unions, then, "Changing to Organize, Organizing for Change" presents two options. We call the first, with its predisposition to organizing at all costs, *organizational combustion*. We call the second, with its merely rhetorical acceptance that organizing is a legitimate function, *organizational evolution*. Given the choice, it is no surprise that local union leaders often prefer the latter.

The fieldwork reported in this paper provides evidence that both approaches are fraught with difficulties. Proponents of organizational evolution conveniently underestimate the potential that resistance to organizing from members, staff, and elected leaders will halt any progress, especially when the push is modest from the start. For their part, those who argue that organizational combustion will generate its own solutions deny the political base of local leaders and the possibility of counterrevolution. Creating a series of crises and picking up the pieces is akin to shoving in nitroglycerin until there is an explosion. The results will not be pretty.

We propose that attention be devoted to building a third alternative that looks strategically at the entire organization and recognizes the complexity of balancing organizing needs with representational realties. Lasting change at the local level will take place only as the result of a multilayered process. Yes, the enthusiasm of local leaders is essential, but there also must be a mass base within the membership that understands and advances the organizing priority. This will not occur spontaneously but must be cultivated by leaders with vision and supported by an educational initiative that goes beyond an appeal to self-interest. Furthermore, the reticence of staff must be respected and steps must be taken to engage them as productive contributors to the change process. We think of this uncharted alternative as *organizational transformation*.

The change to organizing requires more than a shift in resources. It is difficult to imagine a sustained commitment to organizing at the grass roots unless locals have the tools, skills, and strategic perspective necessary to mount successful organizing campaigns. Ultimately the commitment to building the labor movement inherent in the organizing priority challenges unions to alter organizational cultures that are often deeply imbued with traditional and conservative approaches to trade unionism. The struggle to succeed at organizing, to maintain representation, and to alter union culture is forcing national unions to define their role in this process and to reassess their relationships with locals. A key objective of the research reported here is to help clarify the issues at stake in the process of the change to organizing at the local level. Although there are few definitive answers, the experiences of locals struggling with the realities of juggling organizing and representational responsibilities should guide the search for sustainable conversion.

Research Methodology

Because far too little is known about the impact of the change to organizing on the life of the union at the grass roots, in 1996 the AFL-CIO Education and Organizing Departments invited national unions to send representatives to a meeting devoted to the topic. The initial discussion centered on the impact of organizing on local unions' representational functions, especially collective bargaining and contract enforcement. The group decided to meet periodically to exchange information and to sponsor field research on the topic. Over time the emphasis of the discussions and the research gradually expanded to the whole range of experiences of locals with an organizing priority, and the title "Organizational Change Working Group" was adopted. Members of the group were especially interested in lessons that could help national unions promote successful change at the local level. Sixteen national unions from diverse jurisdictions participated in the project. The authors of this paper were involved from the start, Fletcher as convener of the discussions and Hurd as research coordinator.

The field research extended prior work of the authors in cooperation with the Service Employees International Union (SEIU) during 1995–96 (see Fletcher and Hurd 1998, 1999). The common focus was on the representational practices of local unions with a commitment to external organizing. The shared methodology was site visits to the locals to gather information and conduct interviews with elected leaders, staff, and activist members. The survey instrument designed for the SEIU interviews was modified and extended based on input from the participating unions.

Members of the Organizational Change Working Group nominated thirty possible cases of which fourteen were chosen for site visits. The selected cases came from a broad range of industries and included some locals with established organizing programs and others that only recently committed to external organizing. Included were ten local unions and four multiunit collections (district, council, joint board). Membership in these fourteen "locals" ranged from one thousand to sixty thousand. Most site visits included two full days of interviews. Additional interviews with regional staff or elected leaders were conducted in four of the cases. The field research was conducted in 1997–98, with follow-up telephone interviews in 1998–99.

Analysis of the cases was informed by the SEIU project, by the authors' respective experiences working with other unions on changing to organize, and especially by feedback and discussion with the participants in the Organizational Change Working Group. Thus, the conclusions and observations we offer are based on more than the fourteen cases alone. The research we report is clearly qualitative, interpretive, and inductive. With a diversity of views represented on the working group, we started with no consensus regarding a priori hypotheses.

Social Movements and Organizational Change

Voss and Sherman (1998) have contributed a very interesting analysis of local union organizing strategy based on fieldwork conducted at about the same time as the research reported here. Their conclusions are consistent with and sympathetic to the approach we have labeled organizational combustion. They explain how local unions that have adopted innovative organizing tactics differ from other locals with less innovative programs, and explore implications for organizational change.

Voss and Sherman first review the work of social movement scholars and identify consensus on two broad conclusions: (1) tactically innovative movement organizations are almost always informally organized and (2) such movements are likely to try new disruptive tactics only when political opportunity structures are favorable (Voss and Sherman 1998, 3).

Contrary to these expectations, Voss and Sherman find that local unions with the most innovative organizing programs are formally structured and operate in environments with declining political opportunities. Unions they call "full innovators" are locals operating aggressive organizing programs that rely on a tactical repertoire, including "intensive worker organizing, corporate campaigns, strategic targeting, and obtaining union recognition without the NLRB election" (Voss and Sherman 1998, 8). Adoption of the full repertoire of innovative organizing tactics is associated with changes in the organizational structure to support organizing, including (1) creation of an organizing department, (2) recruitment of members to serve as volunteer organizers, (3) a substantial resource shift to support organizing, and (4) a reduction in services for current members (Voss and Sherman 1998, 15).

These full innovators exemplify top-down change to organizing. In each case there is a strong presence from the national union, either in the form of a trusteeship or direct support to a progressive new leader who has embraced organizing and is intent on setting a new direction for the local (Voss and Sherman, 1998, 30, 35). The overriding commonality is that organizing takes priority over all other concerns. The message is that innovation on the organizing front seeps backward into the local, and fires are put out as they arise. The problem of recalcitrant staff is dealt with by importing more militant staff from outside the local and often from outside the labor movement (Voss and Sherman, 1998, 20, 35).

Although we find their inquiry extraordinarily useful because it sets forth the rationale for organizational combustion, enigmas linger. Voss and Sherman (and other supporters of this approach) attend almost exclusively to external organizing, and as a result do not deal directly with the full range of challenges facing local unions that embark on a radical reorientation. It is difficult to see how militant innovation on the organizing front translates into building a social movement. Selections from the organizational change literature offer a constructive framework for further investigation.

We turn first to authors who concentrate their attention on situations involving radical organizational change. Their theme is that the more radical the change, the more essential it is to develop a strategic approach based on careful assessment and thorough preparation. Allaire and Firsirotu (1985) emphasize strategic analysis and goal setting regarding the organization's culture and structure. They conclude that modifying the structure without a corresponding shift in the mindset of organization members is ineffective or even counterproductive.

Nord and Tucker (1986) identify four characteristics that are required with radical organizational change: (1) those leading the effort must have sufficient internal political power to overcome opposition, (2) members of the organization must have the technical skills required to handle new duties or approaches, (3) those responsible for implementing change must have a role in deciding how to proceed, and (4) the organization must be flexible enough to adapt to challenges as they arise. The point is, as for other organizations attempting to move in a new direction, it is important for local unions to assess all aspects of current practice and to identify and address cultural, structural, and technical impediments to the change to organizing.

The literature on organizational readiness provides further guidance. As summarized by Armenakis, Harris, and Mossholder (1993), the consensus of this stream of research is that a program to create organizational readiness is a necessary precursor to a successful change effort. Three components of a comprehensive readiness program are (1) effective internal communication by leaders regarding both the need for and feasibility of change, (2) dissemination of credible external information that demonstrates the urgency to change, and (3) a program to actively involve members of the organization in preparing for and implementing change (Armenakis, Harris, and Mossholder 1993, 688–89). In unions, organizational readiness translates into building political will among members and staff to support an organizing priority (Fletcher and Hurd 1999).

A model of strategic organizational change offered by Tichy (1982) is particularly helpful. Tichy identifies three key strands of an organization's strategic rope—the technical strand, the political strand, and the cultural strand. According to the model, successful organizational change requires attention to all three strands. An organization may prepare technically for change by marshalling all of the necessary resources and acquiring relevant skills, but if the change does not fit the organization's culture or is not supported politically, the strategic rope will unravel. Similarly, cultural and political readiness for change will not be enough if the organization is not able to meet technical requirements.

Although Tichy's model makes sense on its own, we believe that it is even more telling if applied in conjunction with Poulantzas (1973).

An important contribution of Poulantzas to Marxian analysis of the class struggle is the thesis that power exists in a capitalist society along multiple dimensions. Gaining power along only one dimension is insufficient for successful revolution. In this regard he refers specifically to economic power, political power, and ideological power.

This analysis, if we apply it to a particular organization, is similar to Tichy's strategic rope. Economic power is associated with the technical strand, political power with the political strand, and ideological power with the cultural strand. Thinking about unions engaged in the change to organizing, shifting resources, hiring organizers, and developing effective organizing strategies attend only to the technical strand and economic power within the organization. No matter how effective an effort is along this dimension, organizational change may unravel because of political or cultural/ideological opposition. Similarly, a union may have all political forces lined up to support the change to organizing, but deficiencies in resources or technical organizing skills may undermine the effort; at least as likely, the change may fail because the culture of the union does not fit, or the ideology of the members and staff is inconsistent with the organizing priority. Organizational change can succeed only if all three strands of the organization are intertwined and all power bases are aligned.

We can use the Tichy/Poulantzas model to further elucidate differences among the three approaches to organizational change in local unions. In Table 8-1 each row corresponds to an organizational strand, and each column corresponds to a local union function (for simplicity we limit ourselves to organizing and representation, but it would be reasonable to add columns for political action, coalition building, etc.).

Table 8-1 Change to organizing: Local union strategic rope

| | *Local Union Functions* | |
Organizational Strands	*Representation*	*Organizing*
Technical/Economic	Skills	Skills
	Resources	Resources
Political	Parent union	Parent union
	Local leaders	Local leaders
	Members	Members
Cultural/Ideological	Servicing model	Self-interest
	vs.	vs.
	organizing model	Social movement

If we look exclusively at the representation column, for the technical/economic strand to be strong, staff and activist members need to have the skills necessary to protect members on the job and to bargain good contracts, and the local needs sufficient resources to maintain representational quality. For the political strand to be strong, the representational priorities of the parent union, elected local leaders, and members need to be aligned. For the cultural/ideological strand to be strong, there must be consensus regarding representational style; in particular, a comfortable mix of reliance on staff and members with expertise (the servicing model) and member mobilization (the organizing model) needs to be worked out. If all three of these strands are strong, then the local's representational strategic rope will be strong.

If we look exclusively at the organizing column, for the technical/economic strand to be strong, staff and member organizers need to have the skills necessary to pursue an effective organizing program, and the local needs sufficient resources to support the effort. For the political strand to be strong, the level of support for organizing from the parent union, elected local leaders, and members needs to be consistent. For the cultural/ideological strand to be strong, consensus must exist regarding the rationale for organizing: Is the organizing effort targeted at increasing bargaining power to benefit current members, or is the objective to reach out a helping hand to unrepresented workers and build the labor movement? In this regard, attention needs to be given to the cultural match between the experiences of workers being organized and life inside the local. This is a particular concern when the organizing targets are not a demographic match for the current membership (Fletcher and Hurd, 2000). Where all three strands are strong, the local's organizing strategic rope will be strong.

It is a special challenge to move to the next level and weave together all of the representational strands and organizing strands to make a powerful strategic rope for the local's overall program. This is particularly difficult because organizing and representation compete for resources and because representational skills are not directly transferable to organizing. It is here that the three approaches to the change to organizing diverge. The organizational evolution approach concentrates on keeping the representational rope strong and tolerates weak strands in the organizing rope. The organizational combustion approach concentrates on strengthening the organizing rope and tolerates unraveling of the representational rope, even running the risk that it will catch fire. The idea behind the organizational transformation approach is to strategically balance representation and organizing so that all strands are strong, although this is a difficult objective to achieve.

Obstacles to Change

The key obstacle to organizational change is the absence of careful evaluation, prioritization, and planning in most locals.[1] Every local we visited had been forced to innovate in order to pursue an organizing agenda while continuing to provide representational assistance to its members. In some cases the innovations were pursued systematically, but more often they evolved from practice as leaders, staff, and activists struggled to respond to crises associated with the change process. In most locals the change was the organizing itself. Resources were shifted, staff were added or reassigned, members were recruited as volunteer organizers, and some effort was initiated to win member support.

Interestingly, in a few cases the shift into organizing was introduced by a newly elected local officer whose ascendance was fueled by poor or inconsistent servicing under the old regime. This leader's first priority was to upgrade representational work, but this was accomplished in the traditional insurance agent mode. The leader bought into the changing-to-organize trend but to some degree as an afterthought. Ultimately, these new leaders encountered the same problems as established leaders who decided to pursue organizing without altering representational practices simultaneously.

The picture that emerged from the cases included in this project was that there is no simple set of specific programs that can be prescribed for locals who want to simultaneously represent members and free resources for organizing. The best practices summarized in the follow-

---

[1] In deference to the willingness of the officers, members, and staff of the unions we studied to share both successes and failures with us, we refrain from identifying specific locals in our discussion of obstacles to change. At any rate, this section covers more than the fourteen cases we studied, as explained in the methodology section.

ing section offer some clues about how various aspects of the challenge may be addressed, but there is no easy formula for success. The experience is more consistent regarding the difficulties locals encounter as they go through organizational change.

Leaders

Two basic barriers to change emanate from local leaders themselves: political concerns and lack of managerial skills. Because local unions are democratic institutions, local leaders must attend to internal politics or face removal from office. In this situation it is not surprising that a leader's commitment to organizing and organizational change may falter if there is a legitimate political threat in the form of a respected officer or staff member committed to traditional servicing, or if there is vocal opposition to organizing from key members. The temptation to pull back will be particularly intense for those leaders whose original support for organizing is based on aspirations for higher office rather than commitment to building the labor movement. Even if the leader's belief in the value of external organizing is strong, political concerns may interfere with a willingness to promote internal organizing and the development of effective rank-and-file leaders. The current leader may be afraid of losing control of the local. Unfortunately, entrenched leaders may surround themselves with dedicated assistants who go overboard and in effect engage in cult building rather than movement building. In all of these situations the net result of political concerns is that the substance does not match the form of organizational change.

The second barrier to change for local leaders is a lack of managerial skills. Most local leaders manage based on instinct and personal style. Because organizing requires resources, effective financial management can be very important and yet most local leaders have neither the interest nor the training to attend to financial matters. Leaders also manage staff without appreciation for basic principles of human resource management, with styles varying from authoritarian to complete delegation of decisions. Of course, these gaps in management expertise are not unique to locals that are changing to organize, but managerial weaknesses tend to be magnified during periods of change. On the flipside, good local managers may be ill equipped to deal with organizational change because the experience is new to them, their staff, and the members. There is a tendency for many local leaders simply to announce or even mandate change, an approach that invites a back-lash and the assumption of failure among those staff and members who do not personally support the new direction.

Staff

There is widespread resistance from representation staff. In some cases this bubbles just beneath the surface, especially when there is a potential political challenge to the current leader that may ultimately reverse the local's course. In some cases the opposition is open, especially when staff members are unionized and therefore have a forum that allows them to resist (in the cases studied this was evidenced only among regional representation staff). Most common, however, is a sort of passive resistance. Representation staff accept and even support the shift to organizing but are concerned that the quality of representational efforts on behalf of current members is suffering as a result. In most organizing locals, representation staff are assigned a heavier load (which they naturally view as a speedup), and in many cases they feel that the attention to organizing diminishes their importance. Some staff are quietly skeptical and support organizing only because they feel that they have little choice.

There also are problems with organizing staff. The most common difficulty encountered is the assignment of staff to organizing who do not have the requisite skills. Staff with experience in servicing may be reassigned to organizing, or rank-and-file activists with little or no organizing experience may be hired as organizers. Often political supporters of the local leader who are chronological contemporaries are assigned to organizing without attention to the demographics of potential organizing targets. The net result is a local staff of organizers with little background in organizing strategy, tactics, or campaign management.

Some locals do hire organizers from the outside, many of whom are younger than other staff and often have limited union experience beyond organizing. Although the locals that follow this practice seem to have greater success in organizing, other problems may arise. The most common is a separation between organizing and representation staff. Usually they simply do not interact, but in some cases representation staff are peeved about organizers ignoring protocol when, for instance, they visit units unannounced to recruit volunteers. Similarly, when thrust together during initial contract negotiations, organizers prefer activist tactics and are frustrated by representatives who want to keep things calm while they try to work out differences at the table. The most extreme criticism representation staff have about organizers is that they do not care about current members, and this is given some credence by the interview responses of a few organizers who displayed a cynical attitude about the apathy in established units and the conservatism of representation staff.

Another difficulty applies to both homegrown and imported organizers. With the rapid increase in demand for experienced organizers, the best local union organizers all too often leave to pursue other opportunities at higher levels of the labor movement, most often within their own national union. Whether these are viewed as promotions or raids, the result is that local unions have a hard time maintaining momentum on the organizing front.

One final observation about staff. When a local union changes to organizing, this almost always means increased pressure on representation staff both because they are expected to accept a greater servicing responsibility and because they are often called upon to help with organizing. For their part, organizers are driven to work long hours and to be available nights and weekends because there is a sense of urgency about the challenge at hand. The organizing values most commonly voiced are justice, dignity, and fair treatment, but it is troubling that these values are seldom operationalized in the treatment of staff in local unions with a strong organizing agenda.

Members

Even in locals with reputations for organizing success, most members are unaware and unconcerned. Acceptance of and tolerance for their union's organizing program is not based on deep support. In most cases, leaders tell us that their members will go along with organizing so long as "telephone calls are returned," in other words, on the condition that traditional servicing is maintained. But active members who serve as stewards sometimes become jealous of their union's focus on organizing, especially if their own contributions to representation are not publicly recognized. They are particularly frustrated when they can't reach their representative when they need assistance. Similarly, members react negatively when shop floor leaders are pulled out too often to work as volunteers on organizing campaigns.

Members, especially activists, are more supportive of organizing when they feel a clear connection to the workers being organized. Thus, it is easier for a local to win support if it is organizing unrepresented units of the same employer at a nearby location in contrast to workers in another industry or a distant city. In short, members are more positive about organizing if they perceive that it will benefit them personally. Unfortunately, locals that have won internal support for organizing based on the premise that bargaining power would increase have begun to experience a backlash from members impatient for a payoff. There have been related problems in construction unions in which some members have turned on new recruits from the nonunion sector who are rated as journeyman who have not completed the union's apprenticeship program. Long-term members are concerned that instead of enhancing power, organizing may be degrading the craft.

The source of member resistance to organizing is attributed by local leaders to a lack of appreciation for unions and union values. It is difficult to achieve participation of members in any activity not directly related to their own situation. Thus, members may get excited about a grievance and often rally in support of contract negotiations, but they are reluctant to get involved in other union activities one step removed. When locals attempt to get members to participate in political action, coalition building, supporting other struggles, or organizing, they often end up relying on the same small core of activists. Members feel little connection to labor as a movement.

Structure

Except for construction locals that operate from a much larger dues base, the smaller locals in this project (those under 5,000) had an extremely steep challenge simply funding an organizing program. With the majority of local unions even smaller than the smallest considered here, it is clear that national unions will have to provide financial subsidies if they expect locals to pursue an organizing agenda. Money alone will not solve the problems faced by organizing locals, but without significant resources, local unions cannot even consider changing to organize.

There is a caveat here. When the national union funds organizing, it typically exercises control over organizers. This can exacerbate some of the staff difficulties delineated above and increase separation between representation staff and organizers. Furthermore, the instability created in local organizing programs may intensify if the national union shifts organizers around from campaign to campaign.

There are nonfinancial structural impediments to organizing as well. The local programs with the least focus and the most problems are those carried on in isolation. Local unions are ill equipped to pursue a strong organizing agenda without support from regional and national staff and leaders. In those cases in which the regional union office is indifferent to organizing and those in which substantive national commitment is lacking, local unions founder. Locals typically lack the expertise to organize effectively and find it difficult to maintain political will without higher-level leaders openly voicing encouragement.

Local Union Best Practices

Before turning to a description of local union innovations, it is important to point out that there are surprisingly few to report. In fact, a description of what these and other organizing locals have *not* done is necessary to set the stage for consideration of the accomplishments.

Few locals have initiated any substantive changes in how they handle grievances and arbitrations. In most cases staff are heavily involved from step 2 onward, often with the assistance of a chief steward or the equivalent. Innovations that have been initiated typically have resulted because a staff member wanted to improve representational efficiency, but they occurred without consideration for organizing or organizational change. Several locals have talked about getting stewards to handle steps 2 and 3, some have made tentative efforts in this direction, and in one case it was mandated. But the results have been modest to date.

Bargaining is also handled in traditional ways. In some cases members' input is solicited, but this is usually informal or only at a special local meeting for this purpose. Most often a small bargaining team is selected to assist the staff member in charge of negotiations. Although some locals regularly develop mobilization networks to support bargaining, most mobilize members only if a crisis is brewing at the table. Other than release time for union business, there are few innovations in contracts that contribute to organizing. Labor-management committees are common but usually are proposed by management and are seldom viewed as sources of leverage by the union.

The story is similar with coalitions and political action. Although several locals have active political programs, they either are quite traditional or focus narrowly on issues directly related to the members' craft or industry. A couple of locals pursue coalitions systematically as part of a movement-building philosophy, but participation by members is infrequent. More often coalitions either are sought sporadically to increase bargaining power in crisis situations or are part of a community services tradition.

The remainder of this section offers "best practices" of the locals we visited in matters of representation and changing to organize. These practices are not presented as part of a recipe for success but as possible approaches for unions that are implementing change. As such they will need to be adapted to specific conditions faced by individual locals.

Grievances

Although the locals participating in this project have not experimented extensively with their grievance- handling process, there are a few best practices that warrant attention. Perhaps the most important innovation was negotiated by American Federation of State, County, and Municipal Employees (AFSCME) Council 31 which covers all of their Illinois state government units. On the surface one step was removed from a five-step grievance procedure, but more was involved. Council 31 leaders have been looking for ways to free staff time from grievance work. The long-term goal is to phase staff out of the grievance process except as trainers and advisers. Under the old contract there were three steps in the unit with the third step handled by the staff representative and a hearing officer from the state. Few grievances were settled before the third step, and about half were appealed to the fourth step in Springfield (the state capital). Under the new contract the third step has been eliminated with the intention of increasing the importance of the first two steps, the only ones at the unit level.

To reinforce the effort to push decisions down to lower levels, Council 31 has developed a training program for the new grievance process. All staff representing state units have been trained in the delivery of the half-day program and are expected to offer training to stewards in all units. The training goes beyond administrative details and emphasizes that "we want to make the grievance procedure work at the unit level." In fact, almost half of the training is devoted to problem analysis and alternatives to the grievance. In other words, the union has used the new procedure to build responsibility at the grass roots and to redefine the staff role as training rather than grievance handling. The preliminary results have been positive: about half of all grievances are resolved at step two (approximately equal to the results at step three of the old process).

Another innovation worthy of attention is the systematic computerized approach of American Federation of Government Employees (AFGE) Local 987 in Warner Robins, GA. Because it represents federal employees, Local 987 not only pursues grievances under its collective bargaining agreement but also represents members who file complaints under federal personnel rules. Furthermore, filing Unfair Labor Practices (ULP) under the Federal Labor Relations Act is another tool that must be utilized regularly given the limited scope of bargaining in the federal sector. To handle the complexity of this broad grievance arena, Local 987 subscribes to several databases and maintains computer archives for all of its own grievances, personnel cases, and ULPs. Stewards are trained by a staff representative in the local's filing system which is meticulously indexed, and they regularly stop by the local office to use a computer station set up specifically to assist their work. Staff specialization in the different sets of regulations reinforces the effectiveness of the local's representation work.

A third innovation in grievance handling has been negotiated by Communications Workers of America (CWA) Local 7777 in their contracts with units of USWest. For discipline and discharge cases various forms of alternative dispute resolution have replaced or augmented the standard grievance and arbitration process. From the perspective of Local 7777 the most effective approach has been the use of advisory bench arbitration. This expedited process has resulted in more prompt resolution of discipline and discharge cases and simultaneously reduced staff time devoted to grievances.

Bargaining

AFSCME District 1199C represents workers at over 150 hospitals and other healthcare facilities in the Philadelphia area. The local has a policy of seeking common expiration dates for all of its contracts, and it has achieved this objective in most cases. When the contract expiration approaches, staff representatives for each facility work on individual contracts while the local president floats from one negotiating table to another. In the final days all bargaining is moved to a central location, usually a downtown hotel. This process has two distinct advantages: First, it allows 1199C to establish a pattern by getting its best deal then applying the pattern to all employers participating in the master negotiations. Second, it affords the opportunity to mobilize all units simultaneously in support of bargaining, culminating in a mass rally as the deadline approaches.

Several other locals also regularly incorporate mobilization into their bargaining strategy. CWA Locals 4309 in Cleveland and 7777 in Denver have standing mobilization structures that are rejuvenated at each major contract negotiation. Local 4309 recruits one mobilizer for each group of twenty members. The key role of mobilizers is to organize workplace actions, signs of solidarity, and rallies in support of the local's bargaining demands. During multilocal negotiations with employers like Ameritech, the CWA District 4 office coordinates mobilization across units to ensure maximum impact. The Local 7777 mobilization structure is permanent and viewed as a two-way communication network between leaders and members. Although active on occasion during the life of the contract when issues affecting the entire unit arise, the mobilization structure goes into full gear during negotiations.

Contract campaigns are not new to the Union of Needletrades, Industrial and Textile Employees (UNITE) nationally, but during 1997 negotiations at two factories in the Tennessee-Kentucky District, mobilization penetrated down to the shop floor. District staff delivered a training program for the leaders and stewards in both locals. Contract committees surveyed members on negotiating priorities, organized members for action, and staged rallies. The district is extending the training to other units in the hopes of revitalizing dormant locals.

In terms of how bargaining is handled, the most notable innovations have been implemented in response to the difficult challenge posed by first contract negotiations. The New York City–based Office and Professional Employees International Union (OPEIU) Local 153's organizing program has added a number of new units over the past several years. To handle the special demands of first contract bargaining, an effective negotiator on staff has been assigned to specialize in first contracts. Similarly, in UNITE's Southern Region only the most experienced negotiators handle first contracts "because it's a war."

Based on the cases reviewed in this project, there seems to be a consensus emerging that organizers should stay on to assist during first contract negotiations at least during a transition period. In AFSCME Council 31 the organizer works with the staff representative to set up a bargaining team and stays through the early stages of negotiations; if there is a fight, the organizer continues to work with the members of the unit to maintain commitment and build activism.

UNITE's New England Joint Board goes one step further. After each of eight election wins over the past five years, the Joint Board has kept the organizer working with new members to conduct a contract campaign in support of bargaining. The organizer works closely with an experienced negotiator to ensure that workplace and public actions are timed appropriately based on developments at the table. This approach has produced contracts for every organizing victory.

CWA's District 4 (Ohio) also has adopted a systematic approach to first contract negotiations. After concluding that it is hard to use a standard contract for initial bargaining because the employer is almost always unwilling, the district devised a standard strategy. A time line was developed to guide staff assigned to negotiate first contracts. A key feature of the time line was the expectation that the organizing committee would be converted to a mobilization committee. The time line essentially required that both the negotiator and the mobilization committee develop and follow a plan that coordinates bargaining and action.

Bargaining to Organize

AFSCME Council 31 has negotiated voluntary recognition for units outside their current membership with some of the large public-sector employers. These agreements have facilitated organizing with what is essentially a card check process. There is also an equal time agreement with one private-sector employer that essentially would allow the union to respond to a captive audience speech, but this arrangement has not yet been tested. Several other unions have reported a range of neutrality provisions, but the consensus is that they do not work well.

What does work is release time. Most of the local unions visited have some allowance for time off for union work (usually unpaid). Although union time is most frequently used for representation work, a few locals have taken advantage of the practice to support organizing. CWA Local 7777's organizing program is coordinated by a full-time organizing director hired from outside the union, but it is staffed by an eight-member organizing committee. All eight members take advantage of the release time provision and are paid by the local for time lost; four members work full time at organizing and four work part time.

UNITE's New England Joint Board has built an extensive volunteer organizers program over the past four years. When initial assessment of an organizing target is positive, a weekend blitz is scheduled. The blitz is staffed by forty to sixty members who take Friday off from work under release time provisions then donate personal time on the weekend. Friday is used for training and coordinating assignments, with the blitz of home visits held Friday night, Saturday, and Sunday. The blitz allows the union to determine whether to file for an election and is viewed as essential to the Joint Board's organizing success. This approach has had a spillover benefit, as participants return to the shop floor with greater appreciation for the union and become more active rank-and-file leaders. At the 1997 regional meeting 80 percent of the delegates had worked as volunteer organizers. To support the program, the Joint Board makes release time a bargaining priority, and it has secured appropriate language in nearly 90 percent of contracts.

Construction locals of the International Brotherhood of Electrical Workers (IBEW) have found another way to use the bargaining relationship with employers to support organizing. IBEW Locals 611 in Albuquerque and 613 in Atlanta have secured the cooperation of union contractors for their campaigns to organize the nonunion sector. A key organizing tactic is to identify and "strip" the most skilled electricians from nonunion sites. After passing an exam designed to assess their skill level, the electricians are rated "intermediate journeyman" and participating contractors place them on union jobs. Contractors also cooperate by allowing the locals to delay responding to a work request in order to keep a salt on a nonunion project and occasionally will allow an electrician to leave a job temporarily to serve as a salt.

Shifting Resources

To fund an organizing program, locals need to free resources. This is facilitated in some instances by growth, as has been the case at AFSCME Council 31. More often, resources need to be shifted from other functions. CWA Local 4309 lost a longtime secretary who accepted a position with the Cleveland Central Labor Council. The local decided to seize the opportunity to expand its organizing efforts. The members voted to replace the half-time paid job with an organizer's position. A successful volunteer organizer from the ranks was hired to work with the District Organizing Director to identify targets and develop an organizing plan.

The most common method used to shift resources into organizing is to reassign staff. Bakery, Confectionery, and Tobacco Workers (BCTW) Local 26 (Colorado) and OPEIU Local 153 both assigned staff to organizing with the open understanding that the servicing load of representation staff would have to increase as a result. AFSCME District 1199C adopted a policy several years ago requiring representation staff (referred to as administrative organizers) to spend 40 percent of their time on organizing. This was increased to 60 percent in 1997.

IBEW Local 177 in Jacksonville, Florida, determined that it needed to win member support to increase resources for organizing. After putting 75 percent of its members through COMET (Construction Organizing Membership Education Training), the president proposed an increase in the local's assessment from 2 percent of pay to 5 percent with the entire increase earmarked for organizing. After members approved the increase, the six-hundred-member local was able to hire three full-time organizers and with organizing success the local has grown to eleven hundred members.

Building Member Support

AFGE Local 987 has used monetary incentives to convince members to support organizing. Because the local operates in the federal sector's open shop environment, the targets for organizing are the coworkers of the members. After joining, a worker must retain membership for at least a year; most stay beyond that. To win member approval for organizing, the local president demonstrated that the local would come out ahead financially even if it spent $50 for each new member. To make the proposal even more appealing, the local offered to pay its members the $50 for each new recruit. The end result was a membership increase of 30 percent over five years.

IBEW's District 5 (Southern states) also won member support for organizing by appealing to self-interest, albeit indirectly. With the help of COMET and MEMO (Membership Education for Mobilization and Organizing), participating locals have convinced members that the only way to increase bargaining power is to take wages out of competition by increasing market share. And to increase market share, traditional top-down organizing must be supplemented by bottom-up organizing. As noted above in reference to Local 177, this message has won support for organizing and in some cases even convinced members to increase dues to pay for it.

UNITE's Southern Region holds an annual summer school for sixty rank-and-file activists. For one intense week these activists live and breathe union values and learn union-building skills. Similarly, at the region's conference, five hundred members celebrate struggle, participate in demonstrations, and attend workshops on organizing and mobilization. The message of the summer school and the conference is that UNITE is an organizing union because it is fighting for justice. Participants take this message back to their locals and the members clearly understand the priorities.

Education and Administration

In some cases educational programs are used primarily to build support for a union's organizing initiative, such as those just mentioned. Similarly, BCTW Local 26 has used an annual education conference to build awareness of and support for organizing and the organizing model among stewards and other unit leaders. But in one case education is an essential everyday ingredient in the union's overall operation. AFSCME District 1199C has secured employer financing for its Training and Upgrading Fund and has supplemented this with external grants.

The District 1199C training program has an annual budget of approximately $4 million. The district considers education and training as important as collective bargaining. The fund serves union members and the public. It offers credit and noncredit classes on union leadership, public speaking, literacy, algebra, and computers. It runs a nurse's aide training program. It administers a job security fund for members who lose their jobs due to restructuring which offers retraining and job search assistance. It operates a hiring hall for laid-off members and training program graduates. And it administers a tuition reimbursement program for members enrolled in college classes.

The 1199C Training and Upgrading Fund demonstrates the potential for unions to operate large-scale programs with huge budgets. On a smaller scale, AFGE Local 987 administers its own operation very efficiently. When a new set of officers was elected in 1992, the local was determined to make changes to operate on a more secure financial footing and to deliver representational services more effectively. A clerical assistant was replaced with a bookkeeper, the local purchased a new union hall and paid for it in four years, and net assets nearly tripled, in part because membership increased by one-third. This was accomplished with financial planning and careful budget management. Similarly, the staff was reorganized and given specialized assignments that improved the quality of representation. This experience demonstrates that locals can operate in a more businesslike manner and simultaneously enhance union strength and effectiveness.

IBEW Local 177 has applied efficient operational techniques to its organizing program. Since 1991 the local has annually updated a strategic organizing plan. Each staff member is required to set goals with action steps annually; these are updated several times a year and reviewed with the local president. This strategic planning and goal-setting process has increased accountability and enhanced the local's organizing success.

Structure

In UNITE, the national union funds all organizing programs. The programs are implemented at the Joint Board level by the Manager, an Organizing Director, and organizing staff and volunteers. The New England Joint Board, then, has its own organizing programs but also participates in national campaigns. The organizing staff, including the Joint Board's Organizing Director and three organizers, report both to the Manager and the national Organizing Director. Although this dual reporting situation adds some complexity to both planning and conducting campaigns, it works because the Manager and the national Organizing Director communicate and coordinate effectively.

In the IBEW, locals are responsible for organizing in their geographic and industry jurisdiction. District 5 supports organizing by providing COMET and MEMO training and by convening retreats for local business managers to develop districtwide strategic organizing plans. Two of the district's ten staff members are assigned full time to organizing. Their role is to work with individual locals on their own organizing plans, to mentor local organizers, and to coordinate organizing across locals.

In CWA District 4 the Organizing Director has set up an Organizing Network which now includes 46 of the district's 201 locals. The network sponsors organizer apprenticeships, an annual educational retreat for local organizers, and a periodic newsletter. Successful volunteer organizers may be sent to an Organizing Institute three-day program or sometimes to a week of training at the George Meany Center. Because most CWA locals are small, the Organizing Network is essential for promoting and supporting local organizing initiatives.

Best or Second Best?

The best practices we have described are positive examples of local union innovation, but taken as a whole they are hardly revolutionary. Because they are seldom conceived as part of a systematic effort to promote permanent organizational change, they may be more appropriately considered second-best solutions to difficult problems. Based on these cases we are struck by how difficult it is for local unions to develop alternative approaches to representation and to manage the shift to an organizing priority in isolation.

Conclusions

The organizational change literature helps us interpret the experiences of local unions attempting to operationalize the organizing priority. It is clear that even under the best of circumstances local unions will confront barriers to such radical change. The challenge is to overcome these obstacles in order to lay the foundation for sustainable growth. At a rudimentary level this involves attention to technical requirements so that representational effectiveness can be maintained while the capacity to organize successfully is developed. As a corollary, sufficient economic resources are needed for both representation and organizing. Even as these basic needs are being met, local leaders must attend to political demands (which come from both above and below) so that the organizing priority can be retained for the long term. Also required are awareness and effective handling of the inevitable cultural transformation in order to sustain organizing momentum. It is essential to recall that in most local unions the organizing activity itself amounts to cultural change; success brings in new members and elevates this change to another level. It is impossible to imagine that this kind of upheaval can be sustained without ideological acceptance from all corners of the organization.

The challenge is complex. Earlier we identified three distinct interpretations of changing to organize: organizational evolution, organizational combustion, and organizational transformation. It is clear to us now that (rhetoric notwithstanding) the organizational evolution approach is common at the local union level. It is also clear that in locals that attempt merely to evolve, traditional representation prevails, organizing efforts are token, and backsliding is common. The obstacles to change are too substantial for this approach to achieve more than minimal results.

In those locals that have experienced the most notable change, the organizational combustion approach seems to be providing a substantial jolt. Shifting resources does force some creativity in representation, and in many settings progress on the organizing front is evident. However, representational innovations are spotty and invite skepticism and a political backlash from existing members. In short, obstacles to change are undermining these efforts, and the political and ideological separation between the organizing priority and the internal life of these locals is troubling. The pressure to retrench is widespread.

We conclude that the organizational transformation approach offers the most hope for lasting change. Local unions need comprehensive programs that attend to all aspects of the organization. Durable transformation presumes technical efficiency, resource reallocation, political will, and cultural change. These dimensions cannot all be addressed successfully without strategic analysis and enlightened leadership. Control over resources and the power to shift resources in support of the organizing priority is indeed important; however, they alone are not sufficient to ensure that other aspects of a union's operation will fall into line. We argue that political and ideological opposition to change should be attacked simultaneously with the resource shift in order to consolidate the momentum for transforming unions.

We are concerned that the change to organizing is too complex for local unions to tackle on their own. National unions cannot promote changing to organize and ask locals to shift resources only to leave the locals to fend for themselves. It is likely that except for large financially secure locals some type of budgetary support will be needed from the national, especially in the early stages. At least as important, local leaders and staff need training in strategic planning and organizing, and they would benefit from access to information on innovative approaches to representation.

Perhaps the most important question is, how can locals build political will among members to embrace organizing as movement building? Education can win support for organizing, but for long-term commitment a movement orientation is required. National unions need to work with locals on building activism, and they can support these efforts with carefully conceived educational initiatives that challenge members to reconsider their worldview and embrace union values. Failure to address ideological issues openly could undermine the potential to achieve the organizational transformation needed to rebuild the labor movement.

In short, there are three mutually reinforcing ingredients that must be present for the change to organizing at the local level to be self-sustaining:

1. Sufficient resources to support new organizing without compromising representational effectiveness;
2. Strategic planning to prepare the local technically, to identify internal barriers, and to address staff deficiencies and reticence; and

3. Member education and mobilization to build political will and prepare the local for cultural change and ideological reorientation.

This set of requisites is consistent with the organizational change literature. The concept of organizational readiness and the lessons drawn from organizations undergoing radical change seem to apply directly to the union experience. Especially relevant is the reminder from Tichy that failure to address technical, political, and cultural challenges simultaneously could undermine the entire effort to transform a local union. Add to this Poulantzas' insight that in a capitalist society power exists along many dimensions and that no revolution can succeed without victory on all fronts, and we can see why a comprehensive effort at organizational transformation is essential. If there is one thing that stands out based on our field research, it is that there are no easy answers, nor any blueprints. The process of developing twenty-first- century trade unionism is a work in progress, and all progressive-minded trade unionists can and must have a role.

Appendix

AFL-CIO Education Department Representation Project Case List

AFGE Local 987, Warner Robbins, GA

AFSCME Council 31, Chicago, IL

AFSCME District 1199C, Philadelphia, PA

BCTW Local 26, Denver, CO

CWA Local 4309, Cleveland, OH

CWA Local 7777, Denver, CO

IBEW Local 611, Albuquerque, NM

IBEW District 5, Birmingham, AL

   Locals 108, 824, Tampa, FL

   Local 177, Jacksonville, FL

   Local 613, Atlanta, GA

OPEIU Local 153, New York, NY

UNITE New England Joint Board, North Dartmouth, MA

UNITE Southern Region, Atlanta, GA

   Tennessee-Kentucky District, Knoxville, TN

PART III

New Strategic and Institutional Orientations

The Evolution of Strategic and Coordinated Bargaining Campaigns in the 1990s

The Steelworkers' Experience

Kate Bronfenbrenner and Tom Juravich

W ith the refocusing of attention of the labor movement on organizing, an increasing number of scholars have been directing
their research toward the nature and practice of current union organizing efforts (Bronfenbrenner, et al. 1998; *Labor Studies Journal* 1999).
These scholars have begun updating a literature that had grown sorely
out of touch with the organizing experience of America's unions and
have provided the foundation for a more sophisticated understanding
of the organizing process.

While we applaud this resurgence in organizing research, there has
not been a comparable resurgence in research on collective bargaining.
Yet the tremendous growth of contract campaigns, or what alternatively have been called coordinated or strategic campaigns, has been
no less significant than the revolution in union organizing. Beginning
with the early efforts of the Oil, Chemical, and Atomic Workers
(OCAW) at BASF and of the United Mineworkers at Pittston Coal to
more recent campaigns such as the Teamsters at United Parcel Service
and the Hotel and Restaurant Employees (HERE) at the Frontier
Hotel, the labor movement has used these campaigns with increasing
success. Although organizing is important for the revival of American
labor, strategic and coordinated contract campaigns are equally essential to labor's effort to rebuild and revitalize the movement. Without
these campaigns, unions will continue to lose as many new workers as

they gain, and newly organized workers will never be able to achieve contractual guarantees for the rights and protections for which they risked so much in the organizing process.

Collective bargaining and contract campaigns matter because they are the focal point for the power and voice that workers can achieve only through unionization. Collective-bargaining campaigns are also the forum in which unions and union members most connect with customers, clients, and the broader public. When successful, these campaigns result in a significant expansion of union organizing opportunities, bargaining leverage, political clout, and a concomitant shift of public support toward unions. When they fail, as the labor movement learned so painfully with the Professional Association of Air Traffic Controllers (PATCO), they undermine labor's efforts for years to come.

Much of the recent collective-bargaining research, however, still clings to an older industrial relations model that focuses either on large industry analyses (Voos 1994), economic cost benefit analysis (Kaufman 1992; Card 1990), behavioral models of bargaining (Walton and McKersie 1991; Wheeler 1985), or strategic-choice models (Kochan, Katz, McKersie 1994; Walton, Cutcher-Gershenfeld, McKersie 1994). There has been an increase in union training materials on contract and strategic campaigns (AFA 1997; AFL-CIO 1985b; SEIU 1988; Rogers 1994) as well as a smaller literature critical of the use of these campaigns by the labor movement (Northrup 1996; DiLorenzo 1996). However, aside from Getman's work on the United Paperworkers International Union (UPIU) strike at International Paper (1998), Rosenblum's book on Phelps Dodge (1995), and our book on the Steelworkers' campaign at Ravenswood Aluminum Corporation (Juravich and Bronfenbrenner 1999), there have been few detailed analytic studies of corporate and strategic campaigns.

In this chapter we trace the evolution of the use of strategic campaigns by the United Steelworkers of America (USWA) over several decades. This research is based on a series of in-depth analyses of six coordinated Steelworker campaigns that occurred between 1985 and 1997. The research began with a major study of the Ravenswood campaign (Juravich and Bronfenbrenner 1999), followed by subsequent studies conducted with our students on campaigns at USX (formerly US Steel) (Batchelor and Clark 1998), the Northern Indiana Public Service Company (Clark and Hammer 1998), Bayou Steel (Seroka 1998), Wheeling Pitt (O'Malley 1998), and Bridgestone/Firestone (Balfour et al. 2000). For the Bridgestone/Firestone campaign we also relied on a study conducted by Nancy Lessin (1998). The research for all six campaigns is based on interviews with major participants and a review and evaluation of campaign documents.

Phelps Dodge: The World Turned Upside Down

Throughout the 1950s, 1960s, and 1970s, the USWA, like most other industrial unions, developed a system of industry-wide pattern bargaining. This allowed them to negotiate with a number of employers simultaneously, using their combined power and leverage to standardize terms and conditions of employment to the highest common denominator. By the 1980s, however, this system of pattern bargaining was under attack.

Early in 1983, the Nonferrous Industry Conference, led by USWA Secretary-Treasurer Frank McKee, met to begin to prepare for a new round of bargaining in the copper industry. From the beginning the union position was clear. Despite the wave of concessions that had plagued the steel industry, the Steelworkers would hold the line in copper. On June 30, 1983, after months of stalled negotiations with industry leader Phelps Dodge, the Steelworkers had had enough. Frank McKee gathered the USWA team together:

> 'Alex [Lopez, chief negotiator for the local union], tell your people we're not getting anywhere,' said McKee. 'PD wants to try and bust us. Can you get your troops together?' Lopez looked over at [Angel] Rodriguez [local union president]. Of course they could get the troops together. Of course they could whip Phelps Dodge (Rosenblum 1995, 80).

Within a month's time, however, it was apparent that this was not going to be just another strike in which labor and management would engage in a ritual form of warfare. It would be an all-out war. Phelps Dodge was undergoing a massive corporate restructuring under President Richard Moolick and was struggling to find a new bottom line. The company had anticipated the strike and, relying on the manual *Operating During Strikes* developed by former GE executive and now Wharton School of Business professor Herbert Northrup, they had no intention of continuing pattern bargaining or conceding to the Steelworkers' demands.

Over the next several months Phelps Dodge brought in replacement workers and armed security guards and, when the workers and their union fought back, convinced the governor to bring in the National Guard. Unprepared for this level of warfare and with little experience with these tactics, the Steelworkers all but lost once the National Guard was brought in. Although the largely Mexican-American workforce fought bravely, by March 1986 the union was decertified. As Jonathan Rosenblum argues in his book, *Copper Crucible* (1995), this strike in a small New Mexico town, even more than the defeat at PATCO, was the struggle in which American corporations pioneered the aggressive anti-union strategy that would become a blueprint for breaking strikes and breaking unions in the decades that followed.

USX: The Steelworkers Fight Back

The loss to Phelps Dodge was devastating to the Steelworkers, who in many ways were already in free fall. Employment in steel had plummeted from more than 450,000 jobs in 1979 to 150,000 by 1987. The combination of foreign competition, badly outdated plants and equipment, unfavorable trade policies, and the resulting glut in the supply of steel left the industry paralyzed. Mirroring the industry, membership in the USWA dropped from 1.4 million in 1980 to just 680,000 by 1986 (Hoerr 1988).

Just as in copper, after thirty years of pattern bargaining the union would have to bargain individually with basic steel companies like USX.[1] They would also face an entirely different corporate structure

---

[1]All information on USX is drawn from Batchelor and Clark (1998) unless otherwise noted.

and model. As Batchelor and Clark explain, "Although US Steel was still the largest steel producer in the country, it found itself at the mercy of Wall Street, and scrambled to fend off several takeover attempts amid continued operating deficits and an increasing debt load" (Batchelor and Clark 1998, 10–11).

US Steel responded to this turbulence by diversifying, moving into the oil and gas industry through the purchase of both Marathon Oil and Texas Oil and Gas. By the summer of 1986, Chairman David Roderick announced a massive restructuring of the company, including a name change to USX. US Steel would now constitute only one of its four divisions.

Central to the union's bargaining strategy was an effort to force steel companies to open their books for union inspection. As USWA chief negotiator Bernie Kleiman recalls, "We had actually looked to a very significant degree into the inside workings for the first time of LTV, Bethlehem, National, Inland, and Armco . . . we were much more in the dark at US Steel and mostly US Steel just kind of laid in the bushes . . . " (Batchelor and Clark 1998, 27–28).

But the company held firm, refusing to disclose any financial information and adamantly insisting on outsourcing union work. In the middle of July the Steelworkers told the press, "The company has put on the table contract changes that would turn back the clock on workers' rights more than fifty years" (Batchelor and Clark 1998, 33). In a last ditch effort, thirteen hours before the contract was set to expire, the union offered to work under the terms of the old agreement, but the company locked them out.

During the first few months of the lockout, the company and the union conducted a public relations war as both sides tried to portray the other as the primary instigator of the conflict. Workers applied for unemployment compensation, which was handled differently by each state in which the 22,000 workers lived.

Even though the company had successfully stockpiled tons of steel, the main strategy of the USWA was to keep USX from shipping metal. Based on an agreement between the company and the union at the Lorain, Ohio, plant, no metal was shipped during the first two months of the lockout. In a good faith move, the USWA even agreed to help ship some metal that had been ordered before the lockout.

But by the end of November, the deal was off. USX decided to ship steel. More than six hundred union members assembled at the plant gate to block the first shipment. Late in the afternoon, just as union officials believed that the company had changed its mind, the trains began to move. The shipment was escorted by more than 170 police in full riot gear who attacked the locked-out workers. USWA District Director Frank Valenta had his nose broken and sustained a shoulder injury.

The local in Gary, Indiana, was no less militant. Early in September more than two hundred locked-out Steelworkers blockaded the main gate. Although forty-three were arrested, they were undaunted. They held their line, intimidating truck drivers willing to cross. As Christmas approached, the picket lines swelled.

This local pressure forced USX back to the bargaining table. An agreement was reached with the assistance of steel mediator Sylvester Garret. Although the union agreed to concessions, they were considerably fewer than those the company originally proposed, and the union won significant protections against contracting out, one of the primary issues in the campaign.

While the battle at USX did not represent a full-fledged strategic campaign, it was important for two reasons. For the first time the USWA saw the bargaining process as an information-gathering process to learn as much as possible about the internal workings of an individual corporation. Particularly in the face of an industry teeming with corporate mergers, takeovers, and reorganizations, it was no longer enough for the union to examine only its own strength as they had done, rather cavalierly, at Phelps Dodge. To move beyond concessionary bargaining, they would need to develop the expertise to identify which employers were truly in trouble and which companies were using economic conditions as a smoke screen for concession bargaining and union busting.

Second, the USX campaign also marked the first time in several decades that the Steelworkers moved outside the traditional legal responses to strikes and lockouts. Although direct action such as at USX was part and parcel of the Steelworkers' union in the 1930s and 1940s, it had all but disappeared as the union came to rely on the legal protections and the social compact between labor and management that had grown and solidified in the postwar era. Although direct action alone would not always prove to be sufficient, USX marked a paradigm shift in the organization, one that would later allow the development of many more sophisticated tactics in other campaigns.

Ravenswood: The Development of a Coordinated Campaign

When the Ravenswood Aluminum Company (RAC) locked out its more than seventeen hundred workers on October 31, 1990, it looked ominous for the Steelworkers.[2] Following the model pioneered at Phelps Dodge, Ravenswood management operated the plant from the first day of the lockout, literally bringing replacement workers in one door as their unionized workforce was leaving the plant by another. The woods surrounding the plant had been cleared, windows were boarded up, and the plant was heavily fortified by a chain link fence and an armed security force. The workers dubbed the plant "Fort RAC."

Over the next three months the Ravenswood lockout began to look more like another long drawn-out defeat for labor. For the USWA, who had watched their influence in the copper industry plummet with the loss at Phelps Dodge, it looked like aluminum might be next. President George Becker (then vice president) described his first visit to the plant three months into the lockout,

> I found that our people were sitting on a picket line with no effective means of putting the company under pressure whatsoever. Our members couldn't even picket in front of the plant. They were under an injunction. They could stand at the side of the road a mile from the gate and that was it. And I found at the time we had about eleven hundred scabs in the plant already. No way to slow them down. No way to stop them. No way to put pressure on them. I found that we had a lot of people fired and people

---

[2]All information on Ravenswood is drawn from Juravich and Bronfenbrenner (1999) unless otherwise noted.

were generally afraid to do anything and were not doing anything. Simply said, nothing was being done that would be effective in pressuring the company to return to the bargaining table (Juravich and Bronfenbrenner 1999, 68).

Despite the dismal outlook, Becker and the USWA decided to win at Ravenswood. They knew victory would take more than staffing picket lines and waiting for the wheels of justice to turn at the National Labor Relations Board (NLRB). It would not be enough to simply fight back as they had done at USX. Both RAC's reorganization and its bargaining strategy had revealed to the union that traditional loyalties and commitments had been tossed aside. The Steelworkers could not depend on RAC to play according to the old rules. The union tactics would need to change as well.

The Steelworkers knew that Ravenswood would require moving beyond the corporate campaign strategy pioneered by Ray Rogers at J. P. Stevens in the late 1970s, which focused primarily on pressuring corporate boards. Despite high hopes for Rogers' corporate campaign model, the Stevens' victory did not translate into a series of easy wins for labor. In the years that followed, unions began experimenting with a number of other tactics, including in-plant strategies, community coalitions, and more rank-and file involvement. Yet, individually none of these tactics proved to be labor's secret weapon. As the Steelworkers began organizing their campaign for Ravenswood, the consensus was emerging that all of these aspects would need to be involved in moving from a corporate to a more coordinated campaign model.

The Ravenswood campaign was built around several basic principles—extensive research, constant escalation of strategically targeted tactics, and the involvement of rank-and-file workers in all aspects of the campaign. The commitment to research was unprecedented. One of the mysteries in Ravenswood was how Emmett Boyle, a former plant engineer and manager who had left the plant when it was still owned by Kaiser Aluminum, returned a few short years later as the new CEO and a major shareholder of the now privately held company.

Boyle was hated by workers who watched him combine jobs, speed up production, and let safety conditions deteriorate to the point at which five workers had been killed in the short time he had owned the plant. Yet the Steelworkers did not make the mistake of earlier corporate campaigns by focusing exclusively on the obvious target. They understood that a strategic campaign needs to do more than just bring pressure to bear. It must direct that pressure toward those who have the power to settle.

The research conducted for the Steelworkers by the Industrial Union Department of the AFL-CIO (IUD) discovered that Boyle was little more than a front man for forces in the industry that existed far beyond company headquarters in West Virginia. Over the next six months the Steelworkers and the IUD combed loan agreements and Emmett Boyle's divorce papers and gleaned whatever information they could from the unionized workforce. Everything pointed to Clarendon Ltd., a subsidiary of Marc Rich A.G., indicating that financier Marc Rich was ultimately in control of Ravenswood. Rich did not actually own Ravenswood but controlled it indirectly through a tangled web of loans, raw materials, and tolling agreements through which he bought and sold molten aluminum produced by others.

Rich was no ordinary metals trader. According to a former Citicorp oil expert, whether plundering state-owned businesses, violating trade sanctions, or making profitable metals trades with Chile's Augusto Pinochet or Romania's Nicolae Ceausescu, Rich and his partners "made a business out of doing business other people would not do," often operating in the shadows of the law (Juravich and Bronfenbrenner 1999, 105). In 1983 the U.S. government issued a fifty-one-count indictment against Rich and his colleagues, charging them with racketeering, mail and wire fraud, tax evasion, and trading with the enemy, primarily for their violation of the U.S. oil embargo with Iran. Rich, who had transferred the ownership of his trading company to the newly formed paper corporation Clarendon, fled the United States, settling in Zug, Switzerland.

But the research did not stop with the connection to Rich. It continued throughout the campaign, identifying an ever-increasing number of areas where pressure could be applied. The campaign targeted beverage and can companies that purchased the finished aluminum can stock from RAC. Local union members waited with their cars gassed up to follow trucks maybe for a few hours or even a few days to identify where can stock was heading. They also developed a safety and health campaign based on years of meticulous records kept by Local 5668 Health and Safety Director Bill Doyle and the horrendous accident and death rate in the plant.

The basic operating principle of the committee was escalation. As Becker suggests,

> The last thing that I wanted that company, Emmett Boyle [and Marc Rich, and Willy Strothotte] to think of before he went to bed at night, Monday, Tuesday, Wednesday, Thursday, Friday, Saturday, and Sunday night . . . is all the problems and difficulties we caused them that day. And the first thing I wanted them to think of when they woke up is, 'Oh, Christ, I've got to go out and face them sons of bitches again. . . . ' We had to get them thinking about the Steelworkers continually, every day . . . if we let an hour go by that our name didn't cross their minds for some reason or another, then we were failing (Juravich and Bronfenbrenner 1999, 132).

By the spring of 1991 the escalation began to pay off. A number of beverage companies, including Stroh's and Budweiser, stopped buying RAC metal; the Occupational Safety & Health Administration (OSHA) ordered an unprecedented wall-to-wall inspection of the Ravenswood plant; and the NLRB issued a complaint against RAC. Success like this would have some unions feeling smug about their accomplishments. Yet, in an effort that distinguished their actions from many early efforts at coordinated campaigns, Becker and the USWA neither gave up nor slowed down the campaign. This was not a one-dimensional strategy but a multifaceted campaign: as one strategy cooled down, another would heat up.

The campaign soon developed far beyond the purview of most union contract battles. During the summer of 1991, the USWA took the campaign and the local union bargaining committee to Marc Rich's backyard. The Steelworkers linked up with the Swiss Metal workers union (SMUV), the International Chemical and Energy Workers (ICEF), and the International Metalworkers Federation (IMF), and began what would be a series of trips to Europe. Through their research they had discovered that Marc Rich's empire depended on his ability to make deals in secret, and the last thing that Rich wanted was publicity. At this point Rich was beginning to move into Eastern Europe and hardly wanted his fugitive status to be highlighted.

Over the next several months the Steelworkers would travel to Switzerland, the Netherlands, England, France, and Romania and put up what USWA Organizing Director Bernie Hostein would call "a picket line around the world" (Juravich and Bronfenbrenner 1999, 169). They met with bank officials who held loans on RAC and leafleted Rich's colleagues and competitors at high-level metals trading conferences with Marc Rich "Wanted" posters. They conducted street theater with oversized street puppets of Mother Jones (an early West Virginia labor heroine) and Marc Rich himself.

Local union members were actively involved in each of these trips to Europe. Perhaps the most novel aspect of the Ravenswood campaign was its linking of rank-and-file militancy and solidarity with the larger strategic goals of the union. In this way it contrasts sharply with many of the early corporate campaigns that tended to marginalize rank-and-file workers while some small group of staff or consultants planned and executed a high-level corporate strategy.

However important the larger union strategy, including the international campaign, the lockout could not have been sustained without the courage and dedication of the locked-out workers and their families. Most had worked in the plant since it first opened in the 1950s, and many came from mineworker families or were former mineworkers themselves. With an average age of 53, they were committed to their union and to each other. Throughout the twenty-month lockout, only seventeen of their seventeen hundred members crossed the line. Long before the international union had gotten involved, the local had set up a system to monitor plant activity by radio, boat, plane, and by tracking trucks. The local union built an assistance center to distribute strike funds according to need, which turned into a full-fledged food bank later in the lockout. Not a single worker went without food, lost their house or car, or was unable to pay their children's tuition bills for the duration of the lockout.

Early in the campaign the workers' wives had also set up a women's support committee, just as their predecessors had in Flint, Michigan, and Pittston Coal. While their locked-out husbands were enjoined from doing little more than symbolic picketing, the women's support committee stepped in. In addition to providing Christmas gifts for the children and food for union events, they snarled traffic in front of the plant, painted antiscab and anti-Boyle graffiti on barns and hillsides, and traveled across the country lobbying politicians and raising funds for their cause.

Local union officers and members were the core of the trips to Europe as well. The union realized that its best representatives were the locked-out workers themselves, and they received tremendous attention across Europe. They not only made the strategy more effective but also brought that strategy home to all the locked-out workers, their families, and the broader Ravenswood community.

By the spring of 1992 the combination of the research, escalating pressure tactics, and the continued solidarity and involvement of rank-and-file members had tightened the screws on Rich and Ravenswood Aluminum. OSHA had issued a several hundred-thousand-dollar fine, an environmental campaign was gaining momentum, can manufacturers continued to drop RAC metal, and Rich was prevented from making secret deals for a hotel in Romania and smelters in Czechoslovakia and Venezuela. Rich also lost his contract to supply copper to the U.S. Mint. The Mint contract, with one of the nations' top ten most-wanted white collar criminals, had prompted a congressional committee to launch an in-depth investigation into Rich's operations. International union actions were being planned by the USWA and labor allies in Bulgaria, Russia, Australia, Finland, Spain, Hong Kong, and Israel for May and June. The NLRB also would soon issue its decision on whether RAC had illegally locked out its workers, making it liable for millions of dollars in back pay plus interest.

By June a settlement was reached. Under the new agreement, the scabs and subcontractors would be dismissed, the health and safety issues would be addressed, and the cost of living adjustment would be maintained. There would be a wage increase of $1.25 over the life of the agreement and $2000 back pay for every worker. Most important, every one of the locked-out workers, except for two workers convicted of felonies, would return to the plant.

It was a tremendous victory not just for the Ravenswood workers but also for their union and the entire labor movement. Through a new model of comprehensive campaigns, the research, the escalating pressure tactics, and the full participation of the members and the broader community locally, nationally, and internationally, seventeen hundred workers in rural West Virginia and their union had taken on one of the most powerful venture capitalists in the world and won.

Bayou Steel: No Easy Replication

In the wake of the Ravenswood victory, the Steelworkers faced an equally tough adversary at Bayou Steel.[3] Bayou was one of the first minimills the Steelworkers organized and brought under contract, and it was extremely important to the union. But by 1993, as bargaining for the union's second agreement broke down, all was in jeopardy. Not unlike the situations at Phelps Dodge and Ravenswood, the USWA was now facing a company controlled by an investor group. Under the leadership of Howard Meyers, the group's primary goal was to restructure Bayou in a manner that would enhance financial returns to investors by expanding rolling capacity, refinancing the debt, and dramatically cutting labor costs.

The group's strategy was to force the union out on strike to either bring their wages and benefits in line with their nonunion competitors or break the union altogether. By the time the agreement expired on March 20, 1993, the company was bargaining backward, replacing wage gains with incentive pay, cutting back on overtime and healthcare benefits, and demanding a unilateral right to contract out work and layoff their workforce.

Learning from their slow start at RAC, the Steelworkers were anxious to get a campaign quickly under way. Within months of the walkout, the union committed extensive staff and financial resources and sent many of the same experts to Louisiana who had run and staffed the Ravenswood campaign. In essence, they simply transferred the Ravenswood strategy and machinery almost in its entirety to Bayou. Once in place, the strategy team quickly hit Bayou on every front: NLRB, OSHA, and environmental charges; truck-tracking and an end-

---

[3]All information on Bayou Steel is drawn from Seroka (1998) unless otherwise noted.

users campaign; shareholder actions; political action; and trips to Europe. The Ravenswood Women's Support Committee even traveled down to Louisiana to help the spouses of the striking Bayou workers set up their own women's support committee, the Hearts of Steel.

Just as in Ravenswood, the Bayou local threw themselves into the fight to save their union. As a newly organized unit in a fiercely right-to-work state, they were proud that 220 of the 300 workers in the bargaining unit were members of the union. At first, nearly all 220 union members and their families aggressively supported the strike. They were comforted and exhilarated by the support provided by the international union and the broader labor movement. Action by action, they watched their strategy wreak havoc on the company. OSHA citations, Environmental Protection Agency investigations, NLRB charges, the end-user campaign, and shareholder and SEC actions were clearly costing the company millions of dollars and seriously damaging their public image.

But each time the leverage appeared to be working and the union and company appeared to be close to settling the strike, Meyers responded in kind, putting something else on the table that he knew the workers and the union couldn't accept. The union had found ways to exert great pressure on Meyers, to get him to think about the union campaign "Monday, Tuesday, Wednesday, Thursday . . . ," but they still had not convinced him or the other Bayou investors that it was in their interest to allow the union back in the plant. Although the Ravenswood tactics were working on one level, they were failing to exert the pressure that they had on RAC and Marc Rich.

As we have argued above, an integral part of the victory at Ravenswood was the development of tactics and strategies that were rooted in careful research and a serious understanding of how power and decision making flowed in Ravenswood and its allied companies. But Bayou was a different company, with a different ownership structure, workforce, and labor history than Ravenswood. Thus, the strategies and tactics that the union so carefully honed at Ravenswood did not have the same impact when transferred to Bayou Steel.

Unlike Ravenswood, where the union had been in place for nearly forty years and where the workers lived in a homogeneous rural community steeped in the mineworker traditions of union militancy and solidarity, Bayou had only been under union contract since February 1986 and had only been in operation since 1981. In contrast to integrated steel or aluminum plants that need thousands of workers to produce their product, minimills such as Bayou are able to produce steel with many fewer workers. The location of the plant in southern Louisiana, with its mix of races, cultures, and union experience was also an important difference.

Meyers, too, had learned from the Ravenswood campaign. Rather than calling the scabs permanent replacements and thereby permitting the union to offer to return to work and transform the strike into a lockout, the company never fired the strikers except for those they charged with picket-line violence. Following a page out of the RAC playbook, in August 1995 Bayou filed a RICO suit naming the international officers, IUD staff, and local officials as coconspirators. Although the suit had no merit, it forced the union to devote extensive staff and financial resources to defend themselves, distracting attention and energy from the campaign itself.

The union continued to escalate the campaign but now moved more cautiously as, in the aftermath of the RICO suit, the union legal staff began to play a larger role. As the campaign dragged on, many of the outside experts moved on to other union struggles, and the Steelworkers began to rely more on their own staff. The campaign began slowly shifting beyond simply replicating the Ravenswood strategy to targeting Bayou's specific vulnerabilities—the ability of Meyers' group to refinance their debt, expand their rolling capacity, and sell stock.

By the fall of 1996, three and a half years into the strike, both sides were exhausted by the continued struggle, but the union had won some major battles. After months of pressure, that summer they forced the company to recognize the union at their new facility in Tennessee and they had made a highly successful trip to Europe where they reminded Meyers that they would follow him everywhere he tried to make new investments or expand his operations. Now, in September, the company faced the NLRB unfair labor practice trial and the potential for extensive negative publicity and massive back-pay liability.

On September 23, 1996, as the unfair labor practice trial opened in New Orleans, the company made a move toward a real settlement. By the end of the day the NLRB case was withdrawn and the contract was settled. The settlement was an important victory for the union after forty-two months, the longest strike in Steelworker history. Still, the victory at Bayou was by no means complete. As Seroka explains, "The incentive plan was still there. Members would be expected to contribute to future healthcare costs and the company was allowed to subcontract work, although with a very restricted list of positions" (Seroka 1998, 132–133). But the hardest thing for the returning workers to swallow was that the scabs would not be laid off, and sixty-five striking workers who had been discharged for picket-line activity, including union president Ron Ferraro, would have to arbitrate their return to work. The RICO suit was left standing and would not be settled until a year after the strike was over.

The Steelworkers, through the will of the international union and the solidarity of the rank and file, had held out at Bayou. But in a certain way they had forgotten the most important lesson of Ravenswood—the need to build a campaign from the inside out. In part, they were not able to do this at Bayou because when the campaign started they had yet to build the in-house capacity to run a Ravenswood-style campaign. They could replicate the Ravenswood strategy but they could not assume the Ravenswood workforce or the Ravenswood corporate vulnerabilities. To tailor the strategy to fit the workers, their community, and their company the way the union had at Ravenswood was much more difficult.

Bridgestone/Firestone: Out of the Ashes

By the end of the Bayou campaign the Steelworkers had dramatically increased their familiarity with and capacity to conduct sophisticated contract campaigns. Because so many Steelworker staff had been involved in multiple capacities in several of these campaigns, they now had the expertise to run the campaigns in-house. Many international staff representatives and district directors who were initially suspicious of the new strategies had gotten a taste of their effectiveness and had come on board. President Becker also dramatically restructured districts, moving aside some of those most resistant to the new models and new strategies.

Part of the increased capacity was not just to develop a single model for coordinated campaigns but, as the Steelworkers had learned from Bayou, to build campaigns that grew from a detailed understanding of

each company and each workforce, and the recognition of the differences in each campaign. After Ravenswood and Bayou, the USWA also
had to demonstrate that coordinated campaigns could be useful in settings other than huge industrial plants or in all-out wars with employers. If they were going to be truly useful as a strategic model, then
coordinated campaigns would have to be applicable to collective bargaining in a host of different settings.

In the summer of 1995, still in the thick of the struggle at Bayou,
the USWA took on an even more difficult challenge. The Steelworkers were not even on the scene when forty-two hundred members of the United Rubber Workers (URW) went out on strike against
Bridgestone/Firestone in July 1994.[4] Although the 1991–94 master
agreement between the URW and Japanese-owned Bridgestone/Fire-
stone was celebrated by the industrial relations community as a model
of labor-management partnership, by 1994 the company had joined
other tire makers in what they secretly called the "War of '94," a comprehensive effort to break pattern bargaining in the tire industry and
severely weaken the URW's power and influence.

Ten months later, in May 1995, faced with the harsh reality of hundreds of "crossovers"—twenty-three hundred permanent replacements—and a seemingly impotent national boycott, the URW called
an end to the strike and made an unconditional offer to return to work
under the terms of the company's final offer. That offer included severe wage and benefit cuts, twelve-hour days, seven-day workweeks,
mandatory work on holidays at reduced pay, and a two-tiered wage
scale. Bridgestone/Firestone responded by hiring back less than a quarter of the workforce, who were then forced to work surrounded by
scabs, without benefit of a union contract.

Within months the URW merged with the United Steelworkers,
who, as part of the merger agreement, had promised to finance and
staff a full-blown comprehensive campaign to get all the striking workers back to work at Bridgestone/Firestone under a union agreement. If
Ravenswood and Bayou seemed difficult, this appeared to be a virtually impossible task.

---

[4]All information on Bridgestone/Firestone is drawn from Balfour et al. (2000) and Lessin
(1998) unless otherwise noted.

The Bridgestone/Firestone strategy included targeting every plant and headquarters facility in the United States and abroad, as well as stockholders, major creditors, and international bodies such as the Organization for Economic Cooperation and Development. Just as in Ravenswood, as part of their international strategy the union sent worker delegations to Japan to meet with labor, religious, and civil rights organizations. But this time, instead of just sending local union leaders and activists, the union decided to send along workers' families, including spouses and children as young as two years old. As USWA campaign coordinator Gerald Fernandez explained

> I wanted to put a human face to the strike. I wanted the Japanese to understand the suffering. I wanted the Japanese people and workers and unions to understand that they had essentially fired twenty-seven hundred people. . . . In these types of things you can't send officials of the union or paid professionals to do that kind of thing. You have to put a face to the struggle (Balfour et al. 2000, 45).

The USWA global campaign was not limited to Japan; delegations of workers and their families traveled to more than a dozen countries in Asia, Europe, and Latin America, and contacts were made in at least seventy more. The international campaign culminated in the summer of 1996, two years into the strike, in what the union called "International Days of Outrage." During a few short weeks, the USWA organized major demonstrations and job actions with their counterparts in Japan, France, Turkey, Brazil, Venezuela, and Argentina. The Days of Outrage closed at the World Conference for the Bridgestone Corporation, organized by the Steelworkers just outside Bridgestone/Firestone's lavish headquarters in Nashville, Tennessee, where George Becker told the assembled crowd, "We intend to develop a global union workers' action plan to counter this company's growing disregard for its workers' interests, and its exploitation of the economies of both Third World and industrially developed nations" (Balfour et al. 2000, 71).

The union also brought pressure to bear on customers such as tire dealerships, automakers, local and state governments who had contracts with Bridgestone/Firestone, and racetracks such as the Indianapolis 500. It was a breathtaking agenda that could have only been undertaken with the experience of campaigns like Ravenswood and Bayou and the capacity the union had built in the process.

As in Ravenswood and Bayou, the union also filed massive health and safety, environmental, and NLRB charges. But, unlike in Ravenswood, at Bridgestone/Firestone a thousand union members had returned to work inside the struck plants, under conditions that some described as a "living hell," and thousands of other USWA members were working under extended contracts at Bridgestone/Firestone plants that were not part of the strike. So in addition to the external campaign, the union launched a full-scale in-plant campaign, replete with solidarity days, mass grievances, phone and fax jamming of corporate offices, and escalating work-to-rule actions and slowdowns. The scope of the combined internal and external campaign was staggering.

> [Three point six] million handbills, nearly a million 'Don't Buy Bridgestone/Firestone' stickers and bumper stickers, 250,000 campaign buttons, 115,000 small black flags, and 15,000 "Don't Buy" T-shirts were distributed; 63,000 yard signs were displayed. Thousands of separate campaign events involved over 60,000 USWA participants and volunteers; 1,100 separate USWA locals were actively involved. Camp Justice (the USWA solidarity campsite) was occupied for 246 days; the campaign reached 86 countries, including 16 visited by replaced Bridgestone/Firestone [workers]; and 43 foreign workers visited the U.S. to lend their support (United Steelworkers of America 1997, 14–15).

By November 1996 Bridgestone/Firestone had had enough. The union reached a tentative agreement, winning immediate reinstatement for all union members, including all but four of those discharged for strike-related misconduct, and major gains on almost every issue that had prompted the strike except for twelve-hour shifts and the elimination of paid hours for union health and safety work. Perhaps most impressive of all, the new contract would expire simultaneously with other master agreements in the industry. In the words of University of Akron professor and tire industry expert David Meyer, the union's accomplishment was "drop-dead, jaw-to-the-floor amazing" (Lessin 1998, 68).

As George Becker later would say, with Bridgestone/Firestone, on the heels of Ravenswood and then Bayou, the Steelworkers had proven to themselves, the labor movement, and corporate America, that they "knew what it takes to win" (Becker 1998). Still, the union steadfastly maintained that their goal was to do everything possible to reach an agreement without engaging in these kinds of all-out struggles. As their postcampaign report, "One Day Longer: The Road to Victory at Bridgestone/Firestone," stated, "We much prefer . . . to resolve our differences through negotiation. . . . But the real lesson here is that the best way to avoid a fight is to be ready for one. Real victory comes when you are too strong for your enemy to attack you. We must create situations in which companies recognize that they cannot destroy unions" (United Steelworkers of America 1997, 16).

From Wheeling Pitt to NIPSCO: Expanding the Scope of Strategic Campaigns

On October 1, 1996, just as the Bridgestone/Firestone campaign was coming to a head, another forty-four hundred Steelworkers went out on strike against Wheeling Pittsburgh Steel Corporation at eight mills scattered across the Ohio and Monongahela River valleys in West Virginia, Pennsylvania, and southern Ohio.[5] The workers were striking to win back the decent benefit pension plan that they had lost eleven years before in the aftermath of concessions, bankruptcy, and a bitter 98-day strike. In the ensuing years, the company had come under the control of Ronald LaBow, a Wall Street bankruptcy specialist, who by the time of the strike had made Wheeling Pitt one of the most profitable companies in the industry, netting him more than $80 million in a few short years.

The Steelworkers went into bargaining in 1996 knowing that it would take a full-scale comprehensive campaign to win a defined benefit pension fund (a pension fund not tied to the ups and downs of the

---

[5]All information on Wheeling Pitt is drawn from O'Malley (1998) unless otherwise noted.

market) from LaBow. Until then almost all USWA campaigns had been reactive in nature, most starting up months into the campaign. This time, when bargaining at Wheeling Pitt broke off at midnight on October 1 with no agreement on the defined benefit plan, the union had a campaign plan ready to go, put together by the International's Strategic Projects department in conjunction with all eight of the Wheeling Pitt local unions.

Just as in Ravenswood and Bridgestone/Firestone, the key to the Wheeling Pitt strategy was a multifaceted approach that escalated pressure on Wheeling Pitt, its parent company WHX, and WHX subsidiaries across the country while keeping the striking workers at each of the plants committed to the strike. Striking Wheeling Pitt workers traveled the country picketing and handbilling outside company headquarters and WHX subsidiaries. Massive NLRB charges were filed, while religious leaders and national politicians weighed in to push LaBow back to the bargaining table.

Six months into the strike LaBow responded by shutting down four WHX plants, three of which were on strike. According to USWA Strategic Projects Director Ron Bloom, rather than having the intended effect of breaking the strikers' resolve, the plant closings "backfired" on the company, making them look "vindictive and nasty . . . they overplayed their hand" (O'Malley 1998, 58). In response, the union escalated the pressure, purchasing airtime on local radio and television stations featuring the personal stories of striking Wheeling Pitt workers and reaching out to each member of WHX's board of directors. The AFL-CIO weighed in as well: President Sweeney announced a "solidarity conference," inviting every central labor council and AFL-CIO affiliate in the three affected states to help "develop some new strategies to deal with Wheeling Pittsburgh and its CEO" (O'Malley 1998, 61).

By May 1997 Wheeling Pitt's stock had dropped from $10 to $6 a share, and the company reported quarterly net losses of more than $30 million. When LaBow still refused to budge, the union embarked on a nationwide "streets and suites" campaign that targeted the top ten institutional investors in WHX stock, including, among others, Merrill Lynch, Barclays Bank, Dewey Square, American Express, and Mellon Bank, and their CEOs. By June, LaBow was back at the table, for the first time seriously talking about pensions, and on August 1, 304 days after the strike began, he finally capitulated and agreed to the union's demand—a defined benefit pension plan in line with the industry standard.

It was a hard-won victory. It was not easy keeping four thousand workers out on what was really a one-issue strike, yet during all 304 days not one Wheeling Pitt worker crossed the line. As Ron Bloom explained, both the union and Ron LaBow had gambled, each day convinced that the other side would break first. In the end, according to Bloom, LaBow "anted up three hundred times and he lost three hundred times and then he said okay" (O'Malley 1998, 83).

That same summer of 1997, while the media and the public were focused on national strikes at United Parcel Service and Wheeling Pitt, the Steelworkers were gearing up for a very different contract battle at NIPSCO, the Northern Indiana Public Service Company.[6] Unlike their union counterparts at Ravenswood, Wheeling Pitt, Bayou, and Bridgestone/Firestone, the 3,562 service, maintenance, clerical, and technical employees of NIPSCO worked at a public utility, not a major industrial plant. Until 1988 their company had been a regional utility providing electric and gas services to residents of Northern Indiana. In 1988 that changed when NIPSCO was transformed into what management called "an energy-based holding company" (Clark and Hammer 1998, 8). By the time the union entered into bargaining in 1998, their utility plant was one of forty-eight different NIPSCO subsidiaries involved in everything from gas and electric services to rail freight, gas storage, commercial lighting, land acquisition, and real estate development. Under the new company structure, the ratepayers for the core gas and electric subsidiaries became the "cash cow" to finance the more risky capital ventures in real estate and land acquisition. If the ventures failed, the utility ratepayers were left to cover the losses. If they succeeded, the profits were put back into additional financial ventures or to line the pockets of the company's new owners and shareholders. In just a few years the new NIPSCO holding company had generated more than $400 million in excess cash, and its shareholders celebrated a 79 percent return on their initial investment (Clark and Hammer 1998, 10).

---

[6]All information on NIPSCO is drawn from Clark and Hammer (1998) unless otherwise noted.

Labor relations had also changed. At the same time utility rates were skyrocketing, staffing at the plant had been cut by more than 21 percent since 1992. Management came to the table in 1996 unbending on wage and staffing issues at the same time they refused to continue the longstanding practice of early negotiations and joint bargaining with the clerical and physical plant locals. Convinced that management could easily recruit a full complement of replacement workers and outlast any membership commitment to a strike, the local unions, with the advice of the International, decided to launch an alternative campaign. The workers would stay on the job, working without a contract, while the union would run a national comprehensive campaign against NIPSCO, targeting customers and shareholders.

The themes of the campaign focused on NIPSCO as the evil empire of Star Wars, with the union joining the customers as the "rebel alliance" fighting for justice. Over and over, in mailings, flyers, meetings, mass rallies, and an in-depth report entitled "Milking the Cash Cow," the campaign focused on skyrocketing utility rates, cuts in staff and service quality, the accumulation of excess cash by NIPSCO's owners, and how the owners and shareholders were lining their pockets at the expense of their customers and their workers.

Throughout, the campaign was defined in terms of corporate greed versus community and class, which resonated easily with the primarily working class NIPSCO customer base in northern Indiana. The union sought to shine a spotlight on the owners and shareholders, their greed and mismanagement, both at NIPSCO and other companies they owned, including the CEO of Welsh Oil and the president of Purdue University, both of whom were NIPSCO directors.

The union also pursued an inside campaign to hold workers together despite constant harassment from management day in and day out in the plants. The company had played on divisions between the primarily female clerical unit and the largely male physical plant unit, so the union made a priority of breaking down those differences and bringing the two groups together. To accomplish this, they brought in Robin Rich from the Steelworkers local at Bethlehem Steel. Rich had coordinated USWA solidarity for the Bridgestone/Firestone workers.

By early October it became clear to management that their attempts to undermine union solidarity had backfired and that the union was winning the war of public opinion with their customers. By mid-month the company came back to the table with a new agreement, including none of the eighty-five wage, benefit, and work rule concessions that had been included in their final offer when bargaining broke down four months earlier. The new agreement, which was easily ratified by the members on October 23, included major gains in wages and benefits, as well as a signing bonus.

Conclusion

Over the past decade there has been a rapid evolution of Steelworker coordinated and strategic campaigns. From the early campaigns at USX and Ravenswood, the Steelworkers have grown tremendously in their capacity to conduct successful campaigns as diverse as Bridgestone/Firestone and NIPSCO.

This evolution has not, however, reflected steady progress in a single direction, forging a unitary model for strategic campaigns. It has not been the evolution of a single, more-developed species. Instead, it might best be characterized by the evolutionary concept of generalized adaptation by which a less-specialized organism can survive in many different environments, in part because it is neither as vulnerable nor as inflexible as a more highly developed form.

Perhaps the most important observation that comes from this review of a half dozen Steelworker collective-bargaining campaigns is their diversity. After the Ravenswood victory, the USWA seemed assured that they had discovered the best model for strategic campaigns. Yet, as the near loss at Bayou showed, no single model was equally effective for every struggle. The Steelworkers learned, or relearned, from their experience at Ravenswood that the campaign had to follow the employer, the workforce, and the circumstances, not the other way around.

This shift marks a true evolution from the early use of corporate campaigns in the late 1970s and early 1980s. Although the coordinated campaign may not be the magic bullet that some believed, the Steelworkers' experience demonstrates the continued relevance and effectiveness of these campaigns, even against rapidly evolving employers in a complex global economy. These were not simply lucky victories over weak employers. Facing the likes of Rich, Meyers, LaBow, and Bridgestone/Firestone CEO Yoichiro Kaizaki, the Steelworkers were up against some of the most powerful and ruthless individuals and organizations in the world. These victories have proven to both unions and employers that in today's economy in which corporate structures focus less on direct corporate ownership and more on a widening sphere of control, these new structures are not impenetrable to workers and their unions.

The USWA also did not win in only one type of setting; they won against large and small employers, with senior, stable workforces and new ones, and in industrial and service industries. Although we have not provided enough data points for a quantitative analysis, these six case studies strongly indicate the applicability of this overall model or approach across different kinds of employers, workplaces, and communities.

Continuing to refer to the Steelworkers' approach as a "model" for comprehensive campaigns may even be a misnomer. One of the major factors behind the continued success of the Steelworkers' campaigns was that they were not comprised of a series of tactics appended onto an existing union structure. Part of the maturation of the post-Ravenswood USWA was the realization that these coordinated campaigns were the building blocks and the very fiber of the union. Although the union strongly embraced the struggle at Ravenswood in an emotional and ideological sense, some years passed before they had actually gone through sufficient organizational change necessary to regularly engage in this level of campaign.

By the time of the Bridgestone/Firestone campaign, a struggle that few other unions would have had the courage to even try, the USWA had the institutional structure in place to make running and winning the campaign possible. By then it was no longer just George Becker and a few Steelworkers' staff trying to convince the rest of the union about the efficacy of this approach. The union now had the organizational commitment and machinery to make the campaign possible without the Herculean start-up costs and delays that had made Ravenswood so challenging. Although the union did learn important lessons about the nuts and bolts of these campaigns along the way, the real evolution was not in the technical aspects of coordinated campaigns but in the organizational and cultural change of the Steelworkers.

The changes were also not just organizational changes at the top. Part of the effectiveness of these changes was that they reverberated throughout the organization, into local unions and into the hearts and minds of local union members. Rather than moving away from the commitment, energy, and militancy of local union members, the coordinated campaign approach embraced their interests and depended on their active participation in building one union rather than layers of interest groups. As much as anything, these changes were about a return to basic values in the USWA and the courage to stand up for justice and dignity for rank-and-file workers.

Each of these victories went far beyond the industrial enterprise. The Steelworkers did not just save thousands of union jobs through their efforts, they changed the balance of power in collective bargaining across the steel, rubber, and aluminum industries. As the Steelworkers have reported in the aftermath of these hard-won victories, many employers came to the table ready to reach a fair agreement without going to war with the USWA.

As we found in our research, the union still has room to stumble along the way. The international union staff and officers coordinating the campaigns too easily start to think that their skills, experience, and ingenuity can supplant the need for full-membership involvement and participation in the campaign. They forget that the participation of the members, their voices, their stories, and their commitment is what inspires and generates support from other workers and allies around the globe. They also forget that no campaign strategy is worth anything if the members cross the line. Most of all, in the desire to win and win quickly, sometimes they forget the real issues that generated the struggles in the first place, and the true costs of some of the concessions necessary to get an agreement.

Despite these concerns, the Steelworkers' success provides tremendous hope for an American labor movement looking to rebuild and reshape itself. After enduring a decade of concessions in industries going through free fall, the Steelworkers have reestablished themselves as a force to be reckoned with at the bargaining table. Although they may have overreached in their initial efforts during which they courageously lunged at their opponents, clearly they have now matured organizationally to make these victories routine. Since NIPSCO they have gone on to win at Newport News, Continental Tire, and MSI, with similar campaigns under way at CFI, Titan Tire, and Kaiser.

There is much that can be learned from these campaigns, not just as it applies to the Steelworkers but to the entire American labor movement. As George Becker suggested in the aftermath of the Ravenswood victory:

Struggles such as this renew the labor movement. The Ravenswood campaign demonstrated what it takes to win even where the employer is determined to bust the Union—perseverance, constant escalation of the battle, and a dogged determination not to quit no matter how bleak the circumstances may look. The labor movement must be constructive, creative, and ever willing to change but it must never, never forget how to fight (Juravich and Bronfenbrenner 1999, 216).

CHAPTER TEN

Union Mergers and Union Revival

Are We Asking Too Much or Too Little?

Gary Chaison

There is no consensus about the role of union mergers in the revival of the American labor movement. Mergers are rarely mentioned in plans for national union resurgence in organizing and bargaining. Yet, proponents of mergers describe them as the surest and fastest way to rebuild the labor movement.

This difference in perspective is not surprising. There is little research on merger outcomes despite the extensive literature on why and how union officers negotiate mergers (e.g., Chitayat 1979; Chaison 1986, 1996a; Waddington 1995; Williamson 1995) and how union members evaluate merger proposals (e.g., Cornfield 1991; McClendon, Kriesky and Eaton 1995; Devine and Reshef 1998). Moreover, merger agreements are usually promoted by union officers with extravagant claims to convince members, local officers, and staff that more can be gained than lost by merger. The technical aspects of proposed mergers (e.g., the calculation of dues, the composition of governing boards) are described in great detail during merger campaigns, but the benefits are presented as a matter of faith that bigger unions are always better unions. For instance, when union officers explained why the Auto Workers, Machinists and Steelworkers should amalgamate, they claimed that the merger would create an enormous union with the power in bargaining and organizing needed to confront employers and the size and experience to make a tremendous political impact. The leaders of the Machinists, for example, declared, "It is time to add a global union to the global marketplace" (Bureau of National Affairs

1998b, C1), and the merger gives workers "the numbers to fight back" (Swoboda 1995, C2). The Unity Agreement (merger declaration) concluded: "Our enduring vision of a world of dignity, security, and prosperity for the many—not just the few—requires nothing less than that we create a new union for a new era" (Bureau of National Affairs 1995a, E1).

Moving beyond the rhetoric of merger campaigns, we find evidence that mergers can play a useful though limited role in union revival. To put this appraisal in context, we first review the recent merger record.

The Form and Frequency of Union Mergers

Table 10-1 shows the frequency of mergers since 1955, the year of the consolidation the American Federation of Labor and the Congress of Industrial Organizations.[1] Table 10-2 lists mergers from 1995 to 1999.[2]

Table 10-1 Frequency and forms of national union mergers, 1955–1999

Year	Amalgamations	Absorptions	Total Mergers	Average Annual Mergers
1955–1959	3	6	9	1.8
1960–1969	5	19	24	2.4
1970–1979	6	21	27	2.7
1980–1989	4	31	35	3.5
1990–1999	2	36	38	3.8
1990–1994	0	21	21	4.2
1995–1999	2	15	17	3.4

Source: 1955–1979, Chaison (1980); 1980–1994, Chaison (1996b); 1995–1997, Gifford (1998); 1998, Bureau of National Affairs (1998a, 1999b,c).

---

[1]Time series of contemporary union merger activity usually start in 1955 because the merger of the two federations in that year opened new possibilities for combinations among affiliates with similar jurisdiction. Previously, mergers between affiliates of the American Federation of Labor and the Congress of Industrial Organizations were discouraged by the federations' officers (Chaison 1980).

[2]Earlier mergers are listed in the appendixes to Chaison (1986, 1996b).

Table 10-2 Union mergers, 1995 to 1999[1]

Year	Merger
1995	Amalgamated Clothing and Textile Workers (129,000 members) and International Ladies Garment Workers Union (123,000 members) to form Union of Needle Trades, Industrial and Textile Employees (UNITE)
1995	Distillery, Wine and Allied Workers (13,000 members) into United Food and Commercial Workers (1.4 million members)
1995	International Brotherhood of Firemen and Oilers (25,000 members) into Service Employees International Union (1 million members)
1995	United Rubber, Cork, Linoleum and Plastic Workers (94,000 members) into United Steelworkers of America (700,000 members).
1995	United Textile Workers (15,000 members) into United Food and Commercial Workers (1.4 million members)
1996	Aluminum, Brick and Glass Workers (40,000 members) into United Steelworkers of America (700,000 members)
1996	International Chemical Workers (34,000 members) into United Food and Commercial Workers (1.4 million members).
1996	International Leather Goods, Plastics and Novelty Workers (5,000 members) into Service Employees International Union (1 million members)
1996	Metal Polishers, Buffers, Platers and Allied Workers (3,000 members) into International Union of Boilermakers (43,000 members)
1997	International Woodworkers of America (19,000 members) into International Association of Machinists (411,000 members)
1997	Mechanics Education Association of America (3,000 members) into United Automobile Workers (766,000 members).
1997	Newspaper Guild (22,000 members) into the Communications Workers of America (504,000 members)
1998	Health and Human Service Employees (57,000 members) into the Service Employees International Union (1.1 million members)
1998	National Maritime Union of the Marine Engineers Benevolent Association (6,000 members) into Seafarers International Union (80,000 members)
1998	Retail, Wholesale and Department Store Union (72,000 members) into the United Food and Commercial Workers (1.1 million members)
1999	American Federation of Grain Millers (25,000 members) into Bakery, Confectionery and Tobacco Workers (110,000 members)
1999	United Paperworkers International Union (240,000 members) and Oil, Chemical and Atomic Workers (80,000 members) to form PACE (Paper, Allied-Industrial, Chemical and Energy Workers International Union)

Source: Gifford (1998, Chart 3 and Schedule 3); Bureau of National Affairs (1998, 1999c,b).

[1]Does not include mergers agreed to in principle by officers but not yet negotiated and approved by members. For example, the amalgamation of the United Automobile Workers, the United Steelworkers of America, and the International Association of Machinists was announced in 1995 and approved in principle by officers and members, but specific terms have yet to be negotiated and approved by members. The officers stated their intent to merge their unions in 2000, but the date has been moved forward and the Machinists have dropped out of merger talks.

The list does not include mergers that were negotiated and approved by members or convention delegates but not finalized because of legal challenges. For example, in 1999 the Textile Processors, Service Trades, Health Care, Professional and Technical Employees agreed by convention vote to merge into the United Food and Commercial Workers, but this was challenged in a class action lawsuit by some of the Textile Processors' members who claimed procedural irregularities (Bureau of National Affairs 1999a).

The list also does not include affiliations of regional unions into national ones.

We distinguish between two types of national union mergers. In an amalgamation, two or more unions combine to form a new union. An absorption is the merger of a small union (the absorbed union) into a larger one (the absorbing union). Amalgamations occur far less frequently. They are extremely difficult to negotiate, because they create unions with new constitutions and governing bodies (Chaison 1980).[3] Absorbed unions, on the other hand, become parts of absorbing ones, usually as semi-autonomous divisions, with only minor changes in the structure or governance of the larger union. Typically, members or convention delegates of all amalgamating unions must approve of the merger, but only those of absorbed unions vote (Chaison 1986).

Tables 1 and 2 do not include affiliations, the mergers of local and regional unions into national unions, because their identities are not widely known. Although there are public announcements when state employee associations join national unions, and some unions (e.g., the Service Employees and the United Food and Commercial Workers) provide lists of their affiliating unions, records of all union affiliations are incomplete, most likely because many involve very small unions. Reviews of available data show affiliations outnumbering national union amalgamations and absorptions (Chaison 1996b). For example, between 1980 and 1993 the Service Employees alone affiliated seven state employees' associations and 47 local unions; during those years there were 52 national union mergers (Service Employees International Union 1993; Chaison 1996b).

Has the merger pace accelerated during the movement for union revival? Assuming that revival efforts began in earnest around 1995 with the election of John Sweeney and his slate of officers to the leadership of the AFL-CIO, merger frequency has fallen. The average annual number of mergers for 1995–1999 was 3.4 compared to 4.2 for 1990–1994.

There was a rising number of mergers starting in the 1980s because of declining union membership and limited growth potential through traditional organizing for most unions (both have been traced to ris-

---

[3]For example, see Clark and Gray's (2000) analysis of the issues that would have to be resolved in an amalgamation of the Auto Workers, Steelworkers, and Machinists.

ing employer opposition to unionism in a highly competitive environment [Chaison and Rose 1991] as well as to the smaller unions' need for economies of scale in operations[4] [Chaison 1986, 1996b]). Merger activity peaked in the early 1990s and nearly returned to the 1980s level in the most recent period. The typical union merger has been and remains an absorption.

It should be understood that the present merger rate is still high relative to possible national union mergers, and it is not sustainable in the long run. If we use the sixty-eight AFL-CIO affiliates in 1999 (Bureau of National Affairs 1999c) as a proxy for total national unions, and assume that no new unions are formed and mergers are absorptions, a merger rate of 3.8 per year (the 1990s rate) will halve the number of national unions in less than a decade.

We should always interpret longitudinal data on mergers with the greatest caution, and it may be too soon to dismiss the impact of the movement for union revival on merger activity. Mergers announced in a given year usually result from officers' contacts and negotiations in earlier years. The time between initial contacts and merger approvals is not uniform and can be quite long. Some merger talks may have been on and off for several years before an agreement was reached for presentation to members for approval, while others may occur as a flurry of activity.[5] The Aluminum Workers and the Steelworkers, for example, had sporadic meetings on their merger over a decade before they agreed on terms in 1996 (McKay 1996). Compare this to the Chemical Workers who discussed merger with seven unions over two years before merging into the United Food and Commercial Workers (UFCW) in 1996 (Moore 1995). An extreme

---

· [4]For unions, having economies of scale means that they have achieved or maintained sufficient membership size and revenues from dues to be able to provide and utilize specialized services and staff (e.g., full-time lobbyists, a health and safety department) and to cover the necessary costs of administration and operating facilities (e.g., paying for a national convention, maintaining a headquarters, publishing a newspaper) (Chaison 1986).

[5]Analysts of merger data on the macro level should also recognize that successfully negotiated mergers are most likely outnumbered by unsuccessful ones, although the exact number of the latter is unknown. Union officers do not publicize their failures; we generally learn of mergers that failed at later stages (e.g., the rejection of a merger proposal by convention delegates) rather than at the earliest stages (informal talks among officers) (Chaison 1986).

example, there were intermittent merger talks between the National Education Association (NEA) and the American Federation of Teachers (AFT) for more than thirty years before a merger agreement was voted down by the NEA's members in 1998. Discussions between the two unions are continuing on state and local levels (Greenhouse 1998d).

In summary, it is difficult to attribute specific mergers to the movement for union revival. Some merger discussions were probably well advanced in 1995. Others may have been languishing before being inspired by union revival efforts and reaching a stage at which tentative agreements could be announced. Others may do this soon.

Merger Outcomes and Union Revival

Most proposals for union revival envision unions becoming more like social movements than narrowly focused bargaining agents, with new priorities, an expanded repertoire of activities, and stronger links with workers (both organized and unorganized) and their communities. Most prominent of the social movement dimensions of union revival are the progression from a service model of unionism that emphasizes the maintenance of the union as an organization and the provision of benefits for present members to an organizing model that devotes a larger share of resources to recruiting new members; a new assertiveness in bargaining coupled with a greater willingness to strike, particularly over issues of job security, and an effort to enlist broad public support during strikes; increased political activity by unions, alone or through community coalitions, for laws that benefit unions as well as workers in general; and the extensive participation of the rank and file in organizing, negotiations, and union governance.[6] Do mergers promote these elements of union revival? Despite the rhetoric of merger advocates, the evidence shows mergers do not always contribute directly and significantly to union revival.

---

[6]For prescriptions for union revitalization see Hurd (1998); Bureau of National Affairs (1997b,c,d; 1998a); Mantsios (1998); The Century Foundation Task Force on the Future of Unions (1999); and Nissen (1999).

Organizing

The unions' rededication to organizing is at the very heart of revival (Bronfenbrenner et al. 1998; Bureau of National Affairs 1997c, 1998a), but research shows only tenuous connections between organizing and union mergers. Chaison's (1981, 106) analysis of mergers and membership changes concluded:

> It would be difficult to say that the growth of some of the larger absorbing unions (e.g., the Teamsters, the Laborers, or Steelworkers) changed principally because they absorbed a small union [beyond the immediate membership gains through the merger]. And there would be no way to determine the post-merger growth of the absorbed unions unless they were established as distinct divisions within the absorbing union.

Even if we isolate the growth of absorbed unions and measure the organizing gains of new unions formed by amalgamation, we would not know if post-merger growth resulted from the merger itself (i.e., the new resources and staff) or from a higher priority on organizing that could have occurred without merger, or a combination of the two (Chaison 1986).

But mergers do create the potential for greater organizing activity and success. Absorptions or affiliations give small unions access to organizing resources and allow larger unions to establish footholds in new occupations or industries. It is traditional for union officers to announce special funds for organizing drives at the signing ceremonies for merger agreements. For example, when the Service Employees absorbed the 9,000-member Committee of Interns and Residents in 1997, it announced a $1.4-million fund for organizing physicians (Bureau of National Affairs 1997e). A $10-million fund for organizing was created when the Textile Workers and the Ladies Garment Workers amalgamated to form the Union of Needletrades, Industrial and Textile Workers (UNITE) in 1995 (Szekely 1995). A $5-million organizing campaign among healthcare workers in New York City was promised as part of the merger of Local 1199, National Health and Human Services Employees into the Services Employees in 1998 (Bureau of National Affairs 1998c). In 1987 the Harvard Union of Clerical and Technical Workers (HUCTW) affiliated with the American Federation of State, County and Municipal Employees (AFSCME) and received financial assistance that was vital to its successful organizing campaign at Harvard University. When the affiliation agreement was announced, HUCTW was given three hundred thousand dollars and the freedom to decide organizing strategies and the allocation of funds (Hoerr 1997). Finally, when the Paperworkers merged with the Oil, Chemical and Atomic Workers in 1999 to form the Paper, Allied-Industrial, Chemical and Energy Workers (PACE), the new union hired a consultant to develop a comprehensive organizing strategy, set up a program to train members to be organizers, and instituted an "organizing tax"—an allocation of fifty cents per month from each member's dues to finance organizing campaigns (Bureau of National Affairs 1999d).

Some observers of the merger scene strongly caution against mergers becoming substitutes for organizing (Chaison 1986, 1996a,b). It can be extremely tempting for large unions to use absorptions and affiliations as their primary growth strategy, but mergers essentially organize unions rather than workers. Through mergers, new members are added to the unions' rolls quickly and inexpensively relative to traditional organizing because evidence of majority employee support does not have to be demonstrated in labor board elections. Employer opposition to merger is minimal because the workplaces are already covered by collective agreements.[7] If unions choose negotiating mergers over organizing workers, individual unions will grow but without an overall expansion of the labor movement. Officers who favor mergers for union growth would be reluctant to increase the share of their budgets for organizing. Members would understandably reject calls to increase dues for greater organizing if there were faster and cheaper ways for their union to grow. Mergers can complement organizing but great care must be taken not to let them become substitutes for organizing.

---

[7]Employer opposition, however, does occur in affiliations and arises from the employers' concerns that a small local or regional union will become more militant and effective in bargaining if it becomes part of a larger union. Cornfield (1991) and McClendon, Kriesky, and Eaton (1995) found that employers' "vote no" campaigns can sway workers' votes and block mergers.

Collective Bargaining

Some recent mergers have been motivated by a clear need to improve collective bargaining performance by gaining access to large strike funds, research departments, and experienced and skilled negotiators.[8] A classic case is the merger of the Rubber Workers into the Steelworkers in 1995. The Rubber Workers union was engaged in a bitter strike against Bridgestone/Firestone which depleted its strike fund and forced it to raise dues and borrow from other unions. Workers returned to their jobs without a contract. After the merger, the Steelworkers concluded an agreement with the company that was considered a victory despite its concessions simply because it was not a complete defeat. The primary reason that the Rubber Workers chose the Steelworkers union was its reputed skill and militancy in bargaining and its $162-million strike fund (Adams 1995; Norton and Narisetti 1995).[9]

Although mergers may increase negotiating effectiveness and bargaining power, they cannot change the context of bargaining. They cannot reverse the impacts of new production technologies and work restructuring, competition and cost cutting in the healthcare industry, the spread of foreign and domestic nonunion competition, and contracting-out and downsizing in both public and private sectors (Chaison 1996b). Mergers can, however, increase the ability of unions to more effectively respond to these trends during negotiations.

Moreover, mergers can help unions adapt to the demands of decentralized negotiations. Reviews of recent union mergers in Australia, New Zealand, and Sweden show how the transition from national and industrywide bargaining to enterprise and plant-level bargaining requires

---

[8]Examples of small unions merging into large ones specifically to strengthen bargaining are the 1,100-member Boston Globe Employees Association into the 33,000-member Newspaper Guild in 1994 ("Globe Union Joins Guild" 1994); the 1,100-member United Transportation Employees into the 83,000-member Oil, Chemical and Atomic Workers in 1996 (Bureau of National Affairs 1996b); and the 1,200-member Employees Mutual Association into the 75,000-member United Mine Workers in 1996 (Bureau of National Affairs 1996a).

[9]For the Steelworkers, the merger with the Rubber Workers produced some much-needed growth; it had lost nearly half of its members since 1980 because of declining employment in its principal industries (Norton and Narisetti 1995).

more and better trained local staff, officers, and member volunteers to negotiate and administer agreements. Small unions have difficulty adjusting to the volume and demands of decentralized negotiations and merge into large unions to gain access to their financial resources and staff (Chaison 1992, 1996b). Some American unions might also seek merger partners for this reason, but their problems are not as pressing because the shift to decentralized bargaining is not as great.

Political Activity

Merger advocates claim that mergers lead to political clout. Larger unions, they believe, wield greater power in terms of members/voters, canvassers for the campaigns of favored candidates, and financial contributions to parties and candidates. But such political influence could also be achieved through participation in coalitions with unions and other organizations sharing labor's interests, such as those of human rights advocates, consumer activists, and environmentalists. For example, unions played a central role in the coalitions that lobbied and demonstrated unsuccessfully against the North American Free Trade Agreement in 1991–93 and successfully against fast-track authority for the president to negotiate trade pacts in 1997. It is difficult to see how the character or outcome of the coalition activities would be different had there been more union mergers. Moreover, for the past few years unions have debated the best political strategy—creating a pro-worker political party, forging closer union ties to moderate Democrats, supporting both Republican and Democratic candidates who favor pro-worker and pro-union issues, or focusing political action on the community level and working through coalitions. Mergers do not figure in these strategies.

However, when greater local or state political power is a primary objective, mergers can be important. For example, when Local 1199 became part of the Service Employees, the two unions pledged to nearly double their spending on New York City politics. Local 1199 was already a major force in city politics, but the Service Employees, despite its national size and militancy, was not politically active in the city. One report concluded, "For the Service Employees, the merger makes sense not only because it increases the union's size, reach and dues income but also because it stands to transform the union from a midget to a mighty player in New York politics" (Greenhouse 1998b, A15). When the 5,000-member Union of American Physicians and Dentists merged into AFSCME, it gained the backing of one of the strongest lobbying organizations in California where its members work and are affected by healthcare legislation (Adelson 1997).[10]

Membership Participation

If labor unions are to function more like social movements—as communities of workers rather than as narrowly focused bargaining agents—they will have to allow for and actively promote greater membership participation in union affairs: attending meetings, voting in elections, serving on committees, running for office (Bronfenbrenner et al. 1998; Nissen 1999). But merger critics often equate increased union size through merger with the diminished ability and interest of members to participate. They claim that mergers create large bureaucratic and autocratic unions with centralized administrations. When a merger combines unions of workers from dissimilar occupations or industries, the merged union becomes an amorphous organization devoid of a common culture and a sense of solidarity or community of interest among members. Leaders are no longer attuned to the needs of members. Members become apathetic (Moody 1995b; Verespej 1995; Chaison 1996b).

On this point, merger critics fail to understand that the relationship between merger, union size, and membership interest and participation is not a direct one. A large union that grew suddenly through a merger or a series of mergers is not the same as one that grew and diversified gradually through organizing. In most affiliations and absorptions, the smaller union forms or becomes part of a

---

[10]Political activity can also derail merger talks. Some state chapters of the National Education Association objected to its proposed merger with the American Federation of Teachers because they wanted to continue their support of both Republicans and Democrats. They felt they would have to abandon their bipartisan approach if the merged union affiliated with the AFL-CIO (Greenhouse 1998a).

separate division or section that controls most governance and bargaining (Chaison 1982). Union officers call this "retaining our identity while coming under the umbrella of the large union" (Garneau 1995, 1). For instance, when the Newspaper Guild was absorbed by the Communications Workers of America (CWA), it became a sector of that union with its own officers, staff, and bylaws. The merger agreement specifies that the sector "shall not be dissolved nor shall its authority, jurisdiction, functions, or bylaws be changed or impeded without its consent" (*Agreement of Affiliation* 1995, 6). Guild locals are successors to all bargaining rights and collective agreements that they had before the merger. The sector holds a conference prior to the annual CWA convention to amend its constitution, elect officers, set policy, pass resolutions, and conduct other business, and it elects delegates to the CWA convention (*Agreement of Affiliation* 1995).

Amalgamations also create regional and industrial or occupational divisions to reduce members' apprehension about the submergence of their interests in the new union. These structures, with their own officers, staff, headquarters, and conventions, have drawn some criticism because they are costly and prevent the amalgamated union from achieving economies of scale in operations. Departments and positions are created rather than combined or eliminated (Chaison 1982, 1996b).

A recent study of a union amalgamation in Sweden shows that mergers can be designed to prevent the deterioration of membership participation even when a large union with a diverse membership is created without industry divisions. When the Swedish Clothing Workers Union and the Swedish Factory Workers Union merged in 1993, officers from both unions sought to protect membership participation. A key objective of the merger was to encourage local officers and members to be trained for and participate in decentralized negotiations and joint decision-making with employers. The officers negotiated a merger agreement that created regional committees for administrative duties previously reserved for national headquarters, maintained regional structures and local staff positions even though greater economies of scale could be achieved without them, and did not force neighboring locals to merge. A survey among members of both unions before and after the merger showed that measures of membership participation did not change despite the creation of a large union with a diverse membership (Chaison, Sverke and Sjöberg 1997).[11]

Revival and Superunions

It is possible that superunions will emerge in the United States and not only dominate the labor movement but press for a greater role for union mergers in the revival effort. Superunions, or megaunions as they are sometimes called (e.g., Verespej 1995), are huge unions that are formed by amalgamations and grow through absorptions and affiliations (Chaison 1996b). Although there are several in Great Britain (for example, UNISON and the Amalgamated Engineering and Electrical Union) because legislation encourages mergers and there is long tradition of unions using sequences of mergers as a growth strategy, arguably none have yet to emerge in the United States. The proposed merger between the Auto Workers, Steelworkers, and Machinists would have formed a superunion. With over 2 million members, it would have accounted for one in eight union members in the United States and have been the predominant union in manufacturing. The leaders of the three unions welcomed other unions to join with them in merger talks (Bureau of National Affairs 1995b), but in June 1999 the Machinists dropped out of the talks because of differences over

---

[11]Chaison, Sverke, and Sjöberg (1997) measured four facets of participation: administrative participation (activities requiring involvement of considerable time and effort, such as holding office), occasional participation (intermittently occurring activities that nonetheless require substantial effort, such as taking part in bargaining); supportive participation (relatively passive activities requiring little time and effort, such as reading the union newsletter), and membership retention (remaining a member when membership is not compulsory). The investigators found that all forms of participation were unchanged and were high after the merger and that the intention to retain membership had actually increased. They concluded:

Apparently, an open and vigorous discussion of membership participation and a merger plan that assigns a high priority to participation can produce results that defy common assumptions about mergers. Participation need not be lost among the many and complex issues of governance and administration that are resolved in an amalgamation (Chaison, Sverke, and Sjöberg 1997, 13).

union government and structure. A merger of the remaining unions, however, would have created a superunion with 1.5 million members (Greenhouse 1999a). Other superunion mergers are possible; for example, officers of the Communications Workers and the United Food and Commercial Workers have informally discussed a merger to form a 2-million member union that could attract other unions (Bureau of National Affairs 1997a).[12]

Superunions are designed for stability through diversity and size. Without large portions of their membership in any particular industry, occupation, or bargaining unit, they are able to weather industry restructuring, technological change, and strikes without major membership or financial losses. Superunions resemble federations because of their separate, semiautonomous industry or occupational conferences that seek to preserve communities of interest among members while attracting future absorption and affiliation partners (Chaison 1996b).[13]

If American superunions emerge and expand through mergers, they will strongly influence federation policy and shape the proposals for union revival. Based on their own experiences and ambitions, the superunions will want mergers to become fundamental to union revival. Revival will become synonymous with reforming union structure by merging small unions (i.e., those with less than fifty thousand members) into large ones and combining unions in similar or neighboring organizing territories (Chaison 1996b). Under such circumstances, the AFL-CIO will have to define its role in affiliates' mergers, and it must do this with the greatest care.

The Role of the Federation in Affiliates' Mergers

The traditional role of the AFL-CIO and its predecessors in affiliates' mergers is that of an honest broker. Federation officers occasionally introduce likely merger partners and mediate merger negotiations at im-

---

[12]The failed merger attempt of the National Education Association and the American Federation of Teachers would have created a union with 3.3 million members, but one confined to education and with limited potential for expansion through additional mergers.

[13]For a discussion of the financial power of superunions see Masters (1997, 180–82).

passe, but they do not actively and openly promote specific mergers. The AFL-CIO can approve or disapprove of an affiliate's merger, but the basis for and consequences of its scrutiny are not well defined (Chaison 1986). The federation's policy can be succinctly stated as encouraging mergers that make sense. Officers can suggest the benefits of the mergers to small affiliates that have limited prospects for growth and have members in roughly similar occupations and industries, but they can go no further. [14] Respect for affiliate autonomy is crucial to the federation's legitimacy among its unions. Autonomy forms a powerful constraint and precludes an activist merger policy. Overt pressure for specific mergers would be rebuffed and considered an inexcusable intrusion into the internal affairs of affiliates (Chaison 1973, 1986). [15]

In the early 1980s, the federation formed a committee to explore merger prospects, gather and disseminate information on the merger process, and assist in merger negotiations. After a few years of infrequent meetings, the committee was disbanded, most likely because it felt its role could be best carried out informally by federation officers (Chaison 1996b). In 1985 the federation proclaimed that it was desirable for small affiliates sharing communities of interest to merge, and it issued guidelines that defined the conditions under which jurisdictions were broadly similar (AFL-CIO 1985a). These guidelines were never applied. At the 1997 meeting of the AFL-CIO Executive Council, John Sweeney, the federation's president, proposed enlarging the federation's

---

[14]For an exception, see Chaison (1996b, 32–38) regarding the AFL-CIO's active opposition to the proposed merger of the International Typographic Union (ITU) into the Teamsters. The federation campaigned against this absorption and for an amalgamation of the ITU with affiliated printing unions because it wanted a single printing trades union to be formed among several declining affiliates and because the Teamsters was not a member of the federation at that time (1983–87) and would gain entry through that merger.

[15]In other countries, such as Australia and Sweden, federations are more powerful than in the United States, primarily because of their importance to centralized bargaining and union-state consultation. These federations (e.g., the Australian Council of Trade or Unions and the Swedish Trade Union Federation [the LO-Landsorganisationen i Sverige]) have actively promoted merger plans intended to end the independent existence of small ineffective unions, thereby reducing overlap between affiliates' jurisdictions and creating a single large union in each major industry. Despite federation pressures, affiliates remain autonomous in the decision whether to merge and with whom to merge. Accordingly, mergers have not always conformed to federation plans and have not introduced economies of scale in operations or the rationalization of union jurisdictions (Chaison 1996b; Chaison, Sverke, and Sjöberg 1997).

role in affiliate mergers but backed off when union officers would not support change in merger policy (Cohn 1997).[16]

Mergers are internal affairs of the greatest consequence to unions because they end their independent existence and affect the status and employment of officers and staff. The federation's role in mergers will always be restricted, particularly by smaller affiliates concerned that federation merger policy is shaped by the expansionist plans of large unions (Shabecoff 1980). However, as we observed earlier, if super-unions evolve, the federation will have to define its role in mergers within the context of union revival. The most acceptable role will that of a merger facilitator. The AFL-CIO could reestablish the merger committee, recruit and train a staff to mediate merger negotiations, distribute materials that explain merger benefits, provide model implementation agreements, and suggest ways to run merger campaigns. Officers could actively encourage affiliations, arguing that such mergers bring unions into the house of labor and improve their effectiveness as worker representatives.

Conclusion

In many ways we ask too much of union mergers. Research in the United States and other countries shows that mergers will not produce a streamlined, compact labor movement of a few large unions without jurisdictional overlap. Mergers will not rationalize union structure by replacing small, specialized unions with industry-based superunions. The choice of merger partners and conditions are made within unions, not by federation officers and policymakers. Mergers are voluntary and opportunistic. The continued employment of officers and staff after a merger or the impact of a merger on dues can be more important to

---

[16]Since 1984 the AFL-CIO has issued and revised guidelines for a minimum degree of postmerger integration. For example, after a local or regional union becomes affiliated with a national union it must be granted a regular charter and its members must regularly pay dues. This is to prevent nonaffiliated unions from merging with AFL-CIO unions in name only to receive automatic coverage under the federation's no-raid agreement (AFL-CIO 1989).

those appraising merger terms than promises of greater bargaining and political power (Chaison 1996b, 1997). And all merger negotiators have to overcome members' fears about the submergence of their interests in a new, larger union. The only acceptable merger terms may be those that expand governing structures and sustain small locals and regional offices despite their inefficiency (Chaison 1982).

Furthermore, mergers cannot resolve many of the problems that caused them. They will not reduce employer opposition during organizing, turn back the technology and industry restructuring that threatens the job and income security of union workers, or reduce the global competition that weakens the unions' bargaining position. But a fair appraisal will show that mergers never intended to do this, despite the overheated rhetoric of some merger advocates. Rather, the mergers' objective is to halt and possibly reverse financial and membership decline, build institutional stability, and preserve or introduce economies of scale in operations. Studies show that mergers generally do this well, or that they at least provide more favorable outcomes than we might expect without merger (e.g., Chitayat 1979; Chaison 1986, 1996b; Williamson 1995).

Affiliations of local and regional unions with national ones rescue small unions from continuing membership decline and its financial consequences. They bring small unions into the mainstream of the labor movement, enabling them to offer more and better services to members, allocate funds to organizing, and possibly become better-informed and more skilled representatives in bargaining.

Low degrees of organizational integration, the most common post-merger arrangement, means that membership participation need not be sacrificed to build a larger union. Moreover, although researchers seldom recognize it and it would be difficult to measure fully, mergers can energize unions. As the most radical structural change that a union can undergo, mergers bring information sharing and cause members to question their unions' structure, system of governance, and priorities. The campaigns against mergers form the basis of opposition to incumbent leadership and the creation of vibrant political factions. Merger proposals invariably lead to debates at local meetings and national conventions because the stakes are so high—constitutions could be radically altered, locals merged, officers' positions created or discontinued.[17] Finally, mergers lead to a sense of optimism among officers and members who were previously discouraged about the chances of their unions' survival.

Mergers can play an important role in union revival but as a way to strengthen and stabilize unions rather than resolve general economic and political problems. Mergers will not revitalize unions by re-creating them as social movements, although they do have the potential to increase membership participation and organizing activity. The federation has to define its position on mergers within this limited context and the overriding importance of respect for affiliate autonomy. The emergence of superunions would make this task imminent. A good starting point would be to recognize that merging cannot be a substitute for rethinking strategies for organizing, bargaining, and political action.

---

[17]For example, see the local officers' comments in Moody (1995b) regarding the need for intensive debate over the structure and direction of the union to be formed by the amalgamation of the Autoworkers, Steelworkers, and Machinists.

CHAPTER ELEVEN

Building the High Road in Metro Areas

Sectoral Training and Employment Projects

Eric Parker and Joel Rogers

The past two decades of corporate restructuring have dramatically transformed the nature of work and employment in ways that are generally unfavorable to workers. The weakening of internal job ladders, subcontracting of entry-level industry positions, and outsourcing and joint production of tasks involving more advanced occupational strata make initial firm attachment and subsequent advancement more difficult. Shorter job tenure and greater job churning in the broader economy result in more highly volatile labor market conditions for achieving work stability, benefit continuity, and upward mobility. While rumors of the "end of the job" that imply a "spot market" or "freelance" view of the labor market remain vastly premature and misleading, there is still little question that workers are less secure within individual firms and rightly less confident that continued employment within them will naturally lead to higher compensation.[1]

The conventional response to such restructuring is to improve education and training opportunities that help workers cope with recent labor market trends and meet employer demand for skills. As an ameliorative strategy for workers, the thought is that better-trained workers will be more secure ones. Even if they are not retained or advanced

---

[1]For an overview, see Cappelli et al. (1997). On job tenure, see Farber (1997). On earnings instability, see Gottschalk and Moffitt (1994). On job instability and mobility, see Bernhardt, et al. (1998). On contingent work, see Houseman (1997).

by their present employer, they will more easily find advancement opportunities elsewhere. As an industrial strategy, the thought is that business is generally demanding increased skills that present training and other institutions are simply not providing. Meeting the demand would surely make the economy more productive and underwrite the plausibility of training as a boon to workers.

Although better education and training certainly wouldn't harm workers, their benefits are not sufficient to reverse recent labor market outcomes. Despite secular shifts in relative demand for more skilled workers, the pervasiveness of increased industry demand is questionable, and inequality and earnings declines have occurred even within highly educated strata. The dramatic increases in returns to schooling evident over the past two decades in fact owes more to declines in the earnings of less educated workers than to increases in the earnings of more educated ones. Labor market interventions limited to the supply side of worker skill may indeed enable certain individuals to get ahead, but absent a happy Say's Law on human capital, they will do little or nothing to improve the quality of employment and advancement opportunities workers face on the demand side of the labor market. At present, these opportunities appear inadequate to ensure widespread opportunity for wage and earnings growth. Intensified competition between firms, institutional and political changes, and low-wage business strategies provide much of the explanation for stagnating wages and rising inequality. Without direct intervention on the demand side, these outcomes will remain well after any "skills mismatch" is resolved.[2]

The steps unions need to take to defend their members and expand their base in this situation are straightforward in theory if not in practice. Using all the tools at their disposal, they need to close off the low road, help pave the high road, and enable workers and firms to navigate from the first to the second. This means organizing more members and recovering some leverage over wage and other norms in the

---

[2]For an overview of recent trends in income, see Gottschalk (1997). For the impact of supply-and-demand factors on wages, see Bound and Johnson (1992); Katz and Murphy (1992); and Autor, Katz, and Krueger (1997). For an overview of institutional factors, see DiNardo, Fortin, and Lemieux (1996), as well as Mishel, Bernstein, and Schmitt (1999).

economy. It means mobilizing labor's own capital in the form of pension assets to encourage higher standards of corporate practice. It means modernizing labor's political operations and making alliance with other voting constituencies to reclaim some political power, particularly at the state and local levels where much action is devolving. But it also means that unions need to insert themselves more directly into the process of industrial restructuring itself, to assert more control of the terms of trade in firm and regional labor markets, and to intervene on the demand side of the skill equation.

To obtain rewards for training, workers need to build the high road with new technologies, work systems, and skills, and to bargaining over the resulting gains. If the "union premium" in organized firms is to survive competition, those firms need to be more productive than their lower-wage nonunion rivals. Retention of the existing union base preserves the leverage that is needed to organize new workers and minimizes the number of additional members that are needed to maintain or expand market share. More broadly, if the economy as a whole is to move toward more high-road production and service delivery, unions need to take explicit leadership of the restructuring process. Although many allies in this fight can be found, no major institution approaches labor's congruent capacity and interest in waging it. An industrial strategy that benefits workers would generally make the process of new organizing and political and other alliance building much easier.[3]

The question is, how might this be done? While there are many parts to a complete answer, we believe one especially promising one is the growing number of labor-led sectoral training and employment projects, which provide a base for further capacity building and experimentation. These initiatives typically coordinate workforce development activity across groups of firms with convergent skill needs in regional labor markets. They seek to bring greater transparency to the regional labor market within their sectors, to enhance employment and training opportunities, to build a presence within area firms to advance

---

[3]For more on this general view, see Rogers (1990, 1992, 1993, 1993a, 1995, 1996, 1996a, 1997, 1997a), Dresser and Rogers (1998, forthcoming), and Rathke and Rogers (1996). For implications for organization and representation, see also Heckscher (1988); Cobble (1991); and Herzenberg, Alic, and Wial (1998).

workers within and between them, and to work with firms to improve their performance.[4]

The labor movement's potential to play such a role may be most evident where state or local structures of the AFL-CIO have become vehicles for affiliates to achieve bargaining, organizing, and public-policy objectives in their areas. In the case of Wisconsin, the state AFL-CIO has developed a comprehensive strategy for industrial unions to improve the livelihoods of working families. A central component of the strategy is the formation of the Wisconsin Regional Training Partnership (WRTP) that builds the capacity of affiliates to retain and develop the current member base. The other component is the development of an organizing campaign that builds the capacity of affiliates to increase the union content of finished products, either by retaining work in-house, upgrading union suppliers, or organizing nonunion shops. Now the state federation is working with affiliates in a wide range of other sectors to develop comprehensive strategies for regaining their respective market shares or entering markets in which unions do not already have a presence.

This chapter first examines the case of the WRTP. It then considers the possibilities and actual experience, first in Milwaukee and then more generally, of building such institutions of high-road industrial governance in sectors other than manufacturing. It concludes with speculation on the promise of such models and their links to other aspects of labor's revitalization program.

High-Road Partnerships

The origins of the WRTP lay in the deep manufacturing recession that devastated the Midwest in the 1980s. Milwaukee County lost about one-third of its durable goods manufacturing jobs between 1979 and 1987. As the region recovered from the debacle, the more advanced firms encountered a skills shortage associated with adoption of new products, technologies, and work processes. Some firms embarked on "low-road" strategies that involved relocating to low-

---

[4]For examples, see Baugh and Hilton (1997), Benner (1996), Carre and Joshi (1997), Dresser and Rogers (1997), Kazis (1998), and Seigel and Kwass (1995).

wage havens within the United States or abroad or extracting concessions from their unions. But others sought to reposition themselves for more advanced production and worked with their unions to upgrade the skills of an age-compressed workforce. They received assistance from the Wisconsin State AFL-CIO that gained the relevant expertise in workforce development policy based on its leadership in the formation of a one-stop assistance center for dislocated workers. The dislocated worker center began to assist employers, unions, and local technical colleges with the creation of workplace learning centers. This network would later become the foundation for building the WRTP.

A prominent Republican business leader who chaired a governor's commission on workforce development and the president of the state federation invited the Center on Wisconsin Strategy (COWS) to recommend strategies for reviving manufacturing in 1991. COWS proposed a jointly governed consortium of employers and unions to support family-sustaining jobs in a new business environment. After some protracted shuttle diplomacy among and between area firms and unions, COWS obtained final approval of an organizational charter the following year. An interim steering committee sponsored a founding conference that established working groups of charter member firms and unions to build consensus on recommendations for action by the end of 1993.[5]

WRTP has since formed partnerships with numerous public-sector agencies and educational institutions to assist member firms and unions with the adoption of new technologies and work processes; worker education and training programs; and future workforce programs involving dislocated, low-income, and young workers. The partnership has grown from an experiment with a handful of workplaces into an association of sixty-three members employing roughly sixty thousand workers in the greater Milwaukee area or one-quarter of the area's industrial workforce. Improvements in quality, cycle time, productivity, and inventory management have resulted in a net

---

[5]For more on the development of the WRTP, see Neuenfeldt and Parker (1994) and Parker and Rogers (1996). The data reported below come from the WRTP (1998a and 1998b).

increase of roughly six thousand jobs among member firms since 1994. Both management and labor representatives generally report better labor-management relations in shops in which the nonsupervisory workforce is represented by industrial unions. Member wages are robust, averaging $17.37 for skilled trades workers and $14.60 for production workers. And of standing importance to building labor-community alliances, these gains are achieved in a diverse workforce: 16 percent African American, 7 percent Latino, and 25 percent female.

Modernization

The WRTP encompasses larger companies making finished products and a growing number of smaller suppliers. Most of these smaller shops depend on the larger ones for at least part of their business. At least 90 percent of sales of member companies with fewer than 500 employees are to other manufacturers. The larger firms have the capacity to exert pressure on many of their suppliers to adopt the advanced industry practices they have already implemented in-house. The WRTP provides a vehicle for them to achieve supply chain optimization.

The WRTP has formed an alliance with the Wisconsin Manufacturing Extension Program whose mission is to assist smaller-to-medium-sized enterprises (less than 500 employees) with modernization. The modernization service assists smaller shops with assessments of their business operations and plans for improving them. The consultants WRTP has assigned to union shops worked with two-dozen shops in 1999 and completed the implementation of modernization plans in eight of them. The program helped prevent two plant closings involving 1,200 family-supporting jobs. Almost all members now have a functioning joint steering committee to guide modernization in their workplaces. Over the past few years nearly all have designed and engineered new products, and four in five have made major investments in new machinery and equipment. Their new production systems are increasingly based on cellular plant layouts and self-directed teams, with workers increasingly responsible for improving product quality, shortening cycle time, increasing productivity, and reducing inventory cost.

Worker Training

Much of the original emphasis of the WRTP has been on the development of jointly administered training programs for incumbent workers. By 1999 the estimated level of employer investment averaged $678 per frontline worker for a total of nearly $21 million. About six thousand nonsupervisory workers obtained education and training services through a combination of workplace learning centers, technical college courses, tuition reimbursement programs, and apprenticeships. People of color accounted for one-fourth of the total.

Most members either have or plan to create an on-site learning center. The centers are generally run by a combination of technical college instructors and in-house personnel. Taken together, employers spend about $2.4 million on their learning centers per year, and about twenty-four hundred workers participate on an annual basis. In addition, roughly 80 percent of member firms contract with local technical colleges for more specialized courses. All members have at least a tuition reimbursement program for twenty-one hundred workers to further their education on their own time. Finally, half the members are revitalizing their apprenticeship programs in the skilled trades, and journey-level workers may go on to complete their degrees. The result is a substantial increase in the number of incumbent workers with an associate or bachelor degree.

A critical mass of employers investing in skill upgrading has enhanced the upward mobility and career security of workers. Higher skills facilitate the transition to high-performance organizations and enable workers to succeed within them, and the transferability of skills allows workers to find new employment whenever they need to. Along with the dislocated worker center and local technical college, the WRTP is conducting a demonstration project to retrain at least 150 unemployed or at-risk workers for higher-skill jobs such as CNC machinist or maintenance mechanic. The demonstration project features a Spanish track for concurrent instruction in communication and technical skills for a rapidly growing immigrant workforce.

Future Workforce

The revival of manufacturing employment and retirement of a highly age-compressed workforce has elevated the importance of the future workforce in recent years. Despite the recent influx of new workers, the average worker is still 43 years old with 18 years of seniority. WRTP has developed future workforce programs involving unemployed, low-income, and young workers. Unions have begun to participate in selecting job candidates in almost two-thirds of the companies and in conducting employee orientation in more half of them. More recently, they have begun working with management to formalize mentoring networks on the shop floor.

The employment and training program has placed nearly five hundred central city residents into family-supporting jobs over the last three years. The average starting wage of more than $10 per hour plus benefits far exceeds the rest of the workforce development system in the region. The participants increase their individual earnings from an average of about $9,000 per year to $23,000 after their first year on the job. The employment retention rate is nearly 70 percent. Now the challenge is to scale up. A Jobs 2000 Campaign is designed to place five hundred residents this year alone. Residents are recruited from a growing network of job centers, welfare-to-work agencies, community and faith-based organizations, community development corporations, and the like. Over 90 percent of the participants are people of color. Half the participants have not completed high school. Their average household income is roughly $12,000 per year.

The program provides a viable alternative to staffing service agencies. Several member companies are converting temporary jobs back into permanent union-represented jobs. Savings on billing rates, finder's fees, and other costs associated with high turnover staffing arrangements (for example, lower quality and productivity) offset the cost of union wages and benefits. The workers get better jobs, the companies get employees, and the unions get more members. It would take the labor movement roughly $100,000 on average to recruit 100 workers, the number of new members that unions are likely to gain from the conversion of temp jobs in 2000.

The program also provides a vehicle for current union members to participate in selecting, orientating, and mentoring new members. The membership is becoming increasingly diverse. The most dramatic example is the transformation of a suburban plant from an all-white workforce to one in which people of color make up 30 percent. The ability to recruit and retain a qualified workforce under tight labor market conditions has enabled the firm and union to bring in a new product line, increase employment and union membership, and enhance the job security of senior members. The first two African Americans have been elected to union leadership in the history of the plant.[6]

Expansion

WRTP has completed a needs assessment survey of 448 shops to document the opportunity for expansion. Taken together, these shops account for 80 percent of union shops in the state. They employ a total of 134,000 employees, including 95,000 (better than 70 percent) in skilled trades or production jobs. Currently the number one barrier to job growth is the difficulty in finding qualified workers under tight labor market conditions. More than half the shops report a need for assistance with the recruitment and retention of new employees. An even larger number need assistance with upgrading the skills of incumbent workers.

To develop an effective response to these needs, WRTP convened a forum for member companies and unions to discuss the skills shortage with state and local officials. The governor appointed the business and labor co-chairs of WRTP to lead a task force on the future of technical education and training in the state. Most of the budget and policy recommendations are currently being implemented. The $40 million package includes a workforce attachment and advancement fund to help low-wage workers achieve upward mobility, a new scholarship fund for youth to attend their local technical colleges, the expansion of local youth apprenticeship initiatives, the expansion of manufacturing extension programs, and other related efforts. WRTP is now working with local workforce development agencies and educational institutions to expand the partnership in manufacturing and replicate it in other sectors.

---

[6]WRTP is increasingly involved with school-to-work programs to prepare youth for high-tech workplaces as well. Half of the membership provides youth apprenticeships or other work-based training to high school students. Members assist schools with the revival of technical education programs, offer professional development opportunities to teachers, and provide mentors at the work site for students. The graduates obtain high-wage production jobs, traditional apprenticeships, advanced standing in technical colleges, and admission into the university system.

Industry Strategies

The success in retaining and building the industrial union base has renewed enough confidence in the future of manufacturing to inspire
new organizing in the state. The same affiliates that are involved in the
WRTP have typically participated in a new coordinated multi-union
campaign to organize suppliers. The state federation has developed the
campaign to help affiliates become much more proactive in governing
supplier relationships in the region. A handful of local unions have already begun to extend the scope of their collective-bargaining agreement and partnership with employers to take a more proactive role in
sourcing decisions. Workers on the shop floor are increasingly engaged
in coordinating production with their peers in supplier firms and participating directly in supplier development and assistance. The objective of local labor leaders is to establish criteria for outsourcing decisions that enable them to keep work in-house, to utilize unionized
suppliers, or ultimately, to leverage nonunion shops.

Wisconsin is one of a handful of sites for coordinated organizing
campaigns that is supported nationwide by the AFL-CIO. The national
AFL-CIO, state federation, and participating affiliates all have representatives on a steering committee that oversees research, education,
and other assistance that builds the capacity of industrial unions to recapture the market share lost to outsourcing. Local labor leaders immediately recognize the serious threat of nonunion suppliers to the employment security and bargaining power of their members. The
strategic focus of the campaign is on a small number of supplier industries that are responsible for taking most of the work out of the
larger union-represented assembly plants and first-tier suppliers in the
state over the last decade.

The state federation has gradually developed a comprehensive strategy for building the capacity of affiliates to improve the livelihoods of
working families in the state. The WRTP builds their capacity to retain and develop good jobs, to transform bad jobs into good jobs, and
to offer access to better jobs. The organizing campaign builds their capacity to strategically target shops for extending worker voice down
the supply chain to key industries. The legislative and political program is being designed for local unions to block the low road, build

the high road, and move firms from one to the other. The final piece is a resource center drawing upon a variety of allies to provide the necessary research and education for affiliates to advance their bargaining, organizing, and public policy agendas in the state.

The industrial sector has become a model for every sector of the labor movement in the state. Every major affiliate has requested assistance from the state federation with the development of strategies for their respective sectors. The WRTP has already begun to assist affiliates and their employers with development of high-road partnerships in the communication, construction, healthcare, hospitality, and transportation sectors. Other sectors are likely to follow in the near future. In many cases there are already examples of new initiatives in other metro areas. What they all have in common is an ability of worker organizations to establish labor market intermediaries that unite the employment and training needs of communities with the workforce development needs of employers and unions.

HOSPITALITY

The San Francisco Hotels Partnership Project resembles the WRTP in many respects.[7] HERE (Hotel Employees and Restaurant Employees International Union) Local 2 started the project with a dozen major first-class hotels in the market to improve the quality of employment and customer service. They developed strategies for achieving mutual objectives such as an industrywide curriculum for core skills, cross-classification procedures, and the revival of a hiring hall. The first phase has delivered 100 hours of on-the-job and classroom training in team-building and communication skills to more than 1,600 of the 5,000 workers covered by the partnership. The core curriculum may underwrite the reclassification of jobs and the transfer, rotation, and promotion of workers to combine the stability workers want with the flexibility management wants. Additional training is provided in the core job clusters of the industry, including housekeeping and food and beverage departments. Funding comes from a combination of the multi-

---

[7]The following section draws upon Parker and Rogers (forthcoming) and references cited above in note 5.

employer bargaining agreement and the state's employment and training fund. While upgrading standards among the large share of properties under contract, the union has obtained card check agreements from new targets and a local ordinance requiring such agreements from publicly subsidized firms such as convention hotels.

HEALTH CARE

In New York, Local 1199, now affiliated with Service Employees International Union (SEIU), has negotiated a multi-employer fund to support mobility within and between hospitals, nursing homes, and other facilities. The progression of proficiency and certification standards in the sector provides clear pathways for workers to advance their careers on an incremental basis. In the context of enormous restructuring brought about by managed care and fiscal austerity, the ability to obtain additional skills and move into new jobs helps workers adjust to volatile conditions. Through joint committees at the work site, the union has been able to shape the reorganization of service delivery systems, including the redesign of work on the inside and the creation of outplacement centers on the outside, in exchange for a commitment to employment security for much of the workforce. Although workers with the least seniority may lose their current jobs, they have the right to further training, income maintenance, and transfers to other facilities under contract. The demonstrated ability of the union to impact the restructuring of the industry and support worker adjustment to inevitable dislocation has become a major selling point for future organizing in the region.

TECHNOLOGY

In technology Communications Workers of America (CWA) has experimented with the development of employment centers in Cleveland, Los Angeles, Seattle, and elsewhere. The union leverages supplier networks of the traditional phone companies to reemploy dislocated workers in emerging jobs in the sector. The prohibition of prehire agreements outside the building trades effectively requires the centers to compete on the open market based on the quality of their workers. They run a newly developed apprenticeship program to qualify their current members and community residents for various kinds of technical work in a rapidly growing field. As in the building trades, the union provides training, employment stability, and continuous benefits for workers who move from one job to the next. The potential for this strategy is evident in northern Jersey where an International Brotherhood of Electrical Workers (IBEW) local has a more established training center, apprenticeship program, and hiring hall. Under tight labor market conditions, the union no longer has to organize the hard way, signing up workers and filing for elections one employer at a time. As employers began to approach the union about signing onto the labor agreement, the number of contractors supplied by the hiring hall increased from 20 to more than 120 in just the last few years. Union leaders believe they would double their share of the market overnight if they could expand the training center fast enough. This is clearly one of a growing number of instances in which employment and training programs could have an immediate impact on labor market organization.

TEMP WORK

Labor is also beginning to organize around temporary work and staffing service agencies. The labor council in Hackensack, New Jersey, sponsors the Bergen Task Force on Temporary Work to improve conditions in the industry. The task force has produced a "Guide to Best Practice Agencies" to help workers get better jobs, employers get better workers, and temp agencies to fulfill their promise of helping meet the needs of both parties in the new economy. The guide has been taken up by a coalition of similar projects around the country for implementation in their labor market areas. The nonprofit arm of the labor council in Silicon Valley, Working Partnerships USA, has conducted extensive research on the industry and just started a pilot project to dispatch temporary workers to public-sector employers in the region. A critical mass of agreements with employers would enable the nonprofit to reach scale, compete on the open market, and perhaps bring for-profit agencies to the bargaining table. A number of affiliates subjected to widespread adoption of contingent work arrangements are supporting the effort.

CHILD CARE

In Philadelphia, Childspace Cooperative Development Inc. (CCDI) and the National Union of Hospitals and Health Care Employees, AFSCME (American Federation of State, County and Municipal Employees) have joined forces to improve the quality of jobs and quality of care in the area. Childspace supports two employee-owned child care centers with about thirty-five workers each. These centers pay a 25 percent premium over the average wage, offer better benefits than the industry does generally, and provide worker voice and training. With 50 percent lower turnover, they are able to recoup their investment in workers and provide greater continuity and quality of care for low- and moderate-income families. In response to unfavorable policy developments and lower-cost competition, CCDI formed an alliance with Local 1199, a large affiliate of AFSCME, to organize the market. The union is organizing the workers while CCDI is organizing the employers to negotiate an industrywide agreement and provide technical assistance to support higher standards. The strategy is to form a partnership between employers, workers, family providers, and parents to raise the level of public investment in the quality of care and employment in the industry with public resources eventually conditioned on certification of the skills and working conditions of providers.

COMMUNITY-LED EFFORTS

Finally, at least some community and faith-based organizations, principally ACORN (Association of Community Organizations for Reform Now) and IAF (Industrial Areas Foundation), have used their political power to establish themselves as labor-market intermediaries working with area businesses and the public sector to impose conditions on work and increase job access and training for their memberships.[8] ACORN has long operated community-based hiring halls that channel members into industries it simultaneously pressures for greater public accountability. IAF's Project QUEST in San Antonio is an in-

---

[8]For more general reviews of the role in community-based organizations engaged in workforce development, see Clark and Dawson (1995) and Harrison and Weiss (1998).

tegrated program of employment-linked training and support for hundreds of low-income community residents. Area employers in lead sectors, including finance and health care, agree to give their living-wage jobs to residents who demonstrate specified skills. Community organizations and area technical colleges then work together to identify candidates for the reserved positions, train them to the required competencies, and support them during the training period with integrated income and other supports. Both ACORN and IAF have been leaders in the "living wage" campaigns, which over the past few years have spread to more than forty sites around the country and have imposed general area wage norms or conditions on public contracting.

Implications

Most of these projects are not yet at the scale that is needed to fundamentally alter employment relations within their target industry, much less change the terms of regional labor market administration. But their growing number and diversity suggests that worker-unfriendly changes in employment relations are creating a new demand for worker support systems that operate on at least a multi-employer basis, clarify the terms of labor-market demand, assist workers in gaining job access and advancement, and set higher standards for firm conduct. This demand is real, manifest, and widely felt among very large portions of the working population.

Unions are uniquely positioned to satisfy this demand (albeit often through structures differing from their conventional ones) given their defining pro-worker institutional interests, knowledge of industry practice, political and economic power, and cross-firm reach in the economy. Those unions or regional labor bodies that have made the effort can point to concrete gains for their members and improved relations with employers and the community. More broadly, their efforts have moved them from being increasingly marginalized subjects of industrial restructuring to visible authors of a new economy exhibiting greater fairness in the distribution of opportunity and reward. Both directly through this work and through how it is seen, unions secure increased capacity and better market and political conditions for organizing new members.

These new labor market institutions are most naturally organized on a sector within regional economies. Such organization provides more or less obvious economies of scale and scope in the delivery of training and modernization assistance, interfirm learning and collective industry capacity for upgrading, and enhanced career opportunities for workers. Of no small political or welfare importance, it also potentially improves the performance of public institutions. For public-training providers, for example, it improves the flow and quality of information on skill needs while again permitting the efficiencies that come from the articulation of industrywide rather than firm-specific training demand. For private industry councils and emerging workforce investment boards, it provides a natural and more representative foundation for their mandated private-sector representation. For any public intervention in regional industrial policy, such organization provides private leverage on public dollars.

Labor movements always struggle between the competing needs to serve their present members and to make a contribution to the general welfare of the sort that will make them attractive to current nonmembers and secure the social cachet and political support they always need to advance in a competitive capitalist economy. The high-road regional partnerships described here offer a possible resolution to that tension by providing manifest benefit to current members and manifest gains to the broader community.

That they are largely occurring in metropolitan areas is not an accident and provides natural linkage to other aspects of the "New Voices" effort at labor revitalization. To a degree long neglected within the labor movement, union membership remains heavily concentrated in metropolitan areas. Just four such regions (Los Angeles, New York, Chicago, Detroit) account for about a quarter of all private-sector membership, and only forty regions account for fully half. These regions yield local union densities well above national averages and provide the critical mass and leverage needed for successful new organizing. Moreover, to the extent we have high-road production in the United States, it is disproportionately concentrated in such urban areas.[9] Putting these facts together, it is no surprise that all the most

---

[9]The links among union density, metro regions, and high-roading are mutual. Denser populations are easier to organize, organization demands the high road, the richer tax base and "agglomeration" effects associated with population and firm density facilitate the high road being taking, and so on. For more on their interactions and evidence of the relative high-road character of U.S. metro areas, see Luria and Rogers (1999).

advanced union efforts to build high-road partnerships have been metropolitan.

What is less commonly appreciated is that metro reconstruction holds the key to national economic reconstruction. Despite their present neglect, metro regions provide the natural pillars of a high-road national economy. And despite continued sprawl and suburbanization, cities and their immediate surroundings of largely working-class suburbs still contain well over half the general population, while producing an even greater share of national wealth. Turn around production and economic policy within those regions and you turn around the country.

The opportunity all this describes for labor is large. To connect the dots: The places of labor's greatest residual strength also happen to be the places most critical to reordering our economy and holding the greatest immediate potential for modeling the high road. The labor markets within them, which are almost infinitely more immobile and spatially bounded than the product and capital flows of the firms that draw upon them, substantially determine regional patterns of production. Asserting control over the terms of those markets and their administration, which can in fact be done as the examples here show, thus gains labor critical leverage in the real economy where it probably counts the most. Finally, such labor-market interventions would give labor a popular visible role in economic stewardship and therefore all the gains to be had in political and other support without the risk of membership resentment. The reason for the absence of resentment is that the interests of current union members in this area, such as labor-market transparency, training opportunities, industrial upgrading, career paths and mobility, and compensation for greater productivity, are virtually identical to the interests of workers generally. Building high-road regional partnerships in metro regions is thus not an extravagance, much less a distraction from other critical elements in labor's revitalization. On the contrary, as a natural starting point in the long fight to improve the economy's performance for workers, it is a natural way of reconciling the imperatives of membership service and movement growth.

PART IV

Politics and Policy

CHAPTER TWELVE

Organized Labor versus Globalization

NAFTA, Fast Track, and PNTR with China

James Shoch

S ince about 1970 the American labor movement has fought, mostly
unsuccessfully, to alleviate the impact of trade competition and
liberalization on its membership. This lengthy battle over one aspect
of a wider process that has come to be called economic "globalization"
reached new levels of intensity in the 1990s, resulting in a see-sawing
set of outcomes.

In late 1993 labor lost a fierce struggle to defeat the proposed North
American Free Trade Agreement. Four years later, however, in November 1997, labor won a significant victory when it defeated President Bill Clinton's bid to regain "fast-track" trade negotiating authority, which requires that trade liberalization agreements be awarded
quick up-or-down votes in Congress without amendments that can
unhinge such pacts. This was the first time that a president had been
denied such negotiating authority since the advent of the fast-track
procedure in 1974. In fact, this was the first time that a trade liberalization proposal had been rejected in the entire post–World War II
era.[1] Ten months later, in September 1998, labor won a second, albeit
less significant victory when it beat back yet another fast-track proposal, this one Republican sponsored.

Labor did not have much time to celebrate its fast-track victories,
however. In the spring of 2000 the unions suffered another major set-
back when, after a bitter fight, the House of Representative approved

---

[1] Reflecting on the political significance of labor's victory, Thomas Edsall went so far as
to suggest that the "unions' formidable efforts to block the 'fast track' trade bill shows that
organized labor has more influence than at any time since 1968, when it nearly elected a president" (Edsall 1997).

"permanent normal trade relations" (PNTR) with China, which were intended to liberalize trade with that country.

How can we explain this shifting pattern of labor's fortunes? To answer this question, in what follows I will first trace the history of labor's trade policy defeats in the 1970s and 1980s. I will then discuss the NAFTA battle of the early 1990s. Next, I will explore the 1997 fast-track battle in more detail, followed by a much briefer discussion of the 1998 fast-track fight. Finally, in a section written literally as this volume was being sent to press, I will analyze the spring 2000 PNTR struggle.

Analytically I will argue that a number of factors combined to determine the ebb and flow of the trade conflicts of the 1990s, including the variable vigor of Bill Clinton's pro-liberalization efforts. Most important, however, was the shifting balance of strength between business and labor, a balance that was due less to differences in the amount of structurally generated resources available to both actors—here business had a consistent advantage—than it was to differences both in the extent to which these resources were mobilized and in the strategic acuity with which these resources were deployed.

Thus, I will argue that following its defeat on NAFTA, labor's subsequent victories in the 1997 and 1998 fast-track fights were due to the movement's heightened ability to marshal and utilize its human and financial resources for political purposes in a context rendered more favorable to labor by the behavior of the business community. This improvement in labor's political capacities was significantly facilitated by the revitalization of the AFL-CIO's political operations under its new president, John Sweeney.

In the 1997 fast-track conflict, labor capitalized on its successes in the 1996 elections, effectively using "inside" and "outside" lobbying tactics—Washington lobbying, coalition building, issue advertising, grassroots mobilization, etc.—to pressure reelection-minded Congress members, especially Democrats, to oppose fast track. Particularly important in this case, however, was a shift of business campaign contributions to the Republicans following the 1994 congressional elections, which left the Democrats relatively more dependent on labor for campaign funds, a dependence that labor was effectively able to exploit during the fast-track battle.

In the 1998 fast-track fight, however, labor's grassroots organizing around both the issue itself and the fast-approaching midterm elections appear to have played a more important role than did union money in sending the Republican proposal down to defeat.

In the titanic PNTR fight that closed the decade and Clinton's presidency, labor's fortunes were again reversed. This time the unions were outgunned by the business community, which stole a leaf from labor's book by waging a massive inside and outside lobbying campaign of its own, simultaneously involving Washington pressure, issue advertising, and grassroots mobilization. At the same time, during the 1999–2000 election cycle, business redirected some of its campaign contributions back to the Democrats, reducing their dependence on labor and making it easier for a substantial number of them to break with the unions to support PNTR.

In a concluding section, I will suggest that in light of labor's defeat in the PNTR battle and the likely prospect that the unions will not be able to simply block future trade liberalization proposals, labor will need to develop new strategies of accommodation with the forces of globalization and liberalization.

Labor and Trade Policy in the Postwar Era[2]

From the passage of the Reciprocal Trade Agreements Act of 1934, which set the United States on its course toward postwar trade liberalization, down through the enactment of the Trade Expansion Act of 1962, organized labor was a mainstay of the dominant and eventually bipartisan free trade coalition. During this period workers in the nation's globally preeminent Fordist mass production industries shared in the benefits of international trade, while the labor leadership saw trade liberalization as a bulwark against the spread of the communist threat to free trade unionism.[3]

---

[2]In this section and in much of the rest of this chapter, I have drawn heavily on Destler (1998a). For a broader overview of U.S. trade policy and politics during the post-war period, see Destler's landmark study, Destler (1995).

[3]On labor's role in the free trade coalition during this period, see Donohue (1992).

With the eventual decline of the American economy relative to its reconstructed West European and Japanese rivals, however, and the later onset of the crisis of Fordism in the late 1960s and early 1970s, organized labor, largely representing unskilled and low-end semiskilled workers in labor-intensive, import-competing industries, began to abandon its earlier support for free trade (Deardorff and Stern, 1979; Midford, 1993, 538–39; 555–57). Backed by northern industrial-state Democrats, much of labor now opposed further trade liberalization initiatives and called for legislation to slow the rising tide of imports.

Labor's efforts went unrewarded. In the early 1970s Congress refused to consider the union-backed Burke-Hartke bill, which would have imposed across-the-board import curbs. Labor also failed to prevent passage of the liberalizing Trade Reform Act of 1974 (which introduced the fast-track procedure) and the Trade Agreements Act of 1979. In all these fights, labor was defeated by the concerted efforts of free-trading Presidents Nixon and Carter, import-export and multinational business interests, and congressional Republicans—many of them from export-dependent farm and Sun Belt states who had become ideologically aligned with and politically reliant upon these internationally oriented interests.

Labor didn't fare much better in the 1980s when the competitive weaknesses of American industry were compounded by the grossly overvalued dollar, leading to new demands for both import curbs and action to pry open closed foreign, especially Japanese, markets. In 1982 and 1983 labor could not even get the Republican-controlled Senate to take up the twice House-passed "domestic content" bill intended to help the beleaguered auto industry.[4] Labor suffered another defeat in 1984 when it failed to seize an opportunity to amend or block a provision in the Senate version of what became the Trade and Tariff Act of 1984 that continued the Generalized System of Preferences (GSP) for developing countries, an arrangement that labor had long opposed.

Labor was more successful in its efforts to shape the huge Omnibus Trade and Competitiveness Act of 1988.[5] The final version of the bill

---

[4]The bill would have curbed the import of cars and car parts and encouraged foreign countries to produce in the United States by limiting the amount of imported auto parts and labor.

[5]For a thorough analysis of this bill and the politics surrounding it, see Schwab (1994).

contained a number of provisions supported by labor, including the Super 301 law, which required the United States Trade Representative (USTR) to identify countries that consistently erected barriers to U.S. exports and to initiate steps to remove those barriers.[6] On the whole, however, labor was quite disappointed with the trade bill. Under business, Republican, and presidential pressure, various labor-backed provisions were dropped or watered down. In particular, the provision in early House drafts of the bill most strongly supported by labor—the so-called "Gephardt amendment,"[7] which would have required the use of quotas and tariffs to penalize countries like Japan than ran large chronic surpluses with the United States—was replaced in the final draft by the Senate's weaker Super 301 plank.

Labor's influence in all these struggles was undermined by postindustrial structural shifts in the economy that together with other factors had begun to erode the movement's social and political strength as early as the mid-1950s.[8] First, the decline of the northern urban industrial workforce led to a drop in union membership. Combined with the growth of the new high technology and white-collar workforce in the suburbs and the Sun Belt, this produced a relative decline in labor's electoral influence. Second, as we shall see in more detail below, labor's decline limited the funds it could contribute to congressional campaigns, while the amount donated by corporate political action committees (PACs) exploded, especially during the 1980s. This benefited the pro-business, pro-free-trade Republicans and forced Democrats in Congress to become relatively more reliant on business for campaign funding. These trends together limited labor's influence on many issues, including trade policy.

---

[6]The bill also contained a tougher and expedited unfair trade practices procedure, including the designation of violations of workers' rights as unfair trade practices, and an expanded training and adjustment assistance program. A measure requiring that advance notification be given of plant closures involving one hundred or more workers, originally included in the bill, was eventually passed as a freestanding piece of legislation.

[7]Sponsored by Rep. Richard Gephardt (D-Mo.).

[8]In his provocative recent book (Dark 1999), Taylor Dark disputes the widely shared view that labor's political influence declined during the post–World War II era, but I think he overstates his case.

The NAFTA Battle: Labor Loses a Tough One

In the 1990s the focus of labor's trade energies shifted away from attempts to pass tough legislation to stem the flow of imports or to pry open closed foreign markets.[9] Now labor found itself battling initiatives to liberalize trade with the developing world that it feared would cost American workers jobs and income. The first of these battles was over the North American Free Trade Agreement.[10]

In early 1991, responding to a proposal from Mexican president Carlos Salinas de Gortari and pursuing a number of economic and political goals of his own, President George Bush notified Congress of his intent to negotiate a regional free trade agreement with Mexico and Canada. To facilitate these negotiations, on March 1 Bush sent a request for a two-year extension of his fast-track authority to Congress.

The battle lines that emerged that spring over Bush's fast-track request had actually been forming for some months.[11] On the pro-NAFTA side first were competitive agricultural exporters and high technology and other manufacturing exporters seeking to realize economies of scale.[12] The strongest business proponents of fast track and an eventual deal, however, were U.S.-based multinational corporations which more than trade liberalization sought the liberalization of Mexico's investment rules. These firms anticipated that NAFTA would enable them to more easily tap Mexico's vast pool of cheap labor to improve their international competitiveness vis-à-vis their European and especially their Japanese rivals.[13] At the same time, corporations could use the increased threat of flight to Mexico to force workers in their American plants to

---

[9]During the 1980s certain formerly protectionist firms in industries such as textiles, automobiles, and steel with fairly mobile capital and relatively cheap access to critical factor inputs responded to declining possibilities for winning protection by opting for a second-most-preferred strategy of adjustment (Lusztig 1998; Hathaway 1998). Along with strong economic growth, this contributed to the reduction of protectionist pressure in the 1990s.

[10]For two extremely useful overviews and analyses, see Mayer (1998) and Grayson (1995).

[11]For the next two paragraphs, see Mayer (1998, 69–77) and Avery (1998).

[12]On general patterns of business support for NAFTA, see Cox (1995).

[13]As Sandra Masur (1991, 101), Director of Public Policy Analysis for Eastman Kodak and leader of the influential Business Roundtable's efforts on behalf of NAFTA, explained, American business supported NAFTA, because "U.S. manufacturing must pursue joint production [with Mexico] to keep costs down and compete against European and Japanese com-

make wage and work rule concessions, still further reducing their costs and boosting their competitiveness and profits.[14]

On the anti-NAFTA side, various labor-intensive, import-competing agricultural and industrial interests strongly opposed an agreement, fearing a wave of cheap imports. The most concerted opposition to a regional trade pact, however, was mounted by the American labor movement. For labor, as for U.S. multinational business interests, NAFTA was more an investment than a trade issue. Industrial unions worried that by liberalizing not just trade but also investment rules, such an agreement would intensify both the actual and threatened flight of manufacturing capital to Mexico in search of cheap labor, thus eliminating U.S. jobs and undercutting American workers' bargaining power and wages.[15]

---

petitors who pursue similar strategies." According to a 1992 Roper poll, 40 percent of some 450 U.S. corporate executives said it was "very" or "somewhat" likely that their companies would "shift some production to Mexico to Mexico . . . if NAFTA is ratified." For large companies the figure was 55 percent (Bowles and Larudee 1993).

[14]In the same 1992 Roper poll, 24 percent of the executives surveyed admitted that it was either very or somewhat likely that "NAFTA will be used by [their] company as a bargaining chip to keep wages down in the U.S." (Bowles and Larudee 1993). On NAFTA as an element of a strategy of industrial restructuring at labor's expense, see Rupert (1995) and Moody (1995).

[15]On a theoretical note, in a study of labor's influence on congressional voting on NAFTA in 1993, John Conybeare and Mark Zinkula (1996) suggest that large sectors of labor can be expected to support protectionism, or to oppose trade liberalization, regardless of whether a "Stolper-Samuelson" or a "specific factors" model of trade policy preference formation is assumed. According to Stolper-Samuelson theories, which assume that factors of production—broadly defined as capital, labor, and land—are perfectly mobile, owners of abundant factors will support free trade while owners of scarce factors will back protectionism. Thus, in an advanced country like the United States, in which labor is the scarce factor of production, labor as a whole should support protectionism. On the other hand, according to specific-factors models, which assume that production factors are immobile or sector specific, thus leading business and labor preferences to be determined at the industry or sector level, most workers should also support protectionism, since a disproportionate share of the workforce is employed in labor-intensive, import-competing industries.

In fact, labor opposition to NAFTA was stronger than either set of models would predict. Both Stolper-Samuelson and specific-factors models assume that capital is geographically immobile. But even if production factors are immobile across different industrial sectors, as assumed in specific-factors models, capital is often internationally mobile and labor is not. Consequently, labor feared that by increasing both the reality and the threat of manufacturing capital flight to low-wage Mexico, NAFTA would have negative domestic employment and wage effects well beyond those created by an increase in imports produced by Mexican-owned firms. On this general point, see Feenstra (1998).

Initially joining labor in its opposition to an agreement were environmentalists who worried that pollution-intensive firms would also relocate manufacturing operations to northern Mexico to take advantage of that country's weakly enforced environmental laws, thus both exacerbating pollution problems along the border and eroding U.S. environmental standards.

To defuse opposition to the proposed pact, on May 1 Bush produced an "action plan" committing himself to an agreement that cushioned workers and upheld environmental standards. Although the plan was not sufficient to change labor's position on fast track, it did help the president win the support of key environmental groups as well as the endorsement of the congressional Democratic leadership. With this new support in hand, White House and business lobbyists were able to outgun their labor adversaries. In mid-May both the House and Senate defeated resolutions to disallow fast-track authority.

The Main Event

NAFTA was completed in August 1992, in time for George Bush to try to use the treaty during the general election phase of the presidential campaign to woo Hispanic voters and business interests in Texas and California. His opponent, Bill Clinton, was a free-trading "New Democrat" who sought to reconstitute his party's coalition to include the expanding suburbanized middle class and internationally oriented business interests, but who also hoped to avoid alienating organized labor, a core Democratic constituency. Thus Clinton straddled the NAFTA issue until early October, when in an effort to bridge the divide within his party, he finally endorsed the pact under the condition that side agreements be negotiated to deal with core labor standards—including laws on worker health and safety, child and prison labor, the rights of unions to organize, etc.—the environment, and the threat of sudden import surges. While labor was critical of Clinton's NAFTA endorsement, it did have hopes that the side agreements would guarantee the effective enforcement of labor and environmental laws in Mexico, thus reducing the incentives for U.S. manufacturers to relocate plants to that country.

At first it appeared that labor's hopes might be realized. After some early waffling which produced an outcry from congressional Demo-

crats, in May 1993 the new Clinton administration presented proposals to Mexican and Canadian negotiators calling for the formation of
independent commissions that would have the power to ensure that
the countries enforced their own labor and environmental laws. These
proposals, however, met with strong opposition from business, congressional Republicans, and the Mexican and Canadian governments.
With labor on the sidelines refusing to involve itself in the negotiating
process, the Clinton administration backed away from its proposals
and in August agreed instead to a much weaker set of enforcement procedures, especially with respect to labor standards.

Appalled by the labor side agreements, the AFL-CIO formally
came out in opposition to the treaty, and labor escalated its battle
against the pact at both the grass roots and in Washington. State and
local union affiliates mounted a grassroots mobilization against the
agreement that was unprecedented in recent memory. At the same
time, the AFL-CIO funded a television, radio, and print media blitz
against the pact. Finally, individual unions threatened to withhold
campaign contributions from Congress members who voted for the
treaty. Joining labor in what was widely termed an "unholy alliance"
of "strange bedfellows" against the pact were some environmentalists, human rights activists, the grassroots Citizens Trade Campaign,
Ross Perot, Jerry Brown, Pat Buchanan, Jesse Jackson, and Ralph
Nader.

With a big jump on its pro-NAFTA opponents and with public
opinion still substantially opposed to the treaty in the fall, this labor-
led coalition was able to enlist the support of an impressive number of
members of Congress, including key Democratic leaders like House
Majority Leader Richard Gephardt (D-Mo.) and House Whip David
Bonior (D-Mich.). For a time it appeared that labor might actually win
this crucial battle over the U.S. orientation toward the emerging global
economy.

This, of course, was before the pro-NAFTA forces had fully swung
into action. The moribund USA*NAFTA, a business coalition supporting the agreement, was revived and began to lobby intensively. The
elite media regularly editorialized in support of the treaty, often citing
the views of leading members of the economics profession. Republican congressional leaders, once assured that Bill Clinton was commit-

ted to the fight, worked hard to win GOP support for the pact. The moderates and free traders of the Democratic Leadership Council (DLC), convinced that the Democrats' future lay in the growing high-tech, middle-class suburbs rather than in the declining industrial cities, saw NAFTA as a defining issue for their party and threw themselves into the struggle for the treaty's approval.

Most important, after some initial hesitation, Bill Clinton engaged himself fully in the fight. Clinton both attempted to win over public opinion on the issue and furiously lobbied members of Congress, especially Democrats, with promises of trade relief and other favors and with persuasive pleas to resist isolationism and the crippling of his wider efforts on behalf of trade liberalization.

The eleventh-hour efforts of Clinton and other NAFTA supporters paid off, and in mid-November 1993 the treaty was approved by the House and Senate by votes of 234–200 and 61–38, respectively. Three-quarters of House Republicans supported the deal, as did 40 percent of House Democrats. Over three-quarters of Senate Republicans backed the treaty along with half of Senate Democrats.

Though defeated, organized labor had a significant influence on the NAFTA vote. In House and Senate voting on the treaty, various studies have shown that the higher the percentage of blue-collar workers and union members in a representative or senator's district or state, the more likely he or she was to vote against NAFTA. Additionally, the bigger labor's share of a legislator's total campaign contributions, again the more likely he or she was to oppose the treaty.[16]

Unfortunately for labor, however, the trends that had limited union

---

[16]Thus, in the House those members who relied most heavily on campaign contributions from union political action committees—all Democrats—cast lopsided votes against NAFTA. More specifically, in districts in which Democratic members received 20 percent or more of their total campaign contributions from labor PACs, 77 percent of those members opposed the treaty. But those Democrats who received more money from business PACs than labor PACs split on the issue, voting against the treaty by a narrow 82 to 88 margin (Healey and Moore 1997, 3183).

Statistical studies that found significant labor effects on either House or Senate NAFTA voting include Conybeare and Zinkula (1996); O'Halloran (1998); Kahane (1996); Box-Steffensmeir, Arnold, and Zorn (1997); Uslaner (1998a); Steagall and Jennings (1996), and Baldwin and Magee (2000).

influence in earlier trade fights again limited the movement's impact during the NAFTA debate, including its impact on Democrats. Labor's diminished political clout, the business mobilization in support of the pact, and Clinton's success in neutralizing public opinion on the issue and in winning Democratic support for the treaty with his deals and persuasion,[17] particularly from moderate and conservative southerners, allowed the pro-NAFTA forces to carry the day.

Four years later, however, the 1997 fast-track battle would break the mold of all previous trade struggles.

The Fast-Track Fights: Labor Wins Two Big Ones[18]

In the fall of 1997 another trade-policy battle royal was fought as the Clinton administration sought to revive the process of American trade liberalization which had ground to a halt since congressional approval of the Uruguay Round GATT treaty in late 1994.[19] Hoping to strengthen his legacy as a champion of liberal trade during his second term, Clinton requested new fast-track authority with the immediate aim of expanding NAFTA to include Chile. But his broader ambition was to negotiate still other free trade agreements with developing nations in Latin America and Asia.

In 1994 the Clinton administration, looking toward an agreement with Chile, had actually already sought such new fast-track authority in its draft of the Uruguay Round implementing legislation. But anxious to heal the rift with labor resulting from the NAFTA fight before the 1996 presidential campaign, USTR Mickey Kantor proposed that

---

[17]On Clinton's success in both moving public opinion and in winning over Democratic legislators, see Uslaner (1998a,b) and Livingston and Wink (1997).

[18]For additional discussion of the events covered in this section through the summer of 1997, see Destler (1997, 1998b).

[19]Because of the complexity of the GATT agreement and the resulting uncertainty as to its effects, the accord did not evoke the visceral responses that NAFTA had from U.S. workers, for whom the flight of manufacturing capital to Mexico had constituted a palpable threat. Consequently, labor largely sat out the fight over the approval of the less controversial GATT deal, and the agreement was eventually passed with substantial bipartisan majorities. Thus, I will not discuss it here.

labor and environmental standards be explicitly included as negotiating goals. Both the business community and its Republican congressional allies were militantly opposed to the inclusion of such standards, so rather than jeopardize the approval of the GATT agreement, the Clinton administration decided to remove the fast-track provision from the implementing legislation. The introduction of a new fast-track proposal was postponed until after the election.

Clinton Tries Again, But Labor Carries the Day

Having secured his reelection, in early 1997 Clinton set out again to win new fast-track authority.[20] This time the administration was willing to consider a "clean" bill, that is, one that ruled out the inclusion of labor and environmental issues in the core of any new trade agreements in order to gain business and GOP support.

The new White House strategy was based on the calculation that the labor movement would not make trade a top priority in 1997. New AFL-CIO president John Sweeney, formerly president of the Service Employees International Union (SEIU), and his close advisers all came out of the service and public sectors, and thus they tended to care less about trade than did the industrial unions. In the end, however, the administration's calculations with respect to labor's intentions proved to be mistaken. Under pressure from the industrial unions, Sweeney eventually overcame his reservations about opposing the renewal of Clinton's fast-track authority, and at its annual February meeting, the AFL-CIO denounced any NAFTA expansion agreement that did not include provisions to raise foreign wages and labor standards.[21]

Presidential election politics now once again intruded into the debate. Aligning himself with labor, potential presidential hopeful and

---

[20]For the next five paragraphs, see Bernstein (1997); Blustein (1997); Maggs (1997); Balz (1997); Corn (1997); and Cohn (1997).

[21]The industrial unions' resolve was heightened by the findings of a study conducted for the U.S., Canadian, and Mexican governments by Cornell University labor economist Kate Bronfenbrenner (1997b). The three-year survey, which the U.S. Labor Department initially sat on, found that 60 percent of union organizing efforts in manufacturing after NAFTA were met by management threats to close the factories, compared with 29 percent before NAFTA.

"old" Democrat Richard Gephardt circulated a twelve-page letter at-
taching a wide range of labor, environmental, and political conditions
to any new free trade agreements. Vice President and "new" Democrat Al Gore had been a strong supporter of Bill Clinton's trade liberalization program, but hoping to avoid a politically damaging fight with
organized labor that might boost Gephardt's candidacy, Gore urged at
least a delay in the submission of the fast-track proposal to Congress
to allow him more time to strengthen his ties to labor.

White House officials had no wish to jeopardize Gore's presidential
chances. Nor did they wish to further offend congressional liberals as
they pursued Clinton's top priority—a balanced budget. Thus, in mid-
May the White House decided to postpone delivery of its fast-track
proposal until the fall.

Clinton finally unveiled his fast-track plan on September 16. In the
proposal, the White House attempted to find a middle ground between
Democrats and Republicans. Labor and environmental standards were
included among the "negotiating objectives" set out in the bill, but
such issues were to be included in trade pacts only if they were "directly
related to trade." Also, the enforcement of such standards was assigned
to multilateral trade institutions such as the World Trade Organization, which had in the past been hostile to linking labor standards and
trade. Commercial issues, however, such as intellectual property, trade
in services, and agriculture, were to be addressed in core trade agreements, where sanctions could be used to enforce them.

Clinton's plan initially satisfied no one. Labor and its Democratic
allies attacked the proposal for not placing enough emphasis on the inclusion of strong labor and environmental standards in future trade accords, while business and Republican critics were angry that the plan
called for any attention at all to labor and environmental issues.

By the time of the October 1 markup of the bill by the pro-free-trade
Senate Finance Committee, the White House, convinced that the fate
of its fast-track proposal lay in Republican rather than Democratic
hands, had agreed to weaken the measure's labor and environmental
provisions enough to mollify most GOP concerns. Thus, the bill was
passed by the committee with only one opposing vote. A week later,
after another round of negotiations with the administration, the House
Ways and Means Committee approved a similar version of the bill. But

heralding the partisan battle to come, only four of the panel's 16 Democratic members voted in favor of the measure.

During the next two months another NAFTA-like battle was waged between the supporters and opponents of further trade liberalization. As in that earlier contest, by the end of the struggle, the pro-fast track coalition—again including internationally oriented business interests, the elite media, the economics profession, the Republican congressional leadership, the DLC, and of course, Bill Clinton—was fighting hard for passage of the bill. On the other side of the trenches, organized labor, environmental and citizens groups, and liberal congressional Democrats were just as strenuously opposing the measure for its neglect of labor and environmental issues. These liberal forces were again joined on the barricades by conservative Republican nationalists concerned about the alleged threat to U.S. "sovereignty."

While the traditionally pro-free-trade Senate would have passed its version of the fast-track bill,[22] this time in the House, labor and its allies emerged victorious. After votes on the fast-track bill were delayed twice, Clinton was forced to withdraw his proposal when it became clear that he lacked the votes in the House to pass it. A number of tallies suggested that the measure would have gotten the support of about 70 to 75 percent of House Republicans but only 21 percent of House Democrats.[23]

Explaining Labor's Victory

Following so soon after NAFTA's approval, how can the defeat of Clinton's fast-track proposal be explained? The secularly deteriorating structural position of organized labor had certainly not improved since 1993. Unions today represent only 13.5 percent of all U.S. workers, down

---

[22]In early November the Senate voted 69 to 31 in favor of a cloture resolution to defeat an attempted filibuster and allow consideration of the fast-track bill. Given the substantial size of many states, protectionist interests are more easily counterbalanced by pro-free-trade interests than is the case in smaller House districts. In addition, states with low levels of unionization are overrepresented in the Senate, again predisposing the upper chamber toward free trade. On the latter point, see Wirls (1998).

[23]Forty-three Democrats and 160 to 170 Republicans would have voted for fast track. For these estimates, see Barfield (1998).

from 35 percent in the 1950s. And despite the AFL-CIO's heightened commitment to organizing following the election of John Sweeney as president in late 1995, at the time of the first fast-track fight, union membership was still down in both relative and absolute terms since early 1996. Additionally, in late 1997, economic growth was strong, unemployment was low, Bill Clinton's popularity was high, and the generally pro-free-trade Republican party was in control of both houses of Congress. What other factors had changed to permit labor's fast-track victory?

First, whereas by the end of the NAFTA fight public opinion on the treaty had been evenly split, by late 1997 the American public was solidly opposed to renewing Clinton's fast-track authority. This was due in large part to the widespread belief, shared by many in Congress, that NAFTA had been a failure. Much of the public believed that (1) with the trade deficit with Mexico rising, NAFTA had cost the United States jobs; (2) jobs gained from increased exports were no better than those lost to imports or foreign investment; (3) competition from Mexico was undermining American workers' bargaining power and wages; and (4) NAFTA had eroded U.S. environmental quality. Such perceptions fueled a more general concern—"globalphobia," as it was termed—that globalization and trade liberalization were adversely affecting American jobs, living standards, and quality of life.[24]

Still, the role of public opinion in stopping fast track should not be exaggerated. Government officials have often pursued free trade policies even when those policies were unpopular (Scherrer 1994). This is especially likely to occur when the public's preferences are not intense, as appears to have been the case with fast track which voters found less salient than NAFTA. Had public opinion as a whole played a pre-

---

[24]A July 1997 *Wall Street Journal*/NBC News poll showed that 42 percent of Americans believed that NAFTA had had a negative impact on the United States—up from 35 percent in mid-1994—while only 32 percent believed it had had a positive impact. Respondents also opposed granting Clinton new fast-track authority by a 62 to 32 percent margin. Other polls also showed that the public was generally skeptical of free trade and by a wide margin supported the use of trade agreements to protect the environment and raise living standards.

For polling results on NAFTA and fast track, see Kosterlitz (1997b) and Schneider (1997). For more general surveys of public opinion on trade and trade policy, see *The Public Perspective* (1997).

dominant role in the demise of fast track, more than 25 to 30 percent of House Republicans should have opposed it.

Second, expert opinion had also shifted to some degree since the NAFTA fight. A number of studies questioned the degree to which NAFTA had benefited the country or different groups within the population,[25] and other analyses argued more broadly that globalization had negatively affected the wages of certain sectors of the labor force as well as the distribution of income (see especially Greider 1997; Rodrik 1997; and Soros 1997). Again, however, most trade and other experts strongly supported the fast-track bill.

Third, business support for fast track was both slower in mobilizing and less enthusiastic than had been the case with NAFTA, whose benefits to business were clearer than those expected to result from the more procedural fast-track bill. In June Americans Lead on Trade, a coalition of about 550 umbrella business organizations, trade associations, and companies was formed to build support for the renewal of fast-track authority (Borrus 1997; Stone 1997). But fearing that Clinton's fast-track proposal might include unacceptable labor and environmental provisions, the coalition refused to endorse the measure until it saw the final Senate and House language, and thus it really didn't start working the bill until late October. Nonetheless, the business push for fast track during the last weeks of the fight was substantial.

Fourth, conservative economic nationalist influences, both electoral and ideological, contributed to the decision of a substantial bloc of Republicans to oppose fast track. After World War II the Republicans, once the party of protectionism, gradually entered into a bipartisan consensus on liberal trade. But following the end of the cold war, working and lower middle class "Reagan Democrats" began to look toward populist and economic nationalist, though not liberal, solutions to the emerging problems of job loss and wage stagnation. Their mounting anger fueled the presidential campaigns of both Pat Buchanan and Ross Perot in 1992 and 1996. They also propelled a wave of radical populist Republicans into the House in the 1994 elections, helping the GOP to capture control of Congress. These firebrands in

---

[25]For discussion of these studies, see Kosterlitz (1997b) and Lewis (1997).

many cases replaced marginal Democrats, especially in the South, whose support for NAFTA and free trade more generally had alienated blue-collar voters. Thus, more than half of the 91 Republicans first elected to the House in 1994 and 1996 opposed the fast-track bill.[26]

In the end, however, the overall impact of conservative economic nationalist influences on the preferences of House Republicans and thus the role of these influences in the defeat of fast track was relatively limited. Fully 70 to 75 percent of the House GOP members supported the fast-track bill, close to the same proportion that had backed NAFTA in 1993. For all their sound and fury, the populist and nationalist bloc of House Republicans did not actively mobilize against the measure, while the House Republican leadership energetically threw itself into the fight for fast track.

Anti-Fast-Track Influences on the Democrats

A number of factors contributed to the defeat of fast track primarily through their influence on the Democrats, whose overwhelming opposition to the measure ultimately doomed it. Whereas 60 percent of House Democrats had voted against NAFTA in 1993, 79 percent of party members opposed fast track in 1997.

To an important extent, the more unified Democratic opposition to fast track in 1997 was an artifact of the more homogeneously liberal composition of the House Democratic caucus.[27] A substantial number of moderate and conservative, mostly Southern and suburban, pro-NAFTA Democrats retired or were defeated in the Democratic rout of 1994 and in the subsequent 1996 election.[28] Surviving Democratic incumbents, on the other hand, were more likely to come from liberal

---

[26]On the rise of Republican populism and economic nationalism, see Judis (1992) and Wildavksy (1995). On the role of this group in the fast-track fight, see Beinart (1997a).

[27]On these points see Barfield (1998), from which most of the accompanying statistics are taken. See also Beinart (1997a) and Barnes and Cohen (1997).

[28]Southern House Democrats had been much more supportive of NAFTA than their colleagues in the rest of the country, backing the deal 53 to 32, while the rest of the caucus opposed it by almost a 3-to-1 margin. Since 1991, however, the number of white Democratic House members from the 13 Southern states had declined from 79 to only 42.

urban or labor-dominated districts where opposition to free trade was strongest.[29] In addition, in 1996 the Democrats won a number of new seats, mostly in liberal northern districts. Only 23 percent of these new Democratic members planned to vote for fast track. Thus, due to electoral shifts, the House Democratic caucus in 1997 was smaller but more consistently liberal than it had been in 1993.

This explanation of heightened Democratic cohesion on fast track is incomplete, however. It cannot explain why among the ranks of Democratic fast-track opponents were both eighteen former NAFTA supporters and some newly elected non-Southern moderates.[30] Included in these two groups were half of the forty-one members of the moderate New Democratic Coalition who sympathized with the views of the DLC. What explains the opposition to fast track among these Democrats who might have been expected to support Clinton's proposal?

First, Clinton's efforts on behalf of fast track were less concerted and effective than they had been during the NAFTA battle, when he had been able to win over a substantial number of undecided and wavering Democratic moderates.[31] Not wanting to call attention to the intra-Democratic split over the issue or to unduly offend labor whose support Al Gore would need in the 2000 presidential campaign, Clinton never took his case to an anxious public which remained highly skeptical of the value of liberalized trade. Instead, Clinton relied exclusively on an "inside-the-beltway" strategy, promising undecided, mostly Democratic Congress members a flurry of last-minute concessions in return for their votes. But his deal making didn't work this time, since his credibility had been diminished by his failure to deliver on most of the promises he had made during the NAFTA fight.

Clinton had also antagonized House Democrats in other ways, perhaps most importantly with the balanced budget deal that he had struck with the Republicans the previous summer. Many Democrats

---

[29]Overall, whereas 40 percent of all House Democrats voted for NAFTA, 54 percent of those party members who were in the House in 1993 but not in 1997 voted for the accord, while only 30 percent of those who were House members in both years voted for the deal.

[30]Only 20 percent of Democrats who were members of the House in both 1993 and 1997 planned to vote for fast track, 10 percent less than the number in this group who supported NAFTA (Barfield 1998).

[31]For more on the points in this paragraph, see Barnes and Cohen (1997), Frisby and Davis (1997), and Dunne (1997).

believed that the concessions on taxes and spending that Clinton had made to reach such an agreement had undermined his ability to create the "social compact" that he had repeatedly promised for those displaced by economic change (Dionne, Jr. 1997).

Nonetheless, toward the end of the controversy Clinton worked hard to win the fast-track battle.

Labor's Decisive Role: Laying the Groundwork in the 1996 Elections

I would argue that the most important factor underlying the Democrats' solid opposition to fast track was the structurally enabled "agency" of organized labor. During the fast-track fight, labor employed a wide range of strategies. But to an important extent, the key to labor's victory was its extensive prior involvement in the 1996 congressional elections. This effort left labor with both an impressive grassroots organizing infrastructure and substantial leverage on congressional Democrats during the fast-track battle the following year.

Shortly after the Republican takeover of Congress in 1994, labor launched a concerted campaign—"Labor '96"—to help the Democrats recapture control of at least the House of Representatives.[32] Individual unions provided tens of thousands of volunteers who educated, registered, and turned out voters to the polls in support of labor-backed candidates. Beyond this, after replacing the quiescent leadership team headed by Lane Kirkland, the revitalized AFL-CIO under new president John Sweeney and new political director Steve Rosenthal waged an independent, $35 million campaign on behalf of Democratic candidates that included a grassroots field effort in 120 congressional districts directed by 135 full-time political coordinators and a multimedia issue advocacy campaign. In addition, union political action committees increased their campaign spending on behalf of their endorsed candidates to better enable those candidates to reach and persuade uninformed or inattentive voters.

Labor's intensified efforts in 1996 were effective. In the 1992 elections, exit polls showed that 19 percent of the electorate was from union households. Two years later, angered by their loss to Clinton on

---

[32]On labor's electoral efforts in 1996, see Dark (1999, 184–87), Barnes and Cohen (1997), Rosenthal (1998), and Gerber (1999).

NAFTA, union activists largely sat out the midterm elections. The result was a decline in the union share of the turnout to only 14 percent. But in 1996, turnout among union households jumped to 23 percent of the electorate. In addition, while 40 percent of union members had voted for Republican congressional candidates in 1994, this figure dropped to 35 percent in 1996.

Labor's campaign contributions also played an important role in the 1996 elections. As usual, business substantially outspent labor in PAC and individual contributions to candidates, this time by a margin of 7 to 1. But with business PACs shifting their contributions toward the Republicans following the GOP takeover of Congress in 1994, the Democrats were left more dependent on labor money to finance their 1996 campaigns. In House races, for example, labor PAC contributions, which totaled roughly 36 percent of all PAC donations to Democratic candidates in 1994, rose to about 48 percent in 1996.[33] Thus, union money helped keep Democratic candidates at least competitive with their Republican rivals in 1996.

Labor's education, registration, and turn-out efforts, together with its PAC contributions, paid real dividends in the 1996 elections. Democratic House candidates defeated forty-five of the 105 Republicans targeted by the AFL-CIO.

The Labor Mobilization against Fast Track and Its Effects

During the fast-track fight a year later, labor sought both to build and capitalize on its efforts in the 1996 elections.[34] First, labor employed a number of "outside" lobbying tactics. Relying on "Labor '96" coordinators who remained in place in many congressional districts, the AFL-CIO mounted an exceptionally effective grassroots and advertising offensive against fast track in targeted districts, while several federation affiliates—especially the Teamsters, the Steelworkers, and the Union of Needle, Industrial, and Textile Employees (UNITE)—undertook their own independent anti-fast-track activities. And it was not just the

---

[33]For these and subsequent PAC contribution figures (unless otherwise indicated), see Stanley and Niemi (1998, 101–103).

[34]For a detailed account of the labor mobilization against fast track, see Glenn (1998). See also Dark (1999), Kosterlitz (1997b), Abramson with Greenhouse (1997), and Meyerson (1997).

industrial unions that waged the battle. The previous summer the industrial unions had backed up their public-sector colleagues in the fight over the balanced budget. Now those same public-sector unions repaid their debt by throwing themselves into the fast-track fight.

Union members opposed to fast track sent hundreds of thousands of letters and postcards to their representatives, placed over ten thousand phone calls to Congress, made hundreds of visits to congressional district offices, distributed thousands of anti-fast-track videos and booklets, and held dozens of teach-ins and rallies on trade. Meanwhile, the AFL-CIO spent about $2 million on TV and radio ads in twenty key congressional districts.

Labor also actively engaged in "inside" lobbying within the Washington beltway. Labor lobbyists regularly met with and pressed House members—mostly Democrats, but also some Republicans—to oppose fast track. Labor also enlisted the active support of key House leaders, especially Minority Leader Richard Gephardt and Minority Whip David Bonior, who both worked hard to convince undecided Democrats to come out against Clinton's proposal. Finally, union staff members also participated actively in the weekly strategy meetings of the Citizens' Trade Campaign, a broad anti-fast-track coalition of labor, environmental, consumer safety, and civil rights organizations.

In waging its anti-fast-track campaign, labor learned from its unsuccessful fight against NAFTA four years earlier. Attempting to combat the charge that it was acting as a narrow "special interest" in defense only of its own members, labor rejected the protectionist label and instead acknowledged the inevitability and even the desirability of global economic integration. But as AFL-CIO president John Sweeney explained, "The question is not . . . whether we are internationalists, but what values our internationalism serves" (Glenn 1998, 199).

Thus, labor and its liberal Democratic allies framed their opposition to Clinton's "clean" fast-track proposal as part of a wider, more positive argument that globalization had to be managed in the general interest of the country and indeed the world as a whole rather than just in the interest of big exporters and multinational corporations. This meant "rules for—not resistance to—globalization," as Richard Gephardt put it (Corn 1997). More specifically, labor and its supporters called for labor and environmental standards in developing nations to be raised to simultaneously improve living conditions in those poverty-ridden countries, create an expanding middle class that could buy American products, and prevent a corporate "race to the bottom" that would erode U.S. jobs, wages, and environmental quality (Koster-litz 1997a).

In pursuit of these goals, during the fast-track fight, labor sought to build what Karl Polanyi termed a broad "protective countermovement" to limit globalization's various adverse and disruptive effects (Polanyi 1944). More concretely, to turn public opinion against fast track, labor cooperated more actively and fully with environmental, human rights, consumer safety, and other groups than they had during the anti-NAFTA campaign and stressed a wide range of both labor and non-labor concerns. "We didn't just want to talk to union members," said Steven Trossman, an anti-fast-track strategist with the Teamsters. "We wanted to talk to a broader audience to say this is bad for families, even if your job is not on the line."[35]

Labor's various outside and inside lobbying activities were productive. Labor's grassroots mobilization and issue advocacy advertising efforts contributed to the movement of public opinion against Clinton's proposal and conveyed information on the public's preferences on the issue to Congress members. At the same time, labor's inside lobbying efforts reinforced the message from the grass roots and also perhaps played some role in altering legislators' personal preferences on the issue.

But labor's campaign did more than convey information on different aspects of the fast-track issue to House members. Labor leaders exerted more forceful pressure by bluntly warning that lawmakers who supported fast track could not expect either union manpower or money for their 1998 campaigns, even if that meant that some Democrats might lose.[36]

This labor pressure had its desired effect. As noted earlier, informal

---

[35]For example, unions held demonstrations with Friends of the Earth and the Sierra Club in a half dozen cities to call attention to NAFTA's environmental effects on Mexican border towns (Abramson with Greenhouse, 1997). See also Glenn (1998) and Beinart (1997a).

[36]"Labor is practicing the politics of intimidation either with outright threats or implied threats . . . that labor will withdraw any campaign support, either financial or otherwise" to fast-track supporters, said California Rep. Calvin M. Dooley, chairman of the New Democratic Coalition (Brownstein 1997). Although such labor warnings were mostly targeted at Democrats, union lobbyists also pressured some two dozen northeastern and midwestern Republicans.

tallies indicated that 79 percent of House Democrats would have opposed Clinton's fast-track bill had it come to a vote. Many Democrats, including moderate members of the New Democratic Coalition, feared that their support for fast track would lead union activists to sit out the 1998 campaign, as many had done in 1994. Thanks largely to labor's mobilization in 1996, the Democrats had benefited from a significant increase in the union vote that year, and many party members were reluctant to risk another depressed labor turnout in 1998 by backing the fast-track bill.[37]

The Crucial Role of Labor Money

I would argue, however, that even more important in convincing Democrats to oppose fast track than the possible loss of union manpower in the 1998 elections was the threatened loss of union money. Although studies of the effects of campaign spending by individual PACs on congressional voting have been inconclusive, it has been demonstrated that broad aggregations of corporate or labor PAC contributions can produce voting effects on issues of general concern to business or labor.[38] In particular, business and labor PAC spending does seem to have significant effects on congressional voting on trade issues.[39] In the specific case of the fast-track fight, the force of labor's threats to reduce or withdraw contributions to Democratic incumbents who voted for Clinton's proposal stemmed from a recent and substantial shift in the sources of Democratic campaign finance.

Beginning in the mid-1970s, business PACs dramatically proliferated, and their total spending on congressional campaigns exploded. At the same time, hoping to scale back the New Deal social welfare and regulatory state, these PACs abandoned their traditional, access-

---

[37]Many lawmakers who opposed fast track studied what had happened to several dozen Democratic Congress members who voted for NAFTA in 1993 and then lost to Republicans in 1994, partly because alienated union members stayed away from the polls (Abramson with Greenhouse 1997).

[38]For studies that find evidence of labor PAC influence on congressional voting on labor issues, see Saltzman (1987), Wilhite and Theilman (1987), and Neustadtl (1990).

[39]See the studies of congressional voting on NAFTA cited in footnote 16 above. For other studies that find PAC effects on congressional trade voting, see Coughlin (1985), Tosini and Tower (1987), Marks (1993), Nollen and Quinn (1994), and Baldwin and Magee (2000).

oriented strategy of donating to candidates of both parties and instead shifted the bulk of their contributions to Republican candidates in the 1978, 1980, and 1982 congressional elections.

Because the number of union PACs grew slowly during this period and because these PACs also regularly ran up against campaign contribution limits, congressional Democrats were left desperately short of funds to conduct their increasingly media- and consultant-intensive campaigns. To regain lost corporate support, the Democrats were forced to adopt more business-friendly and less labor-responsive policy positions, including those on trade issues such as NAFTA (Gais 1996; Clawson, Neustadtl, and Weller 1998; Jackson 1988). This policy shift, along with the Democrats' retention of control of the House of Representatives in the 1982 elections and their recapture of the Senate in 1986, produced a partial shift of business campaign contributions back to the Democrats.[40] Thanks to this new influx of business money, from 1982 to 1992, the business share of House Democrats' total PAC receipts[41] jumped from 41 to 54 percent, while labor's share fell from 43 to 33 percent.

The 1994 elections, however, produced yet another shift in the structure of campaign finance, also with corresponding policy consequences (Barnes and Cohen 1997; Beinart 1997a; Abramson with Greenhouse 1997; Edsall 1997). After the Republican takeover of Congress, business PACs, pressured by the new GOP congressional leadership, again reduced their contributions to the Democrats while substantially increasing their donations to the majority Republicans. Meanwhile, labor PACs increased their contributions to Democratic candidates.[42] Thus, as noted earlier, union PAC contributions, which totaled roughly 36 percent of all PAC donations to Democratic House candidates in 1994,

---

[40]In 1982, business PACs gave only about 39 percent of their contributions in House races to Democrats. By 1992 this had jumped to about 55 percent.

On the advantage in the receipt of corporate PAC contributions enjoyed by members of the House majority party, see Cox and Magar (1999).

[41]These included contributions from both "corporate" and "trade, membership, and health" PACs.

[42]Although business PACs gave $47.5 million to House Democrats in 1994, that figure dropped to $33 million in 1996. Meanwhile, labor PACs increased their contributions to Democrats from $32.5 million in 1994 to $37.3 million in 1996.

rose to about 48 percent in 1996. Still more important, Democratic challengers who won Republican-held seats in 1996 received more than 60 percent of their PAC contributions from labor.[43]

This renewed Democratic dependence on organized labor for campaign funds was further compounded by the fundraising scandals stemming from the 1996 election. Abandoned by many of its major donors, the Democratic National Committee was $15 million in debt, leaving it unable to aid party candidates with "soft," or unregulated, money.[44]

The Democrats' desperate need for union money heightened the credibility of labor's threat to withhold funds from fast-track supporters in the 1998 midterm elections and thus decisively contributed to the defeat of Clinton's proposal.[45] "Labor has obviously increased its influence in the Democratic Party since we've become the minority and the business community is either less engaged or less influential with us than ever before," said one senior House Democrat" (Brownstein 1997a). A House Democratic leadership aide observed, "Your average House Democrat is thinking, 'The DNC is broke, Clinton is helping Gore, Big Business is with the Republicans, all we've got is labor' (Barnes and Cohen 1997). "This is a $200,000 vote for me," another Democrat reportedly told a Clinton aide, explaining why he might not vote for fast track even though he had voted for NAFTA (Harris 1997).

During the fast-track fight, labor's financial clout gave the labor movement influence with Democrats of various ideological stripes, not just pro-union liberals. With business turning away from the Democrats, even the moderates of the New Democratic Coalition were badly in need of money for their 1998 campaigns. Looking to labor for help,

---

[43]The figure for all Democratic challengers, including both winners and losers, was 71 percent.

[44]As the fast-track vote approached, Democrats took note of a recent special election in Staten Island, NY, where a strong Democratic candidate lost because the Republicans were able to spend $800,000 on soft-money-funded ads, while the Democratic Party lacked the funds to reply.

[45]Martha Gibson and Stephen Carter (1998) demonstrate that as in NAFTA voting, the larger labor's share of a member's total PAC contributions, the more likely the member was to oppose fast track. This time the Democrats' heightened dependence on labor money spelled defeat for Clinton's proposal.

half of them opposed the fast-track bill, to the dismay of the leaders of the DLC (Beinart 1997b). "The business community really has to think very hard about ignoring House Democrats," complained DLC president Al From (Abramson with Greenhouse 1997).

Thus, despite its continued long-term decline, by converting and strategically deploying its structurally generated human and especially its financial resources in a temporarily favorable political conjuncture, organized labor was able to win a major battle against the forces of globalization and free trade. At least in this instance, labor's structurally enabled agency triumphed over the structural constraints that so often limit the movement's advance.

The Lines Are Drawn Again

Chastened by his defeat at labor's hands, Bill Clinton decided not to introduce another fast-track proposal until after the 1998 and perhaps even the 2000 election, in both of which Democratic candidates, including likely presidential aspirant Al Gore, would need labor votes, money, and volunteers. In fact, looking ahead to the 2000 campaign in which Clinton hoped to pass his mantle on to his vice president, both Clinton and Gore spent much of 1998 working to repair their ties to the liberal-labor wing of the Democratic Party (Judis 1998).

Thus, it was Republican Speaker of the House Newt Gingrich who in late June surprised observers by announcing a late September vote on a new fast-track proposal containing no strong labor and environmental provisions.[46] Gingrich's motives appear to have been partisan. First, the Speaker hoped to exploit differences on trade among labor, House Democrats, and the White House just before the fall midterm congressional elections. Second, Gingrich wanted to show business that the GOP cared as much about the corporate agenda as it did about the concerns of social conservatives whose strength within the party had recently appeared to be growing. Finally, Gingrich hoped to mend political fences with farmers to make up for phasing out the farm subsidies that once cushioned price drops.

---

[46]On the late summer and fall 1998 fast-track fight, see Magnusson (1998), Kosterlitz (1998a), and Hosansky (1998).

Most House Republicans backed their leader's bill, determined to hold Democrats accountable in the upcoming elections for blocking fast track's passage. In particular, the Republicans hoped to spotlight the Democrats' alleged subservience to labor in regions with concentrations of export-dependent agricultural interests (Eilperin 1998).

The great majority of House Democrats opposed the GOP measure, due mainly once again to pressure from organized labor.[47] On the one hand, labor vociferously attacked and mobilized against the bill. At the same time, wanting to prevent the election of a filibuster-proof Republican Senate, labor mounted another major effort in support of Democratic candidates in the upcoming congressional races. This time, however, labor found itself even more massively outspent by business than in 1996. Labor also faced the threat of a low turnout of its members, who along with other Americans had become increasingly alienated from politics by a succession of scandals. Thus, labor now decided that its route to greater congressional influence lay not primarily in its campaign contributions, which for the most part had already been collected, or even in a media "air war," but rather in a full-scale, get-out-the-vote ground war.[48]

Labor's strategy paid off almost immediately on fast track. Desperate to retain the support of grassroots union activists in order to avoid another depressed turnout of their core labor base in the elections now only six weeks away, both traditional union supporters and other more moderate Democrats opposed Gingrich's fast-track measure.

On September 25 the House decisively defeated the Republican fast-track bill by a vote of 180 to 243, a substantially greater margin than the one by which Clinton's fast-track proposal had been rejected the year before. Only 29 Democrats, or about 15 percent, voted for the measure this time, while 171 opposed it. On the Republican side, 151 members, or about 68 percent, voted for it and 71 voted against it. Labor won yet another major trade policy victory.

---

[47]Bill Clinton also opposed the Republicans' attempt to put Democrats on the spot before the November elections, especially after it became clear that he would need Democratic support to fend off impeachment over the Monica Lewinsky scandal.

[48]Although labor spent only about $5 million on TV ads in 1998, it spent $18 million on a tightly targeted GOTV (get-out-the-vote) effort coordinated by 400 field activists, up from 135 in 1996, and focused on eight Senate races and 45 tight House races, down from over 100 two years earlier (Greenhouse 1998e; Bernstein 1998).

Battling in Seattle and Over China

This chapter was originally written in the fall of 1998. In late 1999 and in the spring of 2000, Bill Clinton made two final attempts to further establish his legacy as a champion of free trade.

First, Clinton journeyed to Seattle to try to convince delegates to a World Trade Organization (WTO) meeting to launch a new "Millennium Round" of international trade negotiations. The talks collapsed, however, amid dramatic, well-organized street protests by anti-WTO activists who built upon their experiences in the NAFTA and fast-track fights. In fact, inside the meeting hall, the discussions fell apart in good measure because Clinton was attending to another element of his legacy: the vindication of his presidency through the election of his vice president, Al Gore, as his successor in the 2000 election.

Once again the key to understanding this development was organized labor, whose support Gore would need in both the primaries and the general election. Labor had been angered in mid-November when, shortly after the AFL-CIO had endorsed Gore, the administration negotiated a trade and investment pact with China to facilitate that country's entry into the WTO. Now labor came in force to Seattle, joining environmental, human rights, and other activists, to demand that any new international trade agreement include core labor standards.

Concerned that a negotiating agenda that made no reference to worker rights would outrage labor and damage Gore's prospects, and finding only a modest level of enthusiasm within the U.S. business community for a new round of trade talks, Clinton proposed that the WTO establish a working group on international labor standards and even suggested that the organization might need to use sanctions to enforce compliance with such standards. The developing nations took great offense at these ideas, seeing in them a thinly veiled protectionist attempt by the United States to exclude their goods from American markets. Thus, the WTO talks collapsed.

The PNTR Struggle

Substantially more important to Clinton and his business allies than a new trade round was the opening of the fabled China market via implementation of the agreement struck with Beijing in November. To achieve this goal, in this case a higher priority for Clinton than Gore's election, administration officials launched a campaign to convince Congress to abandon its cold war practice of granting China "most favored nation" (MFN) trading status on a year-by-year basis, intended to put pressure on Beijing to improve human rights, in favor of awarding China "permanent normal trade relations" (PNTR). This was necessary, the White House maintained, if American firms were to actually receive the various market-opening and investment concessions that China had made to the United States and other countries to get into the WTO.[49] Otherwise, U.S. companies would lose sales in China to their European, Japanese, and other competitors.[50]

The spring of 2000 saw yet another bitter and now familiar trade struggle in the House of Representatives, this one even more furious than the NAFTA and fast-track fights, over Clinton's PNTR proposal.[51] As suggested above, Clinton's principal ally in the battle was the American business community. Dazzled as their forerunners had been a century earlier by the lure of the China market, internationally oriented U.S. business and agricultural interests saw and fought for what they took to be vast export and investment opportunities (Bradsher 2000). Again joining the White House and business in their support for PNTR were the elite media, most professional economists, pro-business House Republican leaders and members, and a smaller group of Democratic free traders aligned with the DLC.

As usual, the energetic opposition to PNTR was led by organized

---

[49]For background on China's efforts to enter the WTO, see Groombridge and Barfield (1999).

[50]In its November 1999 deal with U.S. negotiators, China agreed among other things to cut average tariffs from 24 to 9 percent by 2005; eliminate import quotas and licenses; reduce taxes on imported cars and permit foreign automakers to sell to Chinese customers and to finance their purchases; open up its retail market by allowing foreigners to set up wholly owned distribution and sales subsidiaries; allow minority foreign ownership of telecommunications companies and securities houses; allow foreigners to invest in Chinese Internet businesses; and stop discriminating against foreign banks. In return, the United States agreed to give up its ability to impose unilateral trade sanctions.

[51]All sides expected PNTR to pass the Senate easily, and thus the battle was concentrated in the House.

labor, which once again saw the China deal as more of an investment than a trade agreement, an understanding openly if quietly acknowledged as accurate by leading business supporters of the pact.[52] Labor viewed American firms' intended exploitation of cheap Chinese labor, facilitated by Beijing's repressive labor and human rights practices, as a threat to U.S. workers' jobs, wages, and working conditions. Also opposing PNTR were environmental, human rights, family farm, and consumer groups, many of them members of the Citizens Trade Campaign, and their liberal Democratic allies as well as social and Republican conservatives motivated by national security concerns and anger at China's repression of religious freedoms. The anti-PNTR coalition argued that continued annual review of China's MFN status was necessary if the United States was to retain any leverage with Beijing with respect to human rights.

This time, however, labor was unable to repeat its fast-track victories, and Clinton and his business and Republican allies triumphed in the PNTR struggle as they had in the NAFTA fight seven years earlier. On May 24, the House of Representatives approved the PNTR bill by a handy margin of 237 to 197.

Explaining Labor's Defeat

Why did labor's anti-PNTR campaign fail? There was certainly no great wave of popular support for PNTR. For the vast majority of voters, the issue simply wasn't very salient, and those who did have opinions appear to have been marginally opposed to the bill (Eilperin and Broder 2000; *Poll Track* 2000).

Increased Republican support for free trade cannot explain the outcome either, since the nearly 75 percent of GOP members who backed PNTR was almost identical to the number of Republican supporters of NAFTA in 1993 and fast track in 1997.

Once again, the difference lay on the Democratic side of the aisle, where just over one-third of House Democrats voted for PNTR, up from only 21 percent in the fast-track fight and including 17 party

---

[52]"This deal is about investment, not exports," said Joseph Quinlan, an economist with Morgan Stanley Dean Witter and Co. For this quote and more evidence on this point, see Cooper and Johnson (2000).

members who had voted against NAFTA. What explains this increased Democratic support for free trade?

First, there seemed to have been a few cracks in labor unity during the fight, which may have weakened Democratic opposition to PNTR. Some union locals representing workers in export-dependent industries appear to have broken with their internationals to support the China deal. And some observers suggest that AFL-CIO president John Sweeney and the leaders of certain nonindustrial unions may have waged a less than all-out fight against PNTR to avoid jeopardizing the achievement of two more important goals: the victory of Al Gore in the presidential race and the Democratic recapture of the House in the November congressional elections (Bedard et al. 2000; Burgess 2000).

Still, by all accounts, labor's inside and outside lobbying campaign against PNTR was perhaps the most intense effort of its kind ever undertaken by the unions. Labor leaders and lobbyists heavily pressured Democratic and a few Republican lawmakers in Washington, in some cases threatening to withhold vital support in the upcoming congressional elections from those who voted for PNTR.[53] Labor and its allies also spent about $2 million on ads opposing the trade bill. Most important, labor—especially the Teamsters, the United Auto Workers, and the United Steelworkers—mounted another extensive grassroots mobilization against PNTR. Union members lobbied legislators, wrote letters, manned phone banks, handed out literature at plant gates, and went door to door in targeted congressional districts across the country.

The most important reason for the increase in Democratic support for free trade during the PNTR fight was not the inadequacy of labor's efforts but rather the massive campaign undertaken by the bill's supporters. First, Bill Clinton, whose energies were not fully engaged in the 1997 fast-track fight, threw himself into the PNTR struggle. Clinton repeatedly spoke out on behalf of PNTR, traveled to congressional

---

[53]The Democrats had again profited substantially from the unions' involvement in the 1998 elections. Twenty-four percent of voters who turned out came from union households, and according to an AFL-CIO poll, 71 percent of union members voted Democratic in a year that saw the party pick up five House seats. In 2000 labor undertook an even more extensive grassroots campaign to help the Democrats recapture control of the House.

districts in California and the Midwest, held meetings with over one hundred undecided and wavering House members, especially Democrats, and made scores of phone calls to other members, arguing that granting China PNTR was essential to this country's economic well-being and national security. As in earlier trade fights, Clinton promised legislators various forms of help for their districts in return for their votes. The president's efforts were effectively complemented by those of other White House and executive branch officials,[54] the House Republican leadership, and Democratic free traders, including members of the moderate New Democratic Coalition and the DLC with which the coalition is associated.

The Business Campaign for PNTR: Lobbying, Mobilization, and Money

The real key to the victory of PNTR, however, was the scale and sophistication of the business mobilization on behalf of the bill (Kahn 2000; Magnusson 2000; Phillips 2000; Burgess 2000). This was in contrast to the business effort in support of Clinton's 1997 fast-track proposal, which had started late and proved largely ineffective. Stunned by its defeat in the earlier fight, the business community quickly began to reorient its trade and wider political strategies in ways that would pay off in the PNTR battle.

Beginning in early 1998, a number of major business organizations— including the Business Roundtable, the U.S. Chamber of Commerce, and the Emergency Committee for American Trade (ECAT)— launched grassroots education and lobbying campaigns in targeted congressional districts to persuade American voters and their representatives of the merits of free trade (Kosterlitz 1998b).

These preliminary efforts were dramatically escalated during the PNTR fight. Individual large corporations[55] and small manufacturers; traditional big business associations like the Business Roundtable, the Chamber of Commerce, and ECAT; the ad hoc Business Coalition for

---

[54]Al Gore only quietly supported PNTR for fear of inflaming his labor supporters.

[55]These included Boeing, FMC, Motorola, Citigroup, Federal Express, and United Parcel Service.

U.S.-China Trade; agribusiness interests represented by the American Farm Bureau and the Agriculture Trade Coalition; and, in their first major foray into trade politics (at least since the U.S.-Japan disputes of the 1980s), high-tech groups like the Information Technology Industry Council, the Electronics Industry Alliance, and the American Electronics Association joined together to wage a massive, multifront campaign to put PNTR over the top.

In addition to aggressive Washington lobbying, business stole a page from labor's playbook, mounting powerful advertising and grassroots campaigns directed at undecided and cross-pressured Democrats with constituents employed in both unionized import-competing firms and unorganized export-dependent and often high-tech companies. Business groups spent as much as $10 million on advertisements alone. Still more novel, corporate executives and employees logged hundreds of visits to congress members' district offices, wrote thousands of letters to their representatives, and organized phone banks to mobilize retirees.[56] And business organizations for the first time created Web sites and e-mail distribution lists to coordinate their daily message.

On still another front, many businesses once again reoriented their campaign contribution strategies, at least partly to influence House Democrats on the China vote. In the wake of their 1997 fast-track defeat, many corporate leaders had come to believe that business had made a mistake in so dramatically shifting its support from Democratic to Republican incumbents after the 1994 midterm elections. These leaders worried that the Republicans had become too strongly influenced by social conservatives, small business populists, and economic nationalists hostile to the interests of big multinational companies, especially with regard to trade policy. They also recognized that business would need at least some Democratic allies if it hoped to win on issues like fast track in the future, but this required that labor's renewed position of strength within the party be weakened or

---

[56]The Business Roundtable targeted eighty-eight congressional districts and hired sixty "trade organizers" to work the issue full time. The Chamber of Commerce organized lobbying and advertising in sixty-six districts.

offset. Thus, a range of business interests urged corporate and PAC officials to resume their support of and contributions to both political parties.[57]

Business did in fact begin to rebalance its financial support for the parties in the 1997–98 election cycle, once again reducing the Democrats' financial dependence on labor, as the share of House Democrats' PAC money that came from labor fell to 43.6 percent, down from 48.4 percent two years earlier (Ornstein, Mann, and Malbin 2000, 106).

The 1999–2000 election cycle was characterized by an explosion of contributions to the parties' House and Senate campaign committees, particularly in the area of soft money. Here again, business directed more of its contributions to the Democrats, and in the seventeen months preceding the PNTR fight had just about evenly split its donations to the two parties' committees as it sought both to hedge its bets on a possible Democratic takeover of the House and to influence the Democrats' policy positions, especially in the spring of 2000 on PNTR.[58] Business also directly wrote checks to and organized fundraisers for members of both parties committed to supporting the China deal or open to being persuaded to do so. As usual, business heavily outspent labor in the process, and in some cases threatened to

---

[57]"Some Republicans aren't going to be there on trade issues," said Dan Schnur, a California GOP consultant. "Ultimately, business is going to form relationships with elements of both parties" (Dunham and Borrus 1998). Business interests calling for renewed support for the Democrats included the Business-Industry Political Action Committee (a corporate lobbying coalition), the U.S. Chamber of Commerce, and the editorialists at *Business Week* (1998; Edsall 1998).

[58]Thus, according to figures compiled by the Center for Responsive Politics, during the first half of 1999 the National Republican Campaign Committee (NRCC) and the Democratic Congressional Campaign Committee (DCCC) split all donations from business 50–50. This is in contrast to the 1998 election in which the NRCC collected 63 percent of the business money. More dramatically, looking only at business soft-money contributions to the two House party committees during the whole of 1999, Common Cause, a leading public interest organization, found that the DCCC received about 47 percent of the business donations, compared to only about 34 percent in 1998. Thanks in part to these business contributions and to carefully controlled spending, by the end of the first quarter of 2000, the DCCC had $26.6 million in cash on hand, far more than the NRCC's $15.5 million (Glasser and Eilperin 1999; VandeHei 2000; Carney 2000).

withhold financial support from legislators who voted against PNTR.[59]

The partial shift of business money back to the Democrats was encouraged by the efforts of the New Democratic Coalition, now up to 65 members out of a total of 211 House Democrats, and the DLC (Carney 1997; Phillips 2000; McGregor 2000). In mid-1996, NDC and DLC members formed the New Democratic Network to help push their party in a moderate direction by raising more corporate money for ideologically sympathetic Democratic candidates, thus weaning the party away from its heavy dependence on labor union contributions. Toward this end, the New Democrats aggressively promoted a pro-business agenda for their party, one that was particularly tailored toward high-tech firms, who were rapidly raising their donations to electoral campaigns and whose support was thought to be up for grabs by both parties (Borrus and Dunham 2000).

Topping this agenda in the first half of 2000 was approval of the China deal, the year's most important business and high-tech priority. New Democrats within and without Congress actively worked to pass the PNTR bill, while the New Democratic Network held a series of fundraisers for pro-trade incumbents and candidates.

More important, and more surprisingly given his history, the increase in business contributions to the Democrats was also fostered by House Minority Leader Richard Gephardt, who in his efforts to attract the funds necessary to help his party recapture control of the House promised a more business and especially a more high-tech-friendly Democratic party. Thus, while Gephardt felt compelled to oppose PNTR

---

[59]Again, according to the Center for Responsive Politics, as of May 1, 2000, the two-hundred-plus members of the Business Roundtable had accounted for more than $58 million in soft money, PAC, and individual contributions to federal parties and candidates in the 1999–2000 election cycle, up 32 and 25 percent, respectively, from the two previous cycles. Suggestive of the impact of this spending, Roundtable members contributed an average of $44,000 in PAC and individual contributions to House members who voted in favor of the China bill but only $25,000 to those who voted against it.

Labor spending also appeared to have had an effect on the PNTR vote. House members who supported the China deal received an average of $23,000 in PAC and individual contributions from unions while lawmakers voting against it received an average of $53,000 from labor. There just wasn't enough labor money to tip the vote against PNTR (The Center for Responsive Politics, 2000a,b).

to avoid unduly alienating his and the Democrats' core labor base, he also refrained from actively organizing against the China pact to avoid offending existing and potential business donors (McGregor 2000). Gephardt's relative inactivity on the issue made it easier for cross-pressured Democrats to eventually come down in support of PNTR.

Learning from its failure in the 1997 fast-track struggle, during the PNTR fight, business more effectively mobilized and deployed its superior resources to overwhelm its labor adversaries with a massive inside and outside lobbying effort and campaign contributions distributed move evenly to members of both parties. Working closely with GOP leaders who put heavy pressure on undecided Republicans, business again held the support of almost three-quarters of House Republicans despite opposition from party conservatives. Still more crucial, with energetic help from Clinton, other administration officials, and New Democrats both inside and outside Congress, business was also able to fracture the House Democratic caucus, winning the backing of just over one-third of caucus members.[60]

Looking Ahead

What will the future hold? Has the once-stalled process of trade liberalization been restarted, or will labor and its allies regroup and find ways to block new regional or multilateral free trade initiatives?

On the one hand, it is conceivable that aggressive organizing efforts will allow labor to offset the structural changes that have eroded the movement's social and political weight in the past several decades. Recent organizing successes, described elsewhere in this volume, among

---

[60]The actual construction of a winning majority was facilitated by the addition to the PNTR bill of a proposal developed by Democrat Sander Levin of Michigan and Republican Doug Bereuter of Nebraska that would create a commission to monitor China's performance on human rights, provide assistance to U.S. workers hurt by a surge in Chinese imports, and impose sanctions on China if Beijing violated international trade rules. Some observers credited the proposal, which business supported and labor opposed as a "fig leaf," with providing the winning margin by enlisting votes from twenty Democrats worried about U.S. jobs and ten Republicans concerned about the U.S. loss of influence on human rights in China.

home healthcare workers in Los Angeles, textile workers in North Carolina, public employees in Puerto Rico, graduate student teaching assistants at the University of California, computer programmers in Washington State, and doctors in Pennsylvania provide some evidence for this scenario (Tyson 1999; Kosterlitz 1999; Buhle and Fraser 1999. More generally see Mort 1998). It is also possible that the strong dollar and economic weakness overseas may continue to widen the U.S. trade deficit, raise unemployment in particular industries, generate new demands for protection, and intensify public globalphobia. In such circumstances, a revitalized labor movement with public opinion at its back and allied with liberal congressional Democrats and some Republican nationalists might again be able to prevent or block new presidential trade liberalization initiatives that lack strong labor and environmental standard provisions. Alternatively, labor and its allies might even be able to force the inclusion of such provisions in new trade legislation.

On the other hand, developments may transpire that produce more defeats of the kind that labor suffered on PNTR. First, structural economic changes may continue to erode organized labor's numbers and resources. Second, if domestic economic growth remains steady and unemployment low, and the value of the dollar declines while overseas growth picks up, thus reducing the trade deficit, popular opposition to trade liberalization may recede, further depriving labor of the ally of public opinion. Finally, the improvement in business's inside and outside lobbying efforts in support of free trade and the resumption by business of a more bipartisan campaign contribution strategy may continue to moderate Democratic opposition to further trade liberalization. This in turn may allow free traders to win approval of new trade liberalization legislation containing no serious labor and environmental standards provisions.

A Path for Labor

In weighing these two scenarios in light of labor's defeat on PNTR, I argue that labor is not likely to have sufficient strength to be able to simply block all future liberalizing trade agreements. Beyond this, I maintain that labor should not try to block all such agreements. As for-

mer United Electrical Workers staff member Lance Compa argues elsewhere in this volume (see also Compa 1998), while shifting trade flows
hurt many workers, many others gain from trade, and many more
could benefit from a liberal trading order accompanied by strong labor
standards to protect workers' rights. Compa also argues that if trade
agreements are simply blocked, economic integration will proceed anyway, leaving no international scrutiny on labor rights. Thus, Compa
concludes that rather than oppose such accords outright, labor should
instead engage in the fight for worker rights on many fronts[61] while
remaining ready to compromise for incremental advances. This could
include support for a modified fast-track bill or acceptance of a free
trade agreement containing only modest gains for labor rights.

In its efforts to achieve such compromises, labor would be wise to
continue its recent emphasis on the grassroots mobilization of its membership, since the redirection of corporate campaign funds back to congressional Democrats is likely to continue to dilute the influence of
labor's own financial contributions.

To counter business's newly successful efforts on behalf of free trade,
the labor movement will also need to strengthen its already substantial
commitment to coalition politics. As we have seen, labor has built
strong coalitions with a wide range of organizations in the trade fights
of the past decade. Since John Sweeney's installation as AFL-CIO president in late 1995, unions have also forged other promising alliances,
especially with churches and community organizations in successful
"living-wage" campaigns in more than thirty cities and with students
on dozens of college campuses in fights against American-owned foreign sweatshops (Buhle and Fraser 1999).

Labor's task now, as suggested earlier, is to build a broader and more
durable "protective countermovement" against globalization's harmful
consequences. This in turn is more easily accomplished if labor is able
to oppose capital's accumulation strategies with its own nonprotec-
tionist, counterhegemonic vision for organizing the global economy,
one that involves a series of compromises with capital on labor rights

---

[61] Including filing complaints under U.S. trade laws with labor rights provisions and under
the NAFTA side agreements, working with European Union colleagues under the EU Works
Council Directive, bringing cases to the International Labor Organization, pressing for corporate codes of conduct, filing lawsuits, and other mechanisms.

and other issues while incorporating the concerns of environmentalists, human rights advocates, and others. Such a vision would involve a grand compromise with capital and at least the more democratic developing countries in which these nations would agree to enforceable labor and environmental standards. Such standards would gradually rise from low initial starting levels in step with improvements in productivity in exchange for guaranteed commitments of long-term development aid and debt relief.[62] In fact, there are indications that the AFL-CIO is thinking seriously about such a "progressive internationalist" alternative program.[63]

If such a program and movement can be developed, labor and its allies may be able to force their globalist adversaries to agree to an accommodation that is adapted to the new era we have entered.

---

[62]In an important recent study of ninety-three nations, Dani Rodrik shows that democracies pay higher wages than autocracies for a given level of manufacturing productivity (Rodrik 1999). This suggests that more democratic developing countries might eventually be persuaded to agree to modest international labor standards, since they are at a competitive disadvantage with more repressive developing countries in which wages are lower.

[63]See the sketch of elements of such a program by Thomas I. Palley (1999), assistant director of public policy for the AFL-CIO. For a fuller argument, see Palley (1998). See also Faux (2000) and Reich (2000).

CHAPTER THIRTEEN

Free Trade, Fair Trade, and the Battle for Labor Rights

Lance Compa

C reative new organizing, bargaining, and internal restructuring initiatives make up the core of the U.S. labor movement's revitalization project. But close to the center and growing in importance as global commerce expands is new union advocacy for workers' rights in international trade. Trade unionists in the United States and in many other countries are rallying behind the demand that no country and no company should gain a competitive advantage by killing union organizers, banning strikes, using forced labor or brutalized child labor, or violating any other basic rights of workers.

The movement to link workers' rights and trade draws strength from a renewed labor movement. It also contributes to labor's transformation, driving a new internationalism within trade unions and building ties with allied environmental, human rights, and other social action communities. In the legislative arena, labor rights advocacy gives unions new clout in trade and investment policy battles as they raise demands for enforceable rules in the global trading system against state-sponsored or state-tolerated labor rights violations.

Free-trade proponents condemn unions' call for a labor rights–trade linkage as a veneer for old-fashioned protectionism. Indeed, some unions want to protect their members' jobs from imports. As democratic bodies responsive to constituents' interests, they could hardly do otherwise. Shifting trade and investment flows hurt many workers, especially in import-sensitive sectors like apparel and electronics. Trade also affects workers in these industries and other manufacturing operations such as auto parts and machine tools in which companies can move—or credibly threaten to move—production overseas (Commission for Labor Cooperation 1997). Trade puts downward pressure on jobs and wages in these sectors, with spillover effects for many other workers. Often union jobs with good wages and benefits are those most harmed. These losses drive down standards, making wages and conditions in lower-wage service jobs the new benchmark for workers in local or regional labor markets (Collins 1998).[1]

While some unions stress short-term protection of members' jobs, the broader U.S. labor movement, especially the AFL-CIO, works closely with unions in developed and developing countries worldwide to forge a common program supporting global trade (International Confederation of Free Trade Unions 2000). Unions understand that workers in developing countries need access for their goods to U.S., European, Japanese, and other advanced industrial countries' markets, and that U.S. workers can gain from expanded trade with increased exports to developing countries. The key demand of unions in both developed and developing countries is for labor rights and human rights to be treated as seriously as property rights in the trading system (Mazur 2000).

For decades, global trade and investment policy was the exclusive province of government officials in the Treasury Department; the Commerce Department; the Office of the United States Trade Representative (USTR); of corporate lawyers, bankers, and economists in Washington, New York, Chicago and Boston; and of bureaucrats in the General Agreement on Tariffs and Trade (GATT), the forerunner of the World Trade Organization (WTO); the International Monetary Fund (IMF); the World Bank; and other international bodies. These specialists viewed calls for workers' rights, human rights, environmental protection and other social links to trade as irritants raised by economic simpletons. For much of the last quarter-century they imposed what came to be called the "Washington Consensus" on global trade and investment policy—liberalizing markets, privatizing state enterprises, making labor laws more flexible (most notably by making it eas-

---

[1]Economists dispute the degree, but not the fact, of trade's effect on wages and conditions of working people. Often affected workers are characterized as "unskilled," as if they are a small group that needs only retraining to cope in today's economy. But the so-called unskilled are really a large majority of workers, those without professional or advanced technical training. For a thorough treatment incorporating many points of view, see Susan M. Collins, ed., *Imports, Exports, and the American Worker* (Brookings Institution, 1998).

ier for firms to fire workers), removing conditions on capital flows, and otherwise eliminating constraints on the activities of multinational companies.

By the time the North American Free Trade Agreement (NAFTA) was approved in 1993 and the WTO was created in 1994, the Washington Consensus was rolling and new horizons beckoned. A Free Trade Agreement of the Americas (FTAA) would extend NAFTA throughout the hemisphere. A Multilateral Agreement on Investment (MAI) would extend NAFTA's investor protection clauses worldwide. A new round of WTO trade talks would open services, agriculture, and other economic sectors to Washington Consensus treatment. A new acronym, TINA (There Is No Alternative), overshadowed demands for social considerations in trade policy (Smith 1999). Multinational companies adamantly opposed linking workers' rights and trade (U.S. Council for International Business 1996).

But starting in the mid-1990s, a revitalized labor movement, allied with environmental, human rights, farmers, consumers, and other social action communities, began braking the Washington Consensus train. In 1997 they mustered the political strength in the United States to defeat "fast-track" trade negotiating authority for the president, the first time the White House was denied a free hand to broker new trade deals (Abramson and Greenhouse 1997).[2] The same year saw the creation of the World Bank's Structural Adjustment Participatory Review Initiative (SAPRI) to engage trade unions and nongovernmental organizations in reviews of Bank policy effects on workers and other social actors (Suzman 1997).

In 1998, working on an international scale, free-trade critics stopped the MAI (Kobrin 1998, Drohan 1998, Lawton 1998) and forced FTAA negotiators to open their doors to civil society. In 1999 a massive mobilization halted in its tracks the WTO's plan for a new round of trade negotiations. In 2000 a labor-led alliance mounted a spirited campaign to maintain annual review by Congress of most-favored-nation trade

---

[2]"Fast track" is Washington shorthand for the legislative process by which Congress, empowered under the Constitution to regulate commerce with foreign nations, delegates trade negotiating power to the executive branch. An agreement made by the president is then submitted to Congress for approval or rejection without amendment.

status for China (renamed "permanent normal trade relations" to soften the public impression of what China was being granted) based on human rights and labor rights considerations.

The China trade bill was approved by Congress over union opposition (Schmitt and Kahn 2000). However, the fierceness of the labor movement's resistance yielded new respect for labor's political strength (Greenhouse 2000). The unions' mobilization also made a permanent mark on U.S. trade and labor policy. As a price of passage, Congress created a commission to review human rights and labor rights with a major trading partner. Unions called it a "fig leaf" in the heat of the lobbying battle, but the new commission provides an ongoing forum for continued activism, scrutiny, and pressure for workers' rights in trade. Beyond the creation of a commission, the intensity of labor's campaign ensured that the issue of workers' rights in trade would stay high on the agenda of the 2000 presidential and congressional elections and in policy debates of the new Congress (Peterson 2000).

Labor's new strength in the trade debate is matched by a new corporate fallibility. The Asian financial crisis and its "tequila effect" in Latin America, the Russian economic fiasco, and other economic crises of the late 1990s in what had been highly touted emerging markets fractured the model of untrammeled capital flows promoted by multinational executives and investors. The crisis called into question not only the competence but also the existence of the IMF and World Bank (Elliott 2000, Naim 2000).

Cracks also appeared in the ranks of the trade priesthood. Joseph Stigliz, the chief economist of the World Bank, shocked his counterparts with revelations of Bank and IMF scorn for human rights and the environment (Stiglitz 2000). Stiglitz coupled his critique with a call to incorporate labor standards and environmental protection into trade agreements. After his term as chief economist ended, his candor got him fired as a World Bank consultant, but his voice prompted serious reconsideration of the relationship between social causes and global trade. Even *Fortune* magazine, after April 2000 protests in Washington at the annual meetings of the World Bank and the IMF, said it was time to take seriously the protests of the labor movement and its allies (Useem 2000).

New leadership in the U.S. labor movement played a key role in derailing the Washington Consensus. The AFL-CIO's old regime unsuccessfully challenged the free-trade thrusts of the 1980s and early 1990s, most notably in the NAFTA defeat of 1993. Former leaders could hardly shape an international trade-union consensus and lead a movement for workers' rights when the U.S. federation's international affairs apparatus was viewed around the world as an extension of the U.S. government. For decades the AFL-CIO's "free labor" institutes intervened in foreign labor movements to prop up unions that supported U.S. foreign policy whether or not they were representative or effective. AFL-CIO agents often broke up more radical unions with a broader popular base among workers. From such a foundation, U.S. labor calls for workers' rights in global trade rang hollow.

The Sweeney leadership, however, brought new directors into the AFL-CIO's international affairs department. They replaced the old free-labor institutes with a new Solidarity Center and put new representatives into field offices around the world. Both in Washington headquarters and in the field, many of these new staffers had earlier been active in efforts to create an alternative progressive international current in the labor movement, often in the face of heavy resistance from AFL-CIO officials of the old regime. Buoyed by new blood and a fresh approach to relations with foreign trade unionists, the AFL-CIO's international affairs activities targeted multinational corporations and workers' rights violations around the world with a new focus on labor rights in global trade.

Historical Background

Historical perspective helps clarify the current struggle for labor rights in trade. Current debates on international labor and trade policy reflect disputes that raged a century ago in the domestic sphere. The U.S. economy grew from one grounded in local and regional commerce to a continental scale in the late nineteenth and early twentieth century. A labor movement rooted in local crafts had to respond with a "continentalization" of its own.

In the late nineteenth and early twentieth century, skilled trades workers such as those in railroads and the new electric-power generation industry formed new national unions. Along with industrial groups, such as miners and brewery workers, they built the American Federation of Labor (and a shorter-lived International Workers of the World). The new labor bodies coordinated trade-union action against rapidly consolidating employers that increasingly operated at a regional and national level across state lines.

In the 1930s the idea of industrial unionism took hold. A Congress of Industrial Organizations gathered mass production workers in new unions of steel, auto, rubber, and electrical workers to confront employers on a national stage—and an international stage, where companies had Canadian branches (the reason why many unions today are still called "the international").

Public policy in economic and labor matters followed a similar trajectory. The labor, populist, and other social reform movements of the late nineteenth and early twentieth century made the first breakthroughs across state lines. The 1914 Clayton Act declared that "the labor of a human being is not a commodity or article of commerce." The Railway Labor Act of 1926 set rules for union organizing and bargaining in that important national industry. The Wagner Act of 1935 soon followed, defining unfair labor practices and creating the National Labor Relations Board (NLRB) to enforce the law in private industry throughout United States.

Citing the Commerce Clause of the Constitution, which empowers Congress to regulate interstate trade, the Supreme Court upheld the constitutionality of the Wagner Act in 1937. Congress went on to pass the Fair Labor Standards Act of 1938, which mandated a federal minimum wage, overtime pay after forty hours in a workweek, and limits on child labor. In decades that followed, the same federal jurisdiction was asserted to pass prevailing wage, equal-pay, nondiscrimination, health and safety, plant-closing advance warning, family and medical leave, and other legislation setting federal minimum employment standards for the entire country.

Many labor advocates are swift to argue that these laws are too weak or too weakly enforced. Even so, these norms create a threshold below which individual states cannot go in efforts to attract investment by cutting labor standards. Federal standards block a "race to the bottom" among the states.

Of course, the race continues in other arenas. Unemployment insurance and workers' compensation remain state-based labor standards, and employers aggressively attack these protections, pressuring states to compete with each other with lower benefits and tighter eligibility rules. State labor federations devote much of their work to defending these programs. Furthermore, the federal minimum wage is so low that some states, especially those taking advantage of "right-to-work" laws, still trumpet a low wage, antiunion climate to attract investment. Low-wage countries overseas are hardly the only engine of plant closings and runaway shops, as workers in traditional industrial centers learned when employers moved to other parts of the United States.

The struggle for labor rights and labor standards in yesterday's interstate commerce within the United States foreshadowed today's battles over international trade policies. Workers and trade unions face the challenge of achieving labor rights and labor standards across national borders, just as American workers earlier had to win them across state boundaries. Workers in other countries confronted similar tasks—the United States is not exceptional in fashioning national standards for diverse regional and local jurisdictions. And just as workers and unions confronted nationwide industries and companies, they now are up against multinational banks and corporations with highly mobile capital at their disposal.

The Contemporary Labor Rights Movement

Progress on labor rights in trade did not begin with the advent of new AFL-CIO leadership, even if the most visible markers have been set since 1995. For many years earlier, the labor movement opened many fronts and made headway in the battle for workers' rights. International labor rights advocacy gained ground in four broad arenas.

1. In a unilateral context, American trade-union advocates achieved labor rights amendments in several U.S. trade laws that made respect for workers' rights a condition of foreign countries' duty-free access to the U.S. market and other trade, foreign aid, or development benefits. In a series of labor-rights petitions under these laws, U.S. unionists and allied groups spurred improvements in many countries and applied sanctions where violations continued.
2. Although they viewed NAFTA's passage as a defeat and roundly criticized the trade agreement's labor side agreement, labor activists in the United States, Canada, and Mexico increasingly used the North American Agreement on Labor Cooperation (NAALC) to advance cross-border solidarity.
3. In a global context, the International Labor Organization (ILO), the WTO, the Organization for Economic Cooperation and Development (OECD), the World Bank, and other multilateral institutions became important international forums for asserting workers' rights. Trade unions around the world found creative ways to press these bodies for advances in labor.
4. Private actors, especially trade unions, also operated outside these government-sponsored institutional arrangements and created their own tools to build labor rights into trade and investment systems. International labor-right advocacy has become central to the work of the International Confederation of Free Trade Unions (ICFTU) and regional affiliates such as the Inter-American Regional Organization of Workers (ORIT), and of International Trade Secretariats (ITS's) that join unions across the world by industry or sector.

Labor and human rights groups also pressured multinational companies to adopt codes of conduct for their foreign subsidiaries or suppliers, and are devising creative ways to apply and enforce such codes. Other labor-allied groups used media strategies to expose labor rights violations in countries where firms supply U.S. brand-name products, or promoted "labeling" measures aimed at consumers who want assurance that products are made under decent working conditions.

1. U.S Unilateral Labor Rights Action

In the early 1980s a small group of labor, religious, and human rights activists began meeting with progressive congressional staffers to shape new initiatives in U.S. trade and labor policy. Alarmed by the free-market, free-trade offensives of the Reagan-Thatcher era and frustrated by narrow trade policy responses by unions (often reflected in Labor Day events that featured smashing a Japanese product), they launched a legislative reform effort to insert labor rights amendments into U.S. trade laws.

A first, a modest breakthrough came in 1983 with adoption of the Caribbean Basin Initiative (CBI), a program for preferential access to the U.S. market for Central American and Caribbean countries. The CBI labor rights amendment contained benefits such as duty-free entry into the United States on exporting countries' compliance with internationally recognized worker rights.

In 1984 a farther-reaching labor rights amendment was added to a bill renewing the Generalized System of Preferences (GSP). The GSP program granted developing nations around the world beneficial, duty-free access for selected products entering the U.S. market. "Taking steps to afford" internationally recognized worker rights became a requirement for participation in the GSP. Just as important, the GSP reform act had the USTR set up a petitioning process, something lacking in the earlier CBI legislation. Now trade unions, human rights groups, and others could challenge a country's GSP beneficiary status because of labor rights violations by filing a complaint with the USTR presenting evidence at the public hearing.

The GSP program permits a developing country to export goods to the United States on a preferential, duty-free basis as long as it meets the conditions for eligibility in the program. The "internationally recognized worker rights" defined in the legislation are the following:[3]

---

[3]It is important to note that these standards are not explicitly linked to ILO conventions or any other accepted international norms. The first four items match most formulations of "core" or "human rights" labor standards. However, the U.S. legislative scheme fails to include a universally recognized core standard for nondiscrimination in employment. This element was rejected by Reagan administration officials who negotiated a compromise bill acceptable to the White House with Ways and Means Committee members (Travis 1992).

1. The right of association
2. The right to organize and bargain collectively
3. A prohibition on the use of any form of forced or compulsory labor
4. A minimum age for the employment of children
5. Acceptable conditions of work with respect to minimum wages, hours of work, and occupational safety and health

The United States was not alone in developing a unilateral labor rights regime. Acting as a bloc, the European Union also adopted a labor rights clause in its GSP program that offered enhanced access to European markets for developing countries that respected workers' freedom of association, did not discriminate in hiring because of race or sex, and provided for child labor protection (Buckley 1997).

Since adoption of the GSP labor rights amendment in 1984, worker advocates have filed complaints on labor rights conditions in more than forty countries under the GSP process. The most active petitioners were the AFL-CIO; individual unions including the UE, IUE, and UFCW; and non-governmental organizations (NGOs) such as the International Labor Rights Fund and various divisions of Human Rights Watch—Asia Watch, Africas Watch, and Americas Watch.

Twelve countries were suspended from GSP beneficiary status because of labor rights violations in the 1980s, including military dictatorships in Chile, Paraguay, Burma, and Pakistan. More than a dozen more were placed on continuing review, including repressive regimes in Guatemala, Haiti, Indonesia, and El Salvador. Several of the suspended countries undertook labor reform measures to meet GSP requirements, and the review process persuaded others to make improvements. The benefits cutoff shocked business elites in Chile and Paraguay, and contributed to the partial restoration of democracy, including more freedom for workers.

In Guatemala, pressure generated by the GSP review helped avert a military takeover in 1993, and later helped gain the first union recognition and collective bargaining agreement in that country's *maquila* sector (Frundt 1999). Similar progress was made in the Dominican Republic, where unionism began taking root in the export processing zones (Jessup and Gordon 2000).

This should not suggest that the GSP labor rights amendment, or any other labor rights amendment in U.S. trade laws, has gone from triumph to triumph. Chile and Paraguay are hardly full democracies, and trade unions still face terrible obstacles there. Guatemala has not overcome the legacy of four decades of military terror, and one or two labor contracts in its rapidly growing export sector, like the handful of contracts in the Dominican Republic's *zonas francas,* hardly augurs trade-union dynamism. Still, in concrete measure, and sometimes in life or death cases, unilateral labor rights action by the United States made a difference.

2. NAFTA and the NAALC

The NAFTA labor agreement sets forth eleven "labor principles" that the three signatory countries commit themselves to promote:

1. Freedom of association and protection of the right to organize
2. The right to bargain collectively
3. The right to strike
4. Abolition of forced labor
5. Prohibition of child labor
6. Minimum wage, hours of work, and other labor standards
7. Nondiscrimination
8. Equal pay for equal work
9. Occupational safety and health
10. Workers' compensation
11. Migrant worker protection

The NAALC provides an accessible forum for trade unions and human rights groups to invoke a critical review of a country's labor law and practice. For three of the eleven labor principles (child labor, minimum wage, and safety and health), an arbitration panel can impose trade sanctions for a persistent pattern of failure to effectively enforce national law.

The NAALC labor rights system inspired cross-border initiatives among labor rights advocates in all three NAFTA countries. International coalitions filed more than twenty cases involving union organizing rights, health and safety abuses, discrimination, migrant worker treatment, and other labor rights issues. The cases were submitted to a National Administrative Office (NAO), the agency in each country's labor department that receives complaints of NAALC violations by a NAFTA partner.

Three cases are described here, one on each country, to illustrate the opportunities for, and limitations of, transnational advocacy presented by the NAALC.

THE PREGNANCY TESTING CASE

Two U.S.-based human rights groups, Human Rights Watch and the International Labor Rights Fund, along with the Mexican Democratic Lawyers' Association, filed a complaint with the NAO of the United States in May 1997 alleging "a pattern of widespread, state-tolerated sex discrimination against prospective and actual female workers in the *maquiladora* sector along the Mexico-U.S. border."[4] Companies named as offenders in the case included General Motors, Zenith, Siemens, Thomson, Samsung, Sanyo, Matsushita, Johnson Controls, and other multinational firms.

The submission challenged the common practice of requiring pregnancy testing of all female job applicants and denying employment to those whose test results were positive. The submission also said that employers pressure employees who become pregnant to leave their jobs. Companies do this, labor advocates argued, to avoid the legal requirement of three months' fully paid maternity leave for workers who give birth.

The coalition that filed the complaint argued that pregnancy testing by employers and the failure of the labor authorities to combat it—sometimes by omission, sometimes by overt support of the employers' discriminatory policy—violated Mexico's obligations under the NAALC. The complaint sought a U.S. NAO review, public hearings in cities along the Mexico-U.S. border, and the formation of an Evaluation Committee of Experts to report on employment practices related to pregnancy in Canada, Mexico, and the United States.[5]

---

[4]See U.S. NAO Case No. 9701, *Submission Concerning Pregnancy-Based Sex Discrimination in Mexico's Maquiladora Sector*, at 4.

[5]Ibid., at 7.

In January 1998 the U.S. NAO issued a report confirming widespread pregnancy testing that discriminated against women workers. Concluding ministerial consultations in October 1998, the labor secretaries of Canada, Mexico, and the United States approved a program of workshops for government enforcement officials, outreach to women workers, and an international conference on gender discrimination issues. In the meantime, several U.S. companies in the *maquiladora* zones announced they would halt pregnancy testing, and legislation was introduced by opposition members of Congress to make a prohibition explicit.

At the international conference in Mexico in early March 1999, Mexican government officials acknowledged the unlawfulness of employee pregnancy testing and the failure of government authorities to halt it. They said they would prepare new instructions to labor department officials to put an end to the practice.

It is still too soon to know if a thorough change in policy and practice will take shape. A follow-up report by Human Rights Watch in December 1998 found that several of the firms that said they would unilaterally stop pregnancy testing had not ended it entirely (Human Rights Watch 1998). But the NAALC complaint made an international affair of what had been a decades-long, hidden, entrenched, accepted practice in Mexico's burgeoning *maquiladora* sector. It set in motion a dynamic for changing the practice through new employer policies, proposed legislative changes, and escalated international attention if an evaluation committee of experts formed to address the case. The case and its attendant campaign efforts also elevated the visibility and influence of Mexican women's rights groups that had formerly been marginalized and ignored in their strictly domestic context.

THE WASHINGTON STATE APPLE CASE

In a major case accepted for review by Mexico in July 1998, a coalition of Mexican labor and human rights groups filed a wide-ranging complaint under NAFTA's labor side accord alleging failure of U.S. labor law to protect workers' rights in the Washington State apple industry. The complaint cited the lack of legal protection for farm-worker union organizing and bargaining rights, discrimination against migrant workers, widespread health and safety violations, budget cuts in U.S. enforcement agencies such the NLRB and the Occupational Safety & Health Administration (OSHA), and employers' use of threats and intimidation in union representation elections at two major apple-packing and shipping plants.

Mexican trade unionists sent a delegation to observe two NLRB elections in apple-industry warehouse operations in January 1998, where the Teamsters had signed up a majority of workers into the union. Using anti-union consultants, those companies destroyed the union's majority in both workplaces through a campaign of threats, intimidation, and discrimination against union supporters. Appalled by what they witnessed in the NLRB election campaigns, as well as by pesticide hazards and other conditions among orchard workers whom the United Farm Workers were seeking to organize, the Mexican allies filed a complaint under the NAFTA labor agreement (Greenhouse 1998b).

Over 45,000 workers are employed in the orchards and warehouses of the largest apple-producing industry in the United States. Most workers come from Mexico, which is the largest single export market for Washington State apples. The petitioners asked the Mexican government to pursue avenues of review, consultation, evaluation, and arbitration available under the NAALC for a "persistent pattern of failure" by U.S. labor law authorities to prevent workers' rights violations in the Washington apple industry.

The Washington apple industry complaint prompted the first public hearing in Mexico, with widespread media coverage of the plight of workers and violations of their rights (Moore 1998). Consultations between the two countries' secretaries of labor contemplate further public hearings in both countries. Significantly, this case has the potential to reach a stage of economic sanctions against the industry, since it contains a safety and health count (Conley 1998)

The NAALC case shocked industry representatives. One company leader said that the NAALC should be revised or industry support for future trade agreements would be severely eroded. He called the NAALC "an open invitation for specific labor disputes to be raised into an international question" (Iritani 1998).

The NAO of Mexico issued its report on the case in August 1999, when Mexico's secretary of labor formally requested ministerial consultations with the U.S. secretary of labor. This development sparked a new round of publicity and related attention to the conditions of migrant workers in the industry (Gorlick 1999).

The Washington apple case exemplifies the opportunities for creative use of labor rights clauses in trade agreement, even when they do not provide specific remedies like reinstatement, back wages, or bargaining orders. The case brought together the Teamsters and the Farm Workers unions, along with sympathetic U.S. human rights groups, in coalition with Mexican counterparts in the independent labor and human rights movements. They worked together in the Teamsters' organizing campaign in apple industry warehouses, and together prepared the complaint. Now they are preparing for public hearings, ministerial consultations, and further proceedings under the NAALC and coordinating testimony, media relations, and other campaign efforts. Their goal is to make the Washington State apple industry a model of good labor relations, good wages and benefits, and effective labor law enforcement for all of North American agriculture.

THE MCDONALD'S CASE

Joined by the Quebec Federation of Labor and the International Labor Rights Fund, the Teamsters union and its Quebec affiliates filed a NAALC complaint in October 1998 on the closure of a McDonald's restaurant in St-Hubert, Quebec, shortly before the union was certified to bargain for workers there. This was the first NAALC case implicating labor law in a Canadian jurisdiction.

The coalition argued that McDonald's used loopholes and delaying tactics to extend union representation proceedings before the Quebec labor board for one year. The company prolonged proceedings by arguing falsely that the restaurant was part of a larger chain where workers transferred among different facilities. McDonald's routinely appealed decisions in the union's favor. Finally it shut the restaurant when the union certification was about to be issued.

Although Quebec labor law is generally favorable to workers and unions, it is impotent in dealing with anti-union workplace closures. The Quebec courts have evolved a doctrine allowing employers to close facilities even partially to avoid unionization, and to do it with complete impunity—the only jurisdiction in North America that does so (the U.S. Darlington doctrine prohibits partial closings but allows a total closure of the entire business even for an anti-union motive) (Commission for Labor Cooperation 1997).

In December 1998 the U.S. NAO announced that it had accepted the McDonald's case for review. In April 1999 the case was settled among the NAOs of the United States and Canada, the petitioners, and Quebec Ministry of Labor. Under the settlement, Quebec's government is forming a special commission to review provincial labor law on anti-union plant closings and to develop legislative remedies to the problem. The governments of Canada and Quebec wanted to keep the controversy within a domestic context rather than have it exposed to a public hearing and further international scrutiny. Such interplay of domestic and international interests is a new, important feature of activity under the NAALC.

THE FTAA

Unions in the United States, Canada, and Mexico are applying their heightened collaboration to the hemispheric arena. At a Miami summit meeting in 1994, Western Hemisphere countries made plans for a free trade agreement of the Americas (FTAA), with 2005 as the target year for such an agreement. Trade unions and allied labor rights advocates called for a strong social dimension in any FTAA. At an April 1998 "People's Summit" in Santiago, Chile, alongside an official governmental summit meeting, trade union delegates adopted three major demands. One was for recognition of a labor counterpart to the officially sanctioned Business Forum that meets with FTAA government trade negotiators. Another was to add the International Labor Organization's core labor standards to any FTAA. Finally, the unions called for adoption of a broader social charter in the FTAA that addressed the concerns of nongovernmental organizations outside labor.

Hemispheric trade unions are working mainly through ORIT, the regional trade union affiliate of the ICFTU, to address labor rights in the context of an FTAA. Significantly, unions also expanded links to NGOs in the hemisphere that embraced human rights, women, migrant workers, indigenous peoples, farmers and farm workers, and other grassroots groups.

New space for social concerns in trade was evident at the 1998 heads of state summit in Santiago, in which talk of trade was matched for the first time by substantive talk of social issues. Indeed, what the governmental summit produced was not far from the parallel peoples' summit results. A final document by the heads of state called for a "social action plan" to promote core ILO labor standards, improve education, reduce poverty and inequality, expand democracy, and guarantee human rights.

The governments also agreed to create a committee on civil society to officially hear the views of labor, environmental, and other nongovernmental organizations as FTAA negotiations proceeded. It remains to be seen whose views the committee will hear, or whether the civil society committee will have access commensurate with that of the already-recognized Business Forum. In any case, this is the first formal trade-negotiating process with a role for civil society groups besides business.

3. Multilateral and Global Action on Labor Rights

Just as it arises under U.S. domestic law and in regional contexts like NAFTA and the FTAA, a labor-rights trade link is taking on greater importance at multilateral and global levels. Labor rights and trade are now high on the agendas of the United Nations, the ILO, OECD, WTO, and at international financial institutions such as the World Bank and the IMF.

UNITED NATIONS

The United Nations' Universal Declaration of Human Rights; the International Covenant on Civil and Political Rights; and the International Covenant on Economic, Social and Cultural Rights treat an array of workers' rights. They include both human rights matters (e.g., freedom of association, forced labor, child labor) and economic and social issues (e.g., decent wages, adequate health insurance, periodic holidays with pay). UN human rights complaint procedures are bureaucratic and slow, but they can put hard pressure on countries to improve labor rights under the spotlight of scrutiny in the highest international forum.

ILO

Since its founding in 1919, the ILO has adopted 182 conventions that cover matters ranging from core standards such as freedom of association and nondiscrimination to detailed safety rules for maritime workers. The ILO has no power to compel compliance with its rulings, but it has far-reaching oversight authority with the potential to advance labor rights through the promotion of ILO norms and its investigating and reporting powers (delaCruz, von Potobsky, and Swepston 1996).

Growing concern over labor rights and labor standards in international trade has provoked new interest in the role of the ILO, which earlier had been more of a forum for set-piece clashes between capitalist and socialist countries. At its 1998 conference, the ILO adopted a Declaration of Fundamental Principles and Rights at Work, a set of core labor rights contained in seven conventions that called for the right to bargain collectively, prohibitions on forced labor, limits on child labor, and an end to race and sex discrimination in employment (ILO 1998).

Under the declaration, every member state is bound to respect these norms whether or not the country has ratified the relevant ILO convention. This has particular relevance for the United States. Of the seven core conventions, the United States has ratified one: Convention No. 105 on the abolition of forced labor. Other countries that ratified only one of the core conventions are Bahrain, Cambodia, China, Laos, Qatar, Solomon Islands, United Arab Emirates, and Zimbabwe.

Although the ILO does not have the power to sanction offenders, its powers of investigation and "jawboning" of employers and governments can often produce results. The ILO has been instrumental in freeing many imprisoned unionists around the world, for example. The AFL-CIO is making a new commitment to ILO action by U.S. unionists, backed up with staff and resources to carry it out. This can give more clout to the ILO in its worker rights advocacy. It can also strengthen ties with workers and unions from other countries.

WTO

The emergence of the ILO as a forum for treating labor rights and trade is directly connected to the WTO's reluctance thus far to engage the issue. The WTO fended off direct treatment of labor concerns at its December 1996 trade ministers' meeting. However, the ministers had to concede the link between labor rights and trade, declaring, "We renew our commitment to the observance of internationally recognized core labour standards." They named the ILO as "the competent body to set and deal with these standards." (WTO 1996)

Despite WTO resistance, labor rights advocates continued pressing for a labor rights link within WTO disciplines. Their action culminated in huge protests by labor, human rights, environmental, and other social movements at the WTO ministerial meeting in Seattle in December 1999. The meeting ended in disarray, with no move to further liberalize trade rules. Critics labeled the protesters protectionists and charged that the AFL-CIO was only seeking to protect members' jobs at the expense of workers in developing countries. But mostly unreported and unnoted was the strong alliance between trade unions of both developed and developing countries around a common program for linking labor rights and international trade (ICFTU 2000).

Continued pressure from trade unions and allied groups will ultimately move the WTO off the mark. In the long run—and perhaps in the shorter run, in light of the global economic crisis that arose in 1998 in the "emerging markets" of Asia, Russia, and Latin America—the economists' theoretical case for expanding global trade will have to be matched by political support from working people and their unions. Workers must have confidence that labor rights and labor standards will be integrated into global economic arrangements, especially in the WTO, to block a race to the bottom among trade competitors.

OECD

In 1976 the OECD devised "Guidelines for Multinational Enterprises" for firms operating in member countries. The OECD is the "rich men's club" of the global economy, coordinating policies among governments of the United States, Japan, Australia, Canada, New Zealand, and the developed nations of Europe. In recent years, however, Korea and Mexico joined the OECD, Korea because of its rapid growth to become the world's eleventh industrial power (before the Asian financial crisis of 1997–98), and Mexico on the strength of its NAFTA ties to the United States and Canada.

The guidelines took shape after revelations of misconduct by multinational corporations in the 1960s and 1970s, especially after the revelations came to light in U.S. congressional hearings chaired by Senator Frank Church. The OECD guidelines cover a range of issues including antitrust matters, financial disclosure requirements, taxation, technology, and others. Section 6 of the guidelines covers employment and industrial relations. It provides for the right to organize and bargain collectively and for the affording of information to employee representatives to "obtain a true and fair view" of company performance. It bans discrimination and calls for advance notice of layoffs and cooperation with unions to mitigate the effects of layoffs. Finally, the Guidelines instruct management not to threaten to close or transfer operations to unfairly influence negotiations or interfere with the right to organize.

The OECD guidelines include a de facto complaint procedure, although the body avoids making specific findings of misconduct by individual companies. Instead, it holds an "exchange of views" on the "experience gained" under the guidelines, and issues "clarifications" of the guidelines as they apply to specific labor-management conflicts. Procedurally, unions that take recourse to the OECD must be careful not to accuse employers of outright violations of the guidelines, but to present a description of relevant facts and seek an interpretation. The OECD states explicitly that "observance of the Guidelines is voluntary and not legally enforceable." (OECD 1997)

Despite its limitations, some unions were able to use the OECD guidelines to advance their agenda, though more by public relations or interunion solidarity measures than through pressure brought to bear by the OECD. The United Mine Workers of America (UMWA) turned to the OECD following a 1988 labor dispute over layoff and recall protections at Enoxy Coal Co., a West Virginia mine owned by ENI, the Italian state-run energy company. A complex "exchange of views" was held among the union, the employers (both the U.S. subsidiary and ENI), and U.S. and Italian government "contact points" that obtained the views of their own ministries or departments. Pressure on the Italian government by unions there helped resolve the dispute to the UMWA's satisfaction (Glade and Potter 1989).

In the 1980s a U.S. union faced with antilabor conduct by the local management of a U.S. subsidiary of a Swedish corporation used the OECD contact-point system to have Swedish unions pressure the Swedish government to persuade Swedish parent-company managers to convince their U.S. executives to halt its objectionable conduct (Glade and Potter 1989).

WORLD BANK AND IMF

After years of resistance to any link to social dimensions in their grant and loan programs, the World Bank and the IMF began addressing labor rights. The bank's 1995 World Development Report was devoted to labor market issues, and offered a definition of core workers' rights (World Bank 1995).

In the wake of the Asian financial crisis and particularly in connection with developments in Indonesia, the IMF conceded a need to take workers' rights into account in its lending programs (Brownstein 1997). The United States moved toward new measures that required labor rights considerations as a condition for continued U.S. financial support for the IMF (Sanger 1998).

Again, one should be careful not to overstate the capacity of these multilateral bodies to remedy labor rights violations. They all contain "soft-law" measures involving investigations, reports, recommendations, consultations, and the like, not "hard-law" adjudication and remedies under coercive state power. But they are important forums where aggressive use of oversight mechanisms can get results.

4. Private Sector Action on Labor Rights

The arenas for labor rights advocacy reviewed above involve government-created bodies and mechanisms, but outside of government, trade unions and human rights groups have engaged many companies and industries directly on labor rights.

ITS'S AND LABOR SOLIDARITY

The AFL-CIO is an important affiliate of the ICFTU, which joins central labor federations from around the world. Several individual U.S. unions are members of the ITS's, the sectoral international union bodies that group unions according to branch of industry. They include ITS's in the metalworking, food, energy, textile, transportation, and other key sectors of the global economy.

For decades, the ICFTU and the ITS's undertook international solidarity campaigns. A notable example came in the 1980s when the International Union of Food and Allied Workers (IUF) launched a campaign for workers at the Coca-Cola bottling plant in Guatemala, where successive union leaders had been assassinated and a strike was threatened with military intervention. The IUF's effort led to a peaceful resolution of the conflict with continued bargaining rights for the union, which has since played a key role in reviving civil society in Guatemala (Frundt 1987).

CORPORATE CODES OF CONDUCT

The ICFTU developed a campaign for corporate codes of conduct on international labor rights. Trade union and human-rights-group pressure convinced many companies to issue codes of conduct for their overseas subsidiaries and suppliers. For example, an Apparel Industry Partnership joining human rights organizations and brand-name clothing retailers such as Levi's and Reebok agreed on a code of conduct covering forced labor, child labor, health and safety, discrimination, the right to organize and bargain collectively, wages, and working hours. The apparel industry code requires supplier firms to respect workers' rights or risk losing contracts with the U.S. companies (BNA 1997). The partnership later formed the Fair Labor Association (FLA) to enforce their code and deal with issues such as independent monitoring, public disclosure of findings, and application of sanctions.

Unhappy with corporate involvement in the FLA, several unions and student groups promoted an alternative Workers Rights Consortium (WRC) for universities to monitor suppliers of university-branded apparel and other products. A European labor-human rights coalition generated a similar effort to establish labor rights standards for overseas suppliers to European companies, called the Fair Trade Foundation.

Another code of conduct was initiated by the New York-based corporate accountability group Center for Economic Priorities. Based on the International Standards Organization (ISO) series of quality standards, this code is called "SA8000" (Social Accountability). It sets forth norms to be reviewed by professional accounting firms. Taking another tack, labor, human rights, and consumer groups developed product-specific codes of conduct for handwoven rugs (the Rugmark Foundation) and for soccer balls (the FIFA code, adopted by the International Federation of Football Associations).

A cautionary note is needed for private-sector codes of conduct. Such codes mainly address brand-name retailers concerned about their image among consumers. Their stance on labor rights seems more a response to the degree of uproar in the buying public than a commitment to sustained efforts to promote labor rights for their employees. Such codes are not catching on with companies less dependent on consumer goodwill (Bounds and Stout 1997). High hopes for the Apparel Industry Partnership were tempered by the difficulty in formulating a monitoring and enforcement system (Greenhouse 1998a). Concern that professional accounting firms will be insufficiently rigorous and lack the experience for effective labor rights monitoring calls into question the SA8000 plan. However, creative labor rights advocates found fertile ground for getting their message out through the use of these private mechanisms.

LITIGATION STRATEGIES ON LABOR RIGHTS

Even the time-honored American battle cry "see you in court" found resonance in international labor rights matters. Labor advocates launched innovative lawsuits in U.S. courts to vindicate international labor rights claims. In a path-breaking case in federal courts, a Korean union sued New York-based Pico Products, Inc., after the company abruptly shut its electronics factory near Seoul in February 1989. Three hundred workers, mostly women, lost their jobs in the shutdown. The union contract called for advance notice and severance pay, and the workers were unpaid for their final weeks of actual labor performed.

The suit alleged violation of their labor contract and interference with their contractual relationship by Pico's U.S. management.

Concerned about the strength of the union's case, Pico made a settlement offer that amounted to practically all the monetary damages that the workers could hope to obtain in winning the case. U.S. attorneys recommended accepting the settlement, but the workers chose to go forward to trial. For them, the satisfaction of a judicial determination of guilt was a higher priority than the money to be gained in a settlement with a nonadmission of wrongdoing.

The judge found all the facts favorable to the plaintiffs: a contract violation had occurred and damage to the workers resulted. However, on a technicality of New York corporate law called the "Felsen exception," the court found that the parent company was insulated from the acts of the Korean subsidiary. That decision was upheld on appeal.[6]

Regardless of the outcome of the Pico case, the breakthrough in reaching a full-scale trial in U.S. courts pitting a foreign labor union against a U.S. multinational corporation set an important precedent for future actions. Other lawsuits targeted owners of Guatemalan apparel factories to enforce back-pay judgments for workers there,[7] chemical companies whose workers were poisoned by pesticides banned in the United States,[8] owners of a Tijuana maquiladora plant for sexual harassment,[9] and energy companies in league with forced labor policies of the Burmese government.[10] Substantial damages claims were won in these cases.

---

[6]See *Labor Union of Pico Korea v. Pico Products, Inc.*, 968 F.2d 191 (1992).

[7]Information on this case is available from the International Labor Rights Education and Research Fund in Washington, D.C.

[8]See *Dow Chemical Co. v. Castro-Alfaro*, 786 S.W.2d 674 (1990); see also Emily Yozell, "The Castro Alfaro Case: Lessons for Lawyers in Transcultural Litigation," in Lance Compa & Stephen Diamond, eds., *Human Rights, Labor Rights, and International Trade* (University of Pennsylvania, 1996), p. 273 (toxic tort case involving Costa Rican banana plantation workers).

[9]See "Workers Succeed in Cross-Border Bid for Justice" (*Maquiladora* sexual harassment case in California state court), *Border Lines* (November 1995), at 1.

[10]See International Labor Rights Fund, *Union of Burma v. Unocal*, plaintiffs amended complaint (suit against U.S. energy company for using forced labor in Burma, pending in federal district court in California).

Litigation in U.S. courts was also important defensively. For example, the International Longshoremen's Association successfully fended off secondary boycott charges by nonunion stevedoring companies when the union sought international solidarity from its counterpart in Japan.[11]

Lawsuits are cumbersome, slow, and expensive. Like any of the other forums outlined here, courtroom proceedings are not a single remedy for the array of labor rights violations that confront workers in the global economy. Still, a targeted legal strategy can hit a labor rights violator hard, both with adverse publicity and with punitive damages paid to workers.

Conclusion

Labor rights advocacy is the most direct challenge to the primacy of a marketplace ideology in which efficiency and profit are the highest values. Labor rights advocates promote values of fairness, justice, and solidarity in global commerce. The battle to achieve enforceable hard law that protects workers' rights in the global economy is an important contribution to the labor movement's revitalization.

Can a beleaguered movement take on multinational companies and the governments that appease them on these varied international grounds when there is so much still to do on organizing, collective bargaining, and domestic political action? There really is no choice. International trade policy is now a battleground for workers' rights, just as national economic policy was the focus of the great reform movements of the turn of the century and the New Deal of the 1930s. The multiple arenas of international labor rights controversy are also forums for labor rights advocacy. The opportunities they present are as varied, and potentially as powerful, as the challenges.

---

[11]See *Canaveral Port Authority v. ILA,* Cert. Den. U.S. Sup. Ct. No. 95–381; *ILA v. NLRB,* 56 F.3rd 205 (1995).

Whither the American Labor Movement?

Harry C. Katz

*T*his afterword reviews the discussions in the preceding chapters concerning the likelihood and nature of a revitalization of the American labor movement. I use the chapters as a springboard to present my views regarding the prospects for union revitalization.

The Social Movement Claim

The opening chapters of this volume (Turner-Hurd and Johnston) assert that for the American labor movement to become revitalized it will have to transform itself into "social unionism" and link up with broader social movements occurring across American society. While few would quarrel with the claim that social turbulence in the 1930s and 1960s contributed to the growth spurts that occurred first within private-sector unionism (1930s) and then within public-sector unionism (1960s and early 1970s), there is much debate in the field of industrial relations concerning the social movement proposition.

For one thing, it is not clear that the American labor movement ever amounted to social movement unionism. The social tumult and political activism of the 1930s and 1960s clearly spurred union growth, but did American unions ever have an agenda that favored radical social change? Didn't business unionism dominate (admittedly not exclusively) the character of American unions from the early twentieth century on?

It is also noteworthy that the American style of business unionism, especially after the 1930s, included support for many progressive social policies including Social Security, the minimum wage, and health and safety regulation. So it is not clear that becoming a social- movement-oriented labor movement was critical to the earlier growth in American unionism. Nor is it clear that American unions on the whole ever became the conservative factor the social movement critics condemn.

It is also not obvious what the social movement proposition actually is. At times the social movement position seems to be claiming that social movement unionism is not only a potential route to union strength, it is the only route. Yet, it is not apparent that the union movements in other countries that have maintained large membership bases, such as the German or Swedish labor movements, did so (or do so) on the basis of social movement unionism. Other researchers, such as Swenson (1989), have argued that it was links to the provision of social insurance or other factors that produced the strength found in those labor movements.

Another way to read the social movement proposition is as a claim that the American labor movement has begun in recent years to transform itself into social movement unionism and that this transformation is likely to extend even further in the years ahead. Here the claim is even more dubious. The research presented in this volume and other recent studies clearly show that the American labor movement is making a serious effort to increase and redefine organizing activities. Yet, it is not at all clear that it makes sense to characterize recent union activities as a drift toward social movement unionism. With regard to labor's political agenda, the chapters in this volume by James Shoch and Lance Compa reveal that the American labor movement recently has been engaged in practical and pragmatic political activities and compromises concerning trade and international labor rights and in doing so has met with some success. The value of these pragmatic compromises belies the claims of the social movement proponents that only radical social policies can promote workers' interests.

Similarly, the industrial relations research literature has long noted the progressive and forceful role American unions have played in representing workers' interests on the shop floor. On the shop floor, as well as in broader politics, it is not clear that radical policies are either feasible or effective.

My skepticism regarding the potential value of social-movement-oriented politics stems in part from the lack of evidence of a transfor-

mation in the political orientation of either American unions or workers. Nor do such transformations seem likely in the future. Perhaps the
most surprising development is the fact that neither the deep reces-
sions that occurred from 1974–76 and 1981–83 nor the ongoing economic expansion have spurred American workers to seek radical social
change. So if neither sharp economic contractions nor a sustained economic boom spur social movement unionism, what would?

There is much evidence (for example, see Cappelli et al. 1997 and
Osterman 1999) that workers have borne the burden of layoffs and economic insecurity over the last twenty years, yet there is scant evidence
that this has led these workers to seek radical political change. If anything, it is workers' conservatism rather than the drift toward social
movement activism that is most striking. On this score, social movement supporters seem to be engaged in wishful thinking, basing their
predictions on what they hope will occur rather than on what is suggested by the evidence.

Charles Heckscher presents another bold vision for the American
labor movement when he asserts that the key to the future growth and
success of American unions lies in their ability to create representation
structures that accommodate the needs of the now allegedly pervasive
highly mobile American workforce. Heckscher sides with those who
believe that workers' attachments to any particular firm are likely to be
short-lived, and so new forms of "associational unionism" are needed.
Much of the debate about this view turns on the degree to which one
believes that high-mobility jobs are, or will be, characteristic of the
American labor market (Cappelli 1999).

Are Career Jobs Gone?

Although few would quarrel with Heckscher's claim that the amount
of worker mobility is increasing, there is great debate in the economics literature concerning the extent to which such "hypermobility" is
pervasive. Economic analysis has revealed that while there is some
shortening in the average job tenure experienced by American workers, the sort of hyper job mobility found among high-tech workers in
Silicon Valley or that found among media workers is not typical (Far-

ber, 1998). Rather, as Osterman (1999) notes in his careful analysis of the evidence, what seems to have changed is that workers and managers now fear the possibility of layoff (and do so even if their employer is doing well), although hyper-labor-market mobility is not actually widespread (see also Sanford Jacoby 1999).

The conservative nature of workers' reactions to increased economic insecurity is revealed by the fact that union membership did not grow even though downsizing and reengineering became widespread, and the fear of such events became even more pervasive. To be fair, Heckscher does not claim that American unions are in the midst of the transformation he recommends, nor does he predict they will shortly make such a transformation; rather, his point is that unions need to comprehensively shift their agenda toward the needs of workers facing rapid labor market change.

Sue Cobble, in her chapter in this volume and previous research, makes a more modest, although related, claim by stressing that unions should become more sensitive to the needs of workers who feel strong occupational links rather than ties to a single employer or job site. She also reminds us that early in its history, the American labor movement contained substantial diversity in its organizational forms and representational strategies. Cobble claims that occupational unionism could draw lessons from the craft unionism that stood as a real alternative to the "industrial union" model that came to dominate the post–World War II period.

There is much to commend in this position, in light of the fact that for many service workers, such as waitresses, the very sort of occupational unionism recommended by Cobble seems to make sense. As revealed in the chapters tracing recent organizing in this volume and in recent events, the American labor movement has been responding to this need to some extent in recent years. For example, 75,000 home-care workers were organized in California in 1999 in a union drive that had much of the flavor of the occupational unionism Cobble recommends. Also, active campaigns that promote occupational-type representation structures are under way in Seattle where Washtec (a union affiliated with the Communications Workers of America) is trying to organize computer technicians, and in the Bay Area among Silicon Valley clerical and technical workers in organizing drives led by Amy

Dean, director of the South Bay Area Labor Council (Van Jaarsveld 2000; Greenhouse 2000).

One can point to these efforts to show that the American labor movement already is doing what Heckscher and Cobble recommend, although maybe not as quickly or as much as they prefer. Or, one could look pessimistically at the fledging nature of these campaigns to raise doubts about such occupational unionism ever becoming a basis for extensive unionism. Such skepticism derives from the fact that even though mobility has increased for some in the American workforce and unions have tried to respond, to date there has been relatively modest growth in union or associational membership among these employees. As the research literature on union organizing has long recognized, there are a number of factors that make it difficult to create permanent representational forums among mobile employees (Lawler 1990).

Increased Diversity in Employment Systems

The economic evidence will disappoint those who claim that frequent mobility across employers has come to dominate the work experience of a large fraction of American workers. Yet, it would be a mistake to discount the fact that a significant number of workers now face heightened, if not hyper, labor-market mobility. The way to reconcile these findings is to recognize the diversity of labor-market experience that has become pervasive in the U.S. labor market and in other countries (Katz and Darbishire 2000). A significant number of American workers still have relatively long work careers with a single employer just as there are some employees who frequently change employers. This diversity exists not only with regard to the frequency of cross-employer labor-market mobility, but also in the significant variety of employment practices and systems. The American labor market, for example, has a large and growing number of low-end jobs characterized by low wages, high turnover, ad hoc and autocratic personnel practices, and little training for workers. Yet, there are also progressive employers who use work teams, pay high wages, use contingent compensation, and have formalized complaint and other personnel practices.

It is the growth in this employment system diversity that is most striking, and also most troubling, for the American labor movement. The troubles for the labor movement spring from the fact that representational and other needs are not necessarily identical for the workers facing this diverse array of labor-market experiences. Put more bluntly, unionized auto assemblers, steel workers, public school teachers, and telecommunications technicians do not have the same representational needs of low-paid garment or service workers. The tensions between these two types of workers are particularly glaring when one turns to an assessment of recent efforts within the American labor movement to emphasize and refashion union organizing.

Tensions within the American Labor Movement

A number of the chapters in this volume—Milkman and Wong, Foerster, Kriesky, and Fletcher and Hurd—examine the recent organizing efforts within the American labor movement. They provide rich additions to the growing literature assessing these efforts. What I find most revealing in these chapters are the internal organizational difficulties unions confront as they respond to the pressure to increase or reorient organizing activities. Milkman and Wong, for example, trace the complexities of organizing among low-wage workers in Los Angeles and show that neither top-down nor bottom-up styles provide a simple prescription for success. They also hint at the long-term problems unions face in sustaining activism and cohesion after an organizing victory. Foerster and Fletcher and Hurd report on the tensions created within the ranks of American unions because of the top-down and directive nature of the Organizing Institute and a number of other AFL-CIO initiatives.

My experiences suggest that there is also substantial debate over appropriate organizing strategies going on between those unions representing high-wage workers and those representing low-wage workers. Much of the AFL-CIO's efforts under the Sweeney administration have been focused on efforts to organize the latter. This has amounted to a push to extend the more "rank-and-file" style of organizing that had been developed at the Service Employees International Union (SEIU) and the Union of Needletrades, Industrial, and Textile Employees (UNITE) even before the Sweeney-led insurgency changed the top leadership and strategy of the AFL-CIO. Yet, it is not clear that this rank-and-file style of organizing is well suited to high-wage auto, steel, telecommunications, and other workers.

High-wage and high-skill employees derive bargaining leverage with their employers from their willingness to improve workplace performance. Yet, taking advantage of this leverage requires that these high-wage employees fashion participatory relationships with their employers in contrast to the more traditional job-control unionism or the rank-and-file organizing approach. In the telecommunications industry, for example, in recent years the Communications Workers of America (CWA) has gained much from the card-check recognition and neutrality procedures (that avoid the need for the normal representation election) negotiated with those employers with whom the union has been able to fashion a positive working relationship (e.g., SBC and Bell Atlantic). Even when high-wage employees and employers are unable to sustain this sort of relationship, it is not clear that any union has yet figured out a style of organizing—rank and file or whatever—that can win against a high-wage employer that aggressively resists unionization.

For those who expected an easy transition to revitalization, such internal tensions and conflicts within the American unions may be surprising. However, shouldn't bureaucratic sluggishness and internal differences in interests and opinion be expected? Unions are, of course, large organizations and naturally face the same sort of tensions that arise in any organization that faces major threats to its survival. A task for future research is to clarify how bureaucratic rigidities within unions compare to those within other transforming organizations and what accounts for the similarities and differences.

My sense is that American unions are doing fairly well in facing up to these organizational tensions as they struggle to increase the intensity of organizing activity and reorient to new styles of organizing. They are doing well in that despite conflicts, there has been no open warfare between major segments of the labor movement, and for the most part the debates appear to have been carried out in a civil manner.

Limited Organizing Success to Date

What is perhaps more disappointing are the limited gains in membership that have followed from the labor movement's revitalization efforts. While it is unclear exactly why it continues to be so difficult to organize workers, the fact remains that even in the face of intensified efforts, greater expenditures, and significant changes in the style and modes of organizing, to date these efforts have produced limited increases in union membership. And the recent news is not encouraging. For example, both the number of representation elections held and the number of elections won by unions in the first half of 1999 dropped significantly from the same time in 1998 (*Daily Labor Report* 1999). Furthermore, in 1999 the share of wage and salary workers who were members of unions (13.9 percent) remained unchanged from the prior year (Bureau of Labor Statistics 2000).

There is a long-standing research literature that tries to explain why American unions had such poor success in organizing in the post–World War II period (Freeman 1985, Fiorito and Maranto 1987, Lawler 1990). Paula Voos (1983), for example, claimed that the limited amount of resources unions devoted to organizing was a key explanation for the small amount of successful organizing. Although every national union has not followed the lead of the Sweeney-led AFL-CIO and substantially increased their organizing efforts, the chapters in this volume reveal that much new energy and money is now going toward organizing. Yet, to date, contrary to Voos' hypothesis, the evidence is that increased expenditures have not readily led to significant organizing success. Even as the resource constraint has loosened, a number of the other impediments to organizing success identified in the research literature remain. These include intense managerial resistance during representation election campaigns and the legal framework that allows such resistance, sophisticated human-resource management policies and practices that lessen the demand for unionization over the long term, and the absence of a communitarian ideology within the American workforce.

Previous research had a hard time determining the relative importance of these various factors during the membership decline period

(1952–1995). The chapters in this volume make a start at using the renewed upsurge in union organizing activity to test hypotheses concerning the relative importance of various organizing impediments. But clearly, much research remains to be done on these issues. Research should strive to identify particular sources of organizing success as well as failure. New data will also make it feasible to test whether the increased employment system diversity, which I claim is an additional new burden on union success, is in fact functioning as an obstacle.

The Need for Linkages across Spheres of Union Revitalization Activities

Beyond organizing, there are other changes occurring within the American labor movement, although these efforts are often overlooked in popular accounts. As the chapters by Parker and Rogers, Chaison, and Bronfenbrenner and Juravich show, in recent years American unions have been engaged in a range of new initiatives ranging from mergers to regional training partnerships to new bargaining approaches. Although these case-study analyses of the initiatives under way in particular spheres of union activity, such as organizing or collective bargaining that appear in this volume and elsewhere, are quite interesting, they overlook a key aspect of recent union revitalization. Research I conducted with Rose Batt and Jeffrey Keefe on the revitalization efforts of the CWA found that it was engaged in an aggressive triangular agenda focusing on organizing, politics, and collective bargaining (Katz, Batt, and Keefe 2000). Union activities in any one of these three spheres often interact with, and complement activities in, another sphere. It was, for example, through novel language won in collective bargaining agreements with the Regional Bell Operating Companies that the CWA gained card-check recognition and employer neutrality in representation elections, key parts of the union's organizing initiative. And similarly, the CWA has linked the political pressures it places on regulatory bodies with efforts to strengthen its strike leverage (and win more at the collective bargaining table).

Our analysis of the CWA's revitalization efforts also reveals that the union has built its integrated triangular strategy by drawing on various institutional legacies. These legacies include the quasi-public-sector nature of the old Bell system; the union's long-standing development of member mobilization to counteract its weakening strike leverage, and the union's focus on retraining and career development in response to corporate restructuring and the collapse of internal labor markets. Although similar detailed evidence from other unions documenting their strategic initiatives is not available, I suspect that similar integrative and institutional-based actions hold the key to successful union revitalization.

The International Challenge

Ultimately, the labor movement will have to find a way to extend revitalization sphere linkages into the international arena. The expansion of international trade and the accelerated expansion of multi-national corporations (MNC's) extend the market internationally. In his classic 1909 analysis of early union formation among shoemakers, Commons explained that as the market expanded to counteract "competitive menaces" and retain bargaining power, unions at the beginning of the twentieth century shifted to a national structure. This provided a structure of representation that paralleled the emerging national structure of markets.

The problem now confronting labor movements all over the globe is that they confront the need for cross-national unionism, yet their efforts to create such unionism face incredible barriers. These barriers include divergent interests (i.e., each labor movement wants the employment) and national differences in language, culture, law, and structure. However, unions will need to find an international parallel to the sort of domestic sphere linkages being pursued by the CWA. While one can point to some signs of such linkage in Europe where unions have parlayed their political strength to promote favorable European Union–level regulation, the gains in this and related fronts to date are extremely limited and the barriers remain daunting.

Conclusion

As the chapters in this volume report, there is much that is new in union organizing and other revitalization initiatives. Yet, the chapters also suggest that the labor movement faces a number of new, as well as many of the same old, problems. To be successful, union revitalization will have to link activities across organizing, political, and collective bargaining spheres. And in the process of forging these linkages, the labor movement will have to find ways to address the often differing needs of high-wage and low-wage workers and simultaneously find ways to overcome the power advantage management is gaining from increased globalization. While wishing the American labor movement well, because of the difficult nature of the task at hand, I can only predict that union revitalization will be an extremely difficult uphill struggle.

References

Abramson, Jill, and Steven Greenhouse. 1997. "Labor Victory on Trade Bill Reveals Power." *New York Times,* November 12: A1.

——. 1997. "The Trade Bill: Labor," *New York Times,* November 12: A1.

"Adam's Mark Inks Neutrality Pact with Labor." 1998. *Colorado Labor Advocate* 76(7) April 9: 1.

Adams, Chris. 1995. "Tire Makers Fears Come True With the Steelworkers." *Wall Street Journal,* July 27: A3.

Adelson, Andrea. 1997. "Union for Doctors to Join Forces With Government Workers." *New York Times,* August 27: A18.

AFA (Association of Flight Attendants). 1997. *Contract Campaign Manual.* Washington, DC: AFA.

AFL-CIO. 1973. "Rules Governing Local Central Bodies." Washington, DC: AFL-CIO.

——. 1985a. *The Changing Situation of Workers and Their Unions: Report of the AFL-CIO Committee on the Evolution of Work.* Washington, DC: AFL-CIO.

——. 1985b. "Developing New Tactics: Winning with Coordinated Campaigns." Washington, DC: AFL-CIO Industrial Union Department.

——. 1989. *Report of the AFL-CIO Executive Council.* Washington DC: AFL-CIO.

——. 1997. "Street Heat: Mobilizing to Win: A Guide to Revitalizing the Labor Movement by Mobilizing Members in Communities Across America." Washington, DC: AFL-CIO.

——. 1998. "June 24, 1998—A Day to Make Our Voices Heard, Our Choices Respected: Tools and Resources for Organizers." Washington, DC: AFL-CIO.

——. 1999. "The Long Run." Work in progress. February 22: 1.

——. nd(a). "The Road to Union City: A Guide to Greatness for Local Unions and Their AFL-CIO Central Labor Councils." Pamphlet. Washington, DC: AFL-CIO.

——. nd(b). "Union Cities—Strong Communities." Unpublished handout.

AFL-CIO Department of Field Mobilization. 1997a. "The Road to Union Cities: Your Resources Map to Rebuild the Labor Movement." Washington, DC: AFL-CIO.

——. 1997b. "Union Cities Planning Guide for Central Labor Councils." Unpublished handout.

——. 1997c. "Why Union Cities?" Unpublished draft, February 21.

——. 1998a. "AFL-CIO Central Labor Councils That Have Adopted Union Cities." Unpublished handout, August 14.

——. 1998b. "Agenda." Unpublished agenda for national CLC conference, July 31–August 2.

AFL-CIO Department of Field Mobilization, Northeast Region. 1998. "AFL-CIO CLC Best Practices Conference." Unpublished agenda, June 5–6.

AFL-CIO Department of Field Mobilization. (1998). "Union Cities Progress Survey." Unpublished handout.

AFL-CIO Department of Organization and Field Services and George Meany Center for Labor Studies. nd. *AFL-CIO Handbook for Central Labor Councils.* Washington, DC: AFL-CIO.

AFL-CIO Education Department. 1998. "Common Sense Economics: The Basic Rap." Rev. #2, April 1998. Washington, DC: AFL-CIO.

"AFL-CIO Executive Council Examines New Organizing Methods." 1996. *Daily Labor Report,* May 9.

Agreement of Affiliation and Merger Between The Newspaper Guild, AFL-CIO, CLC and the Communications Workers of America, AFL-CIO, CLC. 1995. Washington, DC: Communications Workers of America.

Albright, Lewis (West Virginia staff, AFL-CIO Department of Field Mobilization). 1998. Telephone interview with author, October 6, 1998.

Allaire, Y., and M. Firsirotu. 1985. "How to Implement Radical Strategies in Large Organizations." *Sloan Management Review* (spring): 19–33.

Allen, Steven G. 1994. "Developments in Collective Bargaining in Construction in the 1980s and 1990s." In *Contemporary Collective Bargaining in the Private Sector,* edited by Paula B. Voos, 411–45. Madison, Wis.: Industrial Relations Research Association.

Alvarez, Joe (Northeast Regional Director, AFL-CIO Department of Field Mobilization). 1998a. Telephone interview with author, September 28, 1998.

———. 1998b. Telephone interview with author, November 30, 1998.

American Federation of Labor. 1897. *Report of the Proceedings of the Seventeenth Annual Convention.* Washington, DC: AFL.

Armenakis, A.A., S.G. Harris, and K. Mossholder. 1993. "Creating Readiness for Organizational Change." *Human Relations* 46(6): 681–701.

Armstrong, Patricia. 1993. "Professional, Unions, or What?: Learning from Nurses." In *Women Challenging Unions,* edited by Linda Briskin and Patricia McDermott, 304–12. Toronto: University of Toronto Press.

Autor, David H., Lawrence F. Katz, and Alan B. Krueger. 1997. "Computing Inequality: Have Computers Changed the Labor Market?" NBER working paper #5956. Cambridge, MA: National Bureau of Economic Research.

Avery, William P. 1998. "Domestic Interests in NAFTA Bargaining," *Political Science Quarterly* 113(2): 281–305.

Baldwin, Robert E. and Christopher Magee. 2000. *Explaining Congressional Trade Votes on Recent Trade Bills: From NAFTA to Fast-Track.* Washington, DC: Institute for International Economics.

Balfour, Jeff, Jen Bloom Ben Francis-Fallon, and Sue McNeil. 2000. "Snatching Victory from Defeat: The Steelworkers' Global Campaign at Bridgestone/Firestone." Unpublished manuscript.

Balz, Dan. 1982. "Organized Labor Follows the Sun." *Washington Post,* March 7: A9.

———. 1997. "The Battle to Seize the Heart and Soul of the Democrats." *Washington Post National Weekly Edition,* June 9: 11–12.

Banks, Andy. 1991. "The Power and the Promise of Community Unionism," *Labor Research Review* 10(2): 17–32.

Barbelet, J.M. 1988. *Citizenship: Rights, Struggle, and Class Inequality.* Minneapolis: University of Minneapolis Press.

Barfield, Claude E. 1998. "Politics of Trade and Fast Track in the United States." Prepared for delivery at the First Academic Colloquium of the Americas, University of Costa Rica, March 12–14, 1998. *AEI Speeches,* www.aei.org/sp/spbarfld.htm.

Barnes, James A., and Richard E. Cohen. 1997. "Divided Democrats." *National Journal,* November 15: 2304–7.

Barnett, William P., and Glenn R. Carroll. 1995. "Modeling Internal Organizational Change." *Annual Review of Sociology* 21: 217–37.

Batchelor, Heather A., and Matthew J. Clark. 1998. "Confronting the Crisis of Big Steel: · The Bittersweet Victory at USX." Unpublished manuscript.

Baugh, Bob, and Margaret Hilton. 1997. "Economic Development: A Union Guide to the High Road." Unpublished manuscript. Washington, DC: AFL-CIO Human Resources Development Institute.

Becker, George. 1998. Interview. Pittsburgh, PA.

Bedard, Paul, Warren P. Strobel, Suzi Parker, and Nancy Bentrup. 2000. "A Labor Mutiny on China Trade." *U.S. News & World Report,* May 22: 11.

Beinart, Peter. 1997a. "The Nationalist Revolt." *New Republic,* December 1: 22–6.

———. 1997b. "Why the Center Can't Hold." *Time,* November 24: 52.

Bell, Daniel. 1973. *The Coming of Postindustrial Society: A Venture in Social Forecasting.* New York: Basic Books.

Bendix, Reinhard. 1964. *Nation-Building and Citizenship.* New York: John Wiley and Sons.

Benner, Chris. 1996. *Shock Absorbers in the Flexible Economic: The Rise of Contingent Employment in Silicon Valley.* San Jose, Calif.: Working Partnerships USA.

Bennett, John. 1998. "Union-Community Activity and Organizing: The Pioneer Valley Central Labor Council—A Case Study." Presented at the 1998 Conference of the UCLEA-AFL-CIO Education Department and University and College Labor Education Association, San Jose, Calif., May 1, 1998.

Bernhartdt, Annette, Martina Morris, Mark Handcock, and Marc Scott. 1998. *Work and Opportunity in the Post-Industrial Labor Market.* New York: Institute on Education and the Economy, Columbia University.

Bernstein, Aaron. 1997. "NAFTA: A New Union-Busting Weapon?" *Business Week,* January 27.

———. 1998. "Labor Helps Turn the Tide—the Old-Fashioned Way." *Business Week,* November 16: 45.

Blustein, Paul. 1997. "Fast-Track Trade Plan Pits White House Against Top Congressional Democrats," *Washington Post,* March 22: A11.

BNA Daily Labor Report. 1997. "Workplace Code of Conduct," April 15: E-5.

Borrus, Amy. 1997. "Business Is in a Hurry for Fast-Track." *Business Week,* September 15: 38–39.

Borrus, Amy, and Richard Dunham. 2000. "Tech: The Virtual Third Party." *Business Week,* April 24: 74–78.

Bound, John, and George Johnson. 1992. "Changes in the Structure of Wages in the 1980s: An Evaluation of Alternative Explanations." *American Economic Review* 82(3): 371–92.

Bounds, Wendy, and Hilary Stout. 1997. "Sweatshop Pact: Good Fit or Threadbare? Industry Could Get a PR Boom, but Activists Worry." *Wall Street Journal,* April 20: A6.

Bowles, Samuel, and Herbert Gintis. 1986. *Democracy and Capitalism.* New York: Basic Books.

Bowles, Samuel, and Mehrene Larudee. 1993. "NAFTA: Friend or Foe?" *New York Times,* November 15.

Box-Steffensmeir, Janet M., Laura W. Arnold, and Christopher J.S. Zorn. 1997. "The Strategic Timing of Position Taking in Congress: A Study of the North American Free Trade Agreement." *American Political Science Review* 91(2): 324–38.

Boyle, Kevin, ed. 1998. *Organized Labor and American Politics, 1894–1994: The Labor-Liberal Alliance.* Albany, N.Y.: State University of New York Press.

Bradley, Tom (Delaware State Director, AFL-CIO Department of Field Mobilization). 1998. Telephone interview with author, October 7, 1998.

Bradsher, Keith. 2000. "Rallying Round the China Bill, Hungrily." *New York Times,* May 21: Sec. 3, 1.

Brecher, Jeremy, and Tim Costello. 1990. *Building Bridges: The Emerging Grassroots Coalition of Labor and Community.* New York: Monthly Review Press.

———. 1996. "A 'New Labor Movement' in the Shell of the Old?" *Labor Research Review* 24: 5–25.

Brody, David. 1980. *Workers in Industrial America: Essays on the Twentieth-Century Struggle.* New York: Oxford University Press.

———. 1993. *Workers in Industrial America.* 2d ed. New York: Oxford University Press.

———. 1995. "Criminalizing the Rights of Labor," *Dissent* (summer): 363–67.

Bronfenbrenner, Kate. 1997a. "The Role of Union Strategies in NLRB Certification Elections." *Industrial and Labor Relations Review* 50: 195–212.

———. 1997b. *Final Report: The Effects of Plant Closings or the Threat of Plant Closings on the Right of Workers to Organize.* Ithaca, N.Y.: ILR Press/Cornell University Press.

———. ed. 1999. "Organizing for Keeps: Building a Twenty-First Century Labor Movement." *Labor Studies Journal,* special conference issue, April: 3–122.

Bronfenbrenner, Kate, Sheldon Friedman, Richard W. Hurd, Rudolph A. Oswald, and Ronald Seeber, eds. 1998. *Organizing to Win: New Research on Union Strategies.* Ithaca, N.Y.: Cornell University Press.

Bronfenbrenner, Kate, and Tom Juravich. 1998. "It Takes More than Housecalls: Organizing to Win with a Comprehensive Union-Building Strategy." In *Organizing to Win: New Research on Union Strategies,* edited by Kate Bronfenbrenner, Sheldon Friedman, Richard W. Hurd, Rudolph A. Oswald, and Ronald L. Seeber, 19–36. Ithaca, N.Y.: Cornell University Press.

Brownstein, Ronald. 1997a. "Trade Is Still the Exception to Clinton's Rule." *Los Angeles Times,* November 7: A24.

———. 1997b. "If Clinton Pushes, Asia's Breakdown Could Drive Labor Reforms Forward." *Los Angeles Times,* December 15: A5.

Buckley, Neil. 1997. "EU to Offer Carrot to Poor States." *Financial Times* (London), October 30: 5.

Buhle, Paul. 1999. *Taking Care of Business: Samuel Gompers, George Meany, Lane Kirkland and the Tragedy of American Labor.* New York: Monthly Review Press.

Buhle, Paul, and Steve Fraser. 1999. "A New Day for Labor." *The Nation,* September 20: 7–8.

Bureau of Labor Stastistics. 2000. "Union Members Summary." Labor Force Statistics from the Current Population Survey. Press release, January 19, www.bls.gov/news.release /union2.nws.htm.

Bureau of National Affairs. 1995a. "Agreement Regarding Merger of UAW, USW, and IAM." *Daily Labor Report,* July 28: E1.

———. 1995b. "Auto, Steel, Machinists Unions Announce Accord to Merge by 2000." *Daily Labor Report,* July 28: AA1–AA2.

———. 1996a. "Independent Union Affiliates with UMW." *Daily Labor Report,* July 22: A14–A15.

———. 1996b. "OCAW Announces Affiliation of Smaller Union." *Daily Labor Report,* September 23: A14–A15.

———. 1997a. "AFL-CIO: Executive Council Adopts Two Programs to Rebuild Labor Movement at Local Level." *Daily Labor Report,* February 21: C2–C3.

———. 1997b. "AFL-CIO National Convention Adopts Strategy to Help Rebuild Labor Movement." *Labor Relations Week,* October 1: 1020–22.

———. 1997c. "AFL-CIO President John J. Sweeney's Keynote Address to AFL-CIO Convention, Sept. 22, 1997" *Daily Labor Report,* September 23: E1–E3.

———. 1997d. "AFL-CIO Won't See Immediate Increase in Members as Restructuring Continues." *Labor Relations Week,* January 22: 55–56.

———. 1997e. "Health Care Employees: CIR Announces Affiliation with SEIU: Groups Earmark $1.4 Million for Organizing." *Daily Labor Report,* June 9: A1–A2.

———. 1997f. "Health Care Employees: Independent Physicians Union Votes to Affiliate With AFSCME." *Daily Labor Report,* August 28: A8.

———. 1998a. "AFL-CIO Says Membership Loss Stabilized by Organizing 400,000 Members in 1997." *Daily Labor Report,* January 30: A15–A16.

———. 1998b. "Auto Workers: UAW Plans to Step Up Organizing Efforts as Merger Talks Advance." *Daily Labor Report,* June 24: C1–C2.

———. 1998c. "Union Affiliations: New York City Health Care Union Affiliates with 1.2 Million-Member SEIU." *Daily Labor Report,* January 8: A1.

———. 1998d. "UTU, BLE Agree in Principle to Unify, Create New Union by January 2000." *Daily Labor Report,* November 25: A9.

———. 1999a. "Affiliation of Independent Textile Processors with UFCW Impacts UNITE Organizing Effort." *Daily Labor Report,* August 23: A4–A5.

———. 1999b. "AFL-CIO Membership Report Prepared for October Convention." *Daily Labor Report,* October 15: E1–E5.

———. 1999c. "AFL-CIO Report Shows Increase in Membership Since 1997 Convention." *Daily Labor Report,* October 15: E1–E5.

———. 1999d. "Simultaneous Conventions Approve Merger of UPIU, OCAW Into 320,000-Member Group." *Daily Labor Report,* January 6: AA–1.

Burgess, John. 2000. "A Winning Combination: Money, Message and Clout." *Washington Post,* May 25: A4.

Burke, William M. 1899. *History and Functions of Central Labor Unions.* New York: Macmillian Co.

Bussel, Bob. 1998. "Telling Our Own Story: Labor-Produced Media in Reading, Pennsylvania." In *Working Together to Revitalize Labor In Our Communities: Case Studies of Labor Education—Central Body Collaboration,* edited by Jill Kriesky. Orono: University of Maine Press.

California Department of Industrial Relations, Division of Labor Statistics and Research, 1957–89. "Union Labor in California." San Francisco.

Cappelli, Peter. 1999. *The New Deal at Work.* Boston: Harvard Business School Press.

Cappelli, Peter, Laurie Bassi, Harry Katz, David Knoke, Paul Osterman, and Michael Useem. 1997. *Change at Work.* New York: Oxford University Press.

Card, David. 1990. "Strikes and Bargaining: A Survey of the Recent Empirical Literature." *AEA Papers and Proceedings* 80(2): 410–15.

Carney, Eliza Newlin. 1997. "What? A Smiling 'New Democrat'?" *National Journal,* December 6: 2476–77.

———. 2000. "The Money Train." *National Journal,* May 6: 1424–26.

Carre, Francoise, and Pamela Joshi. 1997. "Building Stability for Transient Workforces: Exploring the Possibilities of Intermediary Institutions Helping Workers Cope with Labor Market Instability." Working paper no. 1. Cambridge, MA: Radcliffe Public Policy Institute.

The Center for Responsive Politics. 2000a. "A Passage to China Update: House Approves PNTR." *Money in Politics Alert,* May 24: www.opensecrets.org/news/china _house.htm.

———. 2000b. "A Passage to China: The Business Roundtable and PNTR." *Money in Politics Alert,* May 22: www.opensecrets.org/alerts/v5/alert5_47.htm.

Century Foundation Task Force on the Future of Unions. 1999. *What's Next for Organized Labor?* New York: Century Foundation Press.

Chaison, Gary. 1973. "Federation Expulsion and Union Mergers in the United States." *Relations Industrielles* (Industrial Relations) 28 (June): 343–61.

———. 1978. "Criticism and Comment: Union Mergers and Industrial Environment." *Industrial Relations* 17 (February): 119–123.

———. 1980. "A Note on Union Merger Trends, 1900–1978." *Industrial and Labor Relations Review* 34 (October): 114–20.

———. 1981. "Union Growth and Union Mergers." *Industrial Relations* 20 (winter): 98–108.

———. 1982. "Union Mergers and the Integration of Union Governing Structures." *Journal of Labor Research* III (spring): 139–52.

———. 1986. *When Unions Merge.* Lexington, MA: Lexington Books.

———. 1992. "Union Mergers in the United States: Recent Trends and Questions for Research." Paper presented at the Symposium on Emerging Union Structures. Worcester, MA.

———. 1996a. "The Form and Frequency of Union Mergers." *Proceedings of the 1996 Spring Meeting of the Industrial Relations Research Association.* Madison, Wis.: Industrial Relations Research Association, 493–97.

———. 1996b. *Union Mergers in Hard Times: The View From Five Countries.* Ithaca, N.Y.: Cornell University Press.

———. 1997. "Reforming and Rationalizing Union Structure: New Directions and Unanswered Questions." In *The Future of Trade Unionism: International Perspectives on Emerging Trade Union Structures,* edited by Magnus Sverke, 19–33. Aldershot, UK: Ashgate.

Chaison, Gary N., and Dileep G. Dhavale. 1990. "A Note on the Severity of the Decline in Union Organizing Activity." *Industrial and Labor Relations Review* 43: 366–73.

Chaison, Gary, and Joseph B. Rose. 1991. "The Macrodeterminants of Union Growth and Decline." In *The State of the Unions,* edited by George Strauss, Daniel G. Gallagher, and Jack Fiorito, 3–45. Madison, Wis.: Industrial Relations Research Association.

Chaison, Gary, Magnus Sverke, and Anders Sjöberg. 1997. "The Impact of Union Merger on Member Participation." Paper presented at the Third International Conference of Emerging Union Structures. Canberra, Australia.

Chitayat, Gideon. 1979. *Trade Union Mergers and Labor Conglomerates.* New York: Praeger.

Clark, Matthew J., and David Hammer. 1998. "And the Lights Go Out at NIPSCO." Unpublished manuscript.

Clark, Paul, and Lois S. Gray. 2000. "Assessing the Proposed IAM, UAW, and USW Merger: Critical Issues and Potential Outcomes." *Journal of Labor Research* 21 (winter): 65–82.

Clark, Peggy, and Steven Dawson. 1995. *Jobs and the Urban Poor: Privately Initiated Sectoral Strategies.* Washington, DC: Aspen Institute.

Clawson, Dan, Alan Neustadtl, and Mark Weller. 1998. *Dollars and Votes: How Business Campaign Contributions Subvert Democracy.* Philadelphia: Temple University Press.

Cobble, Dorothy Sue. 1991a. *Dishing It Out: Waitresses and Their Unions in the Twentieth Century.* Urbana, Ill.: University of Illinois Press.

———. 1991b. "Organizing the Postindustrial Work Force: Lessons from the History of Waitress Unionism." *Industrial and Labor Relations Review* 44 (April): 419–36.

———. 1994. "Making Postindustrial Unionism Possible." In *Restoring the Promise of American Labor Law,* edited by Sheldon Friedman, Richard W. Hurd, Rudolph Oswald, and Ronald Seeber, 285–30. Ithaca, N.Y.: Cornell University Press/ILR Press.

——. 1996a. "The Prospects for Unionism in a Service Society." In *Working in the Service Society*, edited by Cameron Lynne Macdonald and Carmen Sirianni, 333–58. Philadelphia: Temple University Press.

——. 1996b. "Reviving the Federation's Historic Role in Organizing." Working paper prepared for the Institute for the Study of Labor Organizations. Silver Springs, Md.: George Meany Center for Labor Studies.

——. 1997. "Lost Ways of Organizing: Reviving the AFL's Direct Affiliate Strategy." *Industrial Relations* 36 (July): 278–301.

——. 1999. "'A Spontaneous Loss of Enthusiasm': Workplace Feminism and the Transformation of Women's Jobs in the 1970s." *International Labor and Working-Class History* 56 (fall): 23–44.

Cobble, Dorothy Sue, and Michael Merrill. 1994. "Collective Bargaining in the Hospitality Industry in the 1980s." In *Contemporary Collective Bargaining in the Private Sector*, edited by Paula Voos, 447–89. Ithaca, N.Y.: Cornell University Press/ILR Press.

Cobble, Dorothy Sue, and Leah F. Vosko. 2000. "Historical Perspectives on Representing Nonstandard Workers." In *Nontraditional Work Arrangements and the Changing Labor Market*, edited by Francoise Carre, et al. Madison, Wis.: Industrial Relations Research Association.

Cockburn, Alexander, and Jeffrey St. Clair. 1999. "AFL-CIO at the Crossroads: Where is Sweeney Taking Labor?" *Counterpunch* (online magazine available at www.counterpunch .org/sweeney.html).

Cohn, Jonathan. 1997. "Hard Labor." *New Republic*, October 6: 21–26.

Colburn, Bruce, and Scott Reynolds. 2000. "New Strength: Union Cities and the New Alliance." Unpublished manuscript.

Collins, Susan M., ed. 1998. *Imports, Exports, and the American Worker*. Washington, DC: Brookings Institution.

Commission for Labor Cooperation. 1997. *Plant Closings and Labor Rights*. www .naalc.org.

Commons, John R. 1934. *Institutional Economics: Its Place in Economics*. New York: Macmillan.

Compa, Lance. 1998: "A Fast Track for Labor." American Prospect, September–October: 60–64.

Conley, Paul. 1998. "Labor Dispute May Disrupt Exports." *The Packer*, August 3: 1A.

Conybeare, John A.C., and Mark Zinkula. 1996. "Who Voted Against NAFTA? Trade Unions Versus Free Trade." *World Economy* 19(1): 1–12.

Cooper, Helene, and Ian Johnson. 2000. "Congress's Vote Primes U.S. Firms to Boost Investment in China." *Wall Street Journal*, May 25: A1.

Corn, David. 1997. "Dick Gephardt: Working-Class Hero, On-the-Make Pol or Both?" *The Nation*, July 7: 11–16.

Cornfield, Daniel. 1991. "The Attitude of Employee Association Members Toward Union Mergers: The Effect of Socioeconomic Status." *Industrial and Labor Relations Review* 44 (January): 334–48.

Coughlin, Cletus C. 1985. "Domestic Content Legislation: House Voting and the Economic Theory of Regulation." *Economic Inquiry* 23(3): 437–48.

Cox, Gary W., and Eric Magar. 1999. "How Much Is Majority Status in the U.S. Congress Worth?" *American Political Science Review* 93(2): 299–309.

Cox, Ronald. 1995. "Corporate Coalitions and Industrial Restructuring: Explaining Regional Trade Agreements." *Competition & Change* 1: 13–30.

Crosby, Jeff (AFL-CIO CLC Advisory Board member and President of North Shore [MA] CLC). 2000. Telephone interview with author, May 18, 2000.

Crosby, Jeff. 1998. "So, Where Do We Get the Resources To Do All This?" Unpublished handout.

Dark, Taylor. 1999. *The Unions and the Democrats: An Enduring Alliance.* Ithaca, N.Y.: Cornell University Press.

Davidoff, Al (New York State Director, AFL-CIO Department of Field Mobilization). 1998. Telephone interview with author, October 9, 1998.

Dean, Amy. 1998. "The Road to Union City: Building the American Labor Movement City by City." In *Not Your Father's Union Movement: Inside the AFL-CIO,* edited by Jo-ann Mort. London: Verso.

Deardorff, Alan V., and Robert M. Stern. 1979. "American Labor's Stake in International Trade." In *Tariffs, Quotas, and Trade: The Politics of Protectionism,* edited by Walter S. Adams. San Francisco: Institute for Contemporary Studies.

Deinard, Caitlin, and Friedman, Raymond. 1990. "Black Caucus Groups at Xerox Corporation (A) and (B)." Boston: Harvard Business School.

dela Cruz, Bartolomeo, Geraldo von Potobsky, and Lee Swepston. 1996. The International Labor Organization. Boulder, CO: Westview Press.

DeLeon, Richard Edward. 1992. *Left-Coast City: Progressive Politics in San Francisco, 1975–1991.* Lawrence: University of Kansas Press.

Delgado, Hector. 1993. *New Immigrants, Old Unions: Organizing Undocumented Workers in Los Angeles.* Philadelphia: Temple University Press.

Destler, I.M. 1995. *American Trade Politics,* 3d ed. Washington, D.C.: Institute for International Economics.

———. 1997. *Renewing Fast-Track Legislation.* Washington, D.C.: Institute for International Economics.

———. 1998a. "Trade Politics and Labor Issues: 1953–95." In *Imports, Exports, and the American Worker,* edited by Susan Collins. Washington, D.C.: Brookings Institution.

———. 1998b. "Congress and Foreign Trade." In *The Controversial Pivot: The U.S. Congress and North America,* edited by Robert A. Pastor and Rafael Fernandez de Castro. Washington, DC: Brookings Institution.

Devine, Kay, and Yonatan Reshef. 1998. "Union Merger Support: A Tale of Two Theories." *Relations Industrielles* (Industrial Relations) 53 (summer): 517–33.

DiLorenzo, Thomas J. 1996. "The Corporate Campaign Against Food Lion: A Study in Media Manipulation." *Journal of Labor Research* 17(3, summer): 359–75.

DiMaggio, Paul J., and Walter W. Powell. 1991. "Introduction." In *The New Institutionalism in Organizational Analysis,* edited by Walter W. Powell and Paul J. DiMaggio, 1–38. Chicago: University of Chicago Press.

Dinardo, John, Nicole Fortin, and Thomas Lemieux. 1996. "Labor Market Institutions and the Distribution of Wages, 1973–1992: A Semiparametric Approach." *Econometrica* 64(5): 1001–44.

Dionne Jr., E.J. 1997. "Why the Democrats Bolted." *Washington Post,* November 14: A27.

Donohue, Peter. 1992. "'Free Trade,' Unions and the State: Trade Liberalization's Endorsement by the AFL-CIO, 1943–62." *Research in Political Economy* 13: 1–3.

Dresser, Laura, and Joel Rogers. 1998. "Networks, Sectors, and Workforce Learning." In *Jobs and Economic Development: Strategies and Practices,* edited by Robert P. Giloth, 64–82. Thousand Oaks, Calif.: Sage. (Reprinted in *Institute for Research on Poverty Reprint Series* 783 [Madison, Wis.: Institute for Research on Poverty].)

———. Forthcoming. "Sectoral Strategies of Labor Market Reform: Emerging Evidence from the U.S." In *Vocational and Adult Education in Europe,* edited by Fons van Wieringen. Dordrecht, The Netherlands: Kluwer Academic.

Drohan, Madelaine. 1998. "How the Net Killed the MAI: Grassroots Groups Used Their Own Globalization to Derail Deal." *Toronto Globe & Mail,* April 29: 1.

Drucker, Peter F. 1976. *The Unseen Revolution: How Pension-Fund Socialism Came to America.* New York: Harper & Row.

———. 1993. *The Post-Capitalist Society.* New York: Harper Collins.

Dunham, Richard S., and Amy Borrus. 1998. "Still the Party of Big Business?" *Business Week,* September 14: 150–60.

Dunlop, John T. 1958. *Industrial Relations Systems.* New York: Henry Holt and Co.

Dunne, Nancy. 1997. "Clinton Goes to the Wire to Save Fast-Track." *Financial Times,* November 7: 7.

Early, Steve. 1996. "New Organizing Should Be Membership-Based." *Labor Notes,* April: 12.

Edsall, Thomas B. 1997. "Big Labor Flexes Its Muscle Once Again." *Washington Post National Weekly Edition,* November 24.

———. 1998. "Giving Republicans the Business." *Washington Post National Weekly Edition,* June 22: 10.

Eilperin, Juliet. 1998. "House Defeats Fast-Track Trade Authority." *Washington Post,* September 26: A10.

Eilperin, Juliet, and David Broder. 2000. "Despite UAW Threat, Low Risk Seen in China Vote." *Washington Post,* May 24: A14.

Eimer, Stuart. 1997. AFL and CIO Central Labor Councils: Solidarity Forever? Unpublished Ph.D. dissertation proposal. University of Wisconsin: Madison.

Eisenscher, Michael. 1999. "Critical Juncture: Unionists at the Crossroads." In *Which Direction for Organized Labor? Essays on Organizing, Outreach, and Internal Transformations,* edited by Bruce Nissen. Detroit: Wayne State University Press.

Elder, Klaus. 1993. *The New Politics of Class: Social Movements and Cultural Dynamics in Advanced Societies.* Newbury Park, Calif.: Sage Publications.

Elliott, Larry, 2000. "IMF, World Bank Need to Correct Their Course." *Journal of Commerce,* April 19: 7.

Emspak, Frank. 2000. "AFL-CIO's Bureaucratic Solutions Won't Help Central Labor Councils." *Labor Notes,* February 11.

Farber, Henry S. 1997a. "The Changing Face of Job Loss in the United States, 1981–1995." Working paper no. 382. Industrial Relations Section, Princeton University.

———. 1997b. "Trends in Long-Term Employment in the United States, 1979–1996." Working paper no. 384. Industrial Relations Section, Princeton University.

———. 1998. "Has the Rate of Job Loss Increased in the Nineties?" *Industrial Relations Section,* Princeton University.

Faux, Jeff. 2000. "A New Grand Bargain." *American Prospect,* January 17: 20.

Feenstra, Robert C. 1998. "Integration of Trade and Disintegration of Production in the Global Economy." *Journal of Economic Perspectives* 12(4): 31–50.

Felder, Sandra (Massachusetts State Director, AFL-CIO Department of Field Mobilization). 1998. Telephone interview with author, October 9, 1998.

Fine, Janice. 1998. "Moving Innovation From the Margins to the Center for a New American Labor Movement." In *A New Labor Movement for the New Century,* edited by Gregory Mantsios, 119–45. New York: Monthly Review Press.

Fletcher, Bill Jr., and Richard Hurd. 1998. "Beyond the Organizing Model: The Transformation Process in Local Unions." In *Organizing to Win: New Research on Union Strategies,* edited by Kate Bronfenbrenner, Sheldon Friedman, Richard Hurd, Rudolph Oswald, and Ronald Seeber, 37–53. Ithaca, N.Y.: Cornell University Press.

———. 1999. "Political Will, Local Union Transformation and the Organizing Imperative." In *Which Direction for Organized Labor? Essays on Organizing, Outreach, and Internal Transformations,* edited by Bruce Nissen, 191–216. Detroit: Wayne State University Press.

———. 2000. "Is Organizing Enough? Race, Gender and Union Culture." *New Labor Forum,* no. 6 (spring/summer): 59–69.

Flores, William V., and Rina Benmayor. 1997. *Latino Cultural Citizenship: Claiming Identity, Space and Rights.* Boston: Beacon Press.

Foner, Henry. 1990. "Saul Mills and the Greater New York Industrial Union Council, CIO." *Labor History:* 31.

Forsythe, Edwin J. 1956. "The St. Louis Central Trades and Labor Union, 1887–1945." Columbia: University of Missouri—Columbia, cited in Stuart Eimer, 1997. AFL and CIO Central Labor Councils: Solidarity Forever? Unpublished Ph.D. dissertation proposal. University of Wisconsin, Madison, Wis.

Foweraker, Joe, and Todd Landman. 1997. *Citizenship Rights and Social Movements: A Comparative and Statistical Analysis.* Oxford: Oxford University Press.

Fraser, Steven, and Joshua B. Freeman, eds. 1997. *Audacious Democracy: Labor, Intellectuals and the Social Reconstruction of America.* Boston: Houghton Mifflin.

Freeman, Richard B. 1985. "Why Are Unions Fairing Poorly in NLRB Representation Elections?" In *Challenges and Choices Facing American Labor,* edited by T. Kochan, 45–64. Cambridge: MIT Press.

Freitas, Gregory. 1993. "Unionization among Racial and Ethnic Minorities." *Industrial and Labor Relations Review* 46(2) January: 284–306.

Friedman, Sheldon, Richard W. Hurd, Rudolph A. Oswald, and Ronald L. Seeber, eds. 1994. *Restoring the Promise of American Labor Law.* Ithaca, N.Y.: ILR Press/Cornell University Press.

Frisby, Michael, and Bob Davis. 1997. "Missing in Action: As Trade Vote Looms, Clinton is Hurt by Lack of Steady Supporters." *Wall Street Journal,* November 6: A1.

Friedman, Ray, and Carter, Donna. 1993. "African-American Network Groups: Their Impact and Effectiveness." Boston: Harvard Business School working paper 93–069, May 1993.

Frundt, Henry. 1987. "To Buy the World a Coke." *Latin American Perspectives* 14 (summer 1987): 398–410.

———. 2000. *Trade Conditions and Labor Rights.* Gainesville, FL: University Press of Florida.

Gais, Thomas. 1996. *Improper Influence: Campaign Finance Law, Political Interest Groups, and the Problem of Equality.* Ann Arbor: University of Michigan Press.

Gapasin, Fernando, and Howard Wial. 1998. "The Role of Central Labor Councils in Union Organizing in the 1990's." In *Organizing To Win; New Research On Union Strategies,* edited by Kate Bronfenbrenner, Sheldon Friedman, Richard W. Hurd, Rudolph A. Oswald, and Ronald L. Seeber. Ithaca, N.Y.: Cornell University Press.

Gapasin, Fernando, and Michael Yates. 1997. "Organizing the Unorganized: Will Promises Become Practices?" *Monthly Review,* July: 46–62.

Gareau, George. 1995. "Guild Convention Backs Merger." *Editor & Publisher* (electronic edition), July 8.

Gerber, Robin. 1999. "Building to Win, Building to Last: The AFL-CIO COPE Takes on the Republican Congress." In *After the Revolution: PACs and Lobbies in the Republican Congress,* edited by Robert Biersack, Paul S. Herrnson, and Clyde Wilcox. Boston: Allyn and Bacon.

Getman, Julius. 1998. *The Betrayal of Local 14: Paperworkers, Politics, and Permanent Replacements.* Ithaca, N.Y.: Cornell University Press.

Gibson, Martha L., and Stephen Carter. 1998. "The Politicization of Fast Track." Paper prepared for delivery at the 1998 Meeting of the American Political Science Association, Boston, September 3–6.

Giddens, Anthony. 1982. "Class Division, Class Conflict, and Citizenship Rights." In Profiles and Critiques in Social Theory, edited by Anthony Giddens, 164–80. Berkeley: University of California Press.

Gifford, C.D. 1998. *Directory of U.S. Labor Organizations.* Washington, DC: Bureau of National Affairs.

Glade, B., and E. Potter. 1989. "Targeting the Labor Practices of Multinational Companies." *Focus on Issues,* U.S. Council for International Business, July.

Glasser, Susan B., and Juliet Eilperin. 1999. "GOP Scrambles to Counter Business's Aid to Democrats." *Washington Post,* November 10: A6.

Glenn, David. 1997. "Making Them Flinch." *Dissent* 44: 51.

———. 1998. "Fast Track Derailed." In *Not Your Father's Union Movement: Inside the AFL-CIO,* edited by Jo-Ann Mort. New York: Verso.

"Globe Union Joins Guild." 1994. *Editor & Publisher* (electronic edition), April 9.

Goffman, Erving. 1974. *Frame Analysis: An Essay on the Organization of Experience.* Cambridge: Harvard University Press.

Goldfield, Michael. 1987. *The Decline of Organized Labor in the United States.* Chicago: University of Chicago Press.

Goldstein, John, and Jeff Crosby. 2000. "AFL-CIO's 'New Alliance' Will Rebuild Local Strength." *Labor Notes,* April 12.

Gordon, Jennifer. 1999. "The Campaign for the Unpaid Wages Prohibition Act: Latino Immigrants Change New York Wage Law: The Impact of Non-Voters on Politics and the Impact of Political Participation on Non-Voters." Unpublished paper. Carnegie Endowment Comparative Citizenship Program.

Gorlick, Arthur C. 1999. "State's Apple Hands Abused, Mexico Says: Complaint Could Lead to Special Investigation and Even Sanctions." *Seattle Post-Intelligencer,* September 9: A1.

Gottschalk, Peter. 1997. "Inequality, Income Growth, and Mobility. The Basic Facts." *Journal of Economic Perspectives* 11: 21–40.

Gouldner, Alvin. 1976. *The Dialectic of Ideology and Technology: The Origins, Grammar, and Future of Ideology.* New York: Oxford University Press.

Gray, Lois, and Ronald Seeber. 1998. "The Industry and the Unions: An Overview." In *Under the Stars: Essays on Labor Relations in Arts and Entertainment,* edited by Lois Gray and Ronald Seeber, 15–49. Ithaca, N.Y.: Cornell University Press/ILR Press.

Grayson, George W. 1995. *The North American Free Trade Agreement: Regional Community and the New World Order.* Lanham, Md.: University Press of America.

Green, James R. 1980. *The World of the Worker: Labor in Twentieth-Century America.* New York: Hill and Wang.

Greenhouse, Steven. 1998a. "Two Unions, In Health and Services, Plan to Merge." *New York Times,* January 7: A15.

———. 1998b. "Mexicans Were Denied U.S. Rights, Suit Says." *New York Times,* May 28: A18.

———. 1998c. "Anti-Sweatshop Coalition Finds Itself at Odds on Garment Factory Code." *New York Times,* July 3: A16.

———. 1998d. "Teachers See Close Ballot on Big Merger." *New York Times,* July 5: 8.

———. 1998e. "Republicans Credit Labor for Success by Democrats." *New York Times,* November 6: A28.

———. 1999a. "Three Unions Say Conflicts Will Delay Merger." *New York Times,* June 25: A21.

———. 1999b. "The Most Innovative Figure in Silicon Valley? Maybe This Labor Organizer." *New York Times,* November 14.

———. 2000a. "Labor, In Switch, Urges Amnesty for All Illegal Immigrants," *New York Times,* February 17: A23.

———. 2000b. "Despite Defeat on China Bill, Labor Is on Rise." *New York Times,* May 30: A1.

Greenwood, Royston, and C.R. Hinings. 1996. "Understanding Radical Organizational Change: Bringing Together the Old and New Institutionalism." *Academy of Management Review* 21: 1022–54.

Greider, William. 1997. *One World Ready or Not: The Manic Logic of Global Capitalism.* New York: Simon and Schuster.

Groombridge, Mark A., and Claude Barfield. 1999. *Tiger by the Tail: China and the World Trade Organization* Washington, DC: AEI Press.

Gross, James A. 1974. *The Making of the National Labor Relations Board.* Albany: State University of New York Press.

———. 1995. *Broken Promise: The Subversion of U.S. Labor Relations Policy, 1947–1994.* Philadelphia: Temple University Press.

Habermas, Jurgen. 1979. *Communication and the Evolution of Society.* London: Heinemann.

Hall, Peter A. 1986. *Governing the Economy: The Politics of State Intervention in Britain and France.* New York: Oxford University Press.

Hannan, Michael T., and John Freeman. 1989. *Organizational Ecology.* Cambridge: Harvard University Press.

Hardman, J.B.S., and Maurice Neufeld, eds. 1951. *The House of Labor.* New York: Prentice Hall.

Harris, John F. 1997. "Clinton Hits 'Fast-Track' Opponents." *Washington Post,* October 28: A4.

Harrison, Bennett, and Marcus Weiss. 1998. *Workforce Development Networks: Community-Based Organizations and Regional Alliances.* Thousand Oaks, CA: Sage.

Hathaway, Oona H. 1998. "Positive Feedback: The Impact of Trade Liberalization on Industry Demands for Protection." *International Organization* 52(3): 575–612.

Haveman, Heather. 1992. "Between a Rock and a Hard Place: Organizational Change and Performance under Conditions of Fundamental Environmental Transformation." *Administrative Science Quarterly* 37: 48–75.

Healey, Jon, and Thomas H. Moore. 1997. "Clinton Forms New Coalition to Win NAFTA Approval." *CQ Weekly,* November 20.

Heberle, Rudolf. 1951. *Social Movements: An Introduction to Political Sociology.* New York: Appleton-Century-Crofts, Inc.

Heckscher, Charles C. 1988. *The New Unionism: Employee Involvement in the Changing Corporation.* New York: Basic Books.

———. 1995. *White-Collar Blues: Management Loyalties in an Age of Corporate Restructuring.* New York: Basic Books.

Held, David. 1989. "Citizenship and Autonomy." In *Social Theory of Modern Societies,* edited by David Held and John Thompson, 162. Cambridge: Cambridge University Press.

Herzenberg, Stephen, John A. Alic, and Howard Wial. 1998. *New Rules for a New Economy: Employment and Opportunity in Post-Industrial America.* Ithaca, N.Y.: Cornell University Press.

Hindman, Hugh, and David Patton. 1986. *The Labor Council in the Community: A Guide to Local Central Bodies.* Columbus: Labor Education and Research Service, Ohio State University.

Hirsch, Barry T., and David A. Macpherson. 2000. *Union Membership and Earnings Data Book 1996.* Washington, DC: Bureau of National Affairs.

Hobsbawm, E.J. 1968. *Labouring Men: Studies in the History of Labour.* London: Wiedenfeld and Nicolson.

Hochschild, Arlie. 1983. *The Managed Heart.* Berkeley: University of California Press.

Hoerr, John P. 1988. *And the Wolf Finally Came: The Decline of the American Steel Industry.* Pittsburgh: University of Pittsburgh Press.

——. 1997. *We Can't Eat Prestige.* Philadelphia: Temple University Press.

Horowitz, Sara. 1999. "Working Today." Talk presented to the MIT Task Force for Reconstructing America's Labor Market Institutions. Cambridge: February.

Hosansky, David. 1998. "House Vote Signals a Key Reversal of U.S. Support for Free Trade." *CQ Weekly,* September 26: 2603–04.

Houseman, Susan. 1997. "Temporary, Part-Time, and Contract Employment in the United States: A Report on the W.E. Upjohn Institute's Employer Survey on Flexible Staffing Practices." Kalamazoo, Mich.: W.E. Upjohn Institute for Employment Research.

Huffman, Pauline (Pennsylvania State Acting Director, AFL-CIO Department of Field Mobilization). 1998. Telephone interview with author, October 5, 1998.

Human Rights Watch. 1998. "A Job or Your Rights: Continued Sex Discrimination in Mexico's Maquiladora Sector," December.

Hurd, Richard W. 1976. "New Deal Labor Policy and the Containment of Radical Union Activity." *Review of Radical Political Economics* 8(3, fall): 32–43.

——. 1998. "Contesting the Dinosaur Image: The Labor Movement's Search for a Future." *Labor Studies Journal* 22(4): 5–30.

International Confederation of Free Trade Unions (ICFTU). 2000. "Social Development for All in a Globalising World." Brussels, May, www.icftu.org.

International Labour Organization (ILO). 1998. "Declaration of Fundamental Principles and Rights at Work," Geneva.

Iritani, Evelyn. 1998. "Mexico Charges Upset Apple Cart in U.S." *Los Angeles Times,* August 20: D2.

Isaac, Larry, Larry Christiansen, Jamie Miller, and Tim Nickel. 1998. "Intermovement Relations: Civil Rights Movement Spillover on Labor Militancy from Taft-Hartley to Reagan." Paper presented at the American Sociological Association meeting, San Francisco, August 1998.

Jackson, Brooks. 1988. *Honest Graft: Big Money and the American Political Process.* New York: Alfred A. Knopf.

Jacoby, Sanford M. 1999. "Are Career Jobs Headed for Extinction?" *California Management Review* 42(1, fall): 123–145.

Janoski, Thomas. 1998. *Citizenship and Civil Society.* New York: Cambridge University Press.

Jessup, David, and Michael Gordon. 2000. "The Case of Bibong in the Dominican Republic and Dominican EPZs." Paper prepared for the 2000 AFL-CIO/UCLEA Conference "Unions and the Global Economy," April.

Johnston, Paul. 1994. *Success While Others Fail: Social Movement Unionism and the Public Workplace.* Ithaca, N.Y.: Cornell University Press/ILR Press.

——. 1998. "Social Movement Unionism: Labor as Citizenship Movement." Paper presented at the Conference on Revival of the American Labor Movement: Arguments, Evidence, Prospects. Cornell University: October 16, 1997. Revised version in this volume.

———. 2001. "Citizens of the Future: The Emergence of Transnational Citizenship among Mexican Immigrants in California." In *Citizenship Today: Global Perspectives and Practices,* edited by T. Alexander Aleinikoff and Douglas Klusmeyer. Washington, D.C.: Brookings Institute.

Judis, John B. 1992. "The Tariff Party." *The New Republic,* March 30: 23–25.

———. 1998. "New Labor, New Democrats—New Alliance?" *The American Prospect,* September-October: 12–14.

Juravich, Tom, and Kate Bronfenbrenner. 1999. *Ravenswood: The Steelworkers' Victory and the Revival of American Labor.* Ithaca, N.Y.: Cornell University Press.

Kahane, Leo H. 1996. "Congressional Voting Patterns on NAFTA: An Empirical Interpretation." *American Journal of Economics and Sociology* 5(4): 394–409.

Kahn, Joseph. 2000. "Last-Ditch Effort by 2 Sides to Win China Trade Vote." *New York Times,* May 23: A1.

Katz, Harry C. 1984. "The Impact of Public Employee Unionism on City Budgeting and Employee Remuneration: A Case Study of San Francisco." New York: Garland.

Katz, Harry C., Rosemary Batt, and Jeffrey H. Keefe. 2000. "The Revitalization of the CWA: Integrating Political Action, Organizing, and Collective Bargaining." Unpublished manuscript. NYSSILR-Cornell University, March.

Katz, Harry C., and Owen Darbishire. 2000. *Converging Divergences: Worldwide Changes in Employment Systems.* Ithaca, N.Y.: Cornell University Press.

Katz, Lawrence F., and Kevin M. Murphy. 1992. "Changes in Relative Wages, 1963–87: Supply and Demand Factors." *Quarterly Journal of Economics* 107: 35–78.

Kaufman, Bruce E. 1992. "Research on Strike Models and Outcomes in the 1980s: Accomplishments and Shortcomings." In *Research Frontiers in Industrial Relations and Human Resources,* edited by David Lewin, Olivia S. Mitchell, and Peter D. Sherer, 77–129. Madison, Wis.: Industrial Relations Research Association.

Kazis, Richard. 1998. "New Labor Market Intermediaries: What's Driving Them?" Unpublished manuscript. Boston, MA: Jobs for the Future.

Kelly, John. 1998. *Rethinking Industrial Relations: Mobilization, Collectivism and Long Waves.* London: Routledge.

Kemble, Eugenia (Executive Director, Albert Shanker Institute). Telephone interview with author, April.

Kerchner, Charles, Julia Koppich, and Joseph G. Weeres. 1997. *United Mind Workers: Unions and Teaching in the Knowledge Society.* San Francisco: Jossey-Bass.

Kerr, Clark, Frederick Harbison, John Dunlop, and Charles Myers. 1960. *Industrialism and Industrial Man.* Cambridge: Harvard University Press.

Kobrin, Stephan J. "The MAI and the Clash of Globalizations." *Foreign Policy* (fall): 97–109.

Kochan, Thomas A. 1974. "A Theory of Multilateral Collective Bargaining in City Governments." *Industrial Relations Review* 27(4): 525–42.

———. 1995. "Using the Dunlop Report." *Industrial Relations* 34:3 (July): 350–66.

Kochan, Thomas, Harry C. Katz, and Robert B. McKersie. 1994. *The Transformation of American Industrial Relations.* Ithaca, N.Y.: Cornell University Press/ILR Press.

Kosterlitz, Julie. 1997a. "The Wages of Trade." *The National Journal,* October 18: 2076–79.

———. 1997b. "Muddy Track." *The National Journal,* August 9: 1595.

———. 1998a. "A Vote the Dems Would Like to Trade In." *The National Journal,* September 12: 2108.

———. 1998b. "Trade Crusade." *The National Journal,* May 9: 1054–57.

———. 1999. "Searching for New Labor." *The National Journal,* September 4: 2470–77.

Kotter, John. 1995. "Leading Change: Why Transformation Efforts Fail." *Harvard Business Review* 73(2): 59–67.

Kriesky, Jill. 1998. "The Depth and Breadth of Labor Body-Labor Center Collaboration." In *Working Together to Revitalize Labor In Our Communities: Case Studies of Labor Education—Central Body Collaboration,* edited by Jill Kriesky. Orono: University of Maine Press.

Kriesky, Jill, ed. 1998. *Working Together to Revitalize Labor in Our Communities: Case Studies of Labor Education—Central Labor Body Collaboration.* Orono, Maine: University and College Labor Education Association.

Lawler, John L. 1990. *Unionization and Deunionization.* Columbia: University of South Carolina Press.

Lens, Sidney. 1959. *The Crisis of American Labor.* New York: Sagamore Press, Inc.

Lessin, Nancy. 1998. "The URW/USWA Campaign Against Bridgestone/Firestone: A Tale of Two Bridgestones?" Unpublished manuscript.

Lewis, Diane E. 1997. "Report Hits NAFTA on Jobs." *Boston Globe,* June 27: D1.

Lichtenstein, Nelson. 1995. *Walter Reuther: The Most Dangerous Man in Detroit.* Urbana: University of Illinois Press.

Lipset, Seymour Martin, ed. 1986. *Unions in Transition: Entering the Second Century.* San Francisco: Institute for Contemporary Studies.

Lipset, Seymor Martin, Martin A. Trow, and James S. Coleman. 1956. *Union Democracy: The Internal Politics of the International Typographical Union.* Glencoe, Ill.: Free Press.

Livingston, C. Don, and Kenneth Wink. 1997. "The Passage of the North American Free Trade Agreement in the U.S. House of Representatives: Presidential Leadership or Presidential Luck?" *Presidential Studies Quarterly* 27(1): 52–70.

Lorwin, Lewis. 1933. *The American Federation of Labor: History, Policies, and Prospects.* Washington, DC: The Brookings Institution.

Luria, Daniel D., and Joel Rogers. 1999. *Metro Futures: Economic Solutions for Cities and Their Suburbs.* Boston: Beacon Press.

Lusztig, Michael. 1998. "The Limits of Rent Seeking: Why Protectionists Become Free Traders." *Review of International Political Economy* 5(1): 38–63.

Macdonald, Cameron Lynn, and Carmen Sirianni. 1996. "The Service Society and the Changing Experience of Work." In *Working in the Service Society,* edited by Cameron Macdonald and Carmen Sirianni, 1–28. Philadelphia: Temple University Press.

Maggs, John. 1997. "Trading Places." *The New Republic,* April 14: 15–16.

Magnusson, Paul. 1998. "Newt May Have Put Fast-Track on an Even Slower Boat," *Business Week,* July 13: 49.

———. 2000. "China Trade: Will Clinton Pull It Off?" *Business Week,* May 29: 74–76.

Maitland, Christine. 1999. "Introduction to the NEA 1999 Critical Issues Symposium: Knowledge Workers and Unions in the 21st Century." *Thought and Action: The NEA Higher Education Journal* 15 (fall): 9–10.

Mantsios, Gregory, ed. 1998. *A New Labor Movement for a New Century.* New York: Monthly Review Press.

March, James, and Johan Olsen. 1989. *Rediscovering Institutions.* New York: Free Press.

Marks, Stephen V. 1993. "Economic Interests and Voting on the Omnibus Trade Bill of 1987." *Public Choice* 75(1): 21–42.

Marshall, T.H. 1950. *Citizenship and Social Class and Other Essays.* Cambridge: Cambridge University Press.

Mason, Fred (Maryland State Director, AFL-CIO Department of Field Mobilization). 1998. Telephone interview with author, October 9, 1998.

Masters, Marick. 1997. *Unions at the Crossroads: Strategic, Membership, Financial and Political Perspectives.* Westport, Conn.: Quorum Books.

Masur, Sandra. 1991. "The North American Free Trade Agreement: Why It's in the Interest of U.S. Business." *Columbia Journal of World Business* 26(2).

Mayer, Frederick W. 1998. *Interpreting NAFTA: The Nature of Politics and the Art of Political Analysis.* New York: Columbia University Press.

Mazur, Jay. 2000. "Labor's New Internationalism." *Foreign Affairs.* January-February: 79–93.

McAdam, Doug. 1988. *Freedom Summer.* New York: Oxford University Press.

McAdam, Doug, John D. McCarthy, and Meyer N. Zald, eds. 1996. *Comparative Perspectives on Social Movements.* Cambridge: Cambridge University Press.

McClendon, John A., Jill Kriesky, and Adrienne Eaton. 1995. "Member Support for Mergers: An Analysis of an Affiliation Referendum." *Journal of Labor Research* 16 (winter): 9–23.

McGregor, Deborah. 2000. "The New Economy Spawns the New Democrats." *The Financial Times,* May 12: 4.

McKay, Jim. 1996. "Aluminum Workers Approve Merger With United Steelworkers of America." *Knight/Ridder Tribune Business News* (electronic edition), December 18.

McNichol, Tom. 1998. "My Supermarket, My Friend." *San Francisco Weekly,* November 11.

Melucci, Alberto. 1996. *Challenging Codes: Collective Action in the Information Age.* Cambridge: Cambridge University Press.

Merrill, Michael (Director, Education and Training, New Jersey State Federation of Labor). 1999. Personal interview with Dorothy Sue Cobble, January 12.

Meyerson, Harold. 1997. "No Brainer, No Votes." *The LA Weekly,* November 14–20: 11.

Midford, Paul. 1993. "International Trade and Domestic Politics: Improving on Rogowski's Model of Political Alignments." *International Organization* 7(4).

Midwest Center for Labor Research. 1991. "An Organizing Model of Unionism." *Labor Research Review* 10.

Milkman, Ruth, and Kent Wong. 2000. "Organizing the Wicked City: The 1992 Southern California Drywall Strike." In *Organizing Immigrants: The Challenge for Unions in Contemporary California,* edited by Ruth Milkman, 169–98. Ithaca, N.Y.: Cornell University Press.

Milkman, Ruth, and Kent Wong, eds. 2000. *Organizing Immigrants: Unions and Foreign-Born Workers in Contemporary California.* Ithaca, N.Y.: Cornell University Press.

Mills, C. Wright. 1951. *White Collar.* New York: Oxford University Press.

Millstein, Merilee (Deputy Director, Northeast Region of AFL-CIO Department of Field Mobilization). 2000. Telephone interview with author, May 17, 2000.

Mink, Gwendolyn. 1986. *Old Labor and New Immigrants in American Political Development: Union, Party, and State, 1875–1920.* Ithaca, N.Y.: Cornell University Press.

Mishel, Larry, Jared Bernstein, and John Schmitt. 1999. *The State of Working America 1998–99.* Ithaca, N.Y.: Cornell University Press.

Mollenkopf, John. 1983. *The Contested City.* Princeton, N.J.: Princeton University Press.

Molotch, Harvey, and John Logan, 1987. *Urban Fortunes, the Political Economy of Place.* Berkeley: University of California Press.

Montgomery, David. 1993. *Citizen Worker: The Experience of Workers in the United States with Democracy and the Free Market during the Nineteenth Century.* New York: Cambridge University Press.

Moody, Kim. 1995a. "NAFTA and the Corporate Redesign of America." *Latin American Perspectives* 22(1): 95–115.

——. 1995b. "Union Merger: Is Bigger Better?" *Labor Notes* 198 (September): 1, 14.

———. 1997. "American Labor: A Movement Again?" *Monthly Review* 49: 63–79.

———. 1998. "Up Against the Polyester Ceiling: The "New" AFL-CIO Organizes Itself." *New Politics* 6.

Moore, Janet. 1995. "Experts Predict Merger with Steel Union Will Strengthen United Rubber Workers." *Knight/Ridder Tribune Business News* (electronic edition), July 9.

Moore, Molly. 1998. "Mexican Farmhands Accuse U.S. Firms." *Washington Post*, December 3: A36.

Mort, Jo-Ann, ed. 1998. *Not Your Father's Union Movement: Inside the AFL-CIO*. New York: Verso.

Naim, Moises. 2000. "Washington Consensus or Washington Confusion?" *Foreign Policy*, March 22: 86–103.

Neilsen, Georgia Panter. 1982. *From Sky Girl to Flight Attendant: Women and Making of a Union*. Ithaca, N.Y.: Cornell University Press/ILR Press.

Neuenfeldt, Phil, and Eric Parker. 1996. *Wisconsin Regional Training Partnership: Building the Infrastructure for Workplace Change and Skill Development*. Washington, DC: AFL-CIO Human Resources Development Institute.

Neufeld, Maurice. 1951. "State of the Unions." In *The House of Labor*, edited by J.B.S. Hardman and Maurice Neufeld, 5–23. New York: Prentice Hall.

Neustadtl, Alan. 1990. "Interest Group PACsmanship: An Analysis of Campaign Contributions, Issue Visibility, and Legislative Impact." *Social Forces* 69(2): 549–64.

Niccoli, Barbara (Maine State Director, AFL-CIO Department of Field Mobilization). 1998. Telephone interview with author, October 6, 1998.

Nissen, Bruce, ed. 1999. *Which Direction for Organized Labor?* Detroit: Wayne State University Press.

Nollen, Stanley D., and Dennis P. Quinn. 1994. "Free Trade, Fair Trade, Strategic Trade, and Protectionism in the U.S. Congress, 1987–88." *International Organization* 48(3): 491–525.

Nord, W.R., and S. Tucker. 1986. *Implementing Radical and Routine Innovation*. Lexington, Mass.: Lexington Books.

Northrup, Herbert R. 1996. "Corporate Campaigns: The Perversion of the Regulatory Process," *Journal of Labor Research* 17(3): 346–58.

Norton, Eric, and Raju Narisetti. 1995. "United Rubber Workers Board Approves Merger with United Steelworkers Union." *Wall Street Journal*, May 12: B10.

OECD (Organization for Economic Coordination and Development). 1997. *Guidelines for Multinational Enterprises*, OECD/GD(97)40.

O'Halloran, Sharyn. 1998. "Comment." In *Imports, Exports, and the American Worker*, edited by Susan Collins, 412–20. Washington, DC: Brookings Institution.

O'Malley, Matt. 1998. "Looking Forward: The 1996–97 USWA Campaign Against Wheeling Pittsburgh Steel Corporation." Unpublished manuscript.

Ornstein, Norman J., Thomas E. Mann, and Michael Malbin, eds. 2000. *Vital Statistics on Congress, 1999–2000*. Washington, DC: AEI Press.

Osterman, Paul. 1999. *Securing Prosperity*. New York: Oxford University Press.

Palley, Thomas I. 1998. *Plenty of Nothing: The Downsizing of the American Dream and the Case for Structural Keynesianism*. Princeton, N.J.: Princeton University Press.

———. 1999. "How to Say No to the IMF." *The Nation*, June 21: 21–22.

Parker, Eric, and Joel Rogers. 1996. "The Wisconsin Regional Training Partnership: Lessons for National Policy." Working paper no. 3. Berkeley, Calif.: National Center for the Workforce.

———. 2001. "Sectoral Training Initiatives in the U.S.: Building Blocks of a New Workforce Preparation System?" In *The German System of Skill Provision in Comparative Perspective*, edited by Pepper D. Culpepper and David Finegold. New York: Berghahn Books.

Parsons, Talcott. 1966. Societies: Evolutionary and Comparative Perspectives. Englewood Cliffs, N.J.: Prentice-Hall.

Perlman, Selig, 1928. *A Theory of the Labor Movement.* New York: Macmillan.

Perpena, Shavonne (Connecticut State Director, AFL-CIO Department of Field Mobilization). 1998. Telephone interview with author, October 5, 1998.

Peterson, Jonathan. 2000. "Trade Debate Shows Force of Social Issues." *Los Angeles Times,* May 25: A1.

Phillips, Michael M. 2000. "Big Business Lobbies Hard as House China Vote Nears." *Wall Street Journal,* May 23: A28.

Piore, Michael J. 1979. *Birds of Passage: Migrant Labor and Industrial Societies.* Cambridge: Cambridge University Press.

Piore, Michael, and Charles Sabel. 1984. *The Second Industrial Divide: Possibilities for Prosperity.* New York: Basic Books.

Piven, Frances Fox, and Richard Cloward. 1988. "Popular Power and the Welfare State." In *Remaking the Welfare State: Retrenchment and Social Policy in America and Europe,* edited by Michael K. Brown. Philadelphia: Temple University Press.

Polanyi, Karl. 1944. *The Great Transformation.* New York: Rhinehart.

Poll Track. 2000. "2000 Polling on China." May 19: http://nationaljournal.com/members/polltrack/2000/issues/00china.htm.

Poulantzas, N. 1973. *Political Power and Social Class.* London: Sheed and Ward, Ltd.

Powell, Walter W., and Rebecca Friedkin. 1987. "Organizational Change in Nonprofit Organizations." In *The Nonprofit Sector: A Research Handbook,* edited by Walter W. Powell, 189–92. New Haven: Yale University Press.

Powers, Laura. 1998. "A Role for Occupational Unions in Improving the Returns to Market-Mediated Work." Unpublished seminar paper. New Brunswick, N.J.: Department of Urban Planning and Public Policy, Rutgers University.

The Public Perspective. 1997. (August/September): 36–37.

Rathke, Wade, and Joel Rogers. 1996. "A Strategy for Labor," *Dissent* 43 (fall): 78–84.

Reich, Robert. 2000. "Trade: A Third Way." *The American Prospect,* May 22: 56.

"Representation Election Number and Union Win Rate Declines in 1999." 1999. *Daily Labor Report* 241: C-1.

Rideout, Lucy (Staff Representative, California Teachers Association, Berkeley, Calif.). 1998. Telephone interview with Dorothy Sue Cobble, May 28.

Rodrik, Dani. 1997. *Has Globalization Gone Too Far?* Washington, DC: Institute for International Economics.

———. 1999. "Democracies Pay Higher Wages." *Quarterly Journal of Economics* 114(3): 707–38.

Rogers, Joel. 1990. "Divide and Conquer: Further 'Reflections on the Distinctive Character of American Labor Laws.'" *University of Wisconsin Law Review* 1–147.

———. 1995. "A Strategy for Labor." *Industrial Relations* 34(3): 367–381.

———. 1992. "What Needs to Be Done for Labor to Flourish." *Economic Notes* 60 (July–August 1992): 11.

———. 1993a. "Don't Worry, Be Happy: The Postwar Decline of Private Sector Unionism in the United States." In *The Challenge of Restructuring: North American Labor Movements Respond,* edited by Jane Jenson and Rianne Mahon, 48–71. Philadelphia: Temple University Press.

———. 1993b. "Reforming U.S. Labor Relations." *Chicago Kent Law Review* 69: 97–127. (Reprinted in abridged form in S. Friedman, R.W. Hurd, R.A. Oswald, and R.L. Seeber, eds., *Restoring the Promise of American Labor Law* [Ithaca, N.Y.: ILR Press, 1994]: 15–28; reprinted in full in M.W. Finkin, *The Legal Future of Employee Representation* [Ithaca, N.Y.: ILR Press, 1994]: 95–125.)

——. 1995. "A Strategy for Labor." *Industrial Relations* 34 (July): 367–81.

——. 1996a. "Necessary Complements." *Boston Review* 21 (summer): 11–12.

——. 1996b. "Labor and Economic Development." HRDI (Human Resources Development Institute) Pre-Conference, San Francisco, December.

——. 1997a. "The Folks Who Brought You the Weekend: Labor and Independent Politics." In *Audacious Democracy*, edited by Steve Fraser and Joshua Freeman, 247–61. New York: Houghton Mifflin. (Reprinted in *Working USA* 1 [November/December 1997]: 11–20.)

——. 1997b. "Where Is Your Money and Where Could It Be?" University of California Institute of Industrial Relations conference, "High Performance Pensions: Multi Employer Plans and the Challenges of Falling Pension Coverage and Retirement Insecurity," Berkeley, September.

Rogers, Ray. 1994. "Make Them Fight for a Place at the Table: How to Take on the Insurance Industry," *Social Policy* 24(4, summer): 31–40.

Rondeau, Kristine (Staff Representative, Harvard Union of Clerical and Technical Workers). 1998. Personal interview with author, September 18.

Rosenblum, Jonathan D. 1995. *Copper Crucible: How the Arizona Miners Strike of 1983 Recast Labor-Management Relations in America*. Ithaca, N.Y.: Cornell University Press/ILR Press.

Rosenthal, Steve. 1998. "Building to Win, Building to Last." In *Not Your Father's Union Movement: Inside the AFL-CIO*, edited by Jo-Ann Mort, 99–111. New York: Verso.

Rosier, Sharolyn A. 1996. "Restructuring Keys on State, Local AFL-CIOs." *AFL-CIO News*, May 20: 10.

Rothstein, Arnold J. 1998. "Outsourcing: An Accelerating Global Trend in Engineering." *Engineering Management Journal* 10(1, March): 7–14.

Rozen, Frieda. 1988. "Turbulence in the Air: The Autonomy Movement in the Flight Attendant Unions." Ph.D. diss., Pennsylvania State University.

Rueschemeyer, D., E.H. Stephens, and J. Stephens. 1992. *Capitalist Development and Democracy*. Cambridge: Polity Press.

Rupert, Mark E. 1995. "(Re)Politicizing the Global Economy: Liberal Common Sense and Ideological Struggle in the US NAFTA Debate." *Review of International Political Economy* 2(4): 658–92.

Saltzman, Gregory M. 1987. "Congressional Voting on Labor Issues: The Role of PACs." *Industrial and Labor Relations Review* 40(2): 163–79.

Sanger, David E. 1998. "Loans to Rights Violators Are Attacked in Congress." *New York Times*, April 22: 8.

Scherrer, Christoph. 1994. *Free Trade Elites and Fair Trade Masses: Why Has Public Opinion Mattered So Little?* Berlin: John F. Kennedy-Institut fuer Nordamerikastudien. Working paper no. 65.

Schmitt, Eric, and Joseph Kahn. 2000. "House, In 237–197 Vote, Approves Normal Trade Rights for China." *New York Times*, May 25: A1.

Schneider, William. 1997. "Democrats Battling Over Their Future." *The National Journal*, September 13: 1810.

Schwab, Susan C. 1994. *Trade-Offs: Negotiating the Omnibus Trade and Competitiveness Act*. Boston: Harvard Business School Press.

Scipes, Kim. 1992. "Understanding the New Labor Movements in the 'Third World': The Emergence of Social Movement Unionism." *Critical Sociology* 19(2): 81–101.

Seigel, Beth, and Peter Kwass. 1995. *Jobs and the Urban Poor: Publicly Initiated Sectoral Strategies*. Somerville, Mass.: Mt. Auburn Associates.

Seroka, Mihail. 1998. "The 42-Month War: Bayou Steel and Local 9121." Unpublished manuscript.

Service Employees International Union. 1988. *Contract Campaign Manual.* Washington, DC: SEIU.

———. 1993. "Service Employees International Union Affiliations Since 1970." Washington, DC: SEIU, November.

Shabecoff, Philip. 1980. "Big Labor, Little Labor." *New York Times,* May 11: 19.

Shaffer, Janet (New Hampshire and Vermont State Director, AFL-CIO Department of Field Mobilization). 1998. Telephone interview with author, October 9.

Shesgreen, Deirdre. 2000. "Gephardt Nudges Democrats in Congress Toward More Centrist Positions." *St. Louis Post-Dispatch,* April 2: A12.

Sipchen, Bob. 1997. "Labor of Love." *Los Angeles Times,* March 9: E1, E8.

Slichter, Sumner H., James J. Healy, and E. Robert Livernash. 1960. *The Impact of Collective Bargaining on Management.* Washington, DC: The Brookings Institution.

Smith, Patrick. 1999. "The Trouble with Globalism." *Business Week,* March 29: 15.

Sneiderman, Marilyn. 1996. "AFL-CIO Central Labor Councils: Organizing for Social Justice," *Labor Research Review* 24 (summer).

———. 1998a. Memorandum to UCLEA Members, November 5.

———. 1998b. Remarks given at AFL-CIO CLC Best Practices Conference, Linthicum, Md., June 6.

Soros, George. 1997. "The Capitalist Threat." *The Atlantic,* February: 47–58.

Soysal, Yasemin N. 1994. *Limits of Citizenship: Migrants and Postnational Membership in Europe.* Chicago and London: The University of Chicago.

Stanley, Harold W., and Richard G. Niemi. 1998. *Vital Statistics on American Politics 1997–1998.* Washington, DC: CQ Press.

Steagall, Jeffrey W., and Ken Jennings. 1996. "Unions, PAC Contributions, and the NAFTA Vote." *Journal of Labor Research* 17(3): 515–21.

Steinberg, Marc W. 1995. "The Great End of All Government: Working People's Construction of Citizenship in Early Nineteenth-Century England and the Matter of Class." In *Citizenship, Identity, and Social History,* edited by Charles Tilly. *International Review of Social History* 40, suppl 3: 19–50.

Steinmo, Sven, Kathleen Thelen, and Frank Longstreth, eds. 1992. *Structuring Politics: Historical Institutionalism in Comparative Analysis.* Cambridge: Cambridge University Press.

Stiglitz, Joseph. 2000. "Democratic Development as the Fruits of Labor." Keynote address, Industrial Relations Research Association Annual Meeting, January.

Stone, Clarence. 1989. *Regime Politics.* Lawrence: University of Kansas.

———. 1993. "Urban Regimes and the Capacity to Govern: A Political Economy Approach." *Journal of Urban Affairs* 15(1): 1–28.

Stone, Peter H. 1997. "Business Pushes for Fast-Track." *The National Journal,* September 27: 1903–04.

Sumners, Robert S. 1976. *Collective Bargaining and Benefit Conferral: A Jurisprudential Critique.* Ithaca, N.Y.: Cornell University Press, New York State School of Industrial and Labor Relations, Institute of Public Employment.

Suzman, Mark. 1997. "World Bank to Assess Policy Impact on Poor." *Financial Times* (London), July 15: 5.

Sweeney, John J. 1996a. *America Needs a Raise: Fighting for Economic Security and Social Justice.* Boston: Houghton Mifflin.

———. 1996b. "Labor's Role in a Meaningful Society." *Tikkun* 11(4, July–August): 37–39.

Swenson, Peter. 1989. *Fair Shares: Unions, Pay and Politics in Sweden and West Germany.* Ithaca, N.Y.: Cornell University Press.

Swoboda, Frank. 1995. "3 Merging Unions Invite Others to Join." *Washington Post,* July 28: C2.

Szekely, Peter. 1995. "Two Major Garment Unions Sew Up Merger Deal." Reuters press release, February 20.

Tarrow, Sidney. 1994. *Power in Movement: Social Movements, Collective Action and Politics.* Cambridge: Cambridge University Press.

"There's More Than One Party of Business." 1998. *Business Week,* May 4: 182.

Thompson, E.P. 1974. *The Making of the English Working Class.* Hammondsworth, England: Penguin Books.

Tichy, N.M. 1982. "Managing Change Strategically: The Technical, Political and Cultural Keys." *Organizational Dynamics,* Autumn: 59–80.

Tosini, Suzanne C., and Edward Tower. 1987. "The Textile Bill of 1985: The Determinants of Congressional Voting Patterns." *Public Choice* 54(1): 19–25.

Travis, Karen. 1992. "Women in Global Production and Worker Rights Provisions in U.S. Trade Laws." *Yale Journal of International Law* (winter): 173–94.

Troy, Leo. 1986. "The Rise and Fall of American Trade Unions: The Labor Movement from FDR to RR." In *Unions in Transition: Entering the Second Century.* San Francisco: Institute for Contemporary Studies.

Turner, Bryan. 1986. *Citizenship and Capitalism: The Debate over Reformism.* London: Allen and Unwin.

Tyson, James L. 1999. "In High-Tech Age, Unions Can Score." *Christian Science Monitor,* July 20: 1.

Ulman, Lloyd. 1955. *The Rise of the National Trade Union: The Development and Significance of Its Structure, Governing Institutions, and Economic Policies.* Cambridge: Harvard University Press.

United Steelworkers of America. 1997. *One Day Longer: The Road to Victory at Bridgestone/Firestone.* Pittsburgh: USWA.

U.S. Council for International Business. 1995. "Statement on Trade and Worker Rights."

"US Needs '30,000 New Jobs a Week Just to Break Even': Interview with George Meany, AFL-CIO." 1972. *U.S. News & World Report,* February 21: 27–29.

Useem, Jerry. 2000. "Growing Challenge to the Globalist Consensus: Despite What Some Would Have You Believe, These Protests Aren't Just Freak Shows." *Fortune,* May 15: 232.

Uslaner, Eric M. 1998a. "Let the Chits Fall Where They May? Executive and Constituency Influences on Congressional Voting on NAFTA." *Legislative Studies Quarterly* 23(3): 347–71.

———. 1998b. "Trade Winds: NAFTA and the Rational Public." *Political Behavior* 20(4): 341–60.

Valenzuela, Abel, Kent Wong, and Maurice Zeitlin. 1998. "Helots No More: A Case Study of the Justice for Janitors Campaign in Los Angeles." In *Organizing to Win: New Research on Union Strategies,* edited by Kate Bronfenbrenner, Sheldon Friedman, Richard W. Hurd, Rudoph A. Oswald, and Ronald L. Seeber, 102–19. Ithaca, N.Y.: Cornell University Press.

VandeHei, Jim. 2000. "Democrats Close the 'Soft Money' Gap With Republicans." *Wall Street Journal,* March 14: A32.

Van Jaarsveld, Danielle D. 2000. Nascent Organizing Initiatives Among High Skilled Contingent Workers: An Examination of the WashTech/CWA Case. Unpublished master's thesis, NYSSILR, Cornell University, Ithaca, N.Y.

Van Steenbergen, Bart. 1994. "Towards a Global Ecological Citizen." In *The Condition of Citizenship,* edited by Bart Van Steenbergen, 141–152. London: Sage Publications.

Verespej, Michael. 1995. "Mega-Unions: Mega Headaches: Only If Unions Can Solve Their Leadership Problems." *Industry Week,* September 4: 71–73.

Voos, Leah F. 2000. *Temporary Work: The Gendered Rise of a Precarious Employment Relationship.* Toronto: University of Toronto Press.

Voos, Paula. 1983. "Union Organizing: Costs and Benefits." *Industrial and Labor Relations Review* 36: 576–591.

Voos, Paula, ed. 1994. *Contemporary Collective Bargaining in the Private Sector.* Industrial Relations Research Association Series. Ithaca, N.Y.: Cornell University Press/ILR Press.

Voss, Kim. 1996. "Collapse of a Social Movement: The Interplay of Mobilizing Structures, Framing, and Political Opportunities in the Knights of Labor." In *Freedom Summer,* edited by Doug McAdam, 227–58. New York: Oxford University Press.

Voss, Kim, and Rachel Sherman. 1998. *Breaking the Iron Law of Oligarchy: Tactical Innovation and the Revitalization of the American Labor Movement.* Unpublished manuscript. Berkeley: University of California.

Waddington, Jeremy. 1995. *The Politics of Bargaining: The Merger Process and British Trade Union Structural Development, 1892–1987.* London: Mansell.

Waldinger, Roger, and Mehdi Bozorgmehr, eds. 1996. *Ethnic Los Angeles.* New York: Russell Sage Foundation.

Waldinger, Roger, Chris Erickson, Ruth Milkman, et al. 1994. *Strategic Negotiations.* Boston: Harvard Business School Press.

Walton, R.E., and R.B. McKersie. 1991. *A Behavioral Theory of Labor Negotiations: An Analysis of a Sound Interaction System.* Ithaca, N.Y.: ILR Press.

Walton, R.E., J.E. Cutcher Gershen Geld, and R.B. McKersie. 1994. *Strategic Negotiations.* Boston: Harvard Business School Press.

Waterman, Peter. 1993. "Social Movement Unionism: A New Union Model for a New World Order?" *Review* (Fernando Braudel Center) 16: 245–78.

Wellington, Harry H., and Ralph K. Winter Jr. 1971. *The Unions and the Cities.* Washington, DC: Brookings Institution.

Wever, Kirsten. 1998. "International Labor Revitalization: Enlarging the Playing Field." *Industrial Relations* 37(3, July): 388–407.

Wheeler, Hoyt. 1985. *Industrial Conflict: An Integrative Theory.* Columbia: University of South Carolina Press.

Wildavksy, Ben. 1995. "Going Nativist?" *The National Journal,* May 27: 1278–81.

Wilhite, Allen, and John Theilman. 1987. "Labor PAC Contributions and Labor Legislation: A Simultaneous Logit Approach." *Public Choice* 53(3): 267–76.

Williamson, Lisa. 1995. "Union Mergers: 1985–94 Update." *Monthly Labor Review* 118 (February): 18–24.

Wirls, Daniel. 1998. "The Consequences of Equal Representation: The Bicameral Politics of NAFTA in the 103rd Congress." *Congress & the Presidency* 25(2): 129–45.

Wolfgang, Myra. 1972. "Young Women Who Work: An Interview with Myra Wolfgang." *Dissent* 31–33.

World Bank. 1995. Workers in an Integrating World, World Development Report. New York: Oxford University Press, 78.

World Trade Organization. 1996. "Singapore Ministerial Declaration." Geneva, Dec. 13: Paragraph 3.

WRTP (Wisconsin Regional Training Partnership). 1998a. *1998 Annual Report.* Milwaukee: WRTP.

———. 1998b. *Wisconsin Manufacturing Needs Assessment.* Milwaukee: WRTP.

Zabin, Carol. 2000. "Organizing Latino Immigrants in the Los Angeles Manufacturing Sector: The Case of American Racing Equipment." In *Organizing Immigrants: The Challenge for Unions in Contemporary California,* edited by Ruth Milkman, 150–68. Ithaca, N.Y.: Cornell University Press.

Zieger, Robert H. 1995. *The CIO: 1935–1955.* Chapel Hill: The University of North Carolina Press.

Biographies

Kate Bronfenbrenner is director of Labor Education Research at Cornell University's School of Industrial and Labor Relations in Ithaca, N.Y. She received her Ph.D. in industrial and labor relations from Cornell University in 1993. Bronfenbrenner's primary research and teaching interests focus on union and employer behavior and strategies in organizing, bargaining, and contract administration. She has authored, co-authored, and edited numerous articles and books on current labor issues, most notably *Ravenswood: The Steelworkers' Victory and the Revival of American Labor* (with Tom Juravich) and *Organizing to Win: New Research on Union Strategies* (with Sheldon Friedman et al.).

Gary Chaison is a professor of industrial relations at the Graduate School of Management, Clark University, Worcester, Mass. His research has been in the areas of union structure, government and growth, and comparative industrial relations. Among other works, he has collaborated in several comparative studies of U.S. and Canadian labor relations, and over the past thirty years he has examined the dimensions of union mergers, most recently in *Union Mergers in Hard Times: The View from Five Countries* (Cornell University Press, 1996) and an investigation of the merger process in Sweden.

Dorothy Sue Cobble (Ph.D. Stanford University) is a professor in the Labor Studies and Employment Relations Department at Rutgers University where she teaches labor studies, history, and women's studies. She is the author of *Dishing It Out: Waitresses and Their Unions in the Twentieth Century* (1991) and the editor of *Women and Unions: Forging a Partnership* (1993). She recently received a Woodrow Wilson Fellowship for her current book project on labor women and social policy in modern America.

Lance Compa (J.D. Yale Law School) is a senior lecturer at the School of Industrial and Labor Relations at Cornell University, where he teaches U.S. labor law and international labor rights. He is author of the 2000 Human Rights Watch report "Unfair Advantage: Workers' Freedom of Association in the United States under International Human Rights Standards." Before turning to international labor law practice and teaching, Compa worked for many years as a trade union organizer and negotiator, principally for the United Electrical Workers (UE) and the Newspaper Guild.

Bill Fletcher, Jr., is Assistant to the President of the AFL-CIO. He oversees the Departments of Education, Civil and Human Rights, Safety and Health, and the Working Women's Department. Prior to coming to the AFL-CIO, he served as Assistant to the President for the East and South for the Service Employees International Union. Also, during his service at SEIU, he directed the Public Sector Division, Field Services, and Education. He served as an adjunct faculty member at the University of Massachusetts–Boston, in the Labor Studies Program.

Amy Foerster is an assistant professor of sociology at Pace University. She received her Ph.D. in sociology from Cornell University in 2000 where her dissertation addressed the role of the AFL-CIO Organizing Institute in the larger movement toward labor revitalization. Currently she is working on a research project examining the relationship between New York City's labor unions and the various racial and ethnic groups that comprise the city's labor force.

Charles Heckscher is a professor in the Department of Labor Studies and Employment Relations at Rutgers University. His research focuses on organization change and its consequences for employees and unions and on the possibilities for more collaborative and democratic forms of work. His books include *The New Unionism, The Post-Bureaucratic Organization,* and *White-Collar Blues.* As Director of the Center for Workplace Transformation, he is leading research into the development of collaboration in local unions and corporations. Before coming to Rutgers, he worked for the Communications Workers' Union and taught Human Resources Management at the Harvard Business School.

Richard W. Hurd is professor and director of Labor Studies at Cornell University. He is coeditor of *Organizing to Win* (Cornell University, ILR Press, 1998) and *Restoring the Promise of American Labor Law* (ILR Press, 1994). He has published dozens of papers in books and professional journals. An economist by training, he has served as an Economic Policy Fellow at the Brookings Institution and as Professor of Economics at the University of New Hampshire. He currently holds an elected position on the Executive Board of the Industrial Relations Research Association.

Paul Johnston is a sociologist and author of *Success While Others Fail: Social Movement Unionism and the Public Workplace* (ILR Press, 1994). He was formerly a union organizer with the United Farm Workers and the Service Employees International Union, and an associate professor of sociology at Yale University. He is currently a researcher affiliated with the University of California at Santa Cruz and executive director of the Citizenship Project.

Tom Juravich is professor and director of the Labor Relations and Research Center at the University of Massachusetts–Amherst. He holds a Ph.D. in sociology from the University of Massachusetts–Amherst and is the author of *Chaos on the Shop Floor: A Worker's View of Quality Productivity and Management, Commonwealth of Toil: Chapters in the History of Massachusetts Workers and Their Unions,* and *Ravenswood: The Steelworker's Victory and the Revival of American Labor* (with Kate Bronfenbrenner).

Harry C. Katz is the Jack Sheinkman Professor of Collective Bargaining and Director, Institute of Collective Bargaining, NYSSILR, Cornell University. His books include *Shifting Gears* (1984) and *The Transformation of American Industrial Relations* (with Thomas Kochan and Robert McKersie, 1986). His latest book is *Converging Divergences: Worldwide Changes in Employment Systems* (with Owen Darbishire, Cornell University Press, 2000).

Jill Kriesky is an extension associate professor at the Institute for Labor Studies and Research, West Virginia University. Her work on labor issues includes *Working Together to Revitalize Labor in Our Communities* (1998), an edited volume on labor educators' roles in central labor council and state federation activities; research on the negotiation and use of neutrality and card-check agreements to support union organizing, with Adrienne Eaton; and studies of the unionized pulp and paper industry, also with Adrienne Eaton.

Ruth Milkman is professor of sociology at UCLA and director of the Institute for Labor and Employment, a multicampus research program of the University of California. Her research and writing has ranged over a variety of issues surrounding work and labor organization in capitalist societies. She is the author of *Gender at Work: The Dynamics of Job Segregation during World War II,* which won the 1987 Joan Kelly Prize from the American Historical Association; *Japan's California Factories: Labor Relations and Economic Globalization* (1991); and *Farewell to the Factory: Auto Workers in the Late 20th Century* (1997). She recently edited the volume *Organizing Immigrants: The Challenge for Unions in Contemporary California* (2000). Her current research focuses on immigrant workers and their relationship to labor unionism in contemporary southern California.

Eric Parker is Executive Director of the Wisconsin Regional Training Partnership and Research Associate at the Center on Wisconsin Strategy, University of Wisconsin–Madison. Various aspects of Parker's work on the development of labor market intermediaries are funded by the Anne E. Casey, Ford, Rockefeller, and Russell Sage Foundations.

Joel Rogers is the John D. MacArthur Professor of Law, Political Science, and Sociology at the University of Wisconsin–Madison, where he also directs the Center on Wisconsin Strategy, a research and policy institute, and project incubator, promoting "high road" economic development. Rogers has written widely on American politics and public policy. His most recent book, with Ruy Teixeira, is *America's Forgotten Majority: Why the White Working Class Still Matters.*

James Shoch is an assistant professor of government at Dartmouth College. He has published articles in *Political Science Quarterly, Politics & Society,* and elsewhere on the U.S. industrial policy debate of the early 1980s, the partisan roots of international economic activism in the Reagan-Bush era, and American labor's struggles against trade liberalization. His book, *Trading Blows: Party Competition and U.S. Trade Policy in a Globalizing Era,* is forthcoming from the University of North Carolina Press.

Lowell Turner is professor of international and comparative labor at the School of Industrial and Labor Relations at Cornell University. Among his writings are *Democracy at Work: Changing World Markets and the Future of Labor Unions* (1991) and *Fighting for Partnership: Labor and Politics in Unified Germany* (1998), both from Cornell University Press. He is currently coordinating an international research project on union revitalization strategies in five countries (the United States, Britain, Germany, Italy, and Spain).

Kent Wong is the director of the Center for Labor Research and Education at UCLA, where he teaches labor studies and Asian American studies. He is president of the newly formed United Association for Labor Education. Previously, he served as staff attorney for the Service Employees International Union #660.

Index

ABC. *See* American Builders
and Contractors
Absorption mergers, 241, 242, 248–49.
See also Union mergers
Academic workers. *See* Colleges
ACORN (Association of Community
Organizations for Reform Now),
269, 270
ACTWU. *See* Amalgamated Clothing
and Textile Workers Union
Adam's Mark Hotel, 142
Advertising, 294, 296, 307. *See also*
Publicity pressure
Advisory bench arbitration, 198
Advisory Committee on the Future of Cen-
tral Labor Councils (AFL-CIO), 134
Affiliation mergers, 241, 245n, 248–49, 254.
See also Union mergers
AFGE. *See* American Federation of
Government Employees
AFL-CIO
centralization issue, 171–72, 173–74,
176–80
and central labor councils, 132–33, 147
and fast track battle (1997), 20n, 286,
294, 295
"free labor" institutes, 318
Gore endorsement, 25, 302, 305
Industrial Union Department, 219
international solidarity, 313, 318, 323, 331, 335
labor market interventions, 259, 260
and NAFTA battle, 283
national community campaigns, 138, 154n
political operations funding, 24
research strategy, 219
and Southern California drywall
strike, 119
support for trade liberalization, 315
and union mergers, 251–53
and Vietnam War, 16
Voice@Work campaign, 142
and Wheeling Pitt campaign, 231
See also "New Voice" AFL-CIO program;
Organizing Institute; Union Cities
program; Union structure
interrelationships
*AFL-CIO Handbook for Central Labor
Councils,* 133
AFL-CIO Street Heat: Mobilizing to Win
(AFL-CIO), 136
African Americans
associational unionism, 75n
justice movements, 56
and labor market interventions, 264
public sector, 44
Southern California workforce exodus,
105, 106
See also Racial/ethnic diversity
AFSCME. *See* American Federation of
State, County, and Municipal
Employees
AFT. *See* American Federation of Teachers
Agriculture, 32
civic regime, 48
temporary/contingent workers, 53
and trade liberalization issues, 300, 304,
307
Washington State apple workers NAALC
case, 326–28
Agriculture Trade Coalition, 307
Air wars. *See* Publicity pressure
Allaire, Y., 187–88
Allen, Donald, 124, 126
Aluminum Workers of America, 242

Alvarez, Joe, 147
Amalgamated Clothing and Textile
   Workers Union (ACTWU), 17, 19, 115
Amalgamated Engineering and Electrical
   Union (Great Britain), 250
Amalgamation mergers, 241, 249–50. *See
   also* Union mergers
American Builders and Contractors
   (ABC), 121
American Electronics Association, 307
American Farm Bureau, 307
American Federation of Government
   Employees (AFGE), 198, 204
American Federation of Labor (AFL)
   and central labor councils, 132–33, 152
   creation of, 319
   organizing, 87–90
   See also AFL-CIO
American Federation of State, County, and
   Municipal Employees (AFSCME)
   collective bargaining, 199, 200–201
   educational programs, 203–4
   grievance procedures, 197
   labor market interventions, 269
   lawsuits, 71
   mergers, 248
   and 1960s/1970s social movements, 15,
   17
   organizing, 19, 200–201, 202–3, 245
American Federation of Teachers (AFT),
   16, 86
   merger proposals, 243, 248n, 251n
Americans Lead on Trade, 290
Anticommunism
   and business unionism, 14, 15, 16
   and central labor councils, 132, 152
   and trade liberalization issues, 277
Anti-union consultants, 327
Anti-union strategies. *See* Employer oppo-
   sition; *specific campaigns*
Antiwar movement, 16
A. Philip Randolph Institute (APRI), 138
Apparel industry. *See* Garment industry
Apparel Industry Partnership, 335, 336
APRI. *See* A. Philip Randolph Institute
Arbitration, 196, 198
Armenakis, A. A., 188
Armstrong, Pat, 95
Asian financial crisis, 317, 334

Associational unionism, 74–75, 181, 341
   immigrant workers, 112–13
   temporary/contingent workers, 32, 53, 76
   Working Today, 53, 76–80
Association of Community Organizations
   for Reform Now. *See* ACORN
At the River I Stand, 15
Australia, 91, 246–47, 252n
Auto Workers, Machinists and Steelwork-
   ers merger proposal, 238–39, 250–51

Bahr, Morty, 76, 77
Bail funding, 119–20
Bakery, Confectionery, and Tobacco Work-
   ers (BCTW), 202, 203
Balanced budget deal, 292–93, 295
Bargaining. *See* Collective bargaining
BASF, 211
Batchelor, Heather A., 215
"Battle in Seattle". *See* Seattle WTO
   protests (1999)
Bayou Steel campaign, 223–26
BCTW. *See* Bakery, Confectionery, and
   Tobacco Workers
Becker, George, 217–18, 220, 226, 228, 230,
   237
Bell, Daniel, 91
Bell Atlantic, 345
Benefit portability, 69, 85
Bensinger, Richard, 19, 160, 170
Bereuter, Doug, 310n
Bergen Task Force on Temporary Work,
   268
Bevona, Gus, 110–11
Biotechnology, 64
Blacks. *See* African Americans
Blockades, 216. *See also* Direct action
Bloom, Ron, 231, 232
Blue Cross/Blue Shield, 158
Boeing Company, 306n
Bonior, David, 283, 295
Bottom-up organizing, 102, 103
   Guess campaign, 114, 128
   Los Angeles-Long Beach port truckers
      strike, 122, 123–24, 128
   and Organizing Institute, 169
   Southern California drywall strike, 117
   See also Mobilization; Rank-and-file par-
      ticipation

Boycotts, 73, 114, 117, 227
Boyle, Emmett, 218–19
Bradley, Bill, 77
Bradley, Tom, 110
Brazil, 37
Bridgestone/Firestone Inc., 226–30, 246
Bronfenbrenner, Kate, 102, 217–18, 286n
Brown, Jerry, 283
Buchanan, Pat, 283, 290
Buhle, Paul, 176n
Building maintenance, 32, 48–49, 104–5,
    106, 111. *See also* Justice for Janitors
    campaigns
Building trades, 104–5
    apprenticeship issues, 195
    bargaining to organize, 201–2
    craft unionism, 54, 60
    Southern California drywall strike, 100,
    103, 104–5, 117–21
Burke-Hartke bill, 278
Burma, 337
Bush, George (senior), 280, 282
Business Coalition for U.S.-China Trade,
    306–7
Business-Industry Political Action
    Committee, 308n
Business policies
    campaign contributions, 276, 294,
    297–98
    China PNTR agreement, 303, 306–10
    and fast track battle (1997), 286, 287, 290
    and fast track battle (1998), 301
    NAFTA battle, 280–81, 283, 285
    See also Employer opposition
Business Roundtable, 280n, 306, 307n
Business unionism, 11, 339–40
    and citizenship, 37
    and employer opposition, 22
    historical perspective, 14–17
    and urban political theory, 57

California
    politics, 57
    Southern California drywall strike, 100,
    103, 104–5, 117–21
    union decline, 105
    See also Immigrant workers
California Immigrant Workers' Association
    (CIWA), 119, 120

Campaign contributions
    and labor mobilization, 312
    and 1996 elections, 293, 294
    and trade liberalization issues, 276, 279,
    284n, 297–300, 307–8
Campus sweatshop campaigns, 312, 335–36
Canada, 328–29
Cancellation clauses, 108
Capital flight, 101, 105. *See also* Runaway
    shops
Capitalism, 39–40, 41, 64. *See also*
    Economic restructuring
Card-check recognition, 201, 267, 345, 347
Career mentoring, 69
Caribbean Basin Initiative (CBI), 322
Carpenters Union. *See* United
    Brotherhood of Carpenters and Join-
    ers of America
Carter, Jimmy, 59
Caterpillar, 46
CBI. *See* Caribbean Basin Initiative
CBTU. *See* Coalition of Black Trade
    Unionists
CCDI. *See* Childspace Cooperative Devel-
    opment Inc.
Center for Economic Priorities, 336
Center on Wisconsin Strategy (COWS),
    260
Centralization issue, 171–72, 173–74,
    176–80, 248
Central labor councils (CLCs), 129
    historical perspective, 131–33, 147
    increased power of, 56
    and New Voice AFL-CIO program, 129,
    133–34
    regional differences, 131n
    See also Union Cities program
Central Vermonters for a Livable Wage, 139
CFI, 237
Chaison, Gary, 157, 250n
Changing to Organize campaign, 164, 166
Chavez, Cesar, 49
Chavez-Thompson, Linda, 20. *See also*
    New Voice AFL-CIO program
Chemical Workers, 242
Child care, 269
Childspace Cooperative Development Inc.
    (CCDI), 269
Chile, 324

China PNTR agreement, 275–76, 277,
  302–10, 316–17
  business campaign, 303, 306–10
Church, Frank, 333
CIO. *See* Congress of Industrial Organizations
Citigroup, 306n
Citizenship, 29, 35–43
  and civic regime, 41–42
  cultural, 40–41
  defined, 35–36
  dimensions of, 38–39
  economic, 38–40, 41
  and immigrant workers, 40, 48–53
  as social movement frame, 29, 36–37
  and temporary/contingent workers,
    53–54
  See also Social movement unionism
Citizens' Trade Campaign, 283, 295, 304
Civic regime, 41–42, 48. *See also* Citizen-
  ship
Civil rights, 38, 40
Civil rights movement, 15, 32
Civil society, 39n
Clark, Matthew J., 215
Class-action lawsuits, 116, 120. *See also*
  Lawsuits
Class consciousness, 111, 233
Clayton Act (1914), 319
CLCs. *See* Central labor councils
Clinton, Bill
  and China PNTR agreement, 303, 305–6
  Dunlop Commission, 19, 59
  fast track battle (1997), 275, 287, 288,
    292
  and NAFTA battle, 282, 284
  Seattle WTO meeting, 302
Coalition of Black Trade Unionists
  (CBTU), 138
Coalitions. *See* Community coalitions
Coal miners, 46, 211, 221
Coca-Cola campaign (Guatemala), 335
Cold war, 14, 15, 16
Collective bargaining
  alternatives to, 68, 71
  concession bargaining, 46, 55
  current practices, 196–97, 199–200
  decentralized, 246–47
  new institutional perspective, 22

and organizing focus, 195
  as path to organizing, 200–202
  pattern bargaining, 199, 213, 214, 227
  and research strategy, 216
  and triangular revitalization strategies,
    347–48
  and union mergers, 246–47
  See also Coordinated/strategic contract
    campaigns; Industrial unionism
Colleges
  campus sweatshop campaigns, 312,
    335–36
  graduate student employees, 32
  temporary/contingent workers, 53, 54
COMET program, 202, 203, 205
Commerce Clause, 319
Commission on the Future of Worker-
  Management Relations (Dunlop
  Commission), 19, 59
Committee of Interns and Residents, 244
Committee on Political Education
  (COPE), 133
"Common Sense Economics," 136n, 149
Communication Workers of America
  (CWA)
  bargaining mobilization, 199
  first contract negotiations, 200
  grievance procedures, 198
  labor market interventions, 267–68
  Los Angeles-Long Beach port truckers
    strike, 101, 103, 122, 123–26, 128
  mergers, 249, 251
  and 1960s/1970s social movements, 17
  and occupational unionism, 342
  organizing, 16, 19, 201, 202, 205, 345
  triangular revitalization agenda, 347–48
Communities of workers, 55
  and associational unionism, 79, 80
  and Bayou Steel campaign, 224–25
  early AFL federal locals, 88–89
  immigrant networks, 111, 118, 119, 124,
    127
  and Ravenswood campaign, 221, 224
  and working conditions, 111, 123, 124
Community coalitions, 10, 197
  corporate campaigns, 46–48, 49
  Guess campaign, 117
  and immigrant organizing, 49–50, 117,
    125, 127

importance of, 90–91
and labor market interventions, 269–70
Los Angeles-Long Beach port truckers
  strike, 125
NIPSCO campaign, 233
and public workers, 43–45
and social movement unionism, 32, 37,
  ;4–58
See also Union Cities program
Compa, Lance, 312
Company financial disclosure, 215
Competition
  and employer opposition, 113, 242
  and independent contractors, 122
  and labor market interventions, 257
Comprehensive organizing campaign, 108
Computerization, 198
Computer technology, 64
Concession bargaining, 46, 55
Con Edison, 71n
Congress of Industrial Organizations
  (CIO), 132, 152. *See also* AFL-CIO
Conservative populism, 290–91, 307
Construction workers. *See* Building trades
Consumers
  and labor rights, 321
  NIPSCO campaign, 233, 234
  and publicity pressure, 70
  and trade liberalization issues, 296, 304
Continental Airlines, 93
Continental Tire, 237
Contingent workers. *See* Temporary/con-
  tingent workers
Contreras, Miguel, 107
Conybeare, John, 281n
Coordinated/strategic contract campaigns,
  211–37
  Bayou Steel, 223–26
  Bridgestone/Firestone, 226–30, 246
  importance of, 211–12, 236
  NIPSCO, 232–34
  and organizational change, 235–36
  Phelps Dodge, 213–14
  Ravenswood, 217–23
  USX, 214–17
  Wheeling Pitt, 230–32
  and workplace diversity, 234, 235
COPE. *See* Committee on Political
  Education

Copper Crucible (Rosenblum), 214
Corporate campaign tactics, 218, 221,
  234–35
  and community coalitions, 46–48, 49
Corporate codes of conduct, 312n, 335–36
Correctional officers, 44n
COWS. *See* Center on Wisconsin Strategy
Craft unionism, 84–85, 342
  communities of workers, 80
  and mobile workforce, 60, 69
  and temporary/contingent workers, 53,
    54
  and wages, 73
  See also Occupational unionism
Critical discourse, 42
Cultural citizenship, 40–41
Culture of organizing, 167. *See also* Organi-
  zational change
Customer pressure, 228–29
CWA. *See* Communication Workers of
  America

Darlington doctrine, 329
Davis, Gray, 57
Day to Make Our Voices Heard, Our
  Choices Respected, 138, 154n
Dean, Amy, 342–43
Decentralized negotiations, 246–47
Declaration of Fundamental Principles and
  Rights at Work, 331
Defined benefit pension funds, 230–31, 232
Delgado, Hector, 99–100
Democratic Leadership Council (DLC),
  284, 292, 300
Democratic Party, 18
  and China PNTR agreement, 304–5,
    307–9
  and fast track battle (1997), 287–88,
    291–93, 296–97, 298–99
  and fast track battle (1998), 301
  fundraising scandals, 299
  and NAFTA battle, 284, 285, 292, 298
Democratic social movements. *See* Social
  movements
Deregulation, 105, 122
Dhavale, Dileep G., 157
Direct action, 49, 216–17
Disinvestment, 55
Dislocated worker programs, 260

DLC. *See* Democratic Leadership Council
"Domestic content" bill, 278
Dominican Republic, 323, 324
Dooley, Calvin M., 296n
Doyle, Bill, 220
Drucker, Peter, 71
Due process, 72
Dues, 143
Dunlop Commission. *See* Commission
    on the Future of Worker-
    Management Relations

ECAT. *See* Emergency Committee for
    American Trade
Economic citizenship, 38–40, 41
Economic restructuring, 59–61, 80–81, 256
    and business unionism, 14
    causes of, 64–65
    and labor-market experience diversity,
        33, 343–44
    and Organizing Institute, 180–81
    and trade liberalization issues, 311
    See also Mobile workforce
Edsall, Thomas, 275n
Educational opportunities
    and citizenship, 38, 40
    and mobile workforce, 69, 256–57
Educational sector, 45n
    "new unionism," 86
    organizing, 16
    union merger proposals, 243, 248n, 251n
Elected Leader Task Force on Organizing,
    163–66
Elections. *See* Campaign contributions;
    National elections; Political strategy
Electoral strategies. *See* Campaign contri-
    butions; Political strategy
Electronics Industry Alliance, 307
Emergency Committee for American Trade
    (ECAT), 306
Employee rights. *See* Labor rights
Employer neutrality provisions, 142, 201,
    345, 347
Employer opposition, 345
    and Bridgestone/Firestone, 227
    and competition, 113, 242
    and immigrant organizing, 103, 113, 126
    and NAFTA, 280–81, 286n
    and Organizing Institute, 180

and Phelps Dodge strike, 214
RICO lawsuits, 121
and union decline, 18, 21–22, 105, 122
union mergers, 245
and wages, 73n
See also specific campaigns
Employment programs. *See* Hiring halls;
    Job training; Labor market interven-
    tions
Employment Project, 76
Enoxy Coal dispute, 333–34
Environmental movement, 16, 20n, 282,
    296, 304
Environmental standards, 282
    charges based on, 222, 223, 229
    and fast track battle (1997), 285–86, 287,
        290, 295–96
Escalation, 218, 220, 231. *See also* Coordi-
    nated/strategic contract campaigns
Europe
    Bayou Steel campaign, 225
    international solidarity within, 348
    labor rights, 312n, 323, 348
    Ravenswood campaign, 220–21, 222
    temporary/contingent workers, 65–66
    See also specific countries
European Americans, 105, 106. *See also*
    Racial/ethnic diversity
European Union. *See* Europe

Fair Labor Association (FLA), 335
Fair Labor Standards Act (FLSA), 120, 319
Fair Trade Foundation, 336
Farmworkers. *See* Agriculture
Fast track battle (1997), 20n, 25, 247, 275,
    285–300, 316
    and campaign contributions, 276,
        297–300
    and conservative populism, 290–91
    and Democratic Party, 287–88, 291–93,
        296–97, 298–99
    and expert opinion, 290
    labor mobilization, 293, 294–97
    and 1996 elections, 285–86, 293–94
    and public opinion, 289–90
    and union decline, 288–89
Fast track battle (1998), 277, 300–301
Federal Express, 306n
Felsen exception, 337

Feminism, 56
Fernandez, Gerald, 228
Ferraro, Ron, 226
Field Mobilization Department (AFL-CIO), 133
FIFA code, 336
Financial leverage, 71–72, 110
Financial planning, 69, 76, 77
Firsorotu, M., 187–88
First contract negotiations, 200
FLA. *See* Fair Labor Association
Flexibility, 64–65. *See also* Economic restructuring; Mobile workforce; Temporary/contingent workers
Flight attendants, 93
Flint auto workers' strike (1998), 47, 221
Florida Education Association, 76
FLSA. *See* Fair Labor Standards Act
FMC Corporation, 306n
Fortune magazine, 317
France, 66n
Freddie Mac, 71n
Free Trade Agreement of the Americas (FTAA), 316, 329–30
Friedman, Ray, 75n
Friends of the Earth, 296n
From, Al, 300
Frontier Hotel campaign, 211
FTAA. *See* Free Trade Agreement of the Americas
Funding. *See* Resources for organizing
Fundraising, 143–44
Future workforce programs, 262–64

Gapasin, Fernando, 142
Garment industry
capital flight vulnerability, 101, 105
corporate codes of conduct, 335–36
Guess campaign, 100, 101, 103, 112–17, 128
racial succession, 105, 106
Garret, Sylvester, 216
GATT. *See* General Agreement on Tariffs and Trade
Gender divisions, 233
General Agreement on Tariffs and Trade (GATT), 285, 286, 315
Generalized System of Preferences (GSP), 278, 322–24

General Motors, 325
Gephardt, Richard, 283, 287, 295, 309–10
Gephardt amendment, 279
Germany
environmental movement, 16
labor revitalization, 14
and social movement unionism, 340
temporary/contingent workers, 66n
Gingrich, Newt, 19, 300
Globalization
and citizenship, 54
and fast track battle (1997), 295
protective countermovement, 312–13
public opinion, 289, 311
See also Economic restructuring; International solidarity; Seattle WTO protests; Trade liberalization issues
Goffman, Erving, 27
Gomez, Jesus, 117
Gompers, Samuel, 84
Gordon, Jennifer, 50n
Gore, Al
AFL-CIO endorsement, 25, 302, 305
and China PNTR agreement, 306n
and fast track battles, 287, 300
Grassroots political action. *See* Community coalitions; Mobilization; Rank-and-file participation
Great Britain, 14, 250
Grievances, 196, 197–98. *See also* Unfair labor practices (ULP) complaints
Grocery clerks, 93–94
GSP. *See* Generalized System of Preferences
Guatemala, 323, 324, 335, 337
Guess campaign, 100, 101, 103, 112–17, 128

Harris, S. G., 188
Harvard Union of Clerical and Technical Workers (HUCTW), 94–95, 244–45
Healthcare benefits, 55
and associational unionism, 76, 77, 79
Healthcare industry
collective bargaining practices, 199
home healthcare campaigns, 20n, 32, 100
labor market interventions, 267
organizing, 15–16
Health/safety violations
Bridgestone/Firestone, 229
and Justice for Janitors campaign, 109

Health/saftey violations (*continued*)
and Ravenswood campaign, 218–20, 222
Washington State apple workers
NAALC case, 327
Hearts of Steel, 224
Heberle, Rudolf, 17n
HERE. *See* Hotel Employees and Restaurant Employees (HERE)
High-road programs. *See* Labor market interventions
High-tech sector
and Democratic Party, 309
labor market interventions, 267–68
mobile workforce in, 341
occupational unionism, 342
and trade liberalization issues, 279
Hiring halls, 204
community-based, 269
occupational unionism, 53, 85, 86
Historical perspectives, 13–14
business unionism, 14–17
central labor councils, 131–33, 147
labor rights, 318–20
trade liberalization issues, 277–79
Hochschild, Arlie, 91
Homecare workers, 20n, 100, 342
Home healthcare campaigns, 20n,
32, 100
Hormel Foods Corporation, 46
Hospitality industries, 32, 266–67
Hostein, Bernie, 221
Hotel Employees and Restaurant Employees (HERE)
Frontier Hotel campaign, 211
labor market interventions, 266–67
organizing, 19
working conditions, 92–93
Houston Organizing Project, 158–59, 162
HUCTW. *See* Harvard Union of Clerical and Technical Workers
Human rights groups, 296, 304, 323, 325, 326, 328
Human Rights Watch, 323, 325, 326

IAF. *See* Industrial Areas Foundation
IBEW. *See* International Brotherhood of Electrical Workers
ICEF. *See* International Chemical and Energy Workers

ICFTU. *See* International Confederation of Free Trade Unions
ILGWU. *See* International Ladies' Garment Workers' Union
ILO. *See* International Labor Organization
ILWU. *See* International Longshore Workers Union
IMF. *See* International Metalworkers Federation; International Monetary Fund
Immigrant organizing, 32–33, 99–128
and citizenship, 48–50
and community coalitions, 49–50, 117, 125, 127
consolidation problems, 128
Guess campaign, 100, 101, 103, 112–17, 128
importance of, 32–33
Justice for Janitors campaigns, 48, 49, 100, 107–12, 128
Los Angeles-Long Beach port truckers strike, 102, 103, 104–5, 122–26
Southern California drywall strike, 100, 103, 104–5, 117–21
and union xenophobia, 113
Immigrant workers
and citizenship, 40, 48–53
importance of, 34, 57, 107
increase in, 105–6
industrial relations theory on, 51n
networks, 111, 118, 119, 124, 127
New Voice stance on, 31n, 52, 100, 128
See also Immigrant organizing
Immigration Reform and Control Act (1986), 51
Independent contractors, 89, 101–2, 122
Transport Maritime Association, 124–25, 126
See also Subcontracting
Indonesia, 334
Industrial Areas Foundation (IAF), 269–70
Industrial citizenship. *See* Economic citizenship
Industrial organization diversity, 234, 235
Industrial relations theory, 21–22, 51n, 212, 340. *See also* Industrial unionism
Industrial Union Councils (IUCs), 132, 152
Industrial unionism
and central labor councils, 133
communities of workers, 80

and craft unionism, 60
and labor-economy relationship, 63
and labor rights, 319
new institutional perspective, 22
paternalism of, 67, 68
vs. peer management, 85
See also Industrial unionism, decline of
Industrial unionism, decline of
and community-based corporate
campaigns, 46
as inevitable, 34
and institutional redesign, 83
and mobile workforce, 65, 68
and need for redefinition, 90
Industry-wide activities
bargaining, 60, 199, 213, 214, 227
organizing, 108, 114, 127
See also Labor market interventions; Oc-
cupational unionism
Inflation, 62, 73–74
Information Technology Industry Council,
307
Information workers. *See* Knowledge
workers
In-plant campaigns, 229
Institutional change. *See* Organizational
change
Institutionalist theory, 22–23, 35–36, 39n
Institutional redesign, 82–84
Inter-American Regional Organization of
Workers (ORIT), 321, 329
Inter-city union solidarity, 110–11
Internal restructuring. *See* New Voice AFL-
CIO program; Organizational change;
Rank-and-file participation
International Association of Machinists and
Aerospace Workers, 238–39, 250–51
International Brotherhood of Electrical
Workers (IBEW)
administrative efficiency, 204
labor market interventions, 268
and occupational unionism, 86
organizing, 201–2, 203, 205
International Chemical and Energy Work-
ers (ICEF), 220
International Confederation of Free Trade
Unions (ICFTU), 321, 329, 335
International Covenant on Civil and Polit-
ical Rights, 330

International Covenant on Economic, So-
cial and Cultural Rights, 330
International Labor Organization (ILO),
312n, 321, 329, 331, 332
International Labor Rights Fund, 323, 325,
328
International Ladies' Garment Workers'
Union (ILGWU)
Guess campaign, 100, 103, 112–17
membership density, 105
UNITE merger, 103, 115
International Longshoremen's Association,
338
International Longshore Workers Union
(ILWU), 126
International Metalworkers Federation
(IMF), 220
International Monetary Fund (IMF), 315,
317, 334
International solidarity, 10, 32, 318
and acceptance of trade liberalization,
312–13
Bayou Steel campaign, 225
Bridgestone/Firestone, 228
importance of, 348
Ravenswood campaign, 220–21, 222
and Seattle WTO protests, 26, 332
See also Globalization; Labor rights;
Trade liberalization issues
International Standards Organization
(ISO), 336
International Trade Secretariats (ITSs), 321,
335
International Typographic Union (ITU),
252n
International Union of Electronic, Electri-
cal, Salaried, Machine and Furniture
Workers (IUE), 323
International unions
and central labor councils, 56
support for corporate campaigns, 46, 47
and Union Cities program, 137, 143,
152–53
See also Union structure
interrelationships; *specific unions*
International Workers of the World
(IWW), 319
ISO. *See* International Standards Organiza-
tion

Italy, 14, 333–34
ITSs. *See* International Trade Secretariats
ITU. *See* International Typographic Union
IUCs. *See* Industrial Union Councils
IUE. *See* International Union of
    Electronic, Electrical, Salaried,
    Machine and Furniture Workers
IWW. *See* International Workers of the
    World

Jackson, Jesse, 71, 283
Japan, 65, 227, 228, 338
J for J. *See* Justice for Janitors campaign
Job security, 63, 65. *See also* Mobile work-
    force
Jobs with Justice, 76
Job training
    and economic restructuring, 256–57
    future workforce programs, 262–64
    occupational unionism, 85
    on-site learning centers, 262
    school-to-work programs, 264n
    union programs, 204
    See also Labor market interventions
Johnson Controls, 325
Joint production, 256
J.P. Stevens Company, 218
Juravich, Tom, 217–18
Justice for Janitors campaigns, 48, 49, 100,
    107–12, 128
    research strategy, 108–9
Justice movements. *See* Social movements

Kaiser Aluminum Corporation, 237
Kaiser Permanente, 10
Kantor, Mickey, 285–86
Keynesian economics, 62
King, Martin Luther, Jr., 15
Kirkland, Lane, 33, 293
Kleiman, Bernie, 215
Knowledge workers, 53, 91. *See also*
    Colleges; High–tech sector
Kochan, Tom, 77
Korea, 337–38

"Labeling" measures, 321
"Labor '96" campaign, 293, 294
Labor Council for Latin American
    Advancement (LACLA), 138

Labor councils. *See* Central labor councils
Labor-management partnerships, 10, 18,
    62, 197
    and occupational unionism, 86–87
    public sector, 45
Labor market interventions, 257–72
    child care, 269
    community-based, 269–70
    demand for, 270
    healthcare, 267
    high-tech sector, 267–68
    hospitality industries, 266–67
    and organizing, 259, 265–66
    temporary/contingent workers, 263,
    268
    urban centrality, 271–72
    Wisconsin Regional Training
    Partnership, 259–64
Labor organization
    diversity of, 28–29, 33–35, 83
    and economic structures, 61–64
Labor revitalization
    debate on, 155
    gradual nature of, 31–32
    1990s victories, 20
    and triangular revitalization agenda,
    347–48
Labor rights, 318–38
    Congressional commission, 317
    and fast track battle (1997), 285–86, 287,
    290, 295–96
    and FTAA, 329–30
    historical perspective, 318–20
    multilateral organizations, 321, 330–34
    and NAFTA, 282, 321, 324–29
    as positive aspect of trade liberalization,
    312
    private sector action, 321, 334–38
    U.S. legislation, 71, 72, 75
    U.S. unilateral action, 321, 322–24
    and WTO Seattle meeting, 302
    See also Seattle WTO protests; Trade lib-
    eralization issues
LaBow, Ronald, 230
LACLA. *See* Labor Council for Latin
    American Advancement
Latin American Truckers' Association, 123
Latino immigrants. *See* Immigrant organiz-
    ing; Immigrant workers

Lawsuits
    filed by employers, 116, 120, 121, 225, 226
    international, 312n, 336–38
    and mobile workforce, 71, 72
    Southern California drywall strike, 120,
      126
Layoffs, 65, 116. *See also* Economic restruc-
    turing; Mobile workforce
Leader-initiated organizing. *See* Top–
    down organizing
Leadership
    African American, 44, 264
    Latino, 107, 113, 128
    new activists, 17, 30, 32, 107, 113
    See also Local unions
Legal assistance, 119–20
Legal tactics. *See* Lawsuits; Unfair labor
    practices (ULP) complaints
Levin, Sander, 310n
Levi Strauss & Company, 10, 335
Lewis, John L., 84
Liebmann, Wendy, 70n
Litigation. *See* Lawsuits; Unfair labor prac-
    tices (ULP) complaints
Living Wage campaigns, 32, 50, 55, 270, 312
Lobbying, 295, 296, 307
Local 1199, National Union of Health and
    Human Services Employees, 76, 244,
    247–48, 267
Local communities. *See* Community coali-
    tions
Local labor councils. *See* Central labor
    councils
Local political leaders, 110, 138
Local unions
    and coordinated/strategic contract cam-
      paigns, 236
    grievance procedures, 197–98
    Houston Organizing Project participa-
      tion, 159–60, 162
    innovation scarcity, 196–97
    internal politics, 177–79, 191, 192, 193
    lack of managerial skills, 142–43,
      192–93
    resistance to organizing, 107–8, 118,
      159–60, 162–63, 182, 192
    and Union Cities program, 137, 140
    See also Leadership; Member servicing
      model; Organizational change; Rank-

and-file participation; Staff; Union
    structure interrelationships
Lockouts. *See specific campaigns*
Los Angeles County Federation of Labor,
    107, 110
Los Angeles homecare workers campaign,
    20n, 100, 342
Los Angeles-Long Beach port truckers
    strike (1996), 102, 103, 104–5, 122–26
Low-wage workers, 79, 343–45. *See also* Im-
    migrant workers; Service sector

Machinists. *See* International Association
    of Machinists and Aerospace Workers
MAI. *See* Multilateral Agreement on
    Investment
Managerial skills, 142–43, 192–93
Maquila sectors, 323, 325–26, 337
Market power. *See* Occupational unionism
Marshall, T. H., 38, 39n
Masur, Sandra, 280
Matsushita Electrical Industrial Company,
    325
McDonald's, 328–29
McKee, Frank, 213
Meany, George, 15, 17, 157
Media role, 283. *See also* Publicity pressure
Media sector, 341
Megaunions. *See* Superunions
Member servicing model
    and business unionism, 14
    and Houston Organizing Project, 160
    and internal politics, 191, 192
    and Organizing Institute, 162
    rank-and-file investment in, 194–95
    and resources for organizing, 193, 206
Membership density
    and business unionism, 14
    and citizenship, 50–51
    current levels, 24, 31, 155, 346–47
    and mobile workforce, 342
    Southern California, 104–5
    steelworkers, 214
    and trade liberalization issues, 288–89
    and union mergers, 241–42, 254
    See also Union decline
Membership participation. *See* Rank-and-
    file participation
MEMO program, 203, 205

Memphis sanitation workers strike (1968), 15

Metropolitan areas. *See* Urban areas, centrality of

Mexican Democratic Lawyers' Association, 325

Mexico
citizenship, 37
labor rights lawsuits, 337
pregnancy testing NAALC case, 325–26
and Washington State apple workers NAALC case, 326–28

Meyer, David, 229

Meyers, Howard, 223

Mills, C. Wright, 91

Minimum wage, 25, 320

Mitsubishi Corporation, 71n

Mobile workforce, 80–81, 341–43
and associational unionism, 74–80
causes of, 64–65
and craft unionism, 60, 69
debate on, 341–42
and early AFL organizing style, 89–90
and educational opportunities, 69, 256–57
implications for labor organization, 68–74
and labor-market experience diversity, 343–44
and occupational unionism, 85
and organizing, 181
positive aspects of, 67–68
resistance to, 66–67
See also Economic restructuring; Temporary/contingent workers

Mobilization
and business unionism, 14
and campaign contributions, 312
China PNTR agreement, 305
and Congressional labor rights commission, 317
and fast track battle (1997), 293, 294–97
and fast track battle (1998), 277, 301
Justice for Janitors campaign, 109, 111
NAFTA battle, 283, 295
and New Voice AFL-CIO program, 10–11
obstacles to, 140
and organizing, 137, 142, 143
and pattern bargaining, 199
and political strategy, 10, 25, 32

as support for bargaining, 196–97, 199
Union Cities program, 136, 137, 138–40, 142, 143, 144
See also Bottom-up organizing

Modernization, 261

Montgomery, David, 27

Moolick, Richard, 214

Mossholder, K., 188

Motorola, Inc., 306n

MSI, 237

Multilateral Agreement on Investment (MAI), 316

Multinational corporations
and international solidarity, 348
and labor rights, 316, 325
and NAFTA battle, 280
and OECD, 332–34
See also Business policies; Employer opposition; North American Agreement on Labor Cooperation

NAALC. *See* North American Agreement on Labor Cooperation

Nader, Ralph, 283

National Airlines, 93

National community campaigns, 138, 154n

National Education Association (NEA), 16, 86
merger proposals, 243, 248n, 251n

National elections
1992, 18, 19, 282, 293
1994, 19, 293–94, 298–99
1996, 276, 285–86, 293–94, 299
1998, 296, 297, 300
2000, 286–87, 300, 302, 305, 308–10

National Guard, 214

National Labor Relations Act (NLRA) (1935) (Wagner Act), 13, 22, 319

National Labor Relations Board (NLRB)
alternatives to, 102, 108, 114, 118–19, 127
Bayou Steel campaign, 223, 225
and Bridgestone/Firestone, 229
new institutional perspective, 22
and Ravenswood campaign, 218, 220
unfair labor practices complaints, 109, 115, 120, 198, 225
Washington State apple workers NAALC case, 327
Wheeling Pitt campaign, 231

National Union of Health and Human
    Services Employees, Local 1199, 76,
    244, 247–48, 267
National Union of Hospitals and Health
    Care Employees, 269
National unions. *See* International unions
NEA. *See* National Education Association
Neighborhood movements. *See* Commu-
    nity coalitions
Netherlands, 66n
Neufeld, Maurice, 14n
Neutrality provisions, 142, 201, 345, 347
New Alliance Proposal, 137
New Deal, 62
New Democratic Caucus, 292, 297, 299,
    309
New Democratic Network PAC, 309
New institutionalist theory, 22–23
Newport News, 237
Newspaper Guild, 249
"New unionism," 86. *See also*
    Occupational unionism
New Voice AFL-CIO program, 2
    and central labor councils, 129, 133–34
    and immigrant workers, 31n, 52, 100, 128
    international solidarity, 318, 331
    and Justice for Janitors campaign, 49
    mobilization, 10–11
    and 1960s/1970s social movements, 17,
        20
    and organizational change, 175–76, 182
    and Organizing Institute, 170, 179
    and social movement unionism, 20, 30,
        33
    and trade liberalization issues, 276, 286,
        293, 312, 318
    and union mergers, 241
    and urban centrality, 271
    See also Organizing focus; Union Cities
        program
New Zealand, 246–47
NGOs. *See* Nongovernmental
    organizations
1930s
    employer opposition, 73n
    labor-economics relationship, 62
    social movement unionism, 13, 22, 23
1960s/1970s social movements, 14-16,
    18–19, 23, 59

and New Voice AFL-CIO program, 17,
    20
NIPSCO campaign. *See* Northern Indiana
    Public Service Company (NIPSCO)
    campaign
NLRA. *See* National Labor Relations Act
NLRB. *See* National Labor Relations
    Board
Nonferrous Industry Conference, 213
Nongovernmental organizations (NGOs),
    323, 329–30
Nord, W. R., 188
North American Agreement on Labor
    Cooperation (NAALC), 321, 324–29
    McDonald's case, 328–29
    pregnancy testing case, 325–26
    Washington State apple workers case,
        326–28
North American Free Trade Agreement
    (NAFTA), 247, 275, 280–85
    and Democratic Party, 284, 285,
        292, 298
    and employer opposition, 280–81, 286n
    labor mobilization against, 283, 295
    and labor rights, 282, 321, 324–29
    and 1994 elections, 293–94
    public opinion, 289
    and Washington Consensus, 316
    See also North American Agreement on
        Labor Cooperation
Northern Indiana Public Service Company
    (NIPSCO) campaign, 232–34
Northrup, Herbert, 214
Nurses, 95

OCAW. *See* Oil, Chemical, and Atomic
    Workers
Occupational Safety & Health Administra-
    tion (OSHA), 220, 222, 223, 327. *See
    also* Health/safety violations
Occupational unionism, 53, 84–87, 95,
    342–43
    defined, 84–85
    and individual needs, 95
    legal limitations on, 86
    peer management, 85–86
    See also Craft unionism
OECD. *See* Organization for Economic
    Cooperation and Development

Office and Professional Employees International Union (OPEIU), 200, 202

Oil, Chemical, and Atomic Workers (OCAW), 211, 245

Omnibus Trade and Competitiveness Act (1988), 278–79

"One-size-fits-all" approach, 83

On-site learning centers, 262

OPEIU. *See* Office and Professional Employees International Union

Operating During Strikes (Northrup), 214

Organizational change, 182–208, 345
administrative efficiency, 204
Allaire/Firsorotu model, 187–88
bargaining to organize, 200–202
and centralization issue, 176–80
collective bargaining practices, 196–97, 199–200
constraints on, 174–75
and coordinated/strategic contract campaigns, 235–36
educational programs, 203–4
Elected Leader Task Force on Organizing, 163–66
and funding, 195–96, 202, 206, 207
and grievance procedures, 197–98
and information channels, 174–75
innovation scarcity, 196–97
and managerial skills, 142–43, 192–93
and New Voice AFL-CIO program, 175–76, 182
Nord/Tucker model, 188
organizational transformation approach, 184, 191, 207–8
organizing structures, 204–5
pressure for, 175
rank-and-file attitudes, 194–95, 202–3, 207, 208
readiness literature, 188
research methodology, 185–86
and social movement unionism, 10, 11–12, 22–23, 30–31
and staff, 193–94
and strategic planning, 187–88, 191, 204, 207
styles of, 182–84
Tichy/Poulantzas model, 188–91, 208
and Union Cities program, 137, 139, 141, 151–52

Voss-Sherman model, 186–87

Organizational combustion, 182–83, 184, 186–87, 190–91, 206. *See also* Organizational change

Organizational culture, 167, 206

Organizational evolution, 183, 184, 190, 206. *See also* Organizational change

Organizational transformation, 184, 191, 207–8. *See also* Organizational change

Organization for Economic Cooperation and Development (OECD), 321, 332–34

Organizers
Latino, 113
newly trained, 166, 168–69
outside recruitment, 168–69, 193–94
role in first contract negotiations, 200
scarcity of, 158–59, 160
See also Leadership; Organizing; Organizing focus

Organizing
collective bargaining as path to, 200–202
devaluing of, 157
early AFL, 87–90
early central labor councils, 131–32
high-wage vs. low-wage workers, 344–45
Houston Organizing Project, 158–59, 162
industry-wide, 108, 114, 127
and labor market interventions, 259, 265–66
limited union growth as result of, 241–42, 346–47
monetary incentives, 202–3
top-down, 102–3, 108, 112
and trade liberalization issues, 310–11
Union Cities program, 137, 140–43
See also First contract negotiations; Immigrant organizing; Organizing focus; Resources for organizing; Union Cities program

Organizing focus, 18–19, 32
and collective bargaining, 195
importance of local unions, 165n
limits of, 24, 59
local union resistance, 107–8, 118, 159–60, 162–63, 182, 192
low-wage worker focus, 344–45
and 1994 elections, 19–20
and social movement unionism, 340

structures for, 204–5
and triangular revitalization agenda,
204–48
and union mergers, 244–45
See also Organizational change; Organizing Institute; Resources for organizing
Organizing Institute (AFL-CIO), 19, 156–81
and centralization issue, 173–74, 176–80
and economic restructuring, 180–81
Elected Leader Task Force on Organizing, 163–66
and employer opposition, 180
formation of, 160–61
future of, 166–68
growth pressure, 170
intrusion into local union affairs, 165,
171, 176
local union resistance, 162–63
outside organizer recruitment, 168–69
precursors of, 157–60
research methodology, 156–57n
RTP program, 161–62
"Organizing model," 164
ORIT. *See* Inter-American Regional Organization of Workers
OSHA. *See* Occupational Safety & Health
Administration
Outsourcing, 256
Overnite Transportation Company, 138
Overtime pay, 120
Owner-operators. *See* Independent
contractors

PACE. *See* Paper, Allied-Industrial, Chem-
ical and Atomic Workers
Pacific Rim Drywall Association (PRDA),
120–21
PACs (political action committees). *See*
Campaign contributions
Paper, Allied-Industrial, Chemical and
Atomic Workers (PACE), 245
Paperworkers Union. *See* United
Paperworkers International Union
Paraguay, 324
Parsons, Talcott, 38
PATCO. *See* Professional Association of
Air Traffic Controllers (PATCO)
Paternalism, 67, 68
Pattern bargaining, 199, 213, 214, 227

Paycheck protection, 25
Peer management, 85–86
Pension funds
defined benefit, 230–31, 232
and financial leverage, 71–72, 110
People of color. *See* African Americans; Im-
migrant workers; Immigrant organiz-
ing; Racial/ethnic diversity; Racial
succession
"People's Summit" (1998), 329
Performing artists, 95
Per-load rates, 122–23
Permanent normal trade relations (PNTR).
See China PNTR agreement
Perot, Ross, 283, 290
Phelps Dodge Corporation, 213–14
Philippines, 37
Picketing
and bottom-up organizing, 118–19
injunctions against, 125, 226
See also Strikes
Pico Products, 337–38
Pittston Coal Company, 46, 211, 221
Plant activity monitoring, 219, 221, 223
Plant closings. *See* Workplace closures
Playboy Clubs, 92–93
PNTR. *See* China PNTR agreement
Polanyi, Karl, 296
Political action committees (PACs). *See*
Campaign contributions
Political leverage, 110, 293
Political rights, 38, 40
Political science, 22–23
Political strategy, 18, 25, 32
and Clinton administration, 19
funding for, 24
Gore endorsement, 25, 302, 305
and independent contractors, 124
traditional practices, 197
and triangular revitalization agenda,
347–48
and union mergers, 247–48
See also Campaign contributions; Fast
track battle (1997); Fast track battle
(1998); North American Free Trade
Agreement; Public policy intervention;
Trade liberalization issues
Political strikes, 48. *See also* Justice for Janitors campaign

Poulantzas, N., 188–91, 208
Power, dimensions of, 189
PRDA. *See* Pacific Rim Drywall
  Association
Pregnancy testing NAALC case, 325–26
Productivity, 258
Professional Association of Air Traffic
  Controllers (PATCO), 18, 45, 212
Project QUEST, 269–70
Proposition 187, 51
Psychological support, 69, 94–95
Publicity pressure, 127
  Bayou Steel campaign, 225
  and corporate codes of conduct, 336
  Guess campaign, 114, 115, 116, 117
  Justice for Janitors campaign, 109–10
  and labor rights, 320
  Los Angeles-Long Beach port truckers
    strike, 124
  and mobile workforce, 70, 72
  NIPSCO campaign, 233, 234
  service sector, 94
  Southern California drywall strike, 120
  USX campaign, 215
  Washington State apple workers
    NAALC case, 327, 328
  Wheeling Pitt campaign, 231
Public opinion
  China PNTR agreement, 304
  fast track battle (1997), 289–90, 296
  globalization, 289, 311
Public policy intervention, 132, 154n
  Union Cities program, 136n, 141, 142
  See also Political strategy
Public sector, 43–45
  colleges, 32, 53, 54
  community involvement, 54, 55
  and fast track battle (1997), 295
  NIPSCO campaign, 232–34
  recent initiatives, 32–33
  social movement unionism, 17, 44
  urban political theory on, 57

Quebec Federation of Labor, 328

Racial/ethnic diversity, 34, 83
  and business unionism, 15
  and cultural citizenship, 40–41

and labor market interventions, 262,
  263, 264
  Union Cities program, 138–39
Racial succession, 48, 105, 106
Racketeer Influenced and Corrupt Organi-
  zations (RICO) Act, 121, 225, 226
RAC. *See* Ravenswood Aluminum Com-
  pany
Railway Labor Act (1926), 319
Rank-and-file participation, 10
  coordinated/strategic contract
    campaigns, 218, 221–22, 224
  NLRB as distancing factor, 108
  and organizational change, 194–95,
    202–3, 207, 208
  and SEIU organizing, 344–45
  union democracy movement, 179–80
  and union mergers, 248–50
  See also Bottom-up organizing;
    Mobilization; New Voice AFL-CIO
    program; Social movement unionism
Ravenswood Aluminum Company (RAC),
  217–23
Raymond, Paula, 77
Reagan administration, 18, 322n. *See also*
  Union decline
Recession, 45
Reciprocal Trade Agreements Act (1934), 277
Reebok, 335
Regional Bell Operating Companies, 347
Release time, 95, 201
Replacement workers
  Bayou Steel campaign, 225, 226
  Bridgestone/Firestone, 227
  Los Angeles-Long Beach port truckers
    strike, 125
  NIPSCO campaign, 233
  Phelps Dodge strike, 214
  Ravenswood campaign, 217
  and unfair labor practice strikes, 109,
    115
Republican Party
  and China PNTR agreement, 304
  and fast track battle (1997), 286, 287,
    288, 290–91, 298
  and fast track battle (1998), 301
  and NAFTA, 283–84
  1996 elections, 294

Research as labor strategy
    and Bayou Steel campaign, 224
    Bridgestone/Firestone, 227
    and coordinated/strategic contract
        campaigns, 216, 218–19, 224, 227
    Guess campaign, 114
    Justice for Janitors campaign, 108–9
    Los Angeles-Long Beach port truckers
        strike, 126
    Ravenswood campaign, 218–19
    USX campaign, 216
Resources for organizing, 202, 346
    Guess campaign, 115, 117
    Los Angeles-Long Beach port truckers
        strike, 126
    and managerial skills, 192
    and member servicing model, 193, 206
    and Union Cities program, 142
    and union mergers, 244
    and union structure interrelationships,
        195–96
Reuther, Walter, 16, 176n
Rich, Marc, 219, 220–21, 222
Rich, Robin, 233
RICO lawsuits, 121, 225, 226
Rifkin, Jeremy, 77
Right to Organize Day of Action, 142
"Right-to-work" laws, 55, 320
Roderick, David, 215
Rodrik, Dani, 313n
Rogers, Ray, 218
Rondeau, Kris, 94–95
Roosevelt, Franklin D., 13
Rosenblum, Jonathan, 214
Rosenthal, Steve, 293
Rugmark Foundation, 336
Rules Governing Local Central Bodies
    (AFL-CIO), 133
Runaway shops, 259–60, 320
    and Guess campaign, 101, 113–15, 116
    and NAFTA, 280–81
    and trade liberalization issues, 280–81,
        314–15
    and union decline, 105
Russian economic crisis, 317

SA8000 (Social Accountability) code,
    336

Safety violations. *See* Health/safety
    violations
Salinas de Gortari, Carlos, 280
Samsung, 325
San Francisco Hotels Partnership Project,
    266–67
Sanyo, 325
SAPRI. *See* Structural Adjustment Partici-
    patory Review
SBC, 345
Scabs. *See* Replacement workers
Schnur, Dan, 308n
School-to-work programs, 264n
Scientific invention, 64
Seattle WTO protests (1999), 9, 155, 302,
    316, 332
    and social movement unionism, 25–26
    and Union Cities program, 151
Seroka, Mihail, 226
Service Employees International Union
    (SEIU), 15–16
    building maintenance workers, 48–49
    inter-city solidarity, 110–11
    labor market interventions, 267
    lawsuits, 71
    Local 1199 merger, 244, 247–48, 267
    Los Angeles homecare workers
        campaign, 20n, 100, 342
    and 1960s/1970s social movements, 17
    organizing initiatives, 19, 33, 107, 244,
        344–45
    Southern California membership
        density, 105
    See also Justice for Janitors campaign
Service sector, 34, 91–94, 181, 344
    appearance issues, 92–93
    customer-employee relationship issues,
        91–92, 93–94
    and occupational unionism, 342
    psychological support, 94–95
Serving model. *See* Member servicing
SFWR. *See* Stewardesses for Women's
    Rights
Sherman, Rachel, 186–87
Siemens, 325
Sierra Club, 296n
Sjöberg, Anders, 250n
"Smile rules," 93–94

SMUV. *See* Swiss Metal workers union
Sneiderman, Marilyn, 133
Social compact, 293
Social justice movements. *See* Social
    movements
Social movements, 32
    and citizenship, 36, 42–43
    1960s/1970s, 14–16, 17, 18–19, 20, 23, 59
    vs. social movement unionism, 11–12, 23
    urban political theory on, 56–57
Social movement unionism, 339–41
    vs. business unionism, 11, 14
    and centralization issue, 179–80
    and community coalitions, 32, 37,
        54–58
    current goals, 20–21
    current status, 31
    defined, 28
    and diversity of labor organization,
        28–29, 33–35
    importance of, 29
    local focus of, 54
    need for unifying frame, 27–28, 36–37
    1930s, 13, 22, 23
    and 1960s/1970s social movements, 17,
        18–19, 20
    and organizational change, 10, 11–12,
        22–23, 30–31
    and organizing focus, 340
    postwar era restrictions, 13–14
    prospects for, 24–26
    public sector, 17, 44
    theoretical perspectives, 21–23
    and union mergers, 243
    and worker conservatism, 341
    See also Citizenship
Social Security reform campaign, 154n
Social wage, 40
Social welfare rights, 38
Sociology, 23
Solidarity Day march, 59
South Africa, 37
South Bay Area Labor Council, 343
Southern California drywall strike, 100,
    103, 104–5, 117–21
South Korea, 37, 337–38
Spain, 66n
Specific factors model of trade policy
    preference, 281n

Speed-ups, 218
Staff
    and coordinated/strategic contract
        campaigns, 226
    and organizational change, 193–94
    Union Cities program, 144
    See also Local unions; Organizers
State federations, 140
Steelworkers. *See* United Steelworkers of
    America
Stewardesses for Women's Rights (SFWR),
    93
Stigliz, Joseph, 317
Stolper-Samuelson model of trade policy
    preference, 281n
Strategic campaigns. *See* Coordinated/
    strategic contract campaigns
Strategic choice theory, 21–22
Strategic planning
    and organizational change, 187–88, 191,
        204, 207
    Union Cities program, 134
Strawberry Campaign, 138, 142, 154n
Street Heat. *See* Mobilization
Street theater, 221
Strike funds, 119, 125, 221
Strikes, 60
    alternatives to, 70–74, 233
    ambivalence about, 31, 47
    Guess campaign, 115, 117
    political, 48
    public sector, 44n
    recent explosion of, 31, 32
    and unfair labor practices complaints,
        109, 115
    and wages, 73
    See also Coordinated/strategic contract
        campaigns; *specific strikes*
Structural Adjustment Participatory
    Review (SAPRI), 316
Subcontracting, 46, 256
    and immigrant organizing, 102, 114–15,
        127
    See also Economic restructuring; Inde-
        pendent contractors
Super 301 law, 279
Superunions, 250–51, 253
Sverke, Magnus, 250n
Sweatshops. *See* Garment industry

Sweden
  mobile workforce, 65, 66n
  and OECD, 334
  and social movement unionism, 340
  union mergers, 246–47, 249–50, 252n
Sweeney, John
  and Justice for Janitors campaign, 107
  and 1960s generation, 17
  on "one-size-fits-all" approach, 83
  and trade liberalization issues, 295, 305
  and union mergers, 252–53
  and Wheeling Pitt campaign, 231
  See also New Voice AFL-CIO program
Swiss Metal workers union (SMUV), 220

Taft-Hartley Act (1947), 13
Talent Alliance, 76
Team Act, 25
Teamsters Union, 104–5, 122
  and China PNTR agreement, 305
  and fast track battle (1997), 294
  McDonalds NAALC case, 328
  mergers, 252n
  recent leadership changes, 47n
  United Parcel Service strike, 20n, 46–47,
    138, 211
  Washington State apple workers
    NAALC case, 327, 328
Technical resources, 144
Technical workers. *See* High-tech sector
Temporary/contingent workers, 32,
  65–66
  associational unionism, 32, 53, 76
  and citizenship, 53–54
  labor market interventions, 263, 268
  and local focus, 55
  occupational unionism, 53, 85, 86
  and organizing, 180–81
  public justice discourse participation,
    54, 55
  research focus on, 33
  See also Economic restructuring; Mobile
    workforce
Temp unionism. *See* Associational unionism; Occupational unionism; Tempo-
  rary/contingent workers
Texaco, 71n
There Is No Alternative. *See* TINA
Thomson, 325

Tichy, N. M., 188–91
TINA (There Is No Alternative), 316
Titan Tire Corporation, 237
TMA. *See* Transport Maritime
  Association
Top-down organizing, 102–3, 108, 112
Trade Agreements Act (1979), 278
Trade and Tariff Act (1984), 278
Trade liberalization issues, 155, 275–79,
  314–18
  and corporate fallibility, 317
  expert opinion, 290, 317
  future of, 310–13
  historical perspective, 277–79
  labor protectionism, 278, 281n, 314–15,
    322, 332
  and Union Cities program, 151
  Washington Consensus, 315–16, 317–18
  See also China PNTR agreement; Fast
    track battle (1997); Fast track battle
    (1998); Labor rights; Seattle WTO
    protests
Trade Reform Act (1974), 278
Training, 203, 205
  for mobilization, 199
  Union Cities program, 146, 149, 150
  Union Summer program, 162n
  See also Job training
Transport Maritime Association (TMA),
  124–25, 126
Trossman, Steven, 296
Trucking, 101–2, 104–5
  Los Angeles-Long Beach port strike, 102,
    103, 104–5, 122–26
  racial succession, 105, 106
Truck-tracking, 219, 221, 223
Trumka, Rich, 20. *See also* New Voice
  AFL-CIO program
Tucker, S., 188
Two-tier wage systems, 46, 48

UE. *See* United Electrical, Radio and
  Machine Workers of America
UFCW. *See* United Food and Commercial
  Workers
Ulman, Lloyd, 152
ULP complaints. *See* Unfair labor practices
  (ULP) complaints
Unemployment insurance, 320

Unfair labor practices (ULP) complaints,
    198, 225
  and replacement workers, 109, 115
  Southern California drywall strike, 120
Union Cities program, 55–56, 134–54
  CLC leadership responses, 148–49
  inter-council collaboration, 144–45
  mobilization, 136, 137, 138–40, 142, 143, 144
  obstacles, 140, 142–43, 146–47, 148–51
  organizing, 137, 140–43
  outline of, 135
  research methodology, 130–31
  resources, 137, 142, 143–47, 150–51
  strategic planning, 134
  and union structure interrelationships,
    140, 143, 152–53
Union decline
  and business unionism, 14
  and employer opposition, 18, 21–22, 105,
    122
  and fast track battle (1997), 288–89
  and immigrant workers, 105, 106, 107,
    118
  as inevitable, 1
  and social movement unionism, 23
  and Southern California drywall strike,
    117–18
  and trade liberalization issues, 279
Union mergers, 238–55
  and AFL-CIO, 251–53
  and collective bargaining, 246–47
  as energizing factor, 254–55
  forms of, 241
  frequency of, 239–40, 241–43
  and organizing, 103, 115, 244–45
  and political strategy, 247–48
  and rank-and-file participation, 248–50
  superunions, 250–51, 253
Union of American Physicians and
    Dentists, 248
Union of Needletrades, Industrial and
    Textile Employees (UNITE)
  bargaining mobilization, 199
  and fast track battle (1997), 294
  first contract bargaining, 200
  Guess campaign, 100, 103, 115–17, 128
  merger, 103, 115, 244
  organizing, 201, 204–5, 244, 345
  training programs, 203

Union Privilege program, 181
Union structure interrelationships
  centralization issue, 171–72, 173–74,
    176–80, 248
  and early AFL organizing, 90
  limits on central labor councils, 132–33,
    152–53
  need for local empowerment, 90, 95
  and Organizing Institute, 165, 171,
    173–74, 176–80
  and resources for organizing, 195–96
  and Union Cities program, 140, 143,
    152–53
Union Summer program, 162n
UNISON (Great Britain), 250
United Auto Workers (UAW)
  Caterpillar strike, 46
  and China PNTR agreement, 305
  and civil rights movement, 15
  Flint strike, 47, 221
  organizing, 19
  Steelworkers/Machinists merger
    proposal, 238–39, 250–51
United Brotherhood of Carpenters and
    Joiners of America, 104–5
  Southern California drywall strike, 100,
    118–19, 121, 128
United Electrical, Radio and Machine
    Workers of America (UE), 323
United Farm Workers (UFW), 100
  as model for revitalization, 46, 48, 49, 53
  Washington State apple workers
    NAALC case, 327, 328
United Food and Commercial Workers
    (UFCW)
  Coca-Cola campaign, 335
  Hormel strike, 46
  and labor rights, 323
  mergers, 242, 251
  and "smile rules," 93–94
United Mineworkers of American
    (UMWA), 46, 211, 333–34
United Nations, 330–31
United Paperworkers International Union,
    245
United Parcel Service (UPS)
  and China PNTR agreement, 306n
  strike, 20n, 46–47, 138, 211
United Rubber Workers (URW), 227, 246

United Steelworkers of America (USWA)
Auto Workers/Machinists merger proposal, 238–39, 250–51
and China PNTR agreement, 305
and fast track battle (1997), 294
Rubber Worker merger, 242, 246
See also Coordinated/strategic contract campaigns
UNITE. *See* Union of Needletrades, Industrial and Textile Employees
Universal Declaration of Human Rights, 330
UPS. *See* United Parcel Service
Urban areas, centrality of, 55, 271–72
Urban political theory, 56–57
Uruguay Round GATT Treaty, 285, 286
URW. *See* United Rubber Workers
USA*NAFTA, 283
U.S. Chamber of Commerce, 306
US Steel. *See* USX Corporation
USWA. *See* United Steelworkers of America
US West, 198
USX Corporation, 214–17

Valenta, Frank, 216
Vietnam War, 16
Violence against strikers
Latin America, 111, 335
Southern California drywall strike, 119
USX campaign, 216
Voice@Work campaign, 142
Voos, Paula, 346
Voss, Kim, 186–87
"Vote no" campaigns, 245n

Wages
and inflation, 62, 73–74
market conditions clause, 121
minimum wage, 25, 320
and mobile workforce, 72–74
taking out of competition, 60, 108, 114, 203
Wagner Act. *See* National Labor Relations Act
Waiting time, 123, 124
Wal-Mart Stores, Inc., 73n
War Labor Board, 13
Washington Consensus, 315–16

Washington State apple workers NAALC case, 326–28
Washtec, 342–43
Waterfront/Rail Truckers Union (WRTU), 123
Wheeling Pittsburgh Steel Corporation, 230–32
Whites. *See* European Americans
WHX, 231. *See also* Wheeling Pittsburgh Steel Corporation
"Why Union Cities?", 149
Wial, Howard, 142
Wilson, William Julius, 77
Wisconsin Regional Training Partnership (WRTP), 259–64
Wolfgang, Myra, 92
Women
associational unionism, 75n
organizing, 15–16
public sector, 44
service sector, 91–94
support committees, 221–22, 224
Worker harassment, 233, 327
Workers' compensation, 320
Workers' family participation, 221–22, 224, 228
Workers Rights Consortium (WRC), 335–36
Working conditions
and alternative forms of pressure, 72
and communities of workers, 111, 123, 124
service sector, 91–94
Working Partnerships USA, 76, 268
Working Today, 53, 76–80, 87
Workplace closures, 320
and labor market interventions, 261
McDonalds NAALC case, 328–29
and NAFTA, 286n
resistance to, 46, 55
Wheeling Pitt campaign, 231
Workplace participation/empowerment, 67, 72
World Bank
and international economic crises, 317, 334
and labor rights, 321, 334
Structural Adjustment Participatory Review, 316
and Washington Consensus, 315

World Trade Organization (WTO), 287
  and labor rights, 321, 332
  and Washington Consensus, 315, 316
  See also Seattle WTO protests (1999)
WRC. *See* Workers Rights Consortium
WRTP. *See* Wisconsin Regional Training
  Partnership

WRTU. *See* Waterfront/Rail Truckers Union

Xenophobia, 113
Xerox Corporation, 75n

Zenith Data Systems, 325
Zinkula, Mark, 281n